The

SUBMARINES
OF THE WORLD

The Illustrated Directory of

SUBMARINES
OF THE WORLD

David Miller

MBI Publishing Company

A Salamander Book

This edition first published in 2002 by
MBI Publishing Company,
Galtier Plaza, Suite 200, 380 Jackson
Street, St. Paul, MN 55101-3885 USA

© Salamander Books Ltd., 2002

A member of Chrysalis Books plc

The information in this book is true
and complete to the best of our
knowledge. All recommendations are
made without any guarantee on the
part of the author or publisher, who
also disclaim any liability incurred in
connection with the use of this data or
specific details.

We recognize that some words,
model names and designations, for
example, mentioned herein are the
property of the trademark holder. We
use them for identification purposes
only. This is not an official publication

MBI Publishing Company books are
also available at discounts in bulk
quantity for industrial or sales-
promotional use. For details write to
Special Sales Manager at
Motorbooks International
Wholesalers & Distributors,
Galtier Plaza, Suite 200, 380 Jackson
Street, St. Paul, MN 55101-3885 USA

Library of Congress Cataloging-in-
Publication Data Available

ISBN 0-7603-1345-8   7/15

The Author

David Miller is a former officer in the British armed forces, who spent his service in England, the Falkland Islands, Germany, Malaysia, the Netherlands, Scotland, and Singapore. He subsequently worked as a freelance author and for three years as a journalist for Jane's Information Group. He was Editor of the two-volume *Jane's Major Warships*, and has written more than forty other works, many of them related to sea warfare and naval weapons.

Acknowledgements

The publishers are grateful for the help given by many institutions and private individuals who have provided photographs for this book, in particular Anchor Consultancy Photo Library for the photographs on pages 47 (bottom), 159 (bottom), 185, 187, 197, 204-5, 207, 209 (top), 263 (bottom), 322-3, and 479 (bottom).

Credits

Project Manager: Ray Bonds
Designed by: Interprep Ltd.
Colour reproduction by: Anorax Imaging Ltd.
Printed in: Slovenia

Contents

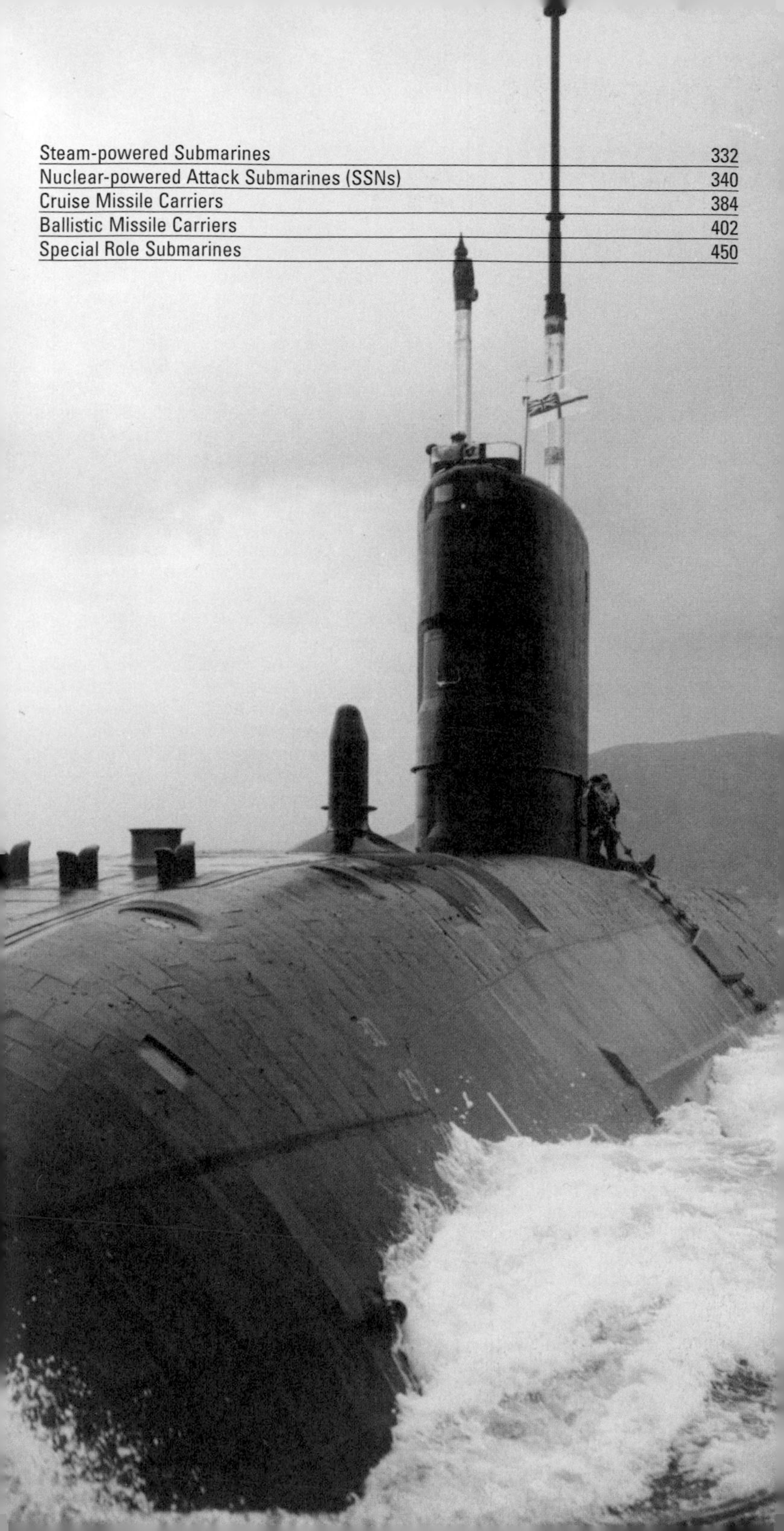

Introduction

The early history of the submarine was similar to that of the aeroplane. From the 15th century onwards a few individuals dreamt of diving and travelling in the depths of the ocean. Who conducted the first successful dive is open to argument, but a Dutchman, van Drebbel, is credited with conducting the first public demonstration, which took place in the River Thames, London, in 1620; it is even suggested that King James I was aboard for one dive. The first person to foresee the potential of the submarine as a weapon of war was an American, David Bushnell, who produced two submersibles to attack the British, the first in 1776 and the second in 1812. He was followed by a Bavarian, Bauer, in 1851, a spate of inventors during the American Civil War, and the Peruvian, Blume. By the 1890s the basic problem of submerging and returning to the surface had been solved, but the question of propulsion was not solved until J. P. Holland established that the solution was the use of electric storage cells, with internal combustion engines being employed on the surface for both propulsion and the recharging of the batteries. Practical use of the various options – petrol, kerosene and diesel – eventually established the latter as the most satisfactory and least dangerous, and for fifty years diesel-electric was the only practicable means of propulsion, with steam an unpopular and dangerous alternative.

In 1914 there were many submarines in service with European, United States and Japanese navies, and it was supposed that their primary use would be against enemy warships. As events unfolded, however, it was their role against merchant shipping that predominated, and the statistics for the twelve months from February 1917 to January 1918 summarise the story. During that period an average of 46 German U-boats were at sea in any one month, sinking a total of 2,684 British merchant ships (6,069,724 tons), a loss which brought the British Empire to the brink of defeat and established the strategic maturity of the submarine for all to see.

The inter-war period saw a few years of consolidation, mixed with a few experiments as navies tested ideas for specialised submarines, such as monitors, aircraft carriers, minelayers and boats that could keep pace with the main surface battlefleet. Many concepts were short-lived and the main focus of attention remained the patrol submarine, which increased steadily in size, and improved in efficiency and capability. However, the vessel itself was still a submersible, spending most of its time on the surface and diving only when it was absolutely necessary to do so. Nor could these boats go very deep, and few could dive to a depth greater than their own length.

During World War II the submarine was again a major element in the combat, although the major navies faced differing strategic situations. Thus, German U-boats in 1939-41 in the Atlantic and in 1942 on the North American coast operated in a "target-rich environment" with thousands of enemy merchant ships to be attacked. For the British, there were few enemy merchant ships to be attacked, except in the Mediterranean where surface traffic between Italy and North Africa offered rich pickings. In the Pacific the Japanese depended upon merchant shipping for movement between captured territories and their homeland and this traffic had been virtually brought to a halt by August 1945. The Japanese operated the most numerous fleet of the largest submarines in the world but achieved indifferent success and were fought to a standstill by the Allies. The Germans and Japanese realised that the basic diesel-electric submarine was capable of better underwater performance if it was streamlined and given greater battery power, but fortunately for the Allies the new classes the Axis powers designed never attained service in significant numbers.

In the immediate post-war period, the former Axis powers were deprived of their submarine fleets, while the victorious navies made do with modernised versions of their wartime boats until a totally new generation of true submarines were ready. The greatest advance came about with nuclear power, with USS *Nautilus* (SSN-571) employing it for the first time on 17 January 1955, but this has proved so expensive that its use is confined to the very few, wealthiest navies. Nevertheless, it is the answer to the dream in which a true submarine can travel in the depths with the only restrictions being the physiological limits of the crew and the amount of supplies that can be carried. The first nuclear submarine powers were the USA, the USSR and the UK, followed by France and then China, although India and Brazil both have active programmes which should result in SSNs by 2020 at the latest.

Meanwhile, the first non-nuclear air-independent propulsion (AIP) boats are coming into service, which will give submarines the capability of remaining submerged for about 14-21 days at a time. There are a number of different systems, but all are used for low-speed cruising, depending upon batteries for high-speed operations. But, just as the number of navies with diesel-electric submarines had increased over the past fifty years, so, too, will the numbers of AIP grow, increasing yet again the threat posed by submarines.

Entries in this book

Submarines are grouped by the country of origin in order to show the development of submarine design within a country and also to show the overall picture as a class. Thus, for example, today's German-built Type 209 is in service with some 15 navies; if each navy's holdings were described individually there would be a great deal of duplication and it would be difficult for the reader to get an overall picture of the class. Thus, the Type 209 is described in one consolidated entry under Germany.

Within the country of origin submarine classes are listed in chronological order of the launch of the first-of-class. The specifications given are for the first-of-class, as built, unless otherwise stated in italics at the foot of the specification table. Where a reasonably accurate figure cannot be discovered, that item is omitted. Individual entries are:

Type = description of primary role.
Total built = grand total for all customers.
Completed = in-service dates of first and last of class.
Displacement = surfaced displacement when fully loaded, and submerged.
Dimensions = overall length and beam between extremities; draught is on the surface at standard displacement.
Propulsion = diesels (number, power per engine); electric motors (number, power per motor); battery (number of cells); shafts.
Performance = surface and submerged speeds as designed; surfaced and submerged ranges are expressed as x nautical miles (nm) at y knots (kt); note that one can be traded against the other; ie, a submarine capable of 11,000nm at 11kt might be capable of 15,000nm at 8kt.
Weapons = torpedoes (tubes by number, location and calibre); guns (by number and calibre). Mines are listed only for specialised minelayers or when special strap-on devices are available; they are not listed where they can be carried in place of torpedoes, as is the case with virtually all modern submarines.
Complement = total crew.

Diesel-Electric Patrol Submarines 1860-1921

There were many attempts during the 19th Century to develop a viable submarine, but one of the major problems preventing complete success was that of underwater propulsion. As described elsewhere in this book, various means were tried, including men turning a crank, and steam, which gave plenty of power but was dangerous in an underwater environment. Compressed air and electric storage batteries were tried as the sole means of propulsion, but both resulted in limited range and the need for the boat to return to harbour to recharge from a shore-based generator. It was the Irish-American inventor, J. P. Holland, who realised that the answer lay in taking an internal combustion engine to sea, where it would both recharge the battery and propel the boat on the surface, thus leaving the battery to provide the power underwater. This battery, which consisted of a large number of individual cells, had to provide power not only for propulsion but also for what is today termed the "hotel load", ie, lighting, heating, operating pumps and valves, raising and lowering the periscopes, operating the cookers, and so on. Thus, the power could rapidly be exhausted and it was one of the captain's many responsibilities to juggle with the problem of speed versus endurance.

Early submarines were powered by gasoline engines, which gave good power for their size but used a fuel which was inherently dangerous, and there were many minor and some major explosions. Realising the danger of gasoline, the Germans used kerosene, but it was extremely pungent and gave off a

*Below: German **U-38** (U-31-class) under the Turkish flag.*

Above: U.S. Navy's first submarine, Holland, October 1901.

dense white exhaust. The answer was found in the diesel and by about 1910 this had become the preferred power source, although a few steam-powered boats were still built. The diesel engine itself took some years to perfect. Early models had a poor power output and the Americans, somewhat uncharacteristically, found it difficult to build a reliable diesel. The engine situation became even more complicated when, on the outbreak of World War I, the export of the best diesels – those from M.A.N. of Nuremburg, Germany – suddenly ceased.

In the years following the launch of Holland's submarine, development was rapid, spurred on by the naval races in Europe between Germany and the UK, and in the Far East between Japan and Russia. Then came World War I in which the stand-off between the great battle fleets and the tight trade embargo imposed by Britain and France led to the extremely rapid development of the patrol submarine, partly as an anti-warship weapon but increasingly in its anti-merchant ship role. The latter was of comparatively limited interest to the Western Powers since the Central Powers (Germany and Austria-Hungary) soon had very few merchant ships left, but was of immense interest to Germany.

Despite their name "submarine" these early boats were in reality "submersibles" – ie, they spent most of their time on the surface and submerged only when actually forced to do so. Then, once submerged, their endurance was strictly limited by the life of the battery, and the boats were both slow moving and difficult to manoeuvre.

Torpedoes

The primary weapon of the submarine was the torpedo. Most submarines entered World War I with 18in (457mm) tubes, but during the war there was a steady increase in calibre. The 21in (533mm) torpedo was introduced into Allied submarines from 1917 onwards, while on the German side the calibre rose from 450mm (17.7in) to 500mm (19.7in), although by the end of the war a 600mm (23.6in) torpedo was under development.

This increase in calibre resulted in both larger warheads and more fuel for greater range, but also meant that larger, heavier tubes were required and greater storage space was needed in the submarine. The real problems with torpedoes, however, were aiming, reliability and accuracy. Aiming depended solely upon the captain, since he alone could see out through the periscope and then had to assess the range and the relative speeds, angles and courses of his own boat and the target. In this era there were no computers to help him. Reliability was a function of a number of systems; first, the torpedo's engine had to be started, then the missile had to be driven down the tube, following which it had to run straight and maintain the correct depth. Finally, if all worked properly and it actually did hit the target, the fuze had to function and explode the warhead.

One of the choices open to the captain was that he could trade the torpedo's speed for range, which in the German G6, for example, could be set for either 1,640yd (1,500m) at 34.5kt, or for 3,380yd (3,000m) at 26kt. Generally, however, captains preferred to keep the range very short and the "rule-of-thumb" for British captains prior to the outbreak of war was that they should launch their torpedo at about three times the length of their own submarine, which, in practical terms, was about 300yd (274m).

Country	Torpedo	IOC	Calibre	Warhead	Maximum Speed	Maximum Range
Austria-Hungary	Whitehead	1911	18in (457mm)	220lb (100kg)	44kt	2,200yd (2,012m)
Germany	C/06	1907	17.7in (450mm)	270lb (123kg)	26kt	3,380yd (3,000m)
	G/6	1911	19.7in (500mm)	235lb (160kg)	35kt	5,470yd (5,000m)
UK	18in Mk VI	1909	18in (457mm)	200lb (91kg)	29kt	6,000yd (5,486m)
	Weymouth 21in Mk II	1914	21in (533mm)	225lb (102kg)	29kt	10,000yd (9,144m)
	21in Mk VI	1917	21in (533mm)	515lb (237kg)	40kt	5,000yd (4,572m)
U.S.	21in U.S.	1917	21in (533mm)	385lb (175kg)	27kt	13,500yd (6,124m)

World War I torpedoes. Note that there was a "trade-off" between speed and range and that to achieve maximum range the speed would be reduced and vice versa.

Various means of launching torpedoes were tried, the most obvious being bow tubes. Early submarines had just one such tube, but this gradually increased to two, then to four, and by about 1918 there were even some with six tubes. Such an increase was primarily intended to enable the captain to fire a number of torpedoes at a time, thus greatly increasing the chance of a hit. The British developed the idea of beam tubes, with a pair of tubes rigidly mounted roughly amidships and pointing, one to each side, at 90 degrees to the boat's axis. The beam had to be increased to accommodate these tubes and the idea did not persist beyond a few classes. Some other navies tried using rotating mounts, which were situated on the upper casing and turned by a mechanical linkage; this proved particularly popular with the French, but was eventually discontinued. The idea of the stern tubes was also introduced, sometimes in a tube outside the pressure hull, but more frequently inside the pressure hull and thus reloadable. Such tubes were mainly intended to fire at chasing warships.

Several navies used metal frames known as "drop collars" of which that designed by the Russian, Drzewiecki, was the most widely used. Such frames were mounted on the upper deck, usually in a recess, and held one torpedo. The torpedo was launched by swinging the frame outboard and then releasing the weapon. Reloading at sea was not possible and the device added considerably to the hydrodynamic resistance of the boat. They were especially popular in the French and Russian navies, but little liked anywhere else.

Guns

The first guns were mounted on submarines in about 1912-13, but they did not become commonplace until about 1916-17. The main requirement was to engage and sink merchant ships, since gun ammunition was far more plentiful than torpedoes. There were very few German merchant ships for Allied submarines to attack, but the British found the guns essential for attacking fleeing U-boats. Early guns were of 3in (76mm) calibre, but this soon increased to 88mm in the German case and 4in (102mm) for the British.

German submarines

Where submarines were concerned, there can be no doubt that the most influential navy in the period 1914-18 was that of Germany. The Germans came late to the submarine field, their previous top priority having been the development of the High Seas Fleet. Indeed, despite the ruthless reputation they subsequently earned, they were ill-prepared for submarine warfare and on the outbreak of war in August 1914 there were just 20 operational U-boats, with another 15 either employed in non-operational tasks (for example, training) or under construction. As soon as it became clear that the war would last much longer than expected the naval staff set in hand a "Mobilisation" (Ms) programme in which they sought to achieve a rapid increase in numbers by economies of scale and also by sticking, so far as was possible, to progressive development of existing designs. Their efforts were, however, beset by a number of problems. First, were the frequent changes in strategic direction concerning U-boat warfare by the government and the High Command, which often meant that the type of U-boat required changed also. But there were also a host of production difficulties, one of the most important being the shortage of skilled manpower, particularly as so many shipyard workers were called-up for Army service. This exacerbated the second problem, which was the difficulties the yards experienced in expanding their capacity to meet the great increase in numbers of U-boats required, as well as the rapid advance in U-boat technology. Further problems were caused by shortages of certain items of equipment, particularly diesel engines. Despite these difficulties, the German Navy brought the U-boat to a degree of size, sophistication, complexity and strategic importance which J. P. Holland could barely have dreamt of only a decade earlier.

U-1/-3/-5 classes   AUSTRIA-HUNGARY

Type: coastal, gasoline/kerosene-electric.

Class	U-1*	U-3	U-5
Total built	2	2	3
Completed	1909	1908	1909-11
Displacement surfaced submerged	230 tons 249 tons	240 tons 300 tons	240 tons 273 tons
Dimensions length beam draught	100ft 0in (30.5m) 15ft 9in (4.8m) 12ft 8in (3.9m)	138ft 9in (42.3m) 14ft 0in (4.5m) 12ft 6in (3.8m)	105ft 4in (32.1m) 13ft 9in (4.2m) 12ft 10in (3.9m)
Propulsion main engines power electric motors power shafts	2 x gasoline 720bhp 2 200shp two	2 x kerosene 600bhp 2 320shp two	2 x gasoline 500bhp 2 230shp two
Performance speed, surface submerged range, surfaced submerged	10.3kt 6kt 950nm at 6kt 40nm at 2kt	12kt 8kt 1,200nm at 12kt 40nm at 3kt	10.8kt 8.5kt 800nm at 8.5kt 48nm at 6kt
Weapons TT location torpedoes guns	3 x 17.7in (450mm) bow-2, stern-1 5 1 x 37mm cannon	2 x 17.7in (450mm) bow-2 3 –	2 x 17.7in (450mm) bow-2 4 –
Complement	17	21	19

* Specifications for U-1/U-2, as built.

Above: Holland design, U-6, was built by Whitehead, Fiume.

History: Work on submarines for the Imperial Austro-Hungarian Navy began in 1904. The first effort was not a success, so it was decided to buy two boats from each of three leading builders; the naval staff laid down the outline specifications, but the design was left to the shipyards. The first pair (U-1, U-2) were designed by the American, Simon Lake, but built under licence at the Naval Yard in Pola. Of typical Lake design, they had a diving chamber under the bow, variable pitch propellers and retractable wheels for running along the seabed; it was the only one of the three designs to feature a gun armament. There were a number of unsatisfactory features, of which the worst were the gasoline engines, which did not reach anything near the advertised power; as a result, the Navy refused to pay for the engines, which were subsequently replaced by diesels. They were employed as training boats during World War I and were then ceded to the Italians who scrapped them in the early 1920s.

The second pair (U-3, U-4) were designed and built by Germania at Kiel, Germany, and then towed to the Mediterranean. This was only Germania's third submarine design. It was remarkably sound, although some difficulties were experienced with the diving planes, while, as in the early German U-boats., the kerosene engine emitted a vast plume of white smoke. However, it was judged to be the most reliable and the most comfortable for the crew, and a revised design subsequently won the competition for a new class. Both took part in World War I, during which U-3 was sunk by a French destroyer, while U-4 sank an Italian armoured cruiser in 1915.

U-5 and U-6 were of a Holland design and were partially built in the USA before being shipped to Whitehead, Fiume, for completion. They were single-hulled boats with a "teardrop" hull and two torpedo tubes, which were completed in 1909. Whitehead then went ahead to build a third boat, an improved version of the Holland design; it was offered to and turned down by various navies, but when war broke out it was finally accepted by Austria-Hungary, who commissioned it as U-12. All three were sunk during the war, although U-5 was raised and rebuilt.

Above: U-4 (U-3-class) – built for Austria by Germania, Kiel.

Above: U-12 (U-5-class), sunk by a mine off Venice in 1916.

Havmanden-class   AUSTRIA-HUNGARY (DENMARK)

Type: coastal, gasoline/diesel-electric.
Total built: 6.
Completed: 1912-14.
Displacement: surfaced 164 tons; submerged 204 tons.
Dimensions: length 127ft 8in (38.9m); beam 11ft 10in (3.6m); draught 7ft 7in (2.3m).
Propulsion: 2 x FIAT/M.A.N. diesel engines, 450bhp; 2 x electric motors, 275shp; one shaft.
Performance: surface – 12kt; submerged – 13kt; range surfaced 1,400nm at 10kt; submerged 23nm at 8kt.
Weapons: 2 x 18in (457mm) TT (bow); 1 x 8mm MG.
Complement: 10.
Specifications, as built.

History: The Royal Danish Navy had already taken delivery of the *Dykkeren* (qv) in 1909, which was designed and built by Fiat at La Spezia, but it had suffered many teething problems. This led them to look elsewhere for their second class of submarines, which was to be built in some numbers and with some, at least, being built in Denmark. The Austrian firm of Whitehead at Fiume had already established its reputation for the design and manufacture of torpedoes, but in the early years of the 20th Century it also designed and built a number of submarines. Most of these were for the Austro-Hungarian Navy, but a number were for export, including this class for Denmark.

The original order was for two, of which the first, *Havmanden*, would be built by Whitehead, while the second, *Havfruen*, would be built at the Copenhagen Navy Yard, using plans purchased from Whitehead. While the first

Above: Havfruen **and** Najaden **(Havmanden-class) in 1914.**

was still under construction a second order was placed, with another two to be built at Whitehead (*Thetis* and *Triton*) and the Copenhagen Navy Yard (*Najaden* and *Nymfen*). One of these, *Triton*, was paid for by popular subscription, an event which happened in a number of countries in the years leading up to World War I, and its name was changed to *2den April*, to commemorate Nelson's Battle of Copenhagen, which was fought on 2 April 1801.

In 1913 the boats were given numbers from #2 to #7 (*Dykkeren* became #1) which were painted on their bridges. This was later changed again and they were redesignated the "A-class" becoming *A-2* to *A-7*. They were stricken and scrapped between 1928 and 1932.

U-10 class

Type: patrol, diesel-electric.
Total built: 4.
Completed: 1915.
Displacement: surfaced 126 tons; submerged 140 tons.
Dimensions: length 91ft 6in (27.9m); beam 16ft 10in (5.2m); draught 8ft 11in (2.7m).
Propulsion: 1 x diesel, 60bhp; 1 x electric motor, 120shp; one shaft.
Performance: surface – 6.5kt; submerged – 5.5kt.
Weapons: 2 x 17.7in (450mm) TT (bow), 2 x torpedoes.
Complement: 17.

History: The outcome of the competition among the first three classes (*U-1, U-3, U-5)*was an order to Germania for five 500-ton boats, to be commissioned into the Austro-Hungarian Navy as *U-7* to *U-11*. However, war broke out before they could be delivered and since the long voyage was considered too

U-20 class

Type: coastal, diesel-electric.
Total built: 4.
Completed: 1916-17.
Displacement: surfaced 173 tons; submerged 210 tons.
Dimensions: length 127ft 2in (38.8m); beam 13ft 0in (4.0m); draught 9ft 0in (2.8m).
Propulsion: 1 x diesel, 450bhp; 1 x electric motor, 160shp; one shaft.
Performance: surface – 12kt; submerged – 9kt.
Weapons: 2 x 17.7in (450mm) TT (bow); 2 x torpedoes.
Complement: 18.

dangerous they were sold to the Germany Navy, who commissioned them as *U-66* to *U-70* (see *U-66* entry). An alternative solution was found in the German UB-1-class, for which the German builder, AG Weser, devised a plan to despatch the boats in sections by rail. The first two boats were duly despatched in sections and rivetted together at Pola. They were then commissioned into the Imperial German Navy as *UB-1* and *UB-15* and operated for several months under the Austrian flag, but manned by German crews and with just one Austrian officer aboard each boat. They were then transferred to the Austrian Navy in mid-1915 as *U-10* and *U-11*, respectively, and manned by Austrian crews. The remaining three, *U-15, -16, -17,* were operated from the start as Austrian units.

As built, none had a deck-gun, but in late 1916 all were armed, *U-11* with a 66mm weapon, the others with a 37mm. *U-16* was sunk during the war, while *U-10* was mined but recovered and rebuilt; she with the other survivors was transferred to Italy in 1920 and scrapped.

History: The Austria-Hungary Navy acquired a number of miscellaneous submarines. One was the French *Curie*, which was sunk trying to enter the main naval base at Pola, and then recovered, repaired and commissioned as *U-14*. Commanded by Oberleutnant Georg Ritter von Trapp, it became one of the most successful boats in the Austrian Navy, while the captain was later immortalised as the hero in the film "The Sound of Music". *U-20* had its origins in a design ordered from Whitehead at Fiume in 1911 by the Royal Danish Navy; three were built and delivered between 1911 and 1913 as the Havmanden-class. On the outbreak of war the Austria-Hungarian Navy seized the design and in March 1915 ordered four boats (*U-20* to *U-22*). Such was the inefficiency of the Austrian system, however, that the boats were not actually commissioned until late 1916/early 1917. All took part in operations in the Adriatic; two were sunk and two survived the war to be ceded to the Allies and scrapped in the early 1920s.

Left: **U-14 (French Curie-class). Captured and rebuilt by the Austrian Navy, her captain was von Trapp, later hero of the film "The Sound of Music".**

U-27 class

Type: coastal, diesel-electric.
Total built: 8.
Completed: 1916-17.
Displacement: surfaced 264 tons; submerged 301 tons.
Dimensions: length 121ft 1in (36.9m); beam 14ft 4in (4.4m); draught 12ft 2in (3.7m).
Propulsion: 2 x diesels, 270bhp; 2 x electric motors, 280shp; two shafts.
Performance: surface – 9kt;submerged – 7kt; maximum operational diving depth 164ft (50m).
Weapons: 2 x 17.7in (450mm) TT (bow); 4 x torpedoes.
Complement: 23.

History: This was the most numerous class of submarines built for the Austria-Hungarian Navy and was essentially the German UB-II design built under licence with a few minor modifications to meet Austrian operational requirements. The order was placed in October 1915, with six to be built at the Pola Naval Yard and two by the Danubius Yard at Fiume. All were delivered in 1917, having taken somewhat longer to build than their German counterparts. The only known variation in the design was *U-41,* the last to be completed, whose hull was extended by 30in (762mm) to accommodate two diesel engines of a different design, which had originally been intended for *U-6.* All served in the Adriatic but only one was lost (due to causes unknown, in early April 1917). After the war the surviviving boats were allocated to France and Italy, who scrapped them.

These were the last boats to be built for the Austria-Hungary Navy. Two UB

Aegir/Rota classes

Type: coastal, diesel-electric.

Class	Ægir (B-class)	Rota (C-class)
Total built	5	3
Completed	1915-16	1918-20
Displacement surfaced submerged	185 tons 235 tons	301 tons 369 tons
Dimensions length beam draught	133ft 2in (40.6m) 12ft 2in (3.7m) 7ft 11in (2.4m)	133ft 2in (47.5m) 14ft 5in (4.4m) 8ft 9in (2.7m)
Propulsion main engines power electric motors power shafts	2 x diesel 450bhp 2 340shp one	2 x diesel 900bhp 2 640shp two

Above: Austrian U-27-class, modified German UB-II-class.

Il-class submarines were operated locally by the German Navy and then sold to Austria in 1917, who commissioned them as *U-43* and *U-47*. Various other designs were either under construction or on the drawing-boards at the time of the Armistice.

Performance		
speed, surface	13.5kt	14.5kt
submerged	9.8kt	10.5kt
Weapons		
TT	3 x 18in (457mm)	4 x 18in (457mm)
location	bow – 2, stern – 1	bow – 2, stern – 1
guns	1 x 57mm	1 x 57mm
Complement	11	17

Specifications in all cases, as built.

History: The Royal Danish Navy's first submarine was *Dykkeren*, which was designed and built by Fiat at La Spezia (see Italy). Driven by two Fiat gasoline engines, it sailed to Denmark where it was accepted in June 1909. It was later given the Danish pennant number "1" and was sunk in collision with a Norwegian steamer in 1916. This was followed by the Havmanden-class, which was designed by Whitehead at Fiume, with six completed between 1911 and 1914, of which three (*Havmanden, Thetis, Triton*) were built at Fiume and three (*Havfruen, Najaden, Nymfen*) under licence at the Copenhagen Navy Yard (see Havmanden- class under Austria-Hungary).

They were later redesignated the A-class. Denmark was neutral during World War I, and all six boats served until being scrapped between 1928 and 1932.

Next came the Ægir-class of five boats, which were designed and built in the Copenhagen Navy Yard. This was the class in production when

Below: C-class submarine, **Rota***, launched August 1918.*

Below right: Danish-built **Neptun** *(B-class) launched in 1915.*

Aigrette-class

FRANCE

Type: harbour-defence, diesel-electric.
Total built: 2.
Completed: 1904.
Displacement: surfaced 178 tons; submerged 253 tons.
Dimensions: length 117ft 7in (35.9m); beam 13ft 3in (4.0m); draught 8ft 7in (2.6m).
Propulsion: 1 x diesel engine, 150bhp; 1 x electric motor, 130shp; one shaft.
Performance: surface – 9.3kt; submerged – 6.2kt; range surfaced 1,300nm at 8kt, submerged 65nm at 3.8kt.
Weapons: 4 x 17.7in (450mm) (2 x Drzwiecki launch cradles, 2 x external cradles).
Complement: 14.

History: The history of French submarine development in the 1890s and early 1900s is one of a bewildering succession of classes, most consisting of one, sometimes two boats, before the Navy and technology moved on. The number of designers in the field can be judged by the fact that when the Navy ran an open competition in 1896 for a 200-ton boat it attracted no fewer than 29 submissions. One of the well-known designers of the day, Maxime Laubeuf (1864-1939), was responsible for a number of sound designs starting with the steam-driven Narval- and Sirène-class (see "Steam" section), which were, in essence, submersible torpedo boats, with twin hulls and ballast tanks between them. Laubeuf's next step was the Aigrette-class, which was based on the Sirène design, but with diesel-electric

Dykkeren was sunk in 1916, and plans were made to build an additional boat to replace it, but although the materials were acquired it was never built.

Fourth in this Danish series was the Rota- or C-class of three boats, designed and built in Denmark. It was originally planned to have a fifth torpedo tube on the upper casing but this could not be made to work properly on the first-of-class and the idea was shelved. All three were scuttled in Danish ports on 29 August 1943 and were later raised and scrapped in the 1950s.

rather than steam power. One feature, typical of the time, was that all four torpedoes were mounted in external launching frames and not in internal tubes. As completed, *Aigrette* had two large girders mounted at an angle, one at the bow, the second above the bridge; they appear to have been intended to deflect the cables used to protect harbour entrances.

It was originally planned to build a total of 13 boats, but in the event only two were completed, *Aigrette* and *Cigogne*. Both served in a harbour defence role in World War I and were scrapped in 1919.

Below: **Aigrette*, with cable-cutters and torpedo in drop-collar.*

Émeraude/Mariotte-classes FRANCE

Type: coastal, diesel-electric.
Total built: 6.
Completed: 1906-08.
Displacement: surfaced 392 tons; submerged 425 tons.
Dimensions: length 147ft 4in (44.9m); beam 12ft 10in (3.9m); draught 12ft 0in (3.6m).
Propulsion: 2 x Sautter-Harlé diesel engines, 600bhp; 2 x electric motors; two shafts.
Performance: surface – 11.5kt; submerged – 9.2kt; range surfaced 2,000nm at 7.3kt, submerged 100nm at 5kt.
Weapons: 6 x 17.7in (450mm) TT (bow – 4; stern – 2); 6 x torpedoes.
Complement: 21.
Specifications for Émeraude-class, as built.

History: The Émeraude-class introduced the French Navy's custom of naming submarines after precious stones, which continues to this day. With a submerged displacement of 425 tons, these were the largest submarines and their armament of six torpedo tubes the heaviest built in France up to this time. They suffered from a number of problems, mainly related to inadequate surface buoyancy and unreliable diesel engines. As built, they had no guns, but in August 1915, two of the class became the first French boats to be armed in this way, each being fitted with a single 37mm cannon.

There was a plan at one stage to produce two boats to a modified Émeraude design in which the hull would have been lengthened by 32ft 9in (10m). Work was actually started on both at Rochfort Arsenal, but seems to

Circé-class FRANCE

Type: coastal, diesel-electric.
Total built: 2.
Completed: 1907.
Displacement: surfaced 351 tons; submerged 491 tons.
Dimensions: length 154ft 6in (47.1m); beam 16ft 1in (4.9m); draught 9ft 10in (3.0m).
Propulsion: 2 x M.A.N. diesel engines, 630bhp; 2 x electric motors, 460shp; two shafts.
Performance: surface – 11.9kt; submerged – 7.7kt; range surfaced 2,160nm at 8kt, submerged 98nm at 3.5kt.
Weapons: 6 x 17.7in (450mm) drop-collars/external cradles, 6 x torpedoes.
Complement: 22.

History: Maxime Laubeuf, who had designed the Narval-, Sirène- and Aigrette-classes, next turned to the Circé-class. Two boats, *Circé* and *Calypso*, were ordered in 1904 and launched three years later in September and October 1907, respectively. This was again a twin-hull design, but this time, however, Laubeuf selected the German firm of M.A.N. to supply the diesel engines.

Above: Saphir *(Émeraude-class), as completed in 1908.*

have proceeded very slowly and all work ceased in 1908.

The design was altered yet again to produce *Mariotte,* which was launched in February 1911. This was even longer, with an overall length of 210ft 3in (64.7m) but had the same power train. Armament was, however, different, with four internal torpedo tubes and two in external Drzwiecki drop-collars; a total of eight 17.7in (450mm) torpedoes was carried. During trials she attained an underwater speed of 11.7kt, a remarkable speed for that era, although how long it was sustained is not recorded. *Mariotte* was employed in the Gallipoli campaign.

Calypso collided with *Circé* off Toulon on 7 July 1914 and was sunk; collisions between submarines were not rare, but it was unusual for a boat to be sunk by its own sister-ship. In May 1917, during World War I, *Circé* sank the German minelayer, *UC-24* (see UC II-class), but was later herself sunk by *U-47* (see U 43-class).

Below: Circé*, a twin-hull Laubeuf design, launched in 1907.*

Brumaire-class

Type: coastal, diesel-electric.
Total built: 16.
Completed: 1911-13.
Displacement: surfaced 397 tons; submerged 551 tons.
Dimensions: length 170ft 11in (52.1m); beam 17ft 9in (5.1m); draught 10ft 2in (3.1m).
Propulsion: 2 x M.A.N. 6-cylinder diesel engines, 840bhp; 2 x electric motors, 660 shp; two shafts.
Performance: surface – 13kt; submerged – 8.8kt; range surfaced 1,7800nm at 10kt, submerged 84nm at 4kt.
Weapons: 1 x 17.7in (450mm) TT (bow), 2 x torpedoes; 4 x Drzwiecki drop-collars, 2 x external cradles, 6 x torpedoes.
Complement: 29.

History: Laubeuf had already been responsible for the 18-strong steam-powered Pluviôse-class (see "Steam" section) and this new class of 16 was essentially a diesel-powered alternative. The main engines were M.A.N.-designed diesels, but manufactured under licence in France by a variety of companies, including Indret, AC Loire, Normand, Sabathé and Sautter-Harlé. All these boats were involved in World War I where they served in the Mediterranean and, in common with most submarines in most navies, they were fitted with a gun on the foredeck in 1916, in this case either a 75mm or a 47mm.

One of the early losses during the war was *Curie*, which was captured by

Clorinde/Amphitrite/ Bellone-classes

Type: coastal, diesel-electric.
Total built: 2.
Completed: 1914.
Displacement: surfaced 413tons; submerged 567 tons.
Dimensions: length 176ft 10in (53.9m); beam 16ft 9in (5.1m); draught 11ft 2in (3.4m).
Propulsion: 2 x M.A.N.-Loire 2-stroke diesels, 800bhp; 2 x electric motors, 700shp; two shafts.
Performance: surface – 13kt; submerged – 9kt; range surfaced 1,300nm at 10kt, submerged 100nm at 5kt.
Weapons: 6 x Drzewiecki drop-collars, 2 x external cradles; 8 x 17.7in (450mm) torpedoes.
Complement: 29.
Specifications for Clorinde-class, as built.

History: A product of the designer M. Hutter, the two boats of the Clorinde-class were developed from Laubeuf's Brumaire-class. *Clorinde* and *Cornélie* were slightly larger than the Brumaire-class and had rather more powerful engines with a designed output power of 1,300bhp, but no more than 800bhp was ever obtained in practice, as a result of which the expected

Above: **Curie*, as built and prior to rebuild by Austrian Navy.***

the Austro-Hungarians, modified and put into service as *U-14* (see U-20 entry above). Two were sunk by mines, *Bernoulli* (February 1918) and *Joule* (May 1915), while *Foucault* was sunk by Austro-Hungarian aircraft in May 1915, one of the earliest examples of aircraft sinking a submarine. A 1917 plan to convert the surviviving boats into minelayers was not pursued and they were stricken at a slow rate, starting with *Coulomb* in 1919 and ending with *Brumaire* in 1930.

15kt surface speed was never realised. Like most contemporary French submarines they did not have any torpedo tubes, being fitted instead with a mix of "drop-collars" designed by the Russian engineer Drzwiecki, and simple frames, all of which were mounted on the upper casing. This was much simpler than torpedo tubes, but they could not be reloaded at sea. Both boats were

Below: French Bellone-class, with unique free-flood casing.

employed in the Atlantic during World War I and both were given a 75mm deck gun at some time in 1916-17. They were stricken in 1926.

The Clorinde-class was followed by eight boats of the Amphitrite-class, which were virtual repeats, but with slight increases in the beam (17ft 9in/5.4m) and in submerged displacement (609 tons). Authorised in the Navy's 1909 programme, they were not laid down until 1911-13 and completed until 1914-15. Two of the class were completed as minelayers, although they did not become available until 1918.

Three more boats were built to an improved and larger design, also by Hutter. The Bellone-class were 216ft 6in (60.6m) long, with a submerged displacement of 788 tons. Their engines had a theoretical output of 1,800bhp, although, again, this was never achieved and the maximum surface speed was just under 15kt against a designed figure of

Armide/O'Byrne-classes   FRANCE

Type: patrol, diesel-electric.

Class	Armide	O'Byrne
Total built	3	3
Completed	1916-17	1919-20
Displacement surfaced submerged	457 tons 670 tons	342 tons 513 tons
Dimensions length beam draught	184ft 5in (56.2m) 17ft 1in (5.2m) 9ft 10in (3.0m)	172ft (52.4m) 15ft 5in (4.7m) 8ft 10in (2.7m)
Propulsion main engines power electric motors power shafts	2 x diesels 2,200bhp 2 900shp two	2 x diesels 1,020bhp 2 400shp two

17kt. *Bellone* was completed in 1915, *Gorgone* in 1916 and *Hermione* in 1917. All three served on in the post-war Navy and all were stricken in July 1935.

***Below:* Artemis *(Amphitrite-class)*with Drzwiecki dropcollars.**

Performance		
speed, surface	17.5kt	14kt
submerged	11kt	8kt
range, surfaced	2,600nm at 11kt	1,850nm at 10kt
submerged	160nm at 5kt	55nm at 5kt
Weapons		
TT	6 x 17.7in (450mm)	4 x 17.7in (450mm)
location	bow	bow
torpedoes	8	6
guns	1 x 47mm	1 x 47mm
Complement	31	25

Specifications in all cases, as built.

History: Maritime nations have traditionally considered it their right on a declaration of war to requisition naval vessels under construction for foreign navies in their shipyards, and it is of little concern whether these were ordered by hostile or friendly nations. Thus, the French naval ministry requisitioned six submarines during the course of World War I, all of them being constructed by Schneider, at Chalon-sur-Saône.

Schneider was building four large, long-range boats, two each for Greece and Japan. These were double-hulled boats with a submerged displacement of 670 tons, designed by Maxime Laubeuf and based on his very successful Pluviôse- and Brumaire-classes. The boats intended for Japan were the S1-class and were to be numbered #14 and #15 by the IJN, but the French requisitioned only the former, which was taken over on 3 June 1915, just before its launch, and commissioned into the French Navy as *Armide*. (The second boat was completed and delivered to the IJN as *#15*). The Greeks had already taken delivery of two Schneider-built boats (see Delfin-class, above) and this second pair were due to be delivered in 1917. They had the temporary Greek designations of *"X"* and *"Ps"* but were taken over by the French on 30 May 1917 and commissioned as *Amazone* and *Antigone*. All three boats served well into the post-war period, before being stricken between 1932 and 1935.

The O'Byrne-class originated in an order from the Rumanian Navy (its first for submarines) placed with Schneider in 1916, at a time when that country was allied to the Western powers. When Rumania was defeated by Germany the French requisitioned the three boats, although they were not actually launched until 1919-20, well after the war's end, but by then Rumania was in no position to pay for them. They were a little smaller than the Greek and Japanese boats; one was stricken in 1928, the other two in 1935.

Right: Built for Rumania, Henri Fournier *was requisitioned.*

Fulton-class   FRANCE

Type: patrol, diesel-electric.
Total built: 2.
Completed: 1917-19.
Displacement: surfaced 870 tons; submerged 1,247 tons.
Dimensions: length 242ft 9in (74.0m); beam 21ft 0in (6.4m); draught 11ft 10in (3.6m).
Propulsion: 2 x Schneider-Carels diesels, 2,700bhp; 2 x electric motors, 1,640shp; two shafts.
Performance: surface – 16.5kt; submerged – 11kt; range surfaced 4,300nm at 10kt, submerged 125nm at 5kt.
Weapons: 8 x 17.7in (450mm) TT; 10 x torpedoes; 1 x 75mm gun.
Complement: 47.

History: These two submarines were originally intended to have steam propulsion, which would have given them a surface speed of 20kt and a range of 2,400nm at 10kt. Construction was approved under the 1914 funding programme, but *Joessel* was not launched until July 1917 and *Fulton* until April 1919, much of this delay being due to the decision, made in the light of wartime experience but while they were under construction, that they should be powered by diesel engines. As a result, the steam units were reallocated to two sloops and the submarines were completed with a pair of Schneider-Carels diesels instead. Both boats also had internally mounted torpedo tubes, the

Above: **Amazone** *(Armide-class), originally built for Greece.*

various external drop-collars and frames having at last been abandoned, and both mounted a 75mm gun. After completion, a much higher bridge structure was added. There was to have been a second batch of six boats, with work starting from May 1915 onwards, but the programme was cancelled. *Fulton* and *Joessel* were both stricken in mid-1935.

Below: Meant for steam, **Joessel** *was completed with diesels.*

La Grange-class

Type: patrol, diesel-electric.
Total built: 4.
Completed: 1918-25.
Displacement: surfaced 920 tons; submerged 1,318 tons.
Dimensions: length 246ft 9in (75.2m); beam 20ft 8in (6.3m); draught 11ft 10in (3.6m).
Propulsion: 2 x Sulzer diesels, 2,600bhp; 2 x electric motors, 1,640shp; two shafts.

Performance: surface – 16.5kt; submerged – 11kt; range surfaced 4,300nm at 10kt, submerged 125nm at 5kt.
Weapons: 8 x 17.7in (450mm) TT; 10 x torpedoes; 2 x 75mm guns.
Complement: 47.

History: As with the Fulton-class, these four boats were ordered just before the outbreak of war and were to have steam propulsion plants, but the Navy decided during construction that this should be changed to diesels. As a result, the steam units were reallocated to sloops and the Lagrange-class fitted with Sulzer

U1-class

Type: coastal, diesel-electric.
Total built: 1.
Completed: 1906.
Displacement: surfaced 238 tons; submerged 283 tons.
Dimensions: length 138ft 9in (42.3m); beam 12ft 6in (3.8m); draught 10ft 6in (3.2m).
Propulsion: 2 x Körting diesel engines, 400bhp; 2 x electric motors, 400shp; battery 396 cells; two shafts.
Performance: surface – 10.8kt; submerged – 8.7kt; range surfaced 1,500nm at 10kt, submerged 50nm at 5kt; maximum operating diving depth 98ft (30m).
Weapons: 1 x 17.7in (450mm) TT (bow); 2 x torpedoes.
Complement: 22.

History: In 1902 Germaniawerft, newly bought by steelmaker Krupp, started to design submarines, their first product, a 17-ton vessel named *Forelle*, being sold to the

Right: The first of the "U-boats," U-1, commissioned in 1906.

diesels. Also as in the Fulton-class, these boats were reconstructed after the war and among other improvements were given higher bridges and much improved periscopes. The boats were completed in a somewhat erratic order: *La Grange* – 1917; *Romazotti* (the last to be ordered) – 1918; *Laplace* – 1919; and *Regnault* – 1924. *La Grange* was stricken in 1935, the remainder in 1937.

Below: La Grange*, following her post-war rebuild.*

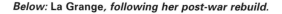

Imperial Russian Navy .The firm then sold a further three larger boats (Karp-class) to Russia and it was only at this point that the Imperial German Navy began to show interest in this new weapon. The order for the first boat was placed in April 1904, with the design being prepared by a Spanish naval architect, d'Equevilley-Montjustin, and construction taking place at Germaniawerft. The design was based on that of the Russian Karp-class, although the Germany naval staff, aware of numerous accidents with petrol engines, insisted on engines driven by kerosene (paraffin). These were certainly safer, but the fuel was far more pungent and there was a major tactical penalty in that the boats emitted a vast cloud of dense white exhaust, which could be seen for miles. The particular type of engines installed in *U-1* could not be reversed, as a result of which she was fitted

---

Forel/Karp-classes   GERMANY (RUSSIA)

Type: coastal, diesel-electric.
Total built: 3.
Completed: 1907.
Displacement: surfaced 207 tons; submerged 235 tons.
Dimensions: length 130ft 0in (39.6m); beam 9ft 0in (2.7m); draught 8ft 0in (2.5m).
Propulsion: 2 Körting kerosene engines, 400bhp; 2 x electric motors, 200shp; two shafts.
Performance: surface – 10kt; submerged – 8.5kt; range surfaced 1,250nm at 10kt, submerged 50nm at 5kt; maximum operating diving depth 98ft (30m).
Weapons: 1 x 18in (457mm) TT (bow); 2 x Drzwiecki drop-collars.
Complement: 28.

History: The Imperial Russian Navy was among the most enthusiastic of submarine pioneers and initially concentrated on its own designs (see Aleksandrowski, Drzwiecki, Delfin/Kasatka), but the outbreak of the Russo-Japanese war (8 February 1904) led to an emergency expansion. Orders were quickly placed to acquire submarines from the United States (see Holland, Lake) and also from Germany. The first to be purchased was the *Forel*, a midget, electrically powered submarine, which had been designed and built by

with controllable-pitch propellers.

The new boat was commissioned in 1906 as *Unterseeboot-1* (submarine number 1), thereby introducing a new (and ominous) term into the international lexicon. *U-1* was subjected to careful testing and then took part in many trials, including a 1910 exercise with *U-3* and *U-4* in which they practised working together against a surface enemy, a tactic which would become known 30 years later as a "wolf-pack".

U-1 was relegated to training duties before the outbreak of World War I and was stricken in 1920. She was then presented to the Deutsches Museum in Munich, where she remains on display to this day, cut-away to reveal the extraordinary hazards and dire conditions endured by the submarine pioneers.

Germaniawerft, Kiel, as a private venture, intended to interest the German Navy in submarine operations. When this failed to happen they sold the vessel to Russia where it was immediately deployed to Vladivostok, but it proved too small to be of any tactical value. Meanwhile, in June 1904 the Russians placed another order with Germaniawerft for three boats. The yard itself was not very experienced in submarine work, but its chief designer, the Spaniard D'Equevilley had worked with Maxime Laubeuf in France and already had several successful designs to his credit. The Russians became considerably annoyed when the German Navy not only placed an order with Germaniawerft for a boat which was virtually identical to their *Karp*, but also ensured that the yard gave such priority to the German boat that although it had been started later was finished before any of the Russian boats.

The three Karp-class boats were delivered to Russia in 1907 and then transferred to the Black Sea by rail. *Kambala* was accidentally rammed and sunk by the Russian battleship *Rostislav* in June 1909, but the remaining two served until 1917, when they were stricken. They became part of the short-lived Ukrainian Navy in 1918, but were then captured by the Germans, only to be surrendered to the British in November 1918, who ordered them to be scuttled.

Below: Russia's three Karp-class boats, built in Germany.

U-13/U-16/U-17 classes   GERMANY

Type: coastal, diesel-electric.

Class	U-13	U-16	U-17
Total built	3	1	2
Completed	1910-11	1911	1912
Displacement surfaced submerged	516 tons 644 tons	489 tons 627 tons	564 tons 691 tons
Dimensions length beam draught	189ft 11in (57.9m) 19ft 8in (6.0m) 11ft 2in (3.4m)	189ft 8in (57.8m) 19ft 8in (6.0m) 11ft 2in (3.4m)	204ft 9in (62.4m) 19ft 8in (6.0m) 11ft 2in (3.4m)
Propulsion main engines power electric motors power shafts	4 x Körting diesels 2 x 350/2 x 250bhp 2 2 x 600shp two		4 x Körting diesels 4 x 350bhp 2 2 x 600shp two

Performance
speed, surface
    submerged
range, surfaced
    submerged
	14.8kt
	10.7kt
	2000nm/14kt
	90nm/5kt
		15.6kt
		10.7kt
		2,100nm/15kt
		90nm/5kt
			14.9kt
			9.5kt
			6,700nm/8kt
			75nm/5kt

Weapons TT location torpedoes	4 x 17.7in (450mm) bow – 2; stern – 2 6		
Complement	29		

History: The U-1-class was followed by steadily improving designs: U-2-class – one boat; U- 3-class – two boats; U-5-class – four 4 boats; and U-9-class – four boats. All were powered by kerosene (paraffin) engines and all were armed with four 17.7in (450mm) torpedo tubes. This first series of boats culminated in the three classes listed here, which were virtually identical, with the U-13-class (three boats) and U-17-class (two boats) built at the Danzig Navy Yard, while the U-16-class (one boat) was built by Germaniawerft. All served during World War I. *U-13*, *U-14*, *U-15* and *U-18* were sunk in 1914-15, and of the two survivors *U-16* sank while on tow to England with only *U-17* managing to reach a breaker's yard. *U-16* and *U-17* both had a 2in (50mm) gun added at some time after 1915.

Right: **U-17** *receives a torpedo at sea; not an easy task.*

Above: U-13, *lead boat in a class of three completed 1910-11.*

Above: U-16; *note plume from kerosene-engine exhaust.*

U-19/U-23/U-27/ U-31/U-43-classes

Type: patrol, diesel-electric.

Class	U-19	U-23	U-27	U-31	U-43
Total built	4	4	4	11	8
Completed	1912-13	1913	1913	1914	1914-15
Displacement surfaced submerged	650 tons 837 tons	669 tons 864 tons	675 tons 867 tons	685 tons 878 tons	725 tons 940 tons
Dimensions length beam draught	210ft 8in (64.2m) 20ft 0in (6.1m) 11ft 10in (3.6m)	212ft 3in (64.7m) 20ft 8in (6.3m) 11ft 6in (3.5m)	212ft 3in (64.7m) 20ft 8in (6.3m) 11ft 6in (3.5m)	212ft 3in (64.7m) 20ft 8in (6.3m) 11ft 10in (3.6m)	213ft 3in (65.0m) 20ft 4in (6.2m) 12ft 2in (3.7m)
Propulsion main engines power electric motors power shafts	2 x M.A.N. 2 x 850bhp 2 2 x 600shp two	2 x Germania 2 x 900bhp 2 2 x 600shp two	2 x M.A.N. 2 x 1,000bhp 2 2 x 600shp two	2 x Germania 2 x 925bhp 2 2 x 600shp two	2 x M.A.N. 2x1000bhp 2 2x 600shp two
Performance speed, surface submerged range, surfaced submerged maximum operational diving depth	14.8kt 10.7kt 2000nm/14kt 90nm/5kt 164ft (50m)	15.6kt 10.7kt 2,100nm/15kt 90nm/5kt 164ft (50m)	14.9kt 9.5kt 6,700nm/8kt 75nm/5kt 164ft (50m)	16.4kt 9.7kt 7,800nm/8kt 80nm/5kt 164ft (50m)	15.2kt 9.7kt 8100nm/8kt 51nm/5kt 164ft (50m)
Weapons TT location torpedoes guns	4 x 17.7in (450mm) bow – 2; stern – 2 6 1 x 88mm				4 x 19.7in (500mm) bow – 2; stern – 2 6 2 x 88mm
Complement	29			35	36

History: The next five classes were very similar to each other. The first in the series, the U-19-class, introduced two major developments, of which the most significant was that surface power was provided by diesel engines rather than the unsatisfactory kerosene engines. Second, it was armed with four tubes for the new 19.7in (500mm) torpedo, which was both more powerful and more reliable than its predecessor. Each class was constructed by one builder: Danzig Naval Yard built the U-19, U-27 and U-43 classes, which were all powered by M.A.N. diesels, while Germaniawerft built the U-23- and U-31-classes and powered them with its own Germania diesels. The great majority of these boats were given deck-guns in 1915-16, which were of two types, either one (or in some cases, two) 3.9in (88mm), or one 4.1in (105mm) (none was known to have mounted two of these heavier weapons). Further, some of those fitted with 88mm weapons in 1915 had them replaced by 105mm guns in 1916-17. These variations almost certainly stemmed from what was available in dockyards, although the desires and persuasiveness of individual captains may have also played a part.

All served throughout World War I, with two achieving different types of distinction. *U-29* was rammed and sunk by HMS *Dreadnought* on 18 March 1915, the only known occasion on which a submarine has been sunk by a battleship. The other boat was *U-35*, which remains the highest scoring submarine of all time, having sunk no fewer that 224 ships (535,000 gross registered tons) in the course of 25 patrols off the British and West African coasts, and in the Mediterranean. This was achieved under the command of four highly skilled officers, of whom the most famous was Kapitän-Leutnant Lothar von Arnauld de la Perrière, whose personal score was 194 ships sunk (453,716 tons); indeed, in one three-week cruise in *U-35* he sank 54 ships (91,000 tons), which was achieved with the expenditure of 900 rounds of ammunition and four torpedoes. Fifteen of the 31 U-boats were war losses and

Below: U-29, photographed from one of her victims.

the surviving boats were broken up by the European Allies, except for *U-46* which went to Japan, where it served as *O-2* until 1922, when it, too, was scrapped.

The one break in the numerical sequence from *U-19* to *U-50* was *U-42*, which was ordered from the Italian company, Fiat, in order to gain knowledge of foreign submarine and diesel engine technology. However, the war broke out before it could be delivered, the boat was requisitioned by the Italian Navy as *Ballila* (qv), and the number 42 in the first series of German numbering remained unused.

Right: U-35, highest scoring submarine in any navy, ever.

U-51/U-57/U-63/ U-81 classes

GERMANY

Type: patrol, diesel-electric.

Class	U-51	U-57*	U-63	U-81
Total built	6	12	3	6
Completed	1915-15	1916-17	1916	1916
Displacement surfaced submerged	715 tons 902 tons	786 tons 954 tons	810 tons 927 tons	808 tons 946 toms
Dimensions length beam draught	213ft 11in (65.2m) 21ft 0in (6.4m) 11ft 10in (3.6m)	219ft 10in (67.0m) 20ft 8in (6.3m) 12ft 6in (3.8m)	224ft 5in (68.4m) 20ft 8in (6.3m) 13ft 2in (4.0m)	230ft 0in (70.1m) 20ft 8in (6.3m) 13ft 2in (4.0m)
Propulsion main engines power electric motors power shafts	2 x M.A.N. 2 x 1,200bhp 2 2 x 600shp 2	2 x M.A.N. 2 x 900bhp 2 2 x 600shp 2	2 x Germania 2 x 1,000bhp 2 2 x 600shp 2	2 x M.A.N. 2 x 1,200bhp 2 2 x 600shp 2

History: The first "Mobilisation" (Ms) type was the U-51-class, six boats (*U-51* to *U-56*) built by Germania, the design being an improved version of the pre-war U-31-class, which had been built by the same company. There were a number of improvements: for example, two more torpedoes were carried, for a total of eight, while the two 88mm deck-guns were mounted during construction (they were later replaced by a single105mm gun in most boats). Two boats were lost in World War I, three survived to be broken up in 1919-22, and the fourth survivor was allocated to Japan where it become *O-3*.

Performance				
speed, surface	17.1kt	14.7kt	16.5kt	16.8kt
submerged	9.1kt	8.4kt	9.0kt	9.1kt
range, surfaced	9,000kt/8nm	7,730nm/8kt	8,100nm/8kt	8,100nm/8kt
submerged	55kt/5nm	55nm/5kt	115nm/5kt	56nm/5kt
maximum operational diving depth	164ft (50m)	164ft (50m)	164ft (50m)	164ft (50m)

Weapons	
TT	4 x 19.7in (500mm)
location	bow – 2; stern – 2
torpedoes	8
guns	2 x 88mm or 1 x 105mm

Complement	
	35

Specifications for U-57 to U-62, as built.

Right: U-53 of the U-51-class at sea in 1917.

The U-57-class consisted of two groups, *U-57* to *U-62*, and *U-99* to *U-104*, both built by AG Weser, at Bremen. These were virtually identical except that the second group had more powerful diesels (2 x 1,200bhp) and could stow a total of 12 torpedoes. Seven were lost in the war: three to surface warships, one to mines, one to another submarine, one cause unknown, and one rammed by the liner *Olympic*; the boats that survived were broken up.

The U-63-class was a further batch of three improved U-51-class boats built by Germania, ordered in May 1915. One was lost in the war, one was scuttled, and one survived to be broken-up.

Finally in these first Ms-boats came the U-81-class, a further batch of six from Germania. Torpedo stowage was again increased, this time to 12. Two survived the war, one being broken-up while the other foundered on the way to the breakers' yard; four were lost during the war, one by a submarine and three by surface warships.

Right: U-86 (U-81-class) at an English port, following her surrender. The forward gun was a 105mm, the after gun an 88mm. Torpedo armament was four 500mm (19.7in) tubes (2 bow, 2 stern) and 12 torpedoes.

U-66-class

GERMANY (AUSTRIA)

Type: patrol, diesel-electric.

Class	U-7 (Austria)	U-66 (Germany)
Total built	0	5
Completed	–	1916-17
Displacement surfaced submerged	695 tons 885 tons	791 tons 933 tons
Dimensions length beam draught	228ft 0in (69.5m) 20ft 8in (6.3m) 12ft 5in (3.9m)	228ft 0in (69.5m) 20ft 8in (6.3m) 12ft 6in (3.8m)
Propulsion main engines power electric motors power shafts	2 x diesels 2 x 1,150bhp 2 2 x 620shp 2	2 x Germania 2 x1,1500bhp 2 2 x 615shp 2

Performance		
speed, surface	17kt	16.8kt
submerged	11kt	10.34kt
range, surfaced	–	6,500nm/8kt
submerged	–	115nm/5kt
maximum operational		
diving depth	164ft (50m)	164ft (50m)
Weapons		
TT	6 x 450mm (17.7in)	5 x 17.7in (450mm)
location	bow – 4; stern – 2	bow – 4; stern – 1
torpedoes	9	12
gun	1 x 66mm	1 x 88mm
Complement	36	36

History: The U-66-class was not part of the German "Mobilisation" (Ms) programme, but was an unsought bonus. Following their early experiences, the Austro-Hungarian Navy stated a requirement for a new type, which was essentially an improved version of the Austrian *U-3*. The competition was won by Germaniawerft of Kiel and five boats were ordered in February 1913 (as the

Austrian *U-7* to *U-11*) for delivery in 1916-17. There was to be a powerful armament of six torpedo tubes and a single 66mm gun, and particular emphasis was placed on a high underwater speed, to achieve which there was to be no bridge while a battery of very powerful cells was installed. On the outbreak of World War I, however, it was considered that the proposed delivery voyage from Kiel to Pola in the Adriatic would be far too hazardous and the boats were much too large to be sent by rail, so they were sold, on

U-87/U-93-classes

GERMANY

Type: patrol, diesel-electric.

Class	U-87 (Project 25)	U-93
Total built	6	24
Completed	–	1916-17
Displacement surfaced submerged	757 tons 998 tons	838 tons 1,000 tons
Dimensions length beam draught	224ft 9in (65.8m) 20ft 4in (6.2m) 12ft 9in (3.9m)	234ft 11in (71.6m) 20ft 8in (6.3m) 12ft 9in (3.9m)
Propulsion main engines power electric motors power shafts	2 x M.A.N. 2 x 1,200bhp 2 2 x 620shp 2	2 x M.A.N. 2 x 1,200bhp 2 2 x 620shp 2

the ways, to Germany. The German Navy then had them modified to German standards, for example by replacing the Austrian 66m gun by a German 88mm and increasing the torpedo load-out to 12, and then completed the work. Three were sunk by British ships and two survived the war, to be broken-up in 1919-21.

Below: **U-70** *was built for Austria, but bought by Germany.*

Performance		
speed, surface	16.9kt	16.8kt
submerged	8.6kt	8.6kt
range, surfaced	8,000nm/8kt	8,300nm/8kt
submerged	56nm/5kt	50/5kt
maximum operational diving depth	164ft (50m)	
Weapons		
TT	6 x 450mm (17.7in)	6 x 450mm (17.7in)
location	bow – 4; stern – 2	bow – 4; stern – 2
torpedoes	12	12
gun	1 x 105mm	1 x 105mm
Complement	36	36

History: The U-87-class, all built by Danzig Naval Yard, was based on *U-50*, the last of the U-43-class, but with the number of forward torpedo tubes increased to four and the torpedo load-out doubled to 12. In addition, the gun armament was changed from two 88mm guns to one 105mm. Six were built, of which four were war losses. Up till now German U-boats had either vertical stems or a backward sloping stem, but a noticeable change in the U-93 class was the adoption of the raked 'clipper' bow. This is generally thought to have been intended to improve sea-keeping when running on the surface (which was certainly one of its effects) but the real reason was that, in combination with the raked and serrated cable-cutter now mounted atop the bow, it was intended to

UB-1-class (Project 34)

Type: coastal, diesel-electric.
Total built: 17.
Completed: 1915.
Displacement: surfaced 127 tons; submerged 142 tons.
Dimensions: length 92ft 2in (28.1m); beam 10ft 6in (3.2m); draught 9ft 10in (3.0m).
Propulsion: 1 x Daimler 4-cylinder diesel, 60bhp; 1 x Siemens-Schuckert electric motor, 120shp; one shaft.
Performance: surface – 6.5kt; submerged – 5.5kt; range surfaced 1,650nm at 5kt, submerged 45nm at 4kt; maximum operating diving depth 164ft (50m).
Weapons: 2 x 17.7in (450mm) TT (bow); 2 x torpedoes; 1 x 8mm MG.
Complement: 14.

History: The speed of the German advance along the North Sea coast in August-September 1914 took the Imperial German Navy by surprise and it found itself faced with a demand for small coastal submarines, but with no assets immediately available to meet it. A design was rushed through and on 15 October an order was duly placed for what was, in essence, a submersible torpedo-boat, with a displacement of about 125 tons and armed with two torpedo tubes. An essential element of the requirement was that the boat had to be transportable by railroad. The result was a neat little craft, single-hulled and with a maximum diameter of 10ft 4in (3.15m), which was imposed by the railway loading limits, and a crew of 14.

The initial order was for eight boats from Germaniawerft (*UB-1* to *UB-8*) and seven boats from AG Weser (*UB-9* to *UB-15*); the former were powered by Daimler diesels, the latter by Körting diesels. This order was, however, quickly increased by two (*UB-16* and *UB-17*) to compensate for the sale of two of the initial order (*UB-1* and *UB-15*) to the Austro-Hungarian Navy. Several years later German ally Bulgaria wanted to buy two of these boats for the defence of its

enable the boat to force its way through anti-submarine nets more effectively. The cable-cutter and raked bow then became a visual characteristic of German U-boat design for the next 20 years.

Below: U-96 shows the smooth lines of 1917-18 U-boats.

Above: The UB-1 class boats were built incredibly quickly.

Black Sea port, Varna; *UB-7* was sunk before it could be handed over, but *UB-8* was delivered in May 1918.

Building time was extraordinarily short, the first boat being completed in just 75 days and the last of the 17 was handed over in May 1915. All but a few boats were then despatched by rail, each requiring three low-loader wagons for the main assemblies (the fore-, centre- and after-sections) plus more for the bridge, engines and cells. Most went to either Antwerp or Hoboken, but a number also went to Pola on the Adriatic coast.

In 1918 four were converted to minelayers, which involved adding a section to increase hull length to 105ft (32.0m) and replacing the torpedo tubes by four 39.4in (1,000mm) mine tubes; eight mines could be carried. A total of seven boats were lost during the war, one was demolished by the Germans as they withdrew from Flanders; the remainder were scrapped in 1919-20.

UB-II-class (Project 39)   GERMANY

Type: coastal, diesel-electric.
Total built: 30.
Completed: 1915-16.
Displacement: surfaced 263 tons; submerged 292 tons.
Dimensions: length 118ft 5in (36.1m); beam 14ft 5in (4.4m); draught 12ft 2in (3.7m).
Propulsion: 2 x Daimler, Körting or Benz diesels, 2 x 140bhp; 2 x electric motors, 280shp; two shafts.
Performance: surface – 9.2kt; submerged – 5.8kt; range surfaced 6,500nm at 5kt, submerged 45nm at 4kt; maximum operating diving depth 164ft (50m).
Weapons: 2 x 19.7in (500mm) TT (bow); 4 torpedoes; 1 x 50mm gun.
Complement: 22.
Specifications for UB-18, as built.

History: The first batch of coastal submarines (see UB-I-class above) was produced remarkably quickly and did all that had been asked of it in the operational requirement, but that was soon out-of-date. Even as the first boats were running trials in early 1915, it was realised that they were too slow and too small. Once they were in service, however, a further problem was revealed; in the current state of development of diesel engines a single engine/single propeller drive system was woefully inadequate and a mechanical problem anywhere in the power-train left the boats wallowing helplessly and very vulnerable. So, the UB-II (Project 39) was developed as a matter urgency, with a larger hull, more powerful electrical cells and a

---

UB-III-class (Project 44)   GERMANY

Type: coastal, diesel-electric.
Total built: 93.
Completed: 1917-18.
Displacement: surfaced 516 tons; submerged 651 tons.
Dimensions: length 181ft 5in (55.3m); beam 19ft 0in (5.8m); draught 12ft 2in (3.7m).
Propulsion: 2 x A.E.G., M.A.N., Körting or Benz diesels, 2 x 550bhp; 2 x electric motors, 2 x 296shp; two shafts.
Performance: surface – 13.5kt; submerged – 7.5kt; range surfaced 9,040nm at 6kt, submerged 55nm at 4kt; maximum operating diving depth 164ft (50m).
Weapons: 5 x 19.7in (500mm) TT (bow – 4; stern – 1); 10 torpedoes; 1 x 105mm gun.
Complement: 34.
Specifications for UB-48, as built.

History: By mid-1915 one of the major problems facing the German Navy was the maintenance of the blockade around the British Isles. There was also a need for boats to carry out patrols in the Mediterranean The large U-boats were in short supply and new ones were taking a long time to build, while the much smaller UB-I and UB-II boats were simply inadequate for the job; their endurance was insufficient, the armament poor and the crew too few in number for protracted patrols in such a harsh environment. A requirement was therefore stated for a U-boat of simple design, displacing some 600 tons and, most importantly, which could be designed and built quickly.
    The new design was based upon that of the UC-II minelayer (qv), but with

Above: UB-40, one of 30 coastal boats of the UB-II-class.

second power-train, all of which added some 270 tons to the surface displacement. Initially, it was accept-ed that these boats could not bemoved by rail, although this was actually achieved, even though it entailed cutting the hull sections longitudinally.

A total of 30 boats were built, 12 by AG Weser in two blocks of six, the remaining 18 by Blohm + Voss. This was Blohm + Voss's first U-boat construction programme. Two were sold to Austria-Hungary in 1917; *UB-43* and *UB-47* kept the same numbers, becoming *U-43* and *U-47*, respectively. Despite their small size and limited capabilities, some of these boats were very successful: *UB-18* sank 126 merchant ships (128,555 tons) while *UB-40* sank fewer ships but with a greater tonnage – 99 ships (131,680 tons). Some 20 boats were lost during the war (surface warships – 10; mines – 7; aircraft – 2; scuttled – 1), leaving 10 which were broken up in 1919-22.

Above: Nine Blue Maxes were won aboard UB-III-class boats.

a totally new forward section and a torpedo compartment in place of the vertical minelaying shafts. This enabled the boats to mount a forward battery of four 19.7in (500mm) torpedo tubes, with a fifth tube in the stern. The deck gun was a naval pattern 88mm gun on a U-boat mounting. The initial orders were issued in May 1916 and a total of 93 boats were built in four yards: Blohm + Voss, Hamburg; AG Weser, Bremen; Vulkan, Hamburg; and Germaniawerft, Kiel, and more were under construction at the war's end. There were many minor differences between the various production batches and by 1918 boats were just over 2ft (0.6m) longer and had increased in displacement by some 5 tons.

UB-III boats served in the waters around the British Isles, as well as the Mediterranean, and of the 29 awards of *Pour le Merite* made to U-boat officers during World War I, no fewer than nine went to men serving aboard UB-III-class boats. Many of these boats were lost in the war, and the relatively small number that survived were handed over to the Allies and broken up.

Kobben/A-2-classes GERMANY (NORWAY)

Type: patrol, kerosene/diesel-electric.

Class	Kobben (A-1)	A-2
Total built	1	3
Completed	1909	1913
Displacement surfaced submerged	206 tons 259 tons	268 tons 353 tons
Dimensions length beam draught	128ft 11in (39.3m) 12ft 2in (3.7m) 9ft 10in (3.0m)	152ft 7in (46.5m) 15ft 9in (4.8m) 8ft 10in (2.7m)

History: The Royal Norwegian Navy (RNorN) was one of the first to show an interest in submarines and sent an officer to watch the trials of USS *Holland* (SS-1) in 1901. Norway's first proposal to build submarines was made in 1902, but it was not until 1907 that the parliament endorsed the Navy's plans. An order was then placed with Germania and the first boat was delivered on 28 November 1909. It was named *Kobben*, but this was changed in 1913 to *A-1*. This boat was generally similar to Germany's *U-1* (qv) and like that boat was powered by two Körting kerosene engines, but had an oval cross-section and an external torpedo tube aft. *Kobben* was used for trials and training, but was used operationally in World War I in defence of Norway's neutrality. She was stricken in 1926 and scrapped in 1933.

In May 1911 Norway next ordered a further three boats to a new design, and these, the A-2-class, were again built by Germania, being launched in 1913 and delivered in early 1914. Norway also placed a further order for a fourth boat in 1912, but this was not launched until May 1914 and was still fitting out when war was declared in August 1914; she was immediately requisitioned by the German Navy and commissioned as *UA*. These four boats had a gyroscopic compass, a wireless installation, and a transverse propeller in the bow for precise positioning when launching torpedoes while the boat was stationary.

The RNorN employed *A-2*, *A-3* and *A-4* as operational boats and they were still in service when Germany invaded Norway in April 1940. Two were unable

Propulsion		
engines	2 x Körting gasoline	2 x Germania diesels
power	2 x 225bhp	2 x 350bhp
electric motor	2	2
power	2 x 150shp	2 x 190shp
shafts	two	two
Performance		
speed, surface	11.9kt	14.5kt
submerged	8.9kt	9.0kt
range, surfaced	1,450nm/9kt	900nm/10kt
submerged	45nm/6.5t	76nm/3.3kt
diving depth	164ft (50m)	164ft (50m)
Weapons		
TT	3 x 18.0in (457mm)	3 x 18.0in (457mm)
location	bow – 2; deck – 1	bow – 2; stern – 1
torpedoes	4	5
Complement	14	17

Above: Norwegian A2, built by Germania, captured by Germany.

to attack the invaders and were scuttled by their crews, but *A-2* was forced to the surface by German ships. She changed hands several times before being broken up. *UA* was employed briefly by the Germans as an operational boat, but was transferred to training in 1916 and was scrapped in the UK in 1919.

Holland-class

Type: harbour defence, gasoline-electric.
Total built: 5.
Completed: 1901-02.
Displacement: surfaced 113 tons; submerged 122 tons.
Dimensions: length 63ft 10in (19.5m); beam 11ft 10in (3.6m); draught 9ft 11in (3.0m).
Propulsion: Wolseley gasoline engine, 160hp; 1 x electric motor, 70hp; one shaft.
Performance: surface – 7.4kt; submerged – 6kt; range surfaced 235nm at 7kt, submerged 20nm at 5kt; maximum operating diving depth 50ft (15m).
Weapons: 1 x 18in (457mm) TT (bow); 3 x torpedoes.
Complement: 8.

History: The Royal Navy watched the development of submarines abroad with growing concern, especially those immediately across the Channel in France, but it was not until the success of the Holland boats in the United States that they decided to take positive action. Thus, when the Electric Boat Co. let the British know that they would be interested in a deal, negotiations were quickly concluded and a contract signed for the construction of a Holland design at the Vickers yard at Barrow-in-Furness. The design was virtually the same as that of the U.S. Navy's Adder-class (qv) and progress was rapid, HMS *No 1* being laid down in February 1901 and launched in October, and all five were in service by 1903. They were to standard Holland pattern, single-hulled, with one torpedo tube in the bows and a gasoline engine for surface propulsion and recharging

A-class

Type: harbour defence, gasoline-electric.
Total built: 13.
Completed: 1902-05.
Displacement: surfaced 190 tons; submerged 207 tons.
Dimensions: length 103ft 3in (31.5m); beam 11ft 10in (3.6m); draught 10ft 1in (3.1m).
Propulsion: 1 x 16-cylinder Wolseley gasoline engine, 350bhp; 1 x electric engine, 125hp; battery 120 cells; one shaft.
Performance: surface – 9.5kt; submerged – 6kt; range surfaced 500nm at 9kt, submerged 20nm at 5kt; maximum operating diving depth 50ft (15m).
Weapons: 1 x 18in (457mm) TT (bow); 3 x torpedoes.
Complement: 11.
Specifications for A-1, as built.

History: The rapid progress made by both Vickers and the Admiralty meant that the sixth of the Holland-class was built to a revised design and became HMS *A-1*, the first of the A-class. She was 40ft (12m) longer and had a much more powerful gasoline engine, but there were numerous changes made to the class during construction. Thus, all boats from *A-2* to *A-13* had a larger hull, 105ft 0in (32.0m) in length, with a 12ft 9in (3.9m) beam and a surface draught of 10ft 8in (3.3m). The output power of the Wolseley gasoline engine was also progressively improved: *A-1* – 350bhp; *A-2* to *A-4* – 450bhp; *A-5* to *A-7* – 550bhp; and *A-8* to *A-12* – 600bhp. The electric motor was also improved, giving 125shp in *A-1* and 150shp in all later boats. Armament was given a significant increase in *A-5* onwards, which had two torpedo tubes, both in the

Above: British Holland inadvertantly displays its lines.

the batteries. They were used to gain experience in the design and operation of such novel warships, but despite the fact that they were worked hard and used for many trials, not one was lost in service. The original intention was to build six units, but progress was so rapid that the sixth was altered while under construction and became the first unit of the British A-class (qv).

All the boats were commissioned in 1902-03 and served for some 10 years. All were sold in 1912-13 and two were broken up. The other three, however, all sank whilst on tow to the breaker's yard, including *No 1* whose wreck was found in April 1981. She was then raised and is now on display at the RN Submarine Museum in Gosport, the only original Holland design to have survived.

Above: Pre-1914 picture of British submarine A-11.

bow, and carried a total of four torpedoes. The last boat, *A-13*, was powered by a Hornsby-Ackroyd six-cylinder, vertical, heavy-oil engine, an interim step in the progress towards a true diesel engine. Other changes included increases in the height of the conning-tower and the introduction of an embryonic bridge.

The A-class was a success and provided a major advance in the Royal Navy's build-up of a submarine arm. Three out of the first four suffered a fate which was all too common in the early days of submarines (and which is by no means unknown today), namely accidental ramming by a surface ship. Thus, *A-1* was lost on 18 March 1904, *A-4* on 16 October 1905 and *A-3* on 2 February 1912, and although all three were raised, none was ever returned to service. *A-7* foundered and was lost in January 1914, but nine boats survived until 1919-20 when they were sold for breaking up, although *A-2* sank en route to the breaker's yard.

B/C-classes

Type: coastal defence, gasoline-electric.
Total built: 11.
Completed: 1904-06.
Displacement: surfaced 287 tons; submerged 316 tons.
Dimensions: length 142ft 2in (43.3m); beam 13ft 7in (4.1m); draught 11ft 7in (3.4m).
Propulsion: 1 x 16-cylinder Vickers gasoline engine, 600bhp; 1 x electric motor, 290shp; battery 166 cells; one shaft.
Performance: surface – 12kt; submerged – 6kt; range surfaced 1,300nm at 9kt, submerged 50nm at 4.5kt; maximum operating diving depth 50ft (15m).
Weapons: 2 x 18in (457mm) TT (bow); 4 x torpedoes.
Complement: 15.
Specifications for B-class, as built.

History: The C-class was a virtual repeat of the B-class, all major characteristics being identical, so the two are treated here together. A total of 11 B-class were launched between 1904 and 1906 and were generally similar in layout to the A-class but appreciably longer and with a much more substantial deck casing to improve surface performance and to make life easier for the crew. The A-class had a single pair of hydroplanes aft, but the B-class had an additional pair mounted on the conning tower in order to improve underwater manoeuvrability, but this was never repeated in a British design.

Six boats (*B-6* to *B-11*) were sent to the Mediterranean and one of these, *B-11*, managed to penetrate the Dardanelles defences and sink the Turkish coastal guardship *Messudieh* (9,120 tons) on 13 December 1914. These six boats became unemployable after 1915 due to lack of essential spares in the theatre, so they were converted at the Italian Navy's Venice dockyard into surface patrol boats. One was, however, destroyed in an Austrian bombing

D-class

Type: coastal, diesel-electric.
Total built: 8.
Completed: 1908-11.
Displacement: surfaced 483 tons; submerged 595 tons.
Dimensions: length 163ft 0in (49.7m); beam 20ft 6in (6.2m); draught 10ft 5in (3.2m).
Propulsion: 2 x 6-cylinder diesels, 2 x 600bhp; 2 x electric motors, 2 x 277shp; battery 210 cells.
Performance: surface – 14kt; submerged – 9kt; range surfaced 1,750nm at 11.2kt, submerged 50nm at 5kt; maximum operating diving depth 100ft (30.5m).
Weapons: 3 x 18in (457mm) TT (bow – 2, stern – 1); 6 x torpedoes.
Complement: 25.
Specifications for D-1, as completed.

History: The D-class incorporated three substantial improvements in British submarine design: the introduction of diesel engines, which resulted in a substantial enhancement in safety for the crews; the first use of saddle tanks, which gave a much higher reserve of buoyancy; and the use of transverse watertight bulkheads, greatly improving survivability in the event of an accident. They were also the first with twin propellers and two engines, the latter being

Above: **C-37** *shows the continuous upper casing now fitted.*

attack while being rebuilt, leaving only five to be employed in the Adriatic. *B-2* was sunk in a collision with a merchant ship, *B-10* was sunk during the war and all the remainder were sold for breaking-up in 1919-21.

No fewer than 38 C-class boats were built, six in the Royal Dockyard at Chatham and all the rest by Vickers, in what was the largest submarine production run up to that time, launches being from July 1906 to February 1910. They were identical to the B-class in most respects, but lacked the amidships hydroplanes and had many detailed improvements.

C-11 was sunk in a peacetime collision with a merchant ship in 1909, but the remainder, although built for coastal work, all had a very busy war. Most were based in the UK, but three (*C-26, C-28, C-35*) were sent to help Russia in 1916, being sent to Archangel by ship, and then by canal barge and rail to the Baltic; all three were scuttled in April 1918 to prevent capture by the Germans.

Above: **D-8**; *note the upper rudder.*

important at a time when engines were none too reliable. All this led to an increase in length – 163ft (49.7m) compared to 142ft (43m) in the B/C-classes – but this meant that a crew of 25 could be accommodated, the extra numbers being needed for the longer operations. The boats were armed with twin 18in (457mm) torpedo tubes in the bows, which were in an "over-and-under" configuration to ensure that the bow was as fine as possible. Only one, *D-4*, ever mounted a gun, a 12-pounder on a "disappearing" mount, which proved clumsy and complicated and was later fixed; as far as can be ascertained this was the first gun to be mounted during construction in any submarine, in any navy. There were marginal differences in length – *D-1* was 163ft (49.7m) long, while *D-2* was slightly shorter at 162ft 1in (49.4m), and *D-3* to *D-9* longer at 167ft 7in (50.2m).

E-class

Type: attack, diesel-electric.

Class	E-1 group	E-9 group
Total built	10*	41**
Completed	1912-13	1913-16
Displacement surfaced submerged	655 tons 796 tons	667 tons 807 tons
Dimensions length beam draught	178ft 1in (54.2m) 22ft 8in (6.9m) 12ft 6in (3.8m)	181ft 0in (55.2m) 15ft 2in (4.6m) 12ft 6in (3.8m)
Propulsion engines power electric motor power shafts	2 x Vickers-Admiralty diesels 2 x 800bhp 2 2 x 420shp two	
Performance speed, surface submerged range, surfaced submerged maximum diving depth	15.25kt 9.25kt 3,000nm/10kt 65nm/5kt 200ft (61m)	
Weapons TT location torpedoes gun	4 x 18in (457m) bow – 1, stern – 1, beam – 2 8 1 x 12pdr (76mm)	5 x 18in (457mm) bow - 2; stern -1; beam - 2 10 1 x 12pdr
Complement	30	34

* Includes two for RAN.
** Does not include six completed as minelayers.

History: The E-class were enlarged and improved versions of the D-class, but the main operational difference resulted from a request by the officers of the Submarine Service, who asked for beam torpedo tubes to be fitted. The problem was that the torpedoes of the time had to be fired at very short ranges; indeed, the teaching was that the boat had to approach to a distance from the target of some three times the length of the submarine – and this meant that in an "end-on" attack the boat then had great difficulty in getting away without colliding with its victim. Some submarine officers held this opinion so strongly that they wanted to do away with bow tubes altogether, but this view did not prevail. The first eight boats (E-1-class) were therefore completed with just one

Above: E-class boat with 12pdr (76mm) on foredeck.

bow tube, one stern tube and two of the new lateral tubes, one on each beam. Exercises, later reinforced by wartime experience, showed that this was not the answer and from *E-9* onwards there were two tubes in the bow, but, unlike the "over-and-under" in the D-class, these were side-by-side.

Although not fitted during construction in the early boats, from 1915 onwards all E- class had a single gun, usually the 12-pdr (76mm), although a 6pdr and the heavier 4in (102mm) was fitted in some boats, a few of them on a "disappearing mount". The E-1 group had two watertight bulkheads, but from *E-9* onwards this was increased to three, but it should be noted that contemporary Italian designs, eg, Fiat-Laurenti, had 10 such bulkheads. The boats were originally classified as having an operational depth of 100ft (31m) but this failed to take account of the stronger hull and the internal bulkheads and was later increased to 200ft (61m). In fact, *E-40* once struck bottom at 318ft (97m) and the only damage was minor leaks at the engine hatch and stern tubes.

The original plan was for the E-class to be succeeded by the larger G-class, but these took longer to build and on the outbreak of war in August 1914 it was decided to order more E-class boats to build up the British submarine force as quickly as possible.

Below: E-31, one of 35 E-class Group III boats built 1915-17.

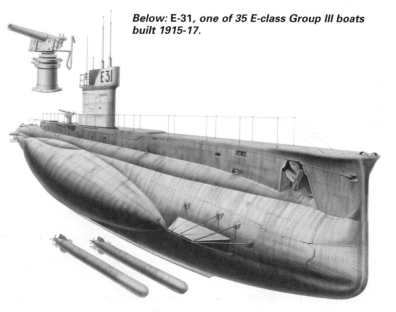

V-class

Type: attack, diesel-electric.
Total built: 4.
Completed: 1914-15.
Displacement: surfaced 386 tons; submerged 453 tons.
Dimensions: length 144ft 0in (43.9m); beam 16ft 6in (5.0m); draught 11ft 6in (3.5m).
Propulsion: 2 x Vickers-Admiralty 8-cylinder diesels, 2 x 450bhp; 2 x electric motors, 2 x 150shp; battery 132 Exide cells; two shafts.
Performance: surface – 14kt; submerged – 8.5kt; range surfaced 3,000nm at 9kt, submerged 50nm at 5kt; maximum operating diving depth 150ft (46m).
Weapons: 2 x 18in (457mm) TT (bow); 4 x torpedoes; 1 x 12pdr (76mm) gun.
Complement: 20.
Specifications for V-1, as built.

History: In 1912 the Admiralty sought two coastal types displacing 250-300 tons, and a committee recommended the Italian Fiat-Laurenti design which was then built by Fiat's UK agents, Scott's of Greenock (see S-type, below). But, despite having plenty of other work on hand, Vickers produced a design of their own, and, somewhat surprisingly, this was accepted.

The V-class had a partial double-hull, which extended over about 75 ft (23m) amidships, and a well designed hull which gave the boats a good underwater speed, although submerged endurance was limited by the electrical capacity of the cells in the battery. There were minor variations between *V-1* and the remaining boats *V-2* to *V-4*, mainly because the latter had two additional 21in

---

F-class

Type: coastal, diesel-electric.
Total built: 3.
Completed: 1915-16.
Displacement: surfaced 353 tons; submerged 525 tons.
Dimensions: length 151ft 0in (46.0m); beam 16ft 1in (4.9m); draught 10ft 7in (3.2m).
Propulsion: 2 x Vickers diesels, 2 x 450bhp; 2 x electric motors, 2 x 200shp; battery 128 New Exide cells; two shafts.
Performance: surface – 14.5kt; submerged – 9kt; range surfaced 3,000nm at 9kt, submerged 90nm at 3kt.
Weapons: 3 x 18in (475mm) TT (bow – 2; stern – 1); 6 x torpedoes; 1 x 2pdr gun.
Complement: 19.

History: The Admiralty placed orders for three different types of coastal submarines in 1912 and early 1913 – S-, V- and W-classes – but despite this it was decided to order yet another class, this time to the Admiralty's own design, resulting in the F-class. The design was based on that of the V-class, but with a number of improvements, including a third (stern) torpedo tube and two additional torpedoes, with a partial double-hull.

The three boats were built at different yards, with long intervals between them, the builders and launch dates being: *F-1* – Chatham Navy Yard, March 1915; *F-2* – J. Samuel White, July 1917; and *F-3* – Thornycroft, February 1916. The three boats were identical except that *F-1* and *F-3* were powered by standard Vickers diesels, while *F-2* was powered by M.A.N. diesels built under licence by J. Samuel White. A further five boats were planned but were

Above: British V-class coastal submarine; four were built.

(0.53m) frames inserted in the centre of the hull and two shorter frames removed forward, which resulted in a net increase in length of 3ft 6in (1.1m) and an increase in submerged displacement of 4 tons. A further difference was that *V-1* had two Laurence Scott electric motors (2 x 150shp) whereas the others had Don Works motors (2 x 190shp).

Two boats served in the English Channel in 1915-16, following which all four operated in the North Sea, being based at Harwich and Great Yarmouth. Two boats were transferred to training duties in 1918, but all four were placed in reserve as soon as the war ended and were sold for scrapping in 1920-21.

Above: F-2 on builder's trials in 1917.

cancelled by Admiral Fisher on his return to the Admiralty as First Sea Lord on the outbreak of war. The three boats served in harbour defence and training duties during the war and were scrapped in the early 1920s.

Nautilus-class

Type: overseas, diesel-electric.
Total built: 1.
Completed: 1915.
Displacement: surfaced 1,441 tons; submerged 2,026 tons.
Dimensions: length 258ft 5in (78.8m); beam 26ft 0in (7.9m); draught 17ft 9in (5.4m).
Propulsion: 2 x Vickers 12-cylinder diesels, 2 x 1,850hp; 2 x electric motors, 2 x 500shp; battery 2 x 176 Exide cells; two shafts.
Performance: surface – 17kt; submerged – 10kt; range surfaced 5,300nm at 11kt, submerged 72nm at 5kt; maximum operating diving depth 200ft (61m).
Weapons: 8 x 18in (457mm) TT (bow – 2; stern – 2; beam – 4), 16 x torpedoes; 1 x 12pdr (76mm) gun.
Complement: 42.

History: The origin of this design lay in a 1912 Admiralty requirement for what was then termed an "overseas submarine" (ie, with longer range and greater endurance than the coastal types), which would have double-hull construction, displace some 1,000 tons and be capable of a surface speed of 20kt. This speed was of great significance, since 20kt was the current speed of the battlefleet and this requirement was to lead in due course to the attempt in many navies to produce a "fleet submarine" capable of moving and cooperating closely with surface ships. Diesel-electric submarines were never able to meet this requirement, steam-electric submarines came a little closer but introduced all sorts of other problems, and it was only the advent of nuclear propulsion that produced the answer.

The requirement went to Vickers, at that time not only Britain's most

G-class

Type: attack, diesel-electric.
Total built: 14.
Completed: 1916-17.
Displacement: surfaced 703 tons; submerged 837 tons.
Dimensions: length 187ft 1in (57.0m); beam 22ft 8in (6.9m); draught 13ft 4in (4.1m).
Propulsion: 2 x Vickers 8-cylinder diesels, 2 x 800bhp; 2 x electric motors, 2 x 420shp; battery 2 x 100 Exide cells; two shafts.
Performance: surface – 14.3kt; submerged – 9kt; range surfaced 2,400nm at 12.5kt, submerged 99nm at 3kt.
Weapons: 1 x 21in (533mm) TT (stern), 2 x torpedoes; 4 x 18in (457mm) TT (bow – 2, beam – 2), 8 x torpedoes; 1 x 3in (76mm) AA gun.
Complement: 30.

History: In 1913 naval intelligence reported that there was a large-scale programme in Germany to build long-range, double-hulled submarines, which would produce a very clear threat to British naval interests. In a somewhat panicked response the Admiralty issued a requirement for a new type with a displacement similar to the E-class (ie, about 800 tons submerged), a partial double-hull, one of the very new 21in (533mm) torpedo tubes forward, and two 18in (457mm) tubes, one on each beam. This resulted in the G-class and between June and November 1914 orders were placed for a total of 15 boats with Chatham Dockyard (five), Armstrong Whitworth (two), Vickers (six), Scott's (one) and White (one). Some of these firms were given permission to install their own choice of suitable diesel, with a view to expanding the knowledge-base on this relatively new type of engine. However, on the

Above: Intended for "overseas" duties, Nautilus was a failure.

experienced submarine builders, but also the most experienced with diesel engines. They responded with a design powered by a new type of 12-cylinder diesel, which, with an output of 1,850bhp, would be capable of driving the boat at 17kt on a displacement of 1,270 tons.

The Admiralty placed an order with Vickers and the *Nautilus* was launched on 31 December 1914, but development of the very advanced big diesel took much longer, especially under wartime conditions, and the boat was not completed until October 1917, by which time she had been re-named *N-1*.

Nautilus was quickly relegated to other uses, first as an instructional ship and then as a floating generator. Although the exercise was an apparent failure the experience gained in building such an advanced and (for the time) large boat and its diesel engines proved invaluable experience for the future. *N-1* was sold for scrap in 1922.

Above: G-10; note gun and large masts for HF radio antenna.

outbreak of war the supply of M.A.N. engines from Germany stopped immediately, while the main alternative came from Sulzer in neutral Switzerland; obtaining the latter might have been possible but could not be guaranteed. The outcome was that all these boats were completed with Vickers engines, except for *G-13*, built by Scott's, which had two Fiat diesels (800bhp each), and even those were unsatisfactory and were later replaced by Vickers engines.

It was originally planned to install the single 21in (533mm) tube in the bows but war experience showed that a minimum of two tubes were needed to secure a good probability of a hit, but for weight reasons it was impossible to install a second of the larger tubes, so the 21in tube was moved to the stern and replaced by two 18in tubes. The gun was a 3in (76mm) weapon on a "disappearing " mount.

One boat was cancelled, so only 14 were completed, 13 in 1916 and one in 1917. All operated in the North Sea, where they sank two U-boats for the loss of three of their own.

J-class

Type: overseas, diesel-electric.
Total built: 7.
Completed: 1916.
Displacement: surfaced 1,204 tons; submerged 1,820 tons.
Dimensions: length 275ft 6in (84.0m); beam 23ft 0in (7.0m); draught 14ft 0in (4.3m).
Propulsion: 3 x Vickers 12-cylinder diesels, 3 x 1,200bhp; 2 x electric motors, 2 x 675shp; battery 232 cells; three shafts.
Performance: surface – 19.5kt; submerged – 9.5kt; range surfaced 5,000nm at 12.5kt, submerged 55nm at 5kt.
Weapons: 6 x 18in (457mm) TT (bow – 4, beam – 2), 12 x torpedoes; 1 x 12pdr (76mm) gun, 1 x 3in (76mm) AA gun.
Complement: 44.

History: In late 1914 the Admiralty received reports that the German Navy was developing U-boats with a surface speed of 22kt, which coincided with yet another request from Admiral Jellicoe, CinC Grand Fleet, for a submarine capable of operating with the main fleet. As a result, Admiral Fisher, who had recently returned to duty as First Sea Lord and had a fascination with speed, determined that the Royal Navy must produce something even faster. At the time Vickers was still trying to get their new, big 1,850hp diesels to run properly (see Nautilus-class) and steam was briefly considered for this new project and then rejected. The only apparent option remaining was to produce a more powerful engine by adding another four cylinders to the existing eight-cylinder

H-class

Type: coastal, diesel-electric.

History: Shortly after the outbreak of war in 1914 the president of Bethlehem Steel visited the UK and secured a contract to supply the Royal Navy with 20 coastal submarines, identical in all respects to the U.S. Navy's H-class (qv). In view of the United States' neutrality, it was arranged that all the parts for the first 10 boats would be delivered to Canadian-Vickers who would then assemble them. The next 10 of the order, however, would be built entirely in the United States, since it was considered at that time that the war would have ended by the time of delivery, so that the question of U.S. neutrality would no longer be relevant. Despite the complexities of manufacturing components all over the USA, sending them to Canada and then assembling them in a yard with no previous submarine experience, the Canadian-assembled boats (*H-1* to *H-10*) were completed in record time, the first being delivered on 26 May 1915, the last on 29 June 1915, and they were immediately commissioned into the RN. *H-1* to *H-4* made the first ever crossing of the Atlantic by submarines, proceeding via the Azores and Gibraltar to the eastern Mediterranean, where they took part in the Gallipoli operations. *H-5* to *H-10* crossed in July but went to the UK where they operated in the North Sea. The U.S.-built boats, numbered *H-11* to *H-20*, were also completed very quickly but the planners prediction of an early end to the war proved to be hopelessly optimistic and the boats were then held in Boston Navy Yard. Six (*H-13* and *H-16* to *H-20*) were released in January 1917 and transferred to Chile in partial compensation for the British having requisitioned a Chilean battleship in 1914. The remaining four did not leave the USA until August 1918; two reached the UK and the other two were

Above: J-class, the first to have the raised gun platform.

Vickers diesel and to install three of these in the new J-class. This gave a maximum surface speed of 19.5kt and also resulted in the only three-shaft submarine ever to be built for the RN. For submerged propulsion there was a battery of 232 cells, driving two electric motors, one on each of the outer shafts; there was no motor on the central shaft. All this resulted in a large hull.

These boats had no stern torpedo tubes, but did have four tubes in the bow, one of the first British boats to do so, which resulted in a great increase in the hit probability in a single salvo. There was one reload torpedo for every tube. The main gun was a 3in (76mm) mounted on the foredeck, but when the boats were transferred to Australia in 1919 a raised gun platform immediately before the bridge was fitted to enable the gun to be fought when proceeding into a head sea.

Above: H-class, one of the most popular to serve in the RN.

presented to the RCN.

The H-class boats were popular in the RN. They were excellent sea-boats, very stable and easy to control, and dived quickly. They had four watertight compartments, their machinery was reliable and the bow battery of four tubes gave them impressive firepower. The first 10 worked hard during the war. Four spent the entire war in the Mediterranean where *H-4* sank the German *UB-52* (23 May 1918), while *H-1* sank numerous Turkish vessels, but then accidentally sank the Italian submarine *H-5* (16 April 1918), ironically also an H-class boat and also built by Canadian Vickers. The only one of the four to be lost was *H-3*, mined on 15 July 1916. Of the remaining six, the British *H-5* was lost in a collision (2 March 1918), *H-6* was stran-ded on the coast of the neutral Nether-lands who later ac-quired it and

Class	H-class	H-21 (Improved H)-class
Total built	20*	23
Completed	1912-13	1917-19
Displacement surfaced submerged	364 tons 434 tons	423 tons 510 tons

Dimensions
    length
    beam
    draught
	150ft 3in (45.8m)
	15ft 4in (4.7m)
	12t 6in (3.8m)
		171ft 9in (52.4m)
		15ft 4in (4.8m)
		13ft 3in (4.0m)

Propulsion engines power electric motors power battery shafts	2 x NLSE diesels 2 x 240bhp 2 2 x 310shp 2 x 60 Gould cells two	

com-missioned it into the RNethN as *O-8*, while *H-10* was lost in the North Sea, cause un-known (19 January 1918).

Popular as the original H-class was, the Improved H-class was even better. This

R-class

GREAT BRITAIN

Type: hunter-killer, diesel-electric.
Total built: 10.
Completed: 1918-19.
Displacement: surfaced 410 tons; submerged 503 tons.
Dimensions: length 163ft 9in (49.9m); beam 15ft 3in (4.7m); draught 11ft 6in (3.5m).
Propulsion: 1 x 8-cylinder diesel, 240bhp; 2 x electric motors, 2 x 600shp; 1 x auxiliary motor, 1x 25bhp; battery 4 x 55 Chloride cells; one shaft.
Performance: surface – 9.5kt; submerged – 15kt; range surfaced 2,000nm at 9kt, submerged 15nm at 14kt; maximum operating diving depth 250ft (76m).
Weapons: 6 x 18in (457mm) TT (bow), 12 x torpedoes.
Complement: 22

History: This was one of the most significant and imaginative submarine designs of World War I, being the first "hunter-killer" in any navy and with an underwater speed not equalled until the mid-1940s. The design resulted from wartime experience which showed the RN that a submarine at periscope depth had a reasonable chance of detecting a German U-boat, but that it was then very difficult to actually catch and sink it, with luck frequently being the decisive factor. So, a requirement was prepared for a submarine purpose-built to find, track and destroy enemy U-boats, for which it would need good detection apparatus, high underwater speed and an effective anti-submarine battery. The result of this extremely perceptive analysis was the R-class, single-hulled boats, with a "body-of-revolution" hull – ie, a spindle form symmetrical about the main axis. There was a minimal superstructure, essentially a bow casing, and a

Performance		
speed, surface	13kt	11.5kt
submerged	11kt	10.5kt
range, surfaced	2,000nm/130kt	2,000nm/13kt
submerged	30nm/5kt	70nm/3kt
maximum diving		
depth	150ft (46m)	150ft (46m)
Weapons		
TT	4 x 18in (457m)	4 x 21in (533mm)
location	bow	bow
torpedoes	8	6
Complement	22	22

*All built for RN, but 2 given to Canada and 6 to Chile (see text)

was the result of a 1917 Admiralty requirement for more of these coastal boats. These incorporated a number of improvements as the result of operational experience, principally four 21in (533mm) tubes for the new, larger and much more powerful torpedoes, as well as a much more powerful radio. The boats had to be some 21ft (6.4m) longer to accommodate the larger torpedoes, and orders were placed for 34, but 10 were cancelled prior to completion as a result of the Armistice. One of the others (*H-41*) sank while fitting out and, although raised, was never completed; thus the number joining the fleet was actually 23. Many of these were sold in the 1930s, but nine served in World War II, during which two were lost; the remainder were scrapped in 1944-45.

Above: R-10, one of the first hunter-killers in any navy.

streamlined fairing around the bridge, with a single propeller and two spade rudders to ensure good manoeuverability. Propulsion was provided by a single diesel engine, identical to that used in the H-class (ie, NLSE design, licence-built in the UK), with two electric motors and – another innovation – a 25hp engine, mounted on the main shaft, for slow speed underwater (what would later be termed a "creep motor"). There were six torpedo tubes, a very heavy battery for this size of submarine, but necessary for its mission. It was originally intended to mount a gun, and a gun platform was actually installed in some boats, but no weapon was ever mounted since it would have reduced the underwater speed. In yet another innovation, five sensitive hydrophones were mounted in the bows in order to detect an enemy submarine while both hunter and hunted were submerged.

L-class

Type: attack, diesel-electric.

Class	L-class	L-9-class	L-50-class
Total built	8	13	7
Completed	1917-18	1918-24	1918-25
Displacement surfaced submerged	891 tons 1,074 tons	890 tons 1,080 tons	960 tons 1150 tons
Dimensions length beam draught	231ft 1in (70.4m) 23ft 6in (7.2m) 13ft 3in (4.0m)	238ft 7in (72.7m) 23ft 6in (7.2m) 13ft 3in (4.0m)	235ft 0in (71.6m) 23ft 6in (7.2m) 13ft 2in (4.0m)
Propulsion main engines power electric motors power shafts	2 x diesels 2 x 1,200bhp 2 2 x 800shp two	2 x diesels 2 x 1,200bhp 2 2 x 800shp two	2 x diesels 2 x 1,200bhp 2 2 x 800shp two
Performance speed, surface submerged range, surfaced	17kt 10.5kt 3,800nm at 10kt	17kt 10.5kt 3,800nm at 10kt	17kt 10.5kt 4,500nm at 8t
Weapons TT - bow torpedoes TT - beam torpedoes guns	4 x 18in (457mm) 8 2 x 18in (457mm) 2 1 x 4in (102mm)	4 x 21in (533mm) 8 2 x 18in (457mm) 2 –	6 x 21in (533mm) 12 – 2 x 4in (102mm)
Complement	35	38	44

History: The L-class originated as a slightly larger development of the E-class, but the first pair, originally designated *E-57* and *E-58*, proved to be sufficiently different to be redesignated the L-class and renumbered as *L-1* and *L-2*. These were followed by an order for six more, and the type then underwent several more major developments. The class can be divided into four groups, the first being the basic design, *L-1* to *L-8*, armed with 18in (457mm) bow and beam torpedo tubes. Like the E-class, these were saddle-tank boats, but 50ft (15.3m) longer, the increase being mainly due to the addition of a further two 18in (457mm) torpedo tubes in the bow battery. This resulted in an increase in displacement of 267 tons but considerable improvements in the diesel engines and electric motors resulted in a better performance. Like the E-class, the L-1-class boats had two beam torpedo tubes, but the stern tubes were deleted.

Next came *L-9* to *L-33*, with the omission of *L-13*, which was never ordered (presumably for reasons of superstition), and six minelayers. The major changes

Above: **L-21*, one of 28 in this very successful class.**

in this group were that the forward armament was upgraded to the new 21in (533mm) tubes (but the 18in/457mm beam tubes were retained), an additional watertight bulkhead was fitted, the length of the pressure hull was increased, and fuel capacity was enlarged. The third group, comprising *L- 14*, *L-17* and *L-24* to *L-27*, is described separately in the Minelayer section.

Finally came the L-50-class, which was developed before *L-1* had even been launched. The hull and machinery were virtually the same as in the earlier boats, but the major change was that the number of bow tubes, all 21in (533mm), was increased to six, with one reload for each tube, and the beam tubes were deleted. *L-50* to *L-55* were ordered in early 1917 (before *L-1* had been launched), followed by an order for a further 19 (*L-56* to *L-74*) two months later. With the end of the war, most were cancelled and only seven were actually completed.

All of the L-1-class, six of the L-9-class and none of the L-50-class were completed before the end of the war, and work then continued at a much slower pace to complete the remainder, the last being *L-23*, which had been laid down at Vickers on 29 August 1917 and launched by them on 1 July 1919, but was later towed to the Naval Dockyard at Chatham, where it was finally completed on 31 October 1924.

The gun armament varied widely. Some of the early boats had no guns at all while others were completed with a single 3in (76mm) deck gun on a disappearing mounting on the deck casing. However, the guns (one in earlier boats, two in the L-50-class) were then mounted at bridge level, resulting in a long bridge structure, with separate trunks for the gun crews and ammunition supply. Although such an arrangement seriously affected the topweight, the reason was that it enable the gun crew to get their weapon into action very much faster – usually before the boat was fully surfaced – than if it was mounted at deck level, which was of particular importance in anti-U-boat engagements. This arrangement, accompanied by a breastwork integrated into the mounting and revolving with it, also enabled the crew to fight the gun more effectively in rough weather than was the possible with a deck gun.

Some of the L-class saw war service in the North Sea and English Channel, during which *L-10* sank a German destroyer (3 October 1918) and *L-12* sank *UB-90* (16 October). The only war loss was *L-10* (3 October 1918), although *L-2* was nearly sunk by

Delfino-class

ITALY

Type: patrol, gasoline-electric.
Total built: 1.
Completed: 1892 (?).
Displacement: surfaced 102 tons; submerged 113 tons.
Dimensions: length 78ft 9in (24.0m); beam 9ft 5in (2.8m); draught 8ft 4in (2.5m).
Propulsion: 1 x gasoline, 130bhp; 1 x electric motor, 65hp; one shaft.
Performance: surface – 6kt; submerged – 5kt.
Weapons: 2 x 14in (356mm) TT.
Complement: 8.

History: Designed by a naval engineer, Giacinto Pullino, this was the Italian Navy's first submarine and the first of very many to be built at La Spezia Navy Yard. There is some uncertainty about the dates of her launch and completion, but it seems that she was at sea by 1892. There was clearly a degree of experimentation, since as built she was powered by batteries, which drove three propellers, one for normal propulsion on the horizontal plane, and two for vertical movement, either to dive or to surface. She was completely rebuilt in 1902, during which the bridge was enlarged, the two 14in (356mm) torpedo tubes were replaced by a single 17.7in (450mm) tube

U.S. warships in February 1918. Three of the class were sent to the Baltic during the "Intervention War" in 1919, during which *L-55* hit a British mine and was lost with all hands (4 June 1919). She was salvaged by the Soviet Navy in 1928, the dead were treated with meticulous correctness, and she was then refitted and returned to service, still bearing the same number. The boats provided the backbone of the submarine service in the 1920s when, since the type had been specifically designed for service in the North Sea, the Admiralty naturally despatched a number to serve on the China Station.

The first of the L-9 group was scrapped in 1927, followed by the majority of the L-1s and L-9s in 1931-32, but with the last of these two early groups holding out until 1937. Four of the L-50s were scrapped in the late 1930s, but three continued to serve throughout World War II when they were employed in either training submarine crews or, in 1944-45, providing targets for ASW frigate crews of the Royal Canadian Navy.

Below: Another view of L-21; *note the high gun position.*

and a gasoline engine added for surface propulsion. Despite her age, Delfino saw service in World War I, but was stricken immediately afterwards.

Below: Delfino, *first of many submarines to be built in Italy.*

Glauco/Foca-classes

Type: patrol, gasoline-electric.
Total built: 5.
Completed: 1905-09.
Displacement: surfaced 157 tons; submerged 240 tons.
Dimensions: length 120ft 9in (38.8m); beam 14ft 1in (4.3m); draught 8ft 8in (2.6m).
Propulsion: 2 x Fiat gasoline engines, 600bhp; 2 x Savigliano electric motors, 170shp; two shafts.
Performance: surface – 13kt; submerged – 6kt; range surfaced 900nm at 8kt, submerged 40nm at 5kt.
Weapons: 3 x 17.7in (450mm) TT (bow).
Complement: 15.
Specifications for Glauco, as built.

History: The Glauco-class was the first design from the drawing board of Cesare Laurenti, an engineering lieutenant who was subsequently to be responsible for many important submarines. This was also the first Italian design to be produced in quantity and there were some differences between the boats: *Glauco* was built with three torpedo tubes, while the remainder had only two; and three had Fiat gasoline engines, while the other two had Thornycroft engines. All served in World War I, providing local defence for Brindisi and Venice, but *Glauco* was stricken in 1916 followed by the remainder in 1918.

Foca, designed and built by Fiat at La Spezia, was a slightly larger

Dykkeren-class

Type: patrol, diesel-electric.
Total built: 1.
Completed: 1909.
Displacement: surfaced 105 tons; submerged 132 tons.
Dimensions: length 113ft 10in (34.7m); beam 10ft 10in (3.3m); draught 7ft 3in (2.2m).
Propulsion: 2 x Fiat gasoline engines; 2 x electric motors, 210hp; two shafts.
Performance: surface – 12kt; submerged – 7.5kt; range surfaced 100nm at 8kt.
Weapons: 2 x 18in (457mm) TT (bow).
Complement: 9.

History: In the early 1900s the Royal Danish Navy decided to add the first submarines to its small fleet and, like a number of other navies, it turned to Italy, whose designers enjoyed a considerable reputation at this time. One of these was Engineer Lieutenant-Commander Cesare Laurenti, whose designs had certain common characteristics, including a double hull for about three-quarters of their length and a high reserve of buoyancy, which made them somewhat skittish in a seaway. They also took a long time to dive, but in those pre-radar days that was not too much of a disadvantage. They also had a remarkable number of internal bulkheads; as many as 10 in some.

The *Dykkeren* design was based on the Italian Glauco- and Foca-classes (qv) and in common with them, the gasoline engines were unreliable and the fuel positively dangerous. *Dykkeren* was armed with two 18in (4567mm) torpedo tubes, but never carried a gun.

Dykkeren was commissioned into the Royal Danish Navy in June 1909 but

Right: Glauco -class, the first design of Lieutenant (Engineer) Cesare Laurenti.

development of the *Glauco*, being 19ft 8in (6m) longer and with a 40-ton increase in submerged displacement. As built, it had three shafts, each powered by a Fiat gasoline engine or a Siemens electric motor. However, the boat suffered an internal explosion in April 1909 while in harbour at Naples, which ignited her fuel and to save the boat she was immediately scuttled. She was later raised and returned to La Spezia, where she was rebuilt, but without the central shaft and gasoline engine/electric motor. This explosion convinced the Italian Navy that gasoline was an inherently dangerous fuel and all later designs were powered by diesel engines. Launched in 1908, *Foca* was stricken in 1918.

Above: Danish Dykkeren *was built by Fiat-Laurenti, Italy.*

experienced many mechanical problems which led to her spending a great deal of time in the Royal Dockyard in Copenhagen. She was sunk on 9 October 1916 in a collision with a Norwegian merchant ship. She was raised in 1917 but did not return to service, being scrapped in 1918. The next class of Danish submarine, the Havmanden-class (qv) was ordered from Whitehead in Fiume.

Medusa-class

Type: harbour defence, diesel-electric.
Total built: 8.
Completed: 1911-13.
Displacement: surfaced 248 tons; submerged 252 tons.
Dimensions: length 147ft 8in (45.1m); beam 13ft 9in (4.2m); draught 9ft 6in (3.0m).
Propulsion: 2 x Fiat/M.A.N. diesels, 650bhp; 2 x Savigliano-Siemens electric motors, 300shp; two shafts.
Performance: surface – 12kt; submerged – 8kt.
Weapons: 2 x 17.7in (450mm) TT (bow); 4 x torpedoes.
Complement: 22.

History: These eight boats were the Italian Navy's first class of diesel-powered submarines, all being driven by Fiat engines and Savigliano electric motors, except for *Velella*, which had M.A.N. engines and Siemens motors. Four were built by Fiat, La Spezia, and two each by Orlando and Riuniti Yard, both at Leghorn. They were well thought-of and considered to have particularly good underwater stability and control.

Two were lost to enemy action: *Medusa* by German U-boat, *UB-15*, disguised as Austrian *U-11* (10 June 1915), and *Jalea* by an Austrian-laid mine (17 August 1915). *Zoea* was driven ashore in a storm in 1917 and, although recovered, was not returned to service. At the war's end one boat, *Argo*, was undergoing conversion to an assault transport to carry troops and frogmen in an attack on the Austro-Hungarian naval base at Pola, but the

Below: The Medusa-class had fine lines for their time.

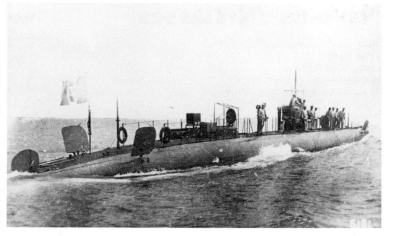

Above: Medusa *was Italy's first diesel-powered submarine.*

attack was cancelled. The six surviving boats were stricken in 1918 and scrapped.

Three other types of small submarine were designed and built for the Italian Navy at this time. One, *Atropo*, was designed and built in Germany and appears to have been an attempt to discover what progress Germany was making in submarine technology. The other two were the two-boat Nautilus-class and six-boat N-class; see next entry.

Nautilus-/N-classes

Type: patrol, diesel-electric.
Total built: 2.
Completed: 1913.
Displacement: surfaced 225 tons; submerged 320 tons.
Dimensions: length 134ft 4in (40.9m); beam 14ft 1in (4.3m); draught 9ft 4in (2.8m).
Propulsion: 2 x Sulzer diesels, 600bhp; 2 x Ansaldo electric motors, 320shp; two shafts.
Performance: surface – 13.2kt; submerged – 8kt; maximum operational diving depth 164ft (50m).
Weapons: 2 x 17.7in (450mm) TT (bow); 4 x torpedoes.
Complement: 19.
Specifications for Nautilus, as built.

History: The Nautilus-class, which entered service just before the outbreak of World War I was the first to be designed by Lieutenant-Commander (Engineer) Curio Bernardis, who went on to became a noted naval architect. The two boats were built in the Venice Navy Yard. Both classes displaced 320 tons and were armed with two 17.7in (450mm) torpedo tubes. Both also had high surface speeds, *Atropo* being capable of just under 15 knots, and all three seem to have been used as submersible torpedo-boats. *Neride* was sunk by Austrian submarine *U-5* (Agust 1915); the other two were stricken in 1919.

Svatoy Georgi/S/ F1-classes

Type: patrol, diesel-electric.

History: The F-1 design was a major success for Italian designer Cesare Laurenti and shipbuilders Fiat-San Giorgio, with a total of 34 built for six navies, including a very prestigious order of three for Britain's Royal Navy. The design originated with the *Svatoy Georgi,* which was ordered by the Imperial Russian Navy in 1912 to a design which was essentially an improved *Medusa* (qv). The improvements included more powerful electric motors, a second periscope, retractable hydroplanes and new signalling equipment. The boat was completed shortly after the outbreak of World War I but before it could be delivered, it was illegally taken over by an impetuous Italian lieutenant who was so desperate to end his country's neutrality that he tried to sail it to the Adriatic where he intended to attack Austrian targets, thus creating a *cassus belli.* The boat was intercepted by the French in Corsica and returned to Italy, who bought the boat from Russia and took it into Italian service as the *Argonauta.* It served until 1928 when it was scrapped, but the Italians also built a replacement for the Russians, which was also named *Svatoi Georgi;* it was handed over in 1916 and delivered to the Arctic Fleet in a voyage lasting two months, calling at Gibraltar, Lisbon and Plymouth en route. It was beached in 1918 and scrapped in 1925.

Meanwhile, the Brazilian Navy decided to buy its first submarine flotilla and placed an order with Fiat-San Giorgio for three boats, together with a specially

Below: N-3 of the six N-class: 277 tons displacement; length 150ft (45.8m); beam 14ft (4.2m); draught 10ft 2in (3.1m); two TT; one gun.

Above: F1-class submarine of the Royal Italian Navy.

designed submarine depot ship, *Ceara* (6,400 tons). These boats were designated the F1-class, were delivered in 1913-14 and served until 1933.

When Italy joined the Allies the Navy was short of small submarines for use in the restricted waters of the Adriatic against the powerful Austro-Hungarian Navy. An order was placed in 1915 for F-class boats, which were again based on the Medusa-class, but incorporating many of the improvements already made in the Russian and Brazilian designs, such as a second periscope, reduced diving time and Fessenden signalling equipment, but with the addition, resulting from wartime experience, of a 76mm (3in) gun. The initial Italian order was for 24 boats but three were sold to Portugal (F-19 to F-21 as *Foca*, *Goldino*, and *Hidra*) and a further three were sold to Spain (F-22 to F-24 as *Narciso Monturiol*, *Cosme Garcia* and *A-3*). These were taken from the Italian order to speed delivery and a further three were then ordered for the Italian Navy, leaving it with 21 boats, plus the virtually identical *Argonauta*.

The British order resulted from a visit by a group of RN officers and Admiralty officials to La Spezia in 1911, when they were impressed by *Medusa* and *Velilla*. Thus, when Fiat's British agent, Scott's Shipyard, offered to built a similar boat for £70,000 the offer was accepted, followed by an order for two more. *S-1* was completed in August 1914, followed by *S-2* in May and *S-3* in September 1915; the designation as "S"-class was out of sequence with the RN's normal system and simply stood for Scott's, the name of the builders. A few changes made to suit British practices, for example in the number and layout of the battery. These boats were unpopular for a variety of reasons, including their slowness in diving, but most probably due to prejudice against foreign ships, and as soon as Italy joined the Allies the RN sold all three to the

Class	Svatoy Georgi	F1	S	F1
Country	Russia	Brazil	UK	Italy, Portugal, Spain
Total built	2	3	3	27 (Italy – 21; Portugal – 3; Spain – 3)
Completed Displacement surfaced submerged	1914 255 tons 306 tons	1913 250 tons 305 tons	1914 265 tons 324 tons	1916-18 262 tons 319 tons
Dimensions length beam draught	148ft 0in (45.1m) 13ft 9in (4.2m) 9ft 10in (3.0m)	150ft 11in (46.0m) 14ft 6in (4.4m) 12ft 2in (3.7m)	148ft 2in (45.1m) 14ft 5in (4.4m) 10ft 4in (3.2m)	149ft 7in (45.6m) 13ft 8in (4.2m) 10ft 2in (3.1m)

Micca-class

Type: patrol, diesel-electric.
Total built: 6.
Completed: 1917-19.
Displacement: surfaced 842 tons; submerged 1,244 tons.
Dimensions: length 207ft 6in (63.2m); beam 20ft 4in (6.2m); draught 14ft 0in (4.2m).
Propulsion: 2 x Fiat diesels, 2 x 1,300bhp; 2 x Ansaldo electric motors, 2 x 2,300shp; two shafts.
Performance: surface – 11kt; submerged – 10kt.
Weapons: 6 x 17.7in (450mm) TT (bow – 4, stern – 2), 8 x torpedoes; 2 x 3in (76mm) guns.
Complement: 40.

History: These were the largest submarines built for the Royal Italian Navy during World War I and suffered from the disadvantage of being designed by a committee, in this case the Navy's Committee for New Ships, although a naval constructor, Lieutenant Virginio Cavalinni, seems to have kept design matters under reasonable control. The order was originally placed with the Venice Naval Yard which actually laid down the first three boats and worked on them for about four months, but the entire order was then passed to the La Spezia Naval Yard. This did not, however, involve the work already done, and the incomplete

Italian Navy, where they retained their "S" numbers. They did not mount a gun while in British service, but appear to have done so when serving with the Italian Navy.

The Japanese F1-class was also a Fiat-Laurenti design, but was considerably larger and the choice of an identical designation appears to have been sheer coincidence – see F1 (Japan).

Propulsion				
diesel engines	2 x Fiat	2 x Fiat	2 x Scott-Fiat	2 x Fiat
power	700bhp	700bhp	2 x 325bhp	670bhp
electric motors	2 x Savigliano	2 x Savigliano	2 x Scott	2 x Savigliano
power	450shp	500shp	2 x 200hp	500shp
shafts	two	two	two	two
Performance				
speed, surface	13.5kt	13.5kt	13.3kt	12kt
submerged	8.8kt	8kt	8.5kt	8.2kt
range, surfaced	950nm/12kt	800nm/13.5kt	1,600nm/8.5kt	1,600nm/8.5kt
submerged	100nm/4kt	18nm/8kt	75nm/5kt	80/4kt
maximum				
diving depth	130ft (40m)	130ft (40m)	130ft (40m)	130ft (40m)
Weapons				
TT	2x7.7in (450mm)	2 x 18in (457mm)	2 x 18in (457mm)	2 x 17.7in (450mm)
location	bow	bow	bow	bow
torpedoes	4	4	4	4
gun	–	–	–	1 x 3in (76mm)
Complement	24	20	18	26

Above: **Angelo Emo**, *laid down in 1914, launched in 1919.*

hulls were simply dismantled. Even now, the building process was so drawn out that although the order was placed in 1914, the first-of-class was not launched until 1917 followed by three in 1918 and two in 1919. As built, these boats had six torpedo tubes and the original intention was to mount a further pair in a rotating mount on the casing, but this was never done. They proved to be unreliable in service and all underwent a partial rebuild in 1923-25. One was stricken in 1928, three in 1930 and the remainder in 1937-38.

Provana-class

Type: patrol, diesel-electric.
Total built: 4.
Completed: 1918-19.
Displacement: surfaced 762 tons; submerged 924 tons.
Dimensions: length 219ft 10in (67.0m); beam 19ft 4in (5.9m); draught 12ft 6in (3.8m).
Propulsion: 2 Fiat diesels, 2,600bhp; 2 x Ansaldo electric motors, 1,400shp; two shafts.
Performance: surface – 16kt; submerged – 9.6kt; maximum operating diving depth 164ft (50m).
Weapons: 6 x 17.7in (450mm) TT (bow – 4, stern – 2), 8 x torpedoes; 2 x 3in (76mm) guns.
Complement: 40.

History: As with the Micca-class, so also with the Provana-class – progress in construction was very slow and even though they were laid down in late 1915, the first boat was not actually launched until November 1917, followed by the other three in January, July and September 1918, and not one actually entered service before the war's end. The design was prepared by Cesare Laurenti and Virginio Cavallini and was very sound, as evidenced by the surface speed of 16kt, the highest of any Italian World War I submarine, although the submerged speed was no more than 9.8kt, rather less than that claimed for the Micca-, Balilla- and Pacinotti-classes. They proved good sea boats and handled well, but as with virtually all Italian boats of this period they

F1-/F2-classes

Type: patrol, diesel-electric.
Total built: 2.
Completed: 1920.
Displacement: surfaced 689 tons; submerged 1,047 tons.
Dimensions: length 215ft 1in (65.6m); beam 19ft 11in (6.1m); draught 13ft 9in (4.2m).
Propulsion: 2 x Fiat diesels, 2,800bhp; 2 x Savigliano electric motors, 1,200shp; two shafts.
Performance: surface – 13kt; submerged – 8kt; range surfaced 3,500nm at 10kt, submerged 75nm at 4kt; maximum operating diving depth 130ft (40m).
Weapons: 5 x 18in (457mm) TT (bow – 3, stern – 2), 8 x torpedoes; 1 x 7.7mm MG.
Complement: 43.
Specifications are for F1-class, as built.

History: The F1-class were the first Italian-designed submarines to be ordered by the Imperial Japanese Navy (IJN), being designed by Fiat-Laurenti and built in Japan by Kawasaki at Kobe. Confusingly, the Japanese designated them as F1-class, but the boats had little, if any, relationship with the Italian F1-class (see page 74), being considerably larger and much more heavily armed. The first two, *No 18* and *No 19* were ordered in 1915 and completed in 1920, when they became the first Japanese submarines with an ocean-going capability. As designed, the cross-section of their pressure hulls was not cylindrical, which was intended to give extra volume, but this was, quite correctly, considered by the IJN to compromise the integrity of the structure, so they added scantlings during construction to provide added strength. The three reload torpedoes

Above: **Andrea Provana,** *nameship of a class of four.*

were very slow to dive and their maximum depth was only 164ft (50m), somewhat less than their overall length.

One boat, *Sebastiano Veniero*, was sunk in a collision with an Italian merchant ship (August 1925) an all too frequent occurrence in the early days of submarines. Two were stricken in 1928, but the fourth, *Giacomo Nani*, survived until 1935.

Above: Italian F1-class submarine.

were all forward; the stern tubes were "one-shot" devices. A 3in (76mm) gun was added in the early 1920s.

The three boats of the F2-class (*Nos 31, 32, 33*) were virtual repeats of the F1-class, except that a different model of Fiat diesel was installed, which actually produced less power and thus reduced the maximum speed to 14kt. The diesels were also notoriously unreliable. This group was especially unpopular in the IJN and had a very short service life. All five boats were affected by the IJN's renumbering exercise in the early 1920s, being categorised as medium (Ro) submarines and numbered *Ro-1* (ex-*No 18*) to *Ro-5* (ex-*No 33*). All were stricken in 1930.

Espadarte/Foca-classes ITALY (PORTUGAL)

Type: patrol, diesel-electric.
Total built: 3.
Completed: 1920.
Displacement: surfaced 260 tons; submerged 389 tons.
Dimensions: length 147ft 9in (45.0m); beam 13ft 10in (4.2m); draught 10ft 6in (3.2m).
Propulsion: 2 x Fiat diesels, 2 x 275shp; 2 x Savigliano electric motors, 2 x 200shp; two shafts.
Performance: surface – 14.2kt; submerged – 8.2kt; range surfaced 3,500nm at 8.5kt, submerged 100nm at 4kt.
Weapons: 2 x 18in (457mm) TT (bow), 4 x torpedoes.
Complement: 21.
Specifications are for Foca-class, as built.

History: Portugal's first submarine was the *Plongeur*, which was built in the early 1890s and scrapped in 1910. The second submarine was *Espadarte*, a Laurenti-Fiat boat, built at La Spezia, launched in December 1912 and handed over in 1913. This boat displaced 300 tons submerged and was 148ft (45.1m) long, powered by two Fiat diesels and armed with two 18in (475mm) torpedo tubes, both in the bows. It was identical, in virtually all respects, to the submarine then building for Russia (see *Svatoy Georgi*). Next came the Foca-class, again designed and built by Fiat-San Giorgio at La Spezia, with three boats delivered in 1917. They were *Foca*, *Golfinho* and *Hidra*, which were essentially repeats of the earlier *Espadarte*, with the same measurements and propulsion system, but with somewhat greater endurance.

K1/-2/-3/-4/KT-classes JAPAN

Type: patrol, diesel-electric.

Class	K-1	K-2/K-3	K-4	KT
Total built	2	9	3	4
Completed	1919	1920-23	1923-24	1923-24
Displacement surfaced submerged	735 tons 1,030 tons	755 tons 1,050 tons	770 tons 1,080 tons	665 tons 1,000 tons
Dimensions length beam draught	227ft 0in (69.2m) 20ft 10in (6.4m) 11ft 3in (3.4m)	230ft 0in (70.1m) 20ft 0in (6.1m) 12ft 1in (3.7m)	243ft 6in (74.2m) 20ft 0in (6.1m) 12ft 1in (3.7m)	243ft 6in (74.2m) 20ft 0in (6.1m) 12ft 1in (3.7m)
Propulsion diesel engines power electric motors power shafts	2 x Sulzer 2,600bhp 2 x Savigliano 1,200shp two	2 x Sulzer 2,600bhp 2 x Savigliano 1,200shp two	2 x Sulzer 2,600bhp 2 x Savigliano 1,200shp two	2 x Sulzer 1,200bhp 2 x Savigliano 1,200shp two

Above: **Espadarte***, Italian Laurenti-Fiat design built for Portugal.*

Performance				
speed, surface	18kt	17kt	17kt	13kt
submerged	9kt	9kt	9kt	8kt
range, surfaced	4,000nm/10kt	6,000nm/10kt	6,000nm/10kt	8,000nm/10kt
submerged	85nm/4kt	85nm/4kt	85nm/4kt	85nm/4kt
Weapons				
TT	6 x 18in (457mm)	6 x 18in (457mm)	4 x 21in (533mm)	4 x 21in (533mm)
location	bow – 4; deck – 2	bow – 4; deck – 2	bow	bow
torpedoes	10	10	8	8
gun	1 x 3in (76mm)	1 x 3in (76mm)	1 x 3in (76mm)	1 x 4.7in (120mm)
			1 x 7.7mm MG	1 x 7.7mm MG
Complement	44	45	45	43

History: For the first decade of its existence the IJN's submarine arm depended upon foreign designs, which were originally built overseas, but then built in increasing numbers in Japanese yards. The IJN became increasingly dissatisfied with these foreign designs, which they considered, with good reason, to be designed to meet very different conditions from those facing the Japanese. In particular, the Japanese found them to have insufficient range for the vast distances of the Pacific, to have hulls lacking the strength to take advantage of the much greater depths of Asian seas, and to have insufficiently precise depth control. This gave rise to a series of K-class (K = *kaigun-chu* = medium, Navy type) designs, which were progressively improved. First in the series, the K1 design was based on the Schneider-Laubeuf S-class, but with a much wider beam (20ft 10in/6.4m compared to 17ft 1in/5.2m) and a stronger hull, consisting of heavy plates and frames reinforced by an exceptional degree (by Western standards) of internal sub-division. The outcome was a hull which could withstand heavy punishment, either from depthcharges or collisions.

The K2 design was essentially a progressive development of the K1 with a slightly longer hull and 10in (0.25m) less beam. Most importantly, fuel oil bunkerage was increased from 60 tons to 75 tons, giving a 2,000nm increase in range. The K3 had the same hull and characteristics as the K2, but with a

Below: K1-class, No 19, was armed with four bow 18in (457mm) torpedo tubes and two drop-collars.

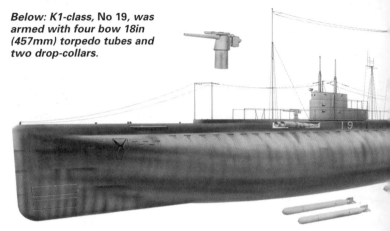

O-classes

NETHERLANDS

Type: patrol, diesel-electric.

Class	O-1	O-2	O-6	O-7
Total built	1	4	1	1
Completed	1906	1911-14	1916	1916
Displacement surfaced submerged	105 tons 124 tons	134 tons 149 tons	192 tons 233 tons	176 tons 206 tons
Dimensions length beam draught	677ft 0in (20.4m) 16ft 0in (4.96.4m) 9ft 23in (2.8m)	105ft 3in (32.1m) 10ft 9in (3.3m) 9ft 10in (2.7m)	117ft 0in (35.7m) 13ft 6in (4.1m) 10ft 2in (3.1m)	112ft 2in (34.2m) 12ft 9in (3.9m) 9ft 6in (2.9m)
Propulsion engines power electric motors power shafts battery	1 x Otto gasoline 160bhp 1 65shp one 60 cells	1 x M.A.N. diesel 280bhp 1 145shp one 60 cells	1 x M.A.N. 375bhp 1 210shp one 60 cells	1 x M.A.N. 350bhp 1 210shp one 60 cells

Above: KT-class, No 69; similar to K4-class but better range.

number of internal improvements; nine were built, making it the most numerous class of IJN submarine up to that time. The K4 had a yet longer hull, 243ft 6in (74.2m) compared to 230ft 0in (70.1m), which was mainly attributable to the introduction of the internationally standard 21in (533mm) torpedo tubes.

The 3in (76mm) gun was also moved forward of the bridge.

The KT (*kai-toku-chu* = medium special, Navy type) was dimensionally identical to the K4-class, but had less powerful Sulzer diesels, which reduced maximum surfaced speed to 13kt; however, bunkerage increased to 116 tons, resulting in an increase in range to 8,000nm at 10kt.

All these boats were renumbered in the "Ro" series in 1923. Most of the K1-, K2- and K3-classes were stricken in 1931-32; a few were retained until 1936. Two of the K4-class were stricken in 1940 but one survived World War II. Only one KT-class survived the war.

Performance				
speed, surface	8.5kt	11kt	12kt	11.5kt
submerged	8kt	8kt	8.5kt	8.5kt
range, surfaced	200nm/8kt	500nm/10kt	750nm/10kt	750nm/10kt
submerged	24nm/6kt	35nm/7kt	42nm/7kt	42nm/7kt
diving depth	82ft (25m)	82ft (25m)	131ft (40m)	131ft (40m)
Weapons				
TT	1 x 9in (250mm)	2 x 17.7in (450mm)	3 x 17.7in (450mm)	3 x 17.7in (450mm)
location	bow	bow	bow – 2; stern – 1	bow – 2; stern – 1
torpedoes	3	4	5	5
Complement	10	10	15	15

History: For many years the Dutch had a unique arrangement. Under this system the Ministry of Defence paid for submarines for use in European waters and these classes were designated *"Onderzeeboot"* (undersea boat = submarine) followed by an Arabic numeral – eg, O-2. But submarines intended for deployment in the Dutch East Indies were paid for by the Colonial Ministry and were designated *"Koloniën"* (colonial), followed by a Roman numeral – eg, K-III. In both cases, however, the procurement policy was the same, with production licences for foreign designs being purchased and all construction taking place in Dutch yards, either De Schelde at Vlissingen or Fijenoord in Rotterdam. There were two sources for the designs in both the "O-" and "K-" series: Hay-Whitehead in Austria (transferred to Hay-Denny, Scotland, after the outbreak of World War I) and the Electric Boat Co., in Groton, Connecticut, whose designs were known as "Holland-type" after the inventor, J. P. Holland. In addition, the preferred source of diesel engines was the German company, M.A.N., but, due to its commitments to the German U-boat programme, this company was unable to supply any more after 1917, after which the Dutch sourced their diesels from the Austrian company, Sulzer.

The first of the O-boats was foisted on a reluctant Navy by the De Schelde yard, which purchased a licence to produce a Holland design from the Electric Boat Co. This private venture, named *Luctor et Energo*, was launched in July 1905 and failed the first round of naval trials, but, due mainly to the persistence of a naval officer, Lt. Koster, and the builder, De Schelde, the boat underwent a second round of trials, which proved successful and she was bought by the Navy in December 1907. Originally powered by a gasoline engine, she was given a 200hp M.A.N. diesel in 1914, and was scrapped in 1920.

This was followed by four boats of the O-2-class built by De Schelde, but to a design by Hay-Whitehead of Fiume in Austria, the only non-Electric Boat design this yard was to build. These were somewhat larger and armed with two 17.7in (450mm) torpedo tubes mounted one above the other in the bows. They also featured the first ever rudimentary air-supply tube that enabled the diesels to be run while the boat was partially submerged – a device which eventually led to the schnorkel ("snort"). They entered service in 1911-13 and were stricken in 1931-35.

The next two boats, *O-6* and *O-7*, are usually described as a two-boat class but, although their armament and machinery were

K-classes (Dutch overseas) NETHERLANDS

Type: patrol, diesel-electric.

Class	K-I	K-II/K-V	K-III/K-VIII
Total built	1	4	4
Completed	1914	1919-21	1919-23
Displacement surfaced submerged	333 tons 358 tons	569 tons 649 tons	649 tons 721 tons
Dimensions length beam draught	159ft 5in (48.6m) 15ft 5in (4.7m) 10ft 2in (3.1m)	188ft 0in (57.3m) 17ft 5in (5.3m) 12ft 6in (3.8m)	211ft 3in (64.4m) 18ft 4in (5.6m) 11ft 10in (3.6m)
Propulsion diesel engines power electric motors power shafts battery	2 x M.A.N. 2 x 850bhp 2 2 x 157shp two 130 cells	2 x Sulzer* 2 x 600bhp 2 2 x 250shp two 120 cells	2 x M.A.N.** 2 x 900bhp 2 2 x 210shp two 132 cells

the same, there were many differences between them. In fact, *O-6*, the larger of the two, was a Holland design built by De Schelde, armed with three torpedo tubes, two in the bows and one mounted externally on the after casing. *O-7*, designed by William Denny & Bros of Dumbarton Scotland, and built by Fijenoord, was slightly smaller, had a quite different hull form and included one very unusual feature, a steering propeller which operated in a transverse duct located just forward of the main propeller. It was stricken in 1939.

Below: Dutch submarine* O-5 *during World War I.

Performance			
speed, surface	17kt	13.5kt	16.5kt
submerged	10.5kt	8kt	8.5kt
range, surfaced	3,500nm/11kt	3,500nm/11kt	3,500nm/11kt
submerged	30nm/8kt	25.5nm/8.5kt	25nm/8.5kt
diving depth	131ft (40m)	131ft (40m)	131ft (40m)
Weapons			
TT	3 x 17.7in (450mm)	4 x 17.7in (450mm)	6 x 17.7in (450mm)
location	bow – 2; stern – 1	bow – 2; deck – 2	bow – 2; stern – 2; deck – 2
torpedoes	6	12	12
gun	–	1 x 75mm; 1 x MG	1 x 75mm
Complement	17	29	31

* *K-II* was powered by two 900hp M.A.N. diesels and was 2kt faster – see notes.

** *K-VII* was powered by two 900hp M.A.N. diesels, *K-IX* and *K-X* by 600hp Sulzers, making them 1kt slower.

History: For several centuries the Netherlands ruled a large colonial empire in the Far East: the Dutch East Indies, modern Indonesia. This huge, sprawling territory required a large naval force, which in turn needed ships and, later, submarines with great range and the ability to operate in conditions of tropical heat. Submarines for the Dutch East Indies were paid for by the Colonial Ministry, and were given "K" (*Koloniën* = colonial) designation, followed by the hull number using Roman numerals.

The first of the overseas boats, *K-I*, was built by De Schelde, Vlissingen, to a Hay-Whitehead design, being laid down in September 1911, launched in May 1913 and commissioned in July 1914. She was powered by two M.A.N. diesels and armed with three torpedo tubes, two in the bows and one in the stern. This boat had little reserve buoyancy and tended to be very uncomfortable when on the surface. It was stricken in 1928.

After this first "colonial" design there were two more classes built by De Schelde to Electric Boat Co. designs. The KIII-class (*K-III, K-IV*) were much larger boats, but there were delays caused by World War I, particularly with the diesels, since M.A.N. could supply only two of the required four 900hp diesels, which were installed in *K-III*. As a result, *K-IV* was powered by two 600hp Sulzers, the loss of power resulting in a 1.5kt reduction in speed. Armament was four torpedo tubes, two in the bows, and two mounted externally on the after casing.

Next from De Schelde/Electric Boat Co. came the K-VIII-class (*K-VIII, K-IX, K-X*) which were to have been armed with six torpedo tubes; two in the bows and two externally on the upper casing abaft the sail, as in the K-III-class, but with two more reloadable tubes aft. However, war experience by other navies had shown that externally mounted tubes were vulnerable in depth-charge attacks, and these were deleted. It had also been planned to mount a 75mm gun but, again, war experience showed a more powerful gun was required and an 88mm was mounted instead. Only *K-VIII* was powered by the planned M.A.N. diesels, the other two having 600hp Sulzers. These were also the first Dutch colonial boats to be of double-hull construction and had a much larger sail than earlier boats.

The two other classes of "colonial" boats were built by Fijenoord to a Hay-Denny design. The first, the single-boat K-II-class was laid down in

Toro-/Ferre-classes   PERU

Type: patrol, diesel-electric.
Total built: 2.
Completed: 1912-13.
Displacement: surfaced ca300 tons; submerged ca400 tons.
Dimensions: length 170ft 11in (52.1m); beam 17ft 9in (5.1m); draught 10ft 2in (3.1m).
Propulsion: 2 x Schneider-Carels 6-cylinder diesel engines; 2 x electric motors; two shafts.
Performance: surface – 13kt; submerged – 8kt; range surfaced 2,000nm at 10kt, submerged ca 80nm at 4kt.
Weapons: 4 x 17.7in (450mm) TT (bow), 6 x torpedoes.
Complement: 21.
Specification for Ferre-class, as built.

History: A submarine pioneer who has received less recognition than his due is the Peruvian Federico Blume (1831-1901), a railroad engineer who prepared his first submarine design in 1864 during the war against Spain. The conflict ended before Blume could complete his boat and nothing more was done until the outbreak of the War of the Pacific (1879-1883), this time against Chile, when Blume, at his own expense, completed a submersible, which he named *Toro* (bull). This vessel was cylindrical in shape with pointed ends and was based on a boiler some 48ft (14.6m) long and constructed from 0.3in (6mm) iron plate, which was then reinforced by appliqué sheets of iron, the whole device being jointed by rivets. Propulsion was by means of a single propeller operated by a long hand crank, which was turned by eight of the 11-man crew.

1915 and launched in 1919, but was not completed until 1922, after the supposedly later K-III-class. This was because M.A.N. was unable to complete the engines, which therefore had to be transported to Vlissingen to be finished by Fijenoord; not surprisingly, this took much more time than had been planned. The very similar K-V-class (*K-V, K-VI, K-VII*) were all powered by Sulzer diesels.

Most of these boats were stricken in the 1930s but the K-VIII-class served on into World War II. *K-X* was scuttled off Soerabaya, but the other two reached Australia, where *K-VIII* was stricken. *K-IX* for a time as a unit of the Royal Australian Navy (RAN) and then reverted to Dutch control as an oiler. She was stricken in 1946.

Below: **K-III**, *designed for operations in the Dutch East Indies.*

Right: Model of the Peruvian **Toro** *of 1864, an ingenious design.*

The vessel submerged by flooding the ballast tanks and surfaced by expelling the water using a manual pump. There was a watertight entrance hatch and there were two hollow retractable masts made of brass to admit air and expel the fumes. Trials started in October 1879 with Blume conducting three weeks of tests and demonstrations; he successfully reached a depth of 72ft (22m) and a submerged speed of 4kt and remained submerged for up to 30 minutes at a time. *Toro* was taken to Callao to attack the Chilean fleet but, warned of this impending attack, the enemy fleet withdrew out of range and *Toro* was later sunk to avoid capture.

There was then a gap of some years. Then, in the early 1900s there was a particularly active French naval mission, which managed to persuade the Peruvian Navy to buy a destroyer and two submarines. The latter were Laubeuf designs and were delivered in 1913, the first modern submarines in any South American navy. These had a rather short operational life, being stricken in 1919, which was primarily due to the difficulty of obtaining spare parts and new cells.

Delfin/Kasatka-classes

Type: harbour defence, gasoline/kerosene.
Total built: 6.
Completed: 1904.
Displacement: surfaced 140 tons; submerged 170 tons.
Dimensions: length 110ft 0in (33.5m); beam 11ft 6in (3.5m); draught 11ft 3in (3.4m).
Propulsion: 1 x kerosene engine, 200bhp; 1 x electric motor, 100shp; one shaft.
Performance: surface – 8.5kt; submerged – 5.5kt; range surfaced 700nm at 8kt, submerged 50nm at 3kt; maximum operational diving depth 150ft (46m)
Weapons: 4 x Drzwiecki drop collars, 4 x torpedoes.
Complement: 24.
Specifications for Kasatka-class, as built.

History: *Delfin*, designed by I. G. Bubnov, ordered in 1901 and completed in 1903, was the Imperial Russian Navy's first operational submarine. It displaced 124 tons, was 64ft (19.6m) long and was armed with two torpedoes in Drzwiecki drop-collars. It was a saddle-tank design. It sank in harbour in June 1904 when grossly overloaded with no fewer than 33 people aboard, a combination of indiscipline and a failure to understand the significance of excess weight in a submarine; no fewer than 21 died and those who survived did so through sheer luck rather than skilled rescue. The boat was raised, refitted and sent to Vladivostock.

Delfin's designer, Bubnov, next produced the Kasatka-class. There were

Osetr (Lake)/Kaiman-classes

Type: patrol, gasoline-electric.

Class	Osetr (Lake)	Kaiman
Total built	6	4
Completed	1905	1907-08
Displacement surfaced submerged	153 tons 187 tons	409 tons 482 tons
Dimensions length beam draught	72ft 0in (22.0m) 12ft 0in (3.6m) 12ft 3in (3.7m)	132ft 0in (40.2m) 14ft 0in (4.3m) 16ft 0in (4.9m)
Propulsion engines power electric motor power shafts	2 x gasoline 2 x 120bhp 2 2 x 60shp two	2 x gasoline 2 x 600bhp 2 2 x 200shp two

Above: Kasatka *saw service in the Russo-Japanese War.*

delays in the supply of the engines so the design was recast for a single propeller and engine; this used kerosene which was very smelly and emitted dense white fumes, but was safer than the gasoline used in *Delfin*. Initially, the type showed some unsatisfactory characteristics, in particular trimming stern-down when submerged, but these were solved by installing floats in the after casing. Four were sent to the Far East for the Russo-Japanese War.

Performance		
speed, surface	8.5kt	10.5kt
submerged	4.5kt	7.0kt
range, surfaced	385nm	1,050nm/8kt
submerged	35nm	40nm/5kt
maximum		
diving depth	96ft (30m)	–
Weapons		
TT	3 x 15in (381mm)	4 x 18in(457mm)
location	bow – 2; stern – 1	bow – 2; stern – 2
Complement	24	34

Specifications apply to first-of-class, as built

History: In its rush to purchase new equipment for the war against Japan, the Imperial Russian Navy bought as many submarines as possible, the basic criterion being that they should reach the theatre of war as rapidly as possible. One element of these orders was the building of six boats designed by the American, Simon Lake, whose company contracted to provide one complete example as a pattern for the construction of a further five in Russia. Several countries showed interest in Lake's *Protector*, which had been built in the United States and was unusual for two reasons: it was the first submarine designed to operate on an even keel when both surfacing and submerging, and it had hydraulically extended wheels for running on the seabed. It arrived in Russia in June 1904 and the other five boats were completed in 1905. *Protector* was renamed *Osetr* and all six were then sent to the Far East as quickly as possible. All were scrapped in 1913-15.

For the Russians the main drawback of the *Osetr* (Lake) boats was that they lacked the range to enable them to operate off the coast of Japan, so an improved-Protector design was prepared and four were built in St. Petersburg as the Kaiman-class. They were completed in 1910, but immediately became the subject of controversy, their shortcomings including failure to meet the performance criteria in various respects (diving time was 10 minutes) and excess weight, and the Russian Navy refused to pay the full contract price,

Below: **Paltus***, an Osetr/Lake-class boat, in about 1907.*

Minoga/Akula/Morzh-class   RUSSIA

Type: patrol, diesel-electric.

Class	Minoga	Akula	Morzh
Total built	1	1	3
Completed	1908	1907	1914-15
Displacement surfaced submerged	117 tons 142 tons	370 tons 475 tons	630 tons 760 tons
Dimensions length beam draught	105ft 9in (32,2m) 9ft 2in (2.8m) 8ft 2in (2.5m)	184ft 0in (56.0m) 12ft 0in (3.7m) 11ft 0in (3.4m)	219ft 8in (67.0m) 14ft 7in (4.5m) 12ft 8in (3.9m)
Propulsion engines power electric motor power shafts	2 x diesel 2 x 120bhp 1 70shp two	3 x diesel 3 x 300bhp 1 225shp three	2 x diesel 2 x 250bhp 2 2 x 400shp two

although they did insist on taking delivery in order to prevent the boats being sold to a third party. The boats were then modified to improve their performance and eventually entered service in the Baltic in late 1911; they carried out some operations in the early part of World War I, but were stricken in 1916 and scuttled in 1918.

Below: Kaiman-class Krokodil; note gap for torpedo drop-collar.

Performance			
speed, surface	11kt	10.6kt	10.8kt
submerged	5kt	6.6kt	8kt
range, surfaced	600nm/10kt	1,900nm	2,500nm
submerged	50nm/3.5kt	38nm/4.8kt	120nm
maximum			
diving depth	96ft (30m)	150ft (46m)	150ft (46m)
Weapons			
TT	2 x 17.7in (450mm)	4 x 18in (457mm)	4 x 18in (457mm)
location	bow	bow – 2; stern – 2	bow – 2; stern – 2
drop collars	–	4	8
torpedoes	2	1 x 47mm	1 x 57mm; 1 x 47mm
Complement	22	34	47

Specifications apply to first-of-class, as built

History: The submarine designer I. G. Bubnov was one of the first to produce a submarine based on the lessons of the Russo-Japanese War (1904-5) and his *Minoga,* launched in October 1908, was a small (155 ton displacement), single-hulled boat. Its significance, however, was that it was the first Russian submarine powered by diesel engines, with two 120hp units driving a single propeller. Unfortunately, this required complicated mechanical control linkages and the boat was not a success, although it did see several years' service.

Bubnov's next design, *Akula*, was essentially an enlarged and improved

Minoga, but with three shafts; indeed, Bubnov seems to have been fascinated by complicated power systems. This system was as fault-prone as the others and all three propellers had to be changed three times and the electric motor once before a satisfactory solution was found. Despite these problems she was considered the most successful of the pre-World War I Russian designs. She was sunk by a mine on 28 November 1915.

Bubnov's next design was the Morzh-class, with three being completed in 1914-15. The design was based on that of the *Akula,* but was not a great success and included a number of inherent faults. The hull design was more like that of a surface ship than that of a submarine, creating even more hydrodynamic drag than usual with submarines of the period and thus reducing submerged speed well below the intended 12 knots. The problems were exacerbated when the outbreak of World War I prevented the German firm of Krupps from delivering the promised diesel engines and the only suitable substitutes which could be found had to be removed from gunboats of the Russian Navy's Amur River flotilla. Despite all these problems the boats were quite successful in service with the Black Sea Fleet, claiming 16 merchantmen sunk and a near miss against *Goeben,* the German/Turkish battlecruiser. *Morzh* failed to return from patrol in May 1917, while *Tyulam* was captured in harbour by the Germans, then handed over to the British and finally taken by the White Russians to Bizerta where she was sold in 1924. *Nerpa* was taken over by the Soviet Navy and was operational from 1922 to 1931, when she was scrapped.

Holland/Narval/AG-classes   RUSSIA

Type: patrol, diesel-electric.

History: In its rush to make good the deficiencies shown up by the Russo-Japanese War, the Imperial Russian Navy ordered submarines from Germany and from both the Electric Boat Co. (Holland) and Simon Lake in the USA. J. P.

Class	Beluga (Holland)	Narval	AG
Total built	7	3	11
Completed	1904-07	1915	1916-21
Displacement surfaced submerged	105 tons 122 tons	673 tons 1,045 tons	355 tons 433 tons
Dimensions length beam draught	65ft 6in (20.0m) 11ft 6in (3.5m) 9ft 6in (2.9m)	230ft 3in (70.2m) 21ft 3in (6.5m) 11ft 8 in (3.6m)	151ft 0in (46.0m) 16ft 0in (4.9m) 12ft 6in (3.8m)
Propulsion engines power electric motor power shafts battery	1 x gasoline 1 x 160bhp 1 70shp one n.k	4 x diesel 4 x 160bhp 2 2 x 225shp two n.k	2 x NLSE diesels 2 x 480bhp 2 2 x 320shp two 2 x 60 cells

Above: **Akula** *looked more like a ship design than a submarine.*

Performance			
speed, surface	8.5kt	10.5kt	12kt
submerged	6kt	11.5kt	10kt
range, surfaced	585nm	1250nm/8.5kt	1,600nm/10kt
submerged	42nm	120nm/7kt	100nm/2kt
maximum			
diving depth	96ft (30m)	150ft (46m)	180ft (55m)
Weapons			
TT	1 x 15.0in (381mm)	4 x 18in (457mm)	4 x 18in (457mm)
location	bow	bow – 2; stern – 2	bow
drop collars	–	4	–
torpedoes	–	–	8
gun	–	1 x 75mm;1 x 63mm	1 x 47mm
Complement	22	47	30

Specifications apply to first-of-class, as built

Holland had a design ready for export with the demonstrator, the *Fulton*, immediately available. A contract was quickly signed and *Fulton* was broken down into sections and despatched to Russia under the guise of a "steam boiler". On arrival it was reassembled, renamed *Som* (catfish) and then used as the pattern for another six which were built at the Nevski Yard in St. Petersburg. Only *Som* and one of the Russian-built boats reached Vladivostok in time to take part in the war against the Japanese; two were sent to the Black Sea and the others served in the Baltic. *Som* was sunk in a collision with a merchant ship in the Baltic, the remainder were stricken in 1916 and scuttled in 1918-19.

The next Holland design to be built for Russia was the three-strong Narval-class, which were built at the Nevski Yard in Nikolayev and launched in 1914, and were by far the largest submarines built for the Tsarist Navy. The specifications for *Narwal* are given in the table but the other two boats had a slightly lower displacement (994 tons) and were more heavily armed, with four additional Drzwiecki drop-collars making a total of eight. It was originally intended that they should be powered by two 850bhp diesels, but these were not available (there was an international shortage of these engines in this period) and four much less powerful units had to be installed instead. All three served in the Black Sea throughout World War I, sinking some 80 enemy ships, and all were scuttled in April 1919.

The last of these three classes was known in the Tsarist Navy as Amerikanskji Golland (AG) (American Holland). They were ordered in 1915 from the Electric Boat Co. at a time when the USA was neutral, and to circumvent this political predicament all parts of the submarines were manufactured in the USA in 1915-16 and then sent by railroad to the Vickers Yard at Montreal in Canada, where an American work-force assembled the boats. The boats were then broken down again into major assemblies and sent by rail to the Canadian West Coast where they were transferred to ships for the voyage to Vladivostok. There they were transferred to rail yet again and sent via the Trans-Siberian railroad to the West for final assembly; five boats were assembled at the Baltic yard, St. Petersburg, and six boats at the Nikolayev Navy Yard. These Russian boats were identical in every respect to those delivered to the U.S. Navy (*SS-28* to *SS-30*), the British Royal Navy (*H-1* to *H-10*) and the navies of Chile and

Below: This Holland design from the Electric Boat Company served in five navies and was one of the most successful types of World War I.

Above: **AG-14**, *one of the successful boats designed in the USA.*

India. The original Russian order was for 18 boats, but only 11 were delivered before the Revolution and the U.S. Navy requisitioned the remaining six, but what happened to the last of the boats, *AG-17*, has never been established. Main armament comprised four 18in (457mm) torpedo tubes, all in the bow; there were no stern tubes or drop-collars. The Baltic boats took part in operations in World War I: one was sunk and the remainder scuttled in April 1918. The AG-class was the last to enter service with the Imperial Russian Navy and although other types were under construction the Revolution overtook them and they were cancelled.

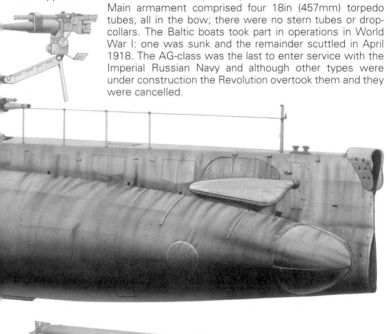

Bars-class RUSSIA

Type: patrol diesel-electric.
Total built: 18.
Completed: 1915-17.
Displacement: surfaced 650 tons; submerged 782 tons.
Dimensions: length 223ft 0in (68.0m); beam 15ft 0in (4.5m); draught 13ft 0in (3.9m).
Propulsion: 2 x diesel engines, 2 x 1,320bhp; 2 x electric motors, 2 x 450shp; two shafts.
Performance: surface – 18kt; submerged – 10kt; range surfaced 400nm at 17kt, submerged 25nm at 9kt; maximum operating diving depth 150ft (46m).
Weapons: 4 x 18in (457mm) TT (bow – 2, stern – 2); 8 x Drzwiecki drop-collars; 1 x 63mm gun, 1 x 37mm AA gun.
Complement: 33.

History: This was the last and most numerous of I. G. Bubnov's designs to enter service in World War I, with orders for 24 being placed in 1912-13. In the event, only 18 were completed as patrol submarines, two were converted to minelayers during construction, and four were never completed due to the Revolution. The design, which was essentially that of the Morzh-class (qv) with an added centre section, promised a powerful armament, high speed both on the surface and submerged, and a long range, but, for a variety of reasons, failed to deliver in all three areas and repeated many of the failings of previous Bubnov designs. A matter outside Bubnov's control was the non-availability of the 1,320hp diesels ordered from Germany, which were replaced from a variety of sources, including new engines from the USA. Some boats used powerplants from Russian patrol boats on the Amur River, but all were considerably less powerful than the German diesels, with the result that the planned surface speed of 18kt was never achieved, few ever exceeding 8kt, and range was also considerably less. There were also problems with the Russian-made (Jevetsky) torpedo tubes, while the Drzwiecki drop-collars were mounted too close to the waterline in the original boats, resulting in an increase

Isaac Peral-/A-/B-classes SPAIN

Type: patrol, diesel-electric.
Total built: 6.
Completed: 1922-23.
Displacement: surfaced 556 tons; submerged 730 tons.
Dimensions: length 210ft 4in (64.1m); beam 17ft 4in (5.6m); draught 11ft 3in (3.4m).
Propulsion: 2 x NLSE diesels, 2 x 700bhp; 2 x electric motors, 2 x 210shp; two shafts.
Performance: surface – 16kt; submerged – 10kt; range surfaced 8,000nm at 10.5kt, submerged 125nm at 4.5kt; maximum operating diving depth 200ft (60m).
Weapons: 4 x 18in (475mm) TT, 8 x torpedoes; 1 x 3in (76mm) gun.
Complement: 28.

History: After the shelving the *Peral* (qv) the Spanish Navy did not order any more submarines until 1915, when one Holland design was built by the Fore River Co. Named *Isaac Peral*, this was very similar to USS *M-1* (SS-47), the U.S. Navy's first double-hulled submarine, which was also built by Fore River and launched in 1915 (see USA M-1-class). The gun was a 3in (76mm) calibre

Above: **Bars; inefficient design caused great underwater drag.**

in drag and a liability to damage (these devices were later removed altogether in most boats and the recesses plated over).

Other problems were, however, of Bubnov's own making. The hull generated considerable hydrodynamic drag so that the underwater speed of 10kt was never achieved, while the lack of internal watertight bulkheads meant that any penetration of the hull was fatal. Less serious, but tactically unsound, was the use of pumps to fill the ballast tanks and the large plumes of water which were generated, which made submerging both slow and easy to spot from a distance.

Most boats saw service during World War I in which four were lost: *Mars* mined (May 1917); two to unknown causes, *Guepard* (October) and *Lvitsa* (June); while *Yedinorog* sank under tow (February 1918). The boats also achieved some successes, sinking eight German transports in the Baltic, of which *Volk* accounted for four. During the Revolution a number were scuttled, but the surviving boats were taken over by the Communists and *Pantera* sank the British HMS *Vittoria* (1,490 tons) on 31 August 1919; the latter was a modern V-class destroyer and remains the largest warship ever sunk by a Russian submarine. The remaining boats served on and were gradually scrapped, except for *Pantera*, which served as a battery hulk until 1955.

Above: The Spanish Isaac Peral *shortly after completion.*

weapon and was on a "disappearing mount" – ie, when not in use the whole apparatus folded back into a cavity in the casing. When boats were given letter designations, *Isaac Peral* became *A-0*. It was scrapped in 1930. Next came three Fiat-Laurenti boats, which were classified as the "A-class" in Spanish service: *Narciso Monturiol* (*A-1*), *Cosme Garcia* (*A-2*) and *A-3* (which did not have a name) – see F-1-class (Italy).

It had always been intended to start submarine construction in Spain and this was achieved with the B-class, construction of which began in 1916, although they were not launched until 1921-23. The design was essentially a

Hajen-/UB-2-/Delfinen-/ Laxen-/Abborren-classes SWEDEN

Type: patrol, diesel-electric.

Class	Hajen	UB-2	Delfinen	Laxen	Abborren
Total built	1	3	1	2	2
Completed	1904	1909	1914	1914-15	1915-16
Displacement surfaced submerged	107 tons 127 tons	138 tons 230 tons	260 tons 370 tons	140 tons 170 tons	174 tons 310 tons
Dimensions length beam draught	70ft 10in (21.6m) 11ft 10in (3.6m) 9ft 10in (3.0m)	87ft 8in (26.8m) 11ft 10in (3.6m) 9ft 10in (3.0m)	139ft 5in (42.5m) 14ft 1in (4.3m) n.k.	87ft 11in (26.8m) 11ft 10in (3.6m) n.k.	101ft 8in (31.0m) 11ft 10in (3.6m) 10ft 2in (3.1m)
Propulsion engines power electric motor power shafts	1 x kerosene 1 x 200bhp 1 70shp one	1 x diesel 4 x 420bhp 1 1 x 200shp one	2 x diesels 2 x 500bhp 2 2 x 150shp two	2 x diesels 2 x 350bhp 2 2 x 100shp two	2 x diesels 2 x 460bhp 2 2 x 140shp two
Performance speed, surface submerged	9.5t 7kt	8.8kt 6.6kt	13.6kt 9.4kt	8.8.kt 6.6kt	9.5kt 7.4kt
Weapons TT location torpedoes	1 x 18.0in (457mm) bow n.k	1 x 18in (457mm) bow 3	2 x 18in (457mm) bow n.k.	1 x 18in (457mm) bow n.k.	2 x 18in (457mm) bow 4
Complement	11	12	21	10	

Specifications apply to first-of-class, as built

History: Two submarines were constructed in Sweden by A. B. Sandahl in 1869 and S. V. Zethelius in 1870, although without apparent success, and it

slightly larger and improved version of the *Isaac Peral* (*A-0*) and like the earlier boat were powered by NLSE diesels, which were M.A.N. designs manufactured under licence in the United States.

All were either sunk or scuttled during the Spanish Civil War. Two were lost in combat in 1936, of which one, *B-5,* was sunk by Nationalist aircraft in June, while the other, *B-6,* was lost to unknown causes, in September. The remainder were scuttled at the end of the Civil War; all were raised and three were scrapped, while the fourth, *B-2,* was used as a battery charging hulk until 1948.

Above: **Delfinen** *photographed while on trials in 1915.*

was left to the arms manufacturer, T. Nordenfelt, to build the nation's first viable submarine in 1883. Like many submarine pioneers he failed to interest his own navy, but did manage to sell one to Greece and two smaller boats to Turkey. The development of the Holland boats in the United States did, however, engage the Navy's interest: they saw the submarine as an effective component in the defence of Sweden's neutrality and in 1900 despatched Commander (Engineer) Carl Richson to see what was going on. On his return parliament voted the funds for the construction of one submarine, *Hajen*, which was designed by Richson based on the Holland principles. It displaced 127 tons and was powered by an Avance kerosene engine, with a Luth & Rosen electric motor for submerged propulsion. *Hajen* was reclassified as a 2nd class submarine in 1909 and in 1916 its Avance engine, which had never been really satisfactory, was replaced by a 135bhp diesel. It was stricken in 1922, but remains on display in Sweden as a museum exhibit.

Following experience with *Hajen* the RSwedN diversified by ordering one submarine from Fiat-Laurenti (see *Hvalen*, below) and three of a developed versions of *Hajen*, which were designated *Underwattensbåten* Nos 2-4 (*Hajen* having been retrospectively designated No 1). They were designed by Carl Richson and built by Motala verkstad, all being launched in 1909. They were somewhat longer than *Hajen*, were better equipped and had a more reliable engine, but had the same armament of one 18in (457mm) torpedo tube and three torpedoes. They were stricken in 1929-30.

Delfinen was a further Richson design, but was much larger, had twin engines/propellers, and was armed with two torpedo tubes. Launched in 1914, it served until 1930 and was then stricken. *Delfinen* was a "one-off" and this development line then reverted to smaller boats. First came the two-boat Laxen-class, which were virtually the same size and layout as the *Underwattensbåten* No 2-class, retaining the single 18in (457mm) torpedo tube, but with twin engines and propellers. The Abborren-class, which followed a year later, was larger, again had twin engines/propellers, but in this case had two torpedo tubes, both in the bows.

Right: **Hajen** *was designed on the* *USS* **Holland** *principles.*

Hvalen/Svårdvisken-classes   SWEDEN

Type: patrol, diesel-electric.

Class	Hvalen	Svårdvisken
Total built	1	2
Completed	1909	1914
Displacement surfaced submerged	186 tons 230 tons	252 tons 370 tons
Dimensions length beam draught	139ft 1in (42.4m) 8ft 10in (2.7m) 13ft 9in (4.2m)	14ft 1in (4.3m) 149ft 3in (45.5m) n.k.
Propulsion engines power electric motor power shafts	3 x gasolene 3 x 250bhp 1 150shp one	2 x diesel 4 x 500bhp 2 1 x 150shp three
Performance speed, surface submerged	14.8kt 6.3kt	14.2kt 8.5kt
Weapons TT location torpedoes gun	2 x 18.0in (457mm) bow 4 –	2 x 18in (457mm) bow 4 1 x 37mm
Complement	17	12

Specifications apply to first-of-class, as built

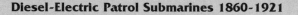

Above: **Svårdvisken*, the first Swedish-built submarine.***

History: In the early years of the 20th century a number of navies sought to acquire the latest submarine technology by buying a very small number of boats from foreign companies. They then absorbed the lessons and either abandoned that particular avenue or decided to set up their own submarine design and construction facilities based on licence production of a development of the original design. Thus, although Sweden had found the American Holland design satisfactory (see previous entry) they purchased a single boat from Italian company, Fiat-San Giorgio, which had established a good reputation at that time. Named *Hvalen,* this was virtually identical to the Italian Navy's Foca-class (qv) and the boat was soon in the world's Press when it sailed from Le Spezia to Stockholm without any accompanying escorts. She served in the RSwedN until 1919 when she was sunk as a target.

In 1910 the Swedish company Kockums of Malmo purchased the Swedish licence from Fiat-San Giorgio, which enabled it to win the next contract for what was now designated a first-class sub-marine. The new class com-prised two boats, *Svårdvisken* and *Tumlaren,* and were slightly larger than *Hvalen,* mainly in order to accommodate two Hesselman six-cylinder diesels in place of the earlier boat's gasoline engines. As com-pleted, both boats mounted a single 37mm gun, which was later replaced by a 57mm weapon. They were both stricken in 1936 but served on as anti-aircraft gun platforms until 1946 when they were scrapped.

Hajen-/Bävern-classes

Type: patrol, diesel-electric.

Class	Hajen	Bävern
Total built	3	3
Completed	1917-18	1921
Displacement surfaced submerged	422 tons 600 tons	472 tons 650 tons
Dimensions length beam draught	177ft 2in (54.0m) 17ft 1in (5.2m) 11ft 6in (3.1m)	187ft 0in (57.0m) 19ft 0n (5.8m) n.k.
Propulsion engines power electric motor power shafts	2 x diesel 3 x 1,000bhp 2 350shp two	2 x diesel 2 x 1,050bhp 2 260shp two

Performance		
speed, surface	15.5kt	15.2kt
submerged	9kt	8.2kt
Weapons		
TT	4 x 18in (457mm)	4 x 18in (457mm)
location	bow	bow
torpedoes	8	n.k.
gun	–	1 x 75mm
Complement	30	31

Specifications apply to first-of-class, as built

History: By the middle of World War I the successes of German U-boats had placed their designers in a pre-eminent position which, coupled with the proximity of Germany just across the Baltic, meant that Sweden looked to that country for its next design. The result was that Kockums bought the licence for a design from one of the most successful German shipyards, Weser AG of Bremen, later to become Deschimag. This was altered to meet Swedish require-ments and the outcome was the Hajen-class, a double-hull design, armed with four 18in (457mm) torpedo tubes and a single 75mm gun. This was followed in 1921 by the improved Bävern-class, also of three boats, which was some 10ft (3m) longer. The Hajen-class was stricken in 1942-43 and the Bävern-class in 1944, except for *Illern,* which was rammed by a merchant ship on 12 August 1944 and sank.

Below:** **Valrossen, one of three boats in the Hajen-class.*

Holland-class

Type: harbour defence, gasoline-electric.
Total built: 1.
Completed: 1897.
Displacement: surfaced 64 tons; submerged 74 tons.
Dimensions: length 53ft 10in (16.4m); beam 10ft 3in (3.1m); draught 8ft 6in (2.6m).
Propulsion: 1 x Otto gasoline engine, 45bhp; 1 x Electro-Dynamics electric motor, 50shp; battery 50 cells; one shaft.
Performance: surface – 8kt; submerged – 5kt; maximum operating diving depth 100ft (31m).
Weapons: 1 x 18in (457mm) TT (bow); 3 x torpedoes; one 8in (203mm) pneumatic gun.
Complement: 7.

History: J. P. Holland was an Irish inventor who produced a series of designs for submarines from 1878 onwards, eventually having that for the *Plunger* accepted by the U.S. Navy in 1895. This was, however, a steam-powered design and Holland, believing that steam would never be suitable, abandoned construction, returned the money to the Navy, and built *Holland Number VI* using his own funds instead. This was by no means the first submarine, but it was certainly the first successful underwater weapons system and included many design features that are still in use today. The design was optimised for underwater performance, with a streamlined "teardrop" hull and a single propeller. Also, she dived with her ballast tanks full, relying for control on her aft-mounted hydroplanes, unlike most contemporary submersibles, which varied the amount of water in their tanks to change depth and, as a result, suffered from instability due to the free-surface effect in their ballast tanks.

Below: USS Holland *1 (SS-1) in Long Island Sound in 1899.*

Above: USS Holland *under repair; note the very clean lines.*

An air-breathing, gasoline-powered drive system provided propulsion on the surface and also charged the batteries, which provided an air-independent propulsion system for submerged operations. Other features, too, have stood the test of time, including the controls and clutches which enabled the petrol engine either to drive the propeller directly, or to recharge the batteries using the motor as a generator, with or without turning the propeller – ie, the batteries could be recharged either while moving at sea or while at rest alongside.

Holland Number VI was constructed at the Crescent Shipyard, Elizabethport, New Jersey, and was launched on 17 May 1897. Trials went well despite a hitch in October that year when a shipyard worker left a valve open while the boat was on the slip, which resulted in her being flooded when the tide came in. Fortunately, actual damage to the electrical system was prevented and the boat passed all her tests.

Main armament was an 18in (457mm) torpedo tube, covered by a watertight cap which was raised for firing by a worm gear. Compensation to maintain the trim when a torpedo was launched was extremely effective. She also mounted a single 8in (203mm) pneumatic gun (also known as a "dynamite" gun) on the bow above the torpedo tube. This was a fixed mount intended to be fired with the muzzle just clear of the water, but, as far as is known, it was never fired.

The boat was purchased by the U.S. Government on 11 April 1900 and named USS *Holland,* subsequently also being allocated the historic number SS-1. She was commissioned on 1 October 1900, the commander being Lieutenant Harry H. Caldwell, USN. *Holland* was used mainly for trials and was also employed as a training boat at the U.S. Naval Academy, Annapolis, until 17 July 1905. She was stricken on 21 November 1910 and sold to a breaker's yard in June 1930. Unfortunately, no trace of this historic boat remains.

A-class

Type: harbour defence, gasoline-electric.

Class	A-class	Holland-class	Holland (Beluga)-class	Holland-class
Country	USA	Japan	Russia	UK
Total built	7	5	7	5
Completed	1901-03	1905	1904-05	1901-02
Displacement surfaced submerged	107 tons 123 tons	103 tons 124 tons	105 tons 122 tons	113 tons 122 tons
Dimensions length beam draught	63ft 10in (19.4m) 11ft 11in (3.6m) 10ft 7in (3.2m)	67ft 0in (20.4m) 11ft 11in (3.6m) 10ft 3in (3.1m)	65ft 6in (20.0m) 11ft 6in (3.5m) 9ft 6in (2.9m)	63ft 10in (19.5m) 11ft 10in (3.6m) 9ft 11in (3.0m)
Propulsion main engines power electric motors power battery shafts	1 x Otto gasoline 160bhp 1 150shp 60 cells one	1 x Otto gasoline 180bhp 1 70shp 60 cells one	1 x gasoline 160bhp 1 70hp 60 cells one	1 x gasoline 160bhp 1 70shp 60 cells one
Performance speed, surface submerged range, surfaced submerged	8kt 7kt – –	8kt 7kt 184nm at 8kt 21nm at 7kt	8.5kt 6kt 585nm 42nm	7.5kt 6kt 500nm at 7kt –
Weapons TT location torpedoes	1x 18in (457mm) bow 3	1 x 18in (457mm) bow 2	1 x 15in (381mm) bow –	1x 18in (457mm) bow 3
Complement	7	13	22	8

History: Following the success of *Holland* (SS-1) four navies built versions of J. P. Holland's next design, a slightly larger development. In the U.S. Navy this new design was known as the A-class (Adder-class), but the British, Japanese and Russian navies gave them the generic title of "Holland-type" boats. The last three are described in their own national entries, but are also included here to show their relationship to the Adder-class. The U.S. Navy's boats were specifically intended for harbour defence, with the crew living either ashore or aboard a tender. Seven were built and were given names as well as hull numbers (SS-2 to SS-8) and class numbers (A-1 to A-7), and to add to the confusion first-of-class *Adder*, which was launched on 22 July 1901, was given hull number SS-3, while the fifth to be launched, *Plunger*, was given the

Above: A-class boat USS Porpoise (SS-7) alongside in 1902.

"senior" numbers of SS-2 and A-1.

The design of the A-class was generally similar to that of *Holland* (SS-1), but with a deck casing stretching from just before the conning tower to the stern. The 8in (203mm) dynamite gun was deleted and the number of torpedoes increased to five. All boats in the class except *Plunger* were shipped to the Philippines in pairs in 1908, 1909 and 1915, where they formed the 1st Submarine Division of the Asiatic Torpedo Fleet, based at the U.S. Navy's major facility at Cavite. *Plunger*'s career was marked by two memorable episodes: first, President Theodore Roosevelt spent several hours submerged in her on 25 March 1905, which he immensely enjoyed; and, second, her last commanding officer was Ensign Chester Nimitz, who was to earn undying fame in World War II. After a period in reserve, *Plunger* was stricken in 1913 and sold for scrap in 1922, while the Philippines-based boats served during World War I, but without seeing any actual combat and were later used as targets; all six were then stricken on 16 January 1922.

The British Holland-class (qv) were built to virtually the same design, but under licence in the Vickers shipyard. Both the Japanese and Russian boats, however, were built in the United States and then broken down into sections and taken across the USA by rail before being shipped across the Pacific to their respective destinations.

Right: Porpoise and Shark in 1905. Note the sailor in the torpedo tube.

B-/C-/D-classes

UNITED STATES OF AMERICA

Type: harbour defence/coastal patrol, gasoline-electric.

Class	B-class	C-class	D-class
Total built	3	5	3
Completed	1906-07	1908-10	1909-10
Displacement surfaced submerged	145 tons 173 tons	238 tons 275 tons	288 tons 337 tons
Dimensions length beam draught	82ft 5in (25.1m) 12ft 6in (3.8m) 10ft 7in (3.2m)	105ft 4in (32.1m) 13ft 11in (4.2m) 10ft 0in (3.0m)	134ft 10in (41.1m) 13ft 11in (4.2m) 12ft 6in (3.8m)

History: These three small classes followed each other, each representing an increase in size and displacement on the original gasoline-engined Holland-class until the D-class. The B-class, like the Holland and A-classes had a single propeller, but the C-class introduce a second shaft and propeller, which arrangement was to endure in U.S. submarines until the *Albacore* in the 1950s. The second power-train made greater horsepower available and improved manoeuvrability, but above all in an era when mechanical reliability was not great, it provided redundancy and ensured that a single fault did not immobilise the submarine at sea.

The B-class were designated "harbor defense" submarines and all three were transferred to the Philippines in 1912, where they joined the A-class. Also like the A-class, they were stricken in 1922. The C-class was actually built in parallel to the B-class, but were larger and had greater range, leading to them being designated coastal defence submarines. In World War I they were deployed in defence of the Panama Canal, and all were stricken in 1920. The D-class followed on from the C-class, being slightly larger and with greater range. All were stricken in 1922.

Right: **Cuttlefish *(SS-11), second of the B-class.***

Propulsion			
main engines	1 x Craig gasoline	1 x Craig gasoline	2 x NLSE gasoline
power	250bhp	500bhp	2 x 300bhp
electric motors	1	1	2
power	150shp	300shp	2 x 260shp
battery	60 cells	120 cells	120 cells
shafts	one	one	two
Performance			
speed, surface	9kt	10.5kt	13kt
submerged	8kt	9kt	9.5kt
range, surfaced	800nm/8kt	800nm/8kt	1,240nm/9kt
submerged	12nm/4kt	80nm/5kt	–
maximum operational diving depth	150ft (46m)	200ft (61m)	200 (61m)
Weapons			
TT	2x 18in (457mm)	2 x 18in (457mm)	4 x 18in (457mm)
location	bow	bow	bow
torpedoes	4	4	4
Complement	10	15	15

E-/F-/H-/K-classes   UNITED STATES OF AMERICA

Type: coastal patrol, diesel-electric.

Class	E-class	F-class	H-class	K-class
Total built	2	4	9	8
Completed	1911	1911-12	1913-18	1913-14
Displacement surfaced submerged	287 tons 342 tons	330 tons 400 tons	358 tons 467 tons	329 tons 521 tons
Dimensions length beam draught	135ft 3in (41.2m) 14ft 7in (4.4m) 11ft 8in (3.6)	142ft 7in (43.5m) 15ft 5in (4.7m) 12ft 2in (3.7m)	150ft 4in (45.8m) 15ft 10in (4.8m) 12ft 5in (3.8m)	153ft 7in (46.9m) 16ft 8in (5.1m) 13ft 1in (4.0m)

History: These four classes represent a steady increase in the refinement and effectiveness of the Holland-type submarine. The E-class was the first in the U.S. Navy to be powered by diesel engines, thus doing away with the inherent danger of the gasoline engines. Even so, these early diesels proved to be a source of constant trouble, which was so severe in the E- and F-classes that the boats had to be withdrawn from service in 1915 and given completely new engines. The E-class were the first U.S. submarines to have bow planes and also the first to have radio equipment and antennas installed in construction.

The F-class was developed and built in parallel with the E-class and was slightly larger. The development train finally came together with the H-class, although only three were actually ordered for the U.S. Navy – *H-1* (SS-28) to *H-3* (SS-30). The type did, however, attract great foreign interest, with large numbers being built for Britain's Royal Navy (see H-class, UK) and the Imperial Russian Navy (see AG-class). At the time of the Russian Revolution six boats remained in the United States awaiting delivery and these were purchased by the U.S. Navy in 1918, being designated *H-4* (SS-147) to *H-9* (SS-152). The K-class succeeded the H-class and was slightly larger.

The two E-class boats both survived World War I, to be stricken in 1922, but the four F-class boats were not so fortunate. *F-4* was the first to be lost, sinking during a diving exercise off Honolulu on 25 March 1915, with the loss of all hands. That was followed by a collision between *F-3* and *F-1* on 17 December 1917 in which the latter sank with the loss of 19 lives. The remaining two boats were stricken and scrapped in 1922. One H-class boat was lost, *Seawolf* (SS-28), which suffered an onboard fire off the Pacific coast and was deliberately run ashore; four men, including the commanding officer were drowned trying to reach the shore and the boat then sank while being hauled off by a repair ship. One of the remaining two original boats was stricken in 1922, while the other boat plus all those from the Russian order were scrapped in 1931.

Right: USS **K-5** *(SS-36), launched in 1914, scrapped in 1931.*

Propulsion				
main engines	2 x NLSE diesels	2 x NLSE diesels	2 x NLSE diesels	2 x NLSE diesels
power	2 x 350bhp	2 x 390bhp	2 x 475bhp	2 x 475bhp
electric motors	2	2	2	2
power	2 x 300shp	2 x 300shp	2 x 300shp	2 x 340shp
battery	120 cells	120 cells	120 cells	120 cells
shafts	two	two	two	two
Performance				
speed, surface	13.5kt	13.5kt	14kt	14kt
submerged	11.5kt	11.5kt	10.5kt	10.5kt
range, surfaced	2,100nm/11kt	2,300nm/11kt	2,300nm/11kt	4,500nm/10kt
submerged	100nm/5kt	100nm/5kt	100nm/5kt	120nm/5kt
maximum				
operational				
diving depth	200ft (61m)	200ft (61m)	200ft (61m)	200ft (61m)
Weapons				
TT	4x 18in (457mm)	4 x 18in (457mm)	4 x 18in (457mm)	4 x 18in (457mm)
location	bow	bow	bow	bow
torpedoes	4	4	8	8
Complement	20	22	28	28

G-class

Type: coastal patrol, gasoline/diesel-electric.

Class	Seal (G-1)	Tuna (G-2)	Turbot (G-3)	Thrasher (G-4)
Pennant No	SS-191/2	SS-27	SS-31	SS-26
Total built	1	1	1	1
Completed	1911	1915	1915	1914
Displacement surfaced submerged	288 tons 337 tons	400 tons 516 tons	393 tons 460 tons	360 tons 475 tons
Dimensions length beam draught	161ft 0in (49.1m) 13ft 1in (4.0m) 12ft 6in (3.8m)	161ft 7in (49.3m) 13ft 1in (4.0m) 12ft 6in (3.8m)	161ft 0in (49.1m) 13ft 1in (4.0m) 12ft 10in (3.9m)	157ft 6in (48.0m) 17ft 6in (5.3m) 10ft 11in (3.3m)

History: These four boats were actually individual designs and were grouped together as the G-class for administrative convenience. Three of them – *G-1*, *G-2* and *G-3* – were designed by Simon Lake. *G-1* and *G-2* were each powered by four gasoline engines, which caused a lot of problems and both spent a great deal of time in maintenance and refits. *G-1* was the first design by Simon Lake to be accepted by the U.S. Navy, being constructed by Newport News (the first submarine to be built there) and commissioned on 28 October 1912, and was unique in the U.S. Navy's numbering system, being given a fractional number – SS-19½ . Her only notable achievement was to carry out a dive of 256ft (78m),

Propulsion				
main engines	4 x gasoline	4 x gasoline	2 x diesels	2 x gasoline
power	4 x 300bhp	4 x 600bhp	2 x 600bhp	2 x 500bhp
electric motors	2	2	2	2
power	2 x 260shp	2 x 260shp	2 x 300shp	2 x 220shp
battery	120 cells	120 cells	120 cells	164 cells
shafts	two	two	two	two
Performance				
speed, surface	14kt	14kt	14kt	14kt
submerged	10kt	10.5kt	95kt	95kt
range, surfaced	2,500nm/8kt	2,500nm/8kt	2,500nm/8kt	2,500nm/8kt
submerged	70nm/5kt	70nm/5kt	70nm/5kt	70nm/5kt
maximum operational diving depth	200ft (61m)	120ft (61m)	200ft (61m)	200ft (61m)
Weapons				
TT	6 x 18in (457mm)	4 x 18in (457mm)	6 x 18in (457mm)	4 x 18in (457mm)
location	bow – 4; deck – 2	bow	bow	bow
torpedoes	8	4	10	8
Complement	24	24	25	24

a record at the time. From 1915 onwards she was used in training and ended her days as an aerial target, being sunk by bombs on 21 June 1920. At one time she was commanded by Lieutenant Charles Lockwood, who as Commander Submarines Pacific (COMSUBPAC) in World War II would mastermind the submarine war against Japan. *G-2* (SS-27), another Lake design, had a relatively short career, being launched in 1911, commissioned in February 1915 and stricken in 1919, which included a lengthy overhaul from March 1916 to June 1917. Most of her career was devoted to experimental and training duties and she then became a target for depth-charges. She was undergoing maintenance on 30 July 1919 when

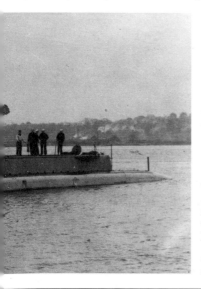

she suddenly sank, drowning three of her crew. *G-3* (SS-31) was the only one of this group of Lake boats to be powered by diesels and served from completion in December 1913 until being stricken in 1922.

G-4 (SS-31), originally named *Thrasher,* was built by Cramp in the USA under licence from Fiat-Laurenti, the only submarine ever to be built for the U.S. Navy to a foreign design. The craft was delivered some three years late and proved generally unsatisfactory, with poor surface range (1,680nm at 8kt), a lack of stability, a very small conning tower and a particularly heavy hull, the latter a consequence of the Laurenti practice of using non-circular frames, which then needed extra bracing.

Left: Seal *(SS-19¹/₂), Lake's first boat for the U.S. Navy.*

L-/M-classes

UNITED STATES OF AMERICA

Type: coastal, diesel-electric.
Total built: 11.
Completed: 1915-17.
Displacement: surfaced 450 tons; submerged 548 tons.
Dimensions: length 167ft 4in (51.0m); beam 17ft 5in (5.3m); draught 13ft 5in (4.1m).
Propulsion: 2 x NLSE diesels, 2 x 600bhp; 2 x electric motors, 2 x 400shp; battery 120 cell; two shafts.
Performance: surface – 14kt; submerged – 10.5kt; range surfaced 3,300nm at 11kt, submerged 150nm at 5kt; maximum operating diving depth 200ft (61m).
Weapons: 4 x 18in (457mm) TT (bow), 8 x torpedoes; 1 x 3in (76mm) gun.
Complement: 28.
Specifications for L-class, as built.

History: There were 11 L-class boats, seven (*L-1* to *L-4, L-9* to *L-11*) to an Electric Boat design, which were built by Fore River at Qunicy, and four to a Lake design, of which three (*L-5* to *L-7*) were built by Lake at Bridgeport and one (*L-8*) at Portsmouth Navy Yard, the latter being the first submarine to be

Right: First of her class, **L-1** *(SS-40) puts to sea.*

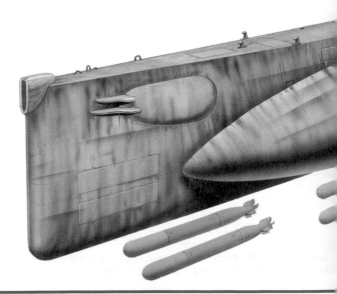

114

Above: USS L-11. Note the "disappearing" mount which left part of the barrel protruding vertically from the foredeck.

built in any U.S. Navy yard. The four Lake boats were marginally smaller than the others, being 165 ft (50.3m) long and with a submerged displacement of 524 tons. These submarines were the first in the U.S. Navy to mount a deck gun, as built, the 3in (76mm) weapon being on a "disappearing" mount, which was unique to the U.S. Navy. To "disappear", the entire mounting swung backwards through 90deg and then lowered into a recess, but leaving the forward 3ft (0.9m) of the barrel protruding vertically above the deck, the muzzle being closed off with a tampion.

L-8 (SS-48), the fourth of the Lake boats, had an unusual history. During World War I it was used in a secret deception scheme, which also involved the four-masted schooner, USS *Charles Whittemore*. The idea was that the *Whittemore* towed the submerged *L-8*, which thus remained hidden but still in close contact with the surface ship by telephone, while the apparently defenceless sailing ship was supposed to attract the attention of a marauding enemy U-boat, whereupon *L-8*, alerted by telephone, would carry out an attack. The British tried a similar idea, but neither navy scored any successes. In 1922

AA (T)-class UNITED STATES OF AMERICA

Type: fleet, diesel-electric.
Total built: 3.
Completed: 1920-22.
Displacement: surfaced 1,106 tons; submerged 1,486 tons.
Dimensions: length 268ft 9in (81.9m); beam 22ft 10in (6.9m); draught 14ft 2in (4.3m).
Propulsion: 4 x NLSE diesels, 4 x 1,000bhp; 2 x electric motors, 2 x 675shp; battery 2 x 60 cells; two shafts.
Performance: surface – 20kt; submerged – 10.5kt; range surfaced 3,000nm at 14kt, submerged 100nm at 5kt; maximum operating diving depth 150ft (46m).
Weapons: 6 x 21in (533mm) TT (bow – 4, deck – 2), 16 x torpedoes; 2 x 3in (76mm) guns.
Complement: 38.
Specifications for T-1 (SS-52), as built.

History: This class was the first of several attempts by the U.S. Navy to produce that ideal sought by a number of the world's largest navies – the "fleet" submarine which could operate with the battle fleet. The first-of-class was authorised in 1914, followed by two more in 1915. The designations require an explanation. The first-of-class was given the class number *SF-1* (SF = Submarine, Fleet-type); the second and third boats were simply given numbers – *SF-2* and *SF-3*. The class designation was then changed to the AA-class, with the boats renumbered *AA-1* to *AA-3*, and finally in 1920 it changed yet again, becoming the T-class (*T-1* to *T-3*). The first-of-class bore the name *Schley* (SS-52), but the other two only ever carried numbers.

The boat had a partial double-hull, with single-hull compartments at each end. *Schley* was one of the first boats in any navy to have trainable torpedo-tube mountings on the upper deck. These had twin 18in (457mm) tubes and the entire mount was

L-8 was deliberately sunk to become a target for magnetic exploders.

During 1917-18 seven boats deployed to Bantry Bay in Ireland, where their bridge dodgers were prominently marked with the letters "AL-" to differentiate them from the British L-class. Although involved in several actions with U-boats, they scored no successes. The Lake-designed boats were scrapped in 1925, while two of the others were stricken in 1922 and the remainder in 1930-32.

The sole M-class submarine, *M-1* (SS-47), had the same weapons as the L-class, but was the first U.S. Navy double-hull submarine and, with an overall length of 196ft 3in (59.8m), she was the longest built for the U.S. Navy up to this time. However, she also had a very narrow beam – 14ft 9in (4.5m) – and was considered to be very crowded and certainly less habitable than contemporary single-hull boats. She also had a habit of taking up a large list when diving or submerging, which, not surprisingly, caused some anxiety among her crew. *M-1* was commissioned on 16 February 1916 and spent almost all of her relatively brief career as a training boat. She was stricken on 15 March 1922 and sold for scrap six months later.

trained from inside the boat by means of handwheels and mechanical linkages on orders from the captain at the periscope. Trials showed this to be not worth the complications and first one and then the other deck mounts were removed from *Schley* and none was ever mounted on the other two boats. *Schley* also initially mounted two 3in (76mm) guns, but this was later changed to a single 4in (102mm). With the deck tubes *Schley* carried the very impressive load of 16 torpedoes and even when the deck tubes were removed all three boats carried 12 torpedoes, which was considerably more than most contemporary submarines, apart from some of the very large U-boats of the German Navy.

To obtain the necessary power, there were four NLSE diesel engines, each with a power output of 1,000bhp, which were mounted in tandem on each shaft, but this caused a great deal of vibration, which, despite many changes of clutches and damping, was never overcome. The third boat, *T-3*, was re-engined with two large M.A.N. diesels, but this proved to be of little benefit.

The boats proved to be just capable of reaching their design speed under ideal conditions, but had so many shortcomings, especially in hull design and propulsion systems, that they were put into reserve in 1922 and scrapped in 1930.

Below: Schley (formerly AA-1), the first "fleet" submarine.

N-class

UNITED STATES OF AMERICA

Type: attack, diesel-electric.
Total built: 7.
Completed: 1916-17.
Displacement: surfaced 348 tons; submerged 414 tons.
Dimensions: length 147ft 4in (44.9m); beam 15ft 9in (4.8m); draught 12ft 6in (3.8m).
Propulsion: 2 x NLSE diesels, 2 x 300bhp; 2 x electric motors, 2 x 150shp; battery 120 cells; two shafts.
Performance: surface – 13kt; submerged – 11kt; range surfaced 3,500nm, submerged 30nm at 5kt; maximum operating diving depth 200ft (61m).
Weapons: 4 x 18in (457mm) TT (bow), 8 x torpedoes.
Complement: 25.
Specifications for N-1 (SS-53), as built.

History: For some years U.S. submarines had suffered from problems with their diesel engines and in the N-class it was decided that, instead of seeking to obtain the greatest possible power from a unit, the designers would deliberately reduce power in order to enhance reliability and reduce the maintenance load. This was tested in the N-class and proved to be such a success that more modest power outputs were adopted in the succeeding classes, while many existing boats were re-engined. Also, for about a decade, U.S. submarines had been given an embryonic bridge, which consisted of a platform mounted on top of the conning tower, usually with a canvas dodger to give some protection to the watchkeepers. The N-class, however, was the first

---

O-class

UNITED STATES OF AMERICA

Type: attack, diesel-electric.
Total built: 16.
Completed: 1918.
Displacement: surfaced 521 tons; submerged 629 tons.
Dimensions: length 172ft 3in (52.2m); beam 18ft 1in (5.5m); draught 14ft 5in (4.4m).
Propulsion: 2 x NLSE diesels, 2 x 440bhp; 2 x electric motors, 2 x 370shp; battery 120 cells; two shafts.
Performance: surface – 14kt; submerged – 10.5kt; range surfaced 5,500nm at 11.5kt; maximum operating diving depth 200ft (61m).
Weapons: 4 x 18in (457mm) TT (bow), 8 x torpedoes.
Complement: 29.

History: The O-class consisted of 16 boats which were built at five different yards. Those built at Portsmouth Navy Yard (1), Puget Sound Navy Yard, Bremerton (1), Fore River, Quincy (7), and California Shipbuilding, Long Beach (3), were identical, but the three from Lake, Bridgeport, were, as usual with this company, different in many minor details. The details of the Lake boats, O-11 (SS-72) to O-13 (SS-74), were: length 175ft 3in (52.4m), beam 16ft 9in (5.1m) and submerged displacement 629 tons. A further difference in the last six boats (ie, Lake and California Shipbuilding) was that they were powered by Sulzer diesels, produced in the United States by Busch-Sulzer.

Two were peacetime losses: O-5 (SS-66) was in collision with a merchant ship on 28 October 1923 and O-9 (SS-70) foundered in 1941. Most boats were employed in the training role from 1928 onwards, although six were stricken in

to follow foreign example and have an all-steel bridge. The N-boats were the last U.S. submarine class to be built without a deck gun until the late 1940s.

Three N-boats were built by Seattle Construction and four by Lake. The latter were 155ft (47.2m) long, and had a 14ft 6in (4.4m) beam, with a submerged displacement of 415 tons. The Lake boats were commissioned in 1918 and decommissioned and sold for scrap in 1922, a remarkably brief service life, whereas the Seattle boats were commissioned in 1917 and served until 1926, after which they were held in reserve until 1930. *N-2* (SS-54) was modified to test the Neff air-independent propulsion system and while the system worked it was considered to offer no significant advances over conventional diesel-electric systems and was not pursued further.

1930 and one in 1938. Seven served through World War II and were scrapped in 1945-46.

O-12 (SS-73), one of those stricken in 1930, was leased by the Australian explorer, Sir Hubert Wilkins (1888-1958), for the sum of $1 per year for five years in order to lead a submarine expedition to the North Pole. *O-12* was converted at Brooklyn Navy Yard, the changes including the addition of a long, curved upper deck, a collapsible bowsprit, and two air-drills capable of drilling holes though up to 100ft (30.5m) of ice. She was renamed *Nautilus* after Jules Verne's fictional submarine and the boat, now with civilian status, was towed across the Atlantic by a U.S. Navy battleship. She set out from Norway in late 1931 and did actually go under the ice, but Wilkins was forced to turn back when still some 450nm (724km) from the Pole. It was a very brave attempt.

R-class

Type: attack, diesel-electric.
Total built: 27.
Completed: 1918-19.
Displacement: surfaced 569 tons; submerged 680 tons.
Dimensions: length 186ft 5in (56.8m); beam 18ft 1in (5.5m); draught 14ft 5in (4.4m).
Propulsion: 2 x NLSE diesels, 2 x 600bhp; 2 x electric motors, 2 x 467shp; battery 120 cells; two shafts.
Performance: surface – 13.5kt; submerged – 10.5kt; range surfaced 4,700nm at 6.2kt; maximum operating diving depth 200ft (61m).
Weapons: 4 x 21in (533mm) TT (bow), 8 x torpedoes; 1 x 3in (76mm) gun.
Complement: 29.
Specifications are for R-1 (SS-78), as built.

History: The 27 R-class boats were built in three yards, Fore River (14), Union Iron Works (6) and Lake (7), and as usual the Lake boats were different. This time they were dimensionally identical to the others, but had a lesser displacement: 510 tons surfaced, 583 tons submerged. Of greater significance was that they had different engines, Busch-Sulzer diesels (2 x 500bhp), and they retained the 18in (457mm) torpedo tubes, whereas all the rest mounted four of the new 21in (533mm) tubes, the first U.S. submarines to do so.

As in the L- and N-classes, the Lake-built boats were the first to be scrapped, in this case in 1930. Three R-boats, *R-3, R-17* and *R-19*, were transferred to Britain's Royal Navy in 1941-42. Of these, the latter, then designated HMS *P-514,* was sunk in a collision with the minesweeper USS *Georgian*, off Cape Race (21 June 1942).

S-class

Type: patrol, diesel-electric.

History: The S-class started with the first submarine-design competition ever run by the U.S. Navy, which resulted in three prototypes: two company designs, *S-1* (SS-105) from the Electric Boat Company and *S-2* (SS-106) from Simon Lake, and a government-designed boat, *S-3* (SS-107), built by Portsmouth Navy Yard. The result of the competition was that the Lake design was considered unsatisfactory and orders were placed for two groups, followed by two separate repeat orders.

Group 1, the Electric Boat design, comprised 25 boats: the prototype, *S-1* (SS105), plus 12 boats each from Fore River (*S-18* to *S-29)* and Union Iron Works (*S-30* to *S-41*). These were single-hulled boats, powered by NLSE diesels, completed between 1919 and 1922.

Group 2, the official Bureau of Ships design, comprised 15 boats, the first of which was the prototype, *S-3*, the production boats being completed by Portsmouth Navy Yard (*S-4* to *S-13)* and Lake (*S-14* to *S-17)*. This group shared the major characteristics of the Group I design, but was double-hulled and was always considered to be much more crowded. Unusually among U.S. submarines of the period, these boats were built with non-folding bow hydroplanes, although they were given folding mechanisms in 1922-24 refits. These boats were powered by a variety of main engines, from NLSE, M.A.N. or Busch-Sulzer.

Group 3 was a development of the Electric Boat design, with

Above: Peruvian R-1*, export version of the U.S. Navy's R-class.*

The only other loss was USS *R-12* (SS-89) which sank during a torpedo exercise off Key West, Florida. The boat was on the surface, preparing to dive, when it suddenly started to flood forward; a warning was sounded but she went down extremely quickly and the only survivors were five men of the bridge crew. The number crew lost was 42, which suggests that she was seriously overmanned, possibly with trainees. The initial cause of the disaster was never determined. *R-12* was one of only two U.S. submarines lost in the Atlantic during World War II.

    R-14 (SS-91) was involved in a famous incident when it ran out of fuel while searching for a missing tugboat south-east of Hawaii in May 1921. Rather than wait to be found the crew sewed blankets and mattress covers together to make a number of square-rigged sails and then proceeded back to Hawaii, an epic voyage that took five days and remains unique in submarine history.

six boats (*S-42* to *S-47*) completed at Fore River in 1923-24.

    Group 4 comprised four boats (*S-48* to *S-51*) completed by Lake in 1922. They were to a C&R design, were longer than the three earlier groups, and had a stern torpedo tube, bringing the number of tubes to five and torpedoes carried to 14.

    The first Lake type, *S-2*, was the original Lake prototype which displaced 977 tons (submerged), was 207ft (63.1m) long, and had speeds of 15kt on the surface and 11.5kt submerged. Although this design was rejected in favour of

Below: S-1 *conducting aircraft-carrying trials in the 1920s.*

	Group 1	Group 2	Group 3	Group 4
Total built	25	15	6	4
Hull Nos	S-1, S-18 – S-41	S-3, S-4 – S-17	S-42 – S-47	S-48 – S-51
Completed	1920-24	1919-23	1924-25	1922
Displacement surfaced submerged	854 tons 1,062 tons	876 tons 1.092 tons	906 tons 1,126 tons	903 tons 1,230 tons
Dimensions length beam draught	219ft 3in (66.9m) 20ft 8in (6.3m) 15ft 9in (4.8m)	231ft 07in (70.4m) 22ft 0in (6.7m) 13ft 1in (4.0m)	225ft 5in (68.7m) 20ft 8in (6.3m) 16ft 1in (4.0m)	240ft 2in (73.2m) 21ft 8in (6.6m) 13ft 5in (4.1m)

the Electric Boat design, and despite its "one-off" status, *S-2* was commissioned into the U.S. Navy and served in the Asiatic Fleet from 1921 to 1929, not being scrapped until 1931.

A total of 51 S-boats entered service between 1918 and 1924, and there were three peacetime losses. *S-4* was rammed by a USCG cutter as she was surfacing and sank with loss of all hands. She was later raised, repaired and returned to service, being stricken in 1931. *S-5* was flooded and sank (1 August 1920) coming to rest on the bottom. The crew managed to raise the stern until it was above the water and then cut a hole through which they all escaped. The hulk was recovered but was not returned to service. The third loss was *S-51* which was rammed by the merchant ship, *City of Rome*, off Block Island, New York (25 September 1925); only three out of the 36 aboard were rescued. The hulk was raised but never returned to service. Two boats of Group 4 and the sole Lake prototype were scrapped in 1931 and a further one Group 1 and six Group 2 boats were stricken and scrapped in 1936-37. The remaining 38 S-

122

Propulsion				
main engines	2 x NLSE diesels	2 x NLSE diesels	2 x BS diesels	2 x BS diesels
power	2 x 600bhp	2 x 1,00bhp	2 x 600bhp	2 x 900bhp
electric motors	2	2	2	2
power	2 x 750shp	2 x 600shp	2 x 600shp	2 x 750shp
shafts	two	two	two	two
battery	120 cells	120 cells	120 cells	120 cells
Performance				
speed, surface	14kt	15kt	14.5kt	14l.5kt
submerged	11kt	11kt	11kt	11kt
range, surfaced	3,420nm/6.5kt	5,000nm/10kt	2,510nm/6.5kt	5,900nm/10kt
submerged	–	–	–	–
maximum operational diving depth	200ft (61m)	200ft (61m)	200ft (61m)	200ft (61m)
Weapons				
TT	4 x 21in (533mm)	4 x 21in (533mm)	4 x 21in (533mm)	5 x 21in (533mm)
location	bow	bow	bow	bow – 4, stern – 1
torpedoes	12	12	12	14
gun	1 x 4in (102mm)	1 x 4in (102mm)	1 x 4in (102mm)	1 x 4in (102mm)
Complement	38	22	38	38

boats all saw service in World War II, six of which (all Group 1) were supplied to foreign navies: Poland – 1 (1941) and UK – 5 (1942). Seven in U.S. service were lost during the war, six Group 1 (*S-26*, *S-27*, *S-28*, *S-36*, *S-37*, *S-39*) and one Group 3 (*S-44*). The remaining boats survived the war and were then either scrapped or expended as targets in 1945-46.

Below: S-48, 2nd Lake Type. Fifty-one S-class were built.

Diesel-Electric Patrol Submarines 1922-1946

World War I transformed the submarine from an interesting novelty into a major weapon of war. Indeed, the manner in which German U-boats had brought the mighty British Royal Navy to the verge of defeat showed clearly how submarines, properly used, could exert a strategic influence out of all proportion to their numbers. Despite the German defeat, the U-boats had established a reputation for effectiveness and sound design, and many Allied navies seized the opportunity to obtain examples in the post-war share-out of U-boat prizes, which were then examined in the most minute detail. In fact, the British were so shaken by their experiences that when they attended the Washington Naval Conference in 1921-22 they proposed the total abolition of the submarine, but this received little support from other navies, although limits were agreed on total tonnage and gun calibres.

Submarine construction continued during the 1920s, albeit at a slow pace, partly due to the Washington limits, but also as a consequence of the increasingly severe financial situation. Thus, most navies built a number of small classes of "patrol" submarines, while some of the larger navies also tried to produce a "fleet submarine" which would be capable of steaming at the same speed as the surface battlefleet. In the 1920s this meant a sustained speed of 20kt, but such a goal proved very elusive, requiring ever larger submarines with increasingly powerful diesels. Then, when the 20kt speed was achieved, it was discovered that the speed of the battlefleet had increased to 28-30kt and by the early 1930s it was appreciated that the concept was flawed and designers' turned to more productive fields.

The technical advances made during the inter-war period were steady rather than spectacular. New steels were introduced, which, coupled with the use of welding in place of riveting, enabled diving limits to be increased and improved watertightness, particularly in fuel tanks. Designs became more sophisticated, although many navies encountered control and stability problems when new classes were introduced.

The 1930s also saw the first attempts to make revolutionary improvements in the submerged performance of submarines. Speed and range had improved only marginally since before World War I, apart, of course, from the British R-class of 1918. The problem was attacked in the 1930s by German and Japanese designers, acting quite independently of each other. The Japanese appear to have been first; their No 71 was launched in 1938 and achieved an underwater speed of 21kt, although they seem not to have tried to find a new air-independent propulsion (AIP) system to take full advantage of these new capabilities. The German inventor, Dr. Walter, produced equally revolutionary prototypes in the late 1920s, although his work also included propulsion systems; however, when he was nearing an operational design which was both streamlined and air-independent, his design was adapted for the diesel-electric Type XXI.

During World War II the Germans fought their Atlantic campaign with the Type VII and Type IX, neither of which was outstanding in any way. However, they were sound designs, and capable of being produced in large numbers; by May 1945 some 705 Type VIIs had been produced, of which 437 were lost in action, while of 194 Type IXs as many as 150 were lost. The U-boats sank large amounts of Allied shipping but they were eventually defeated by a combination of surface and airborne anti-submarine warfare (ASW), coupled with the electronic warfare systems which broke the Enigma code upon which the Germans were so reliant. Two other factors were also of great importance: Allied scientists stayed one step

Right: Loading a torpedo aboard a German Type VIIC which, because of limited space, could carry only 14.

ahead of Axis scientists throughout the war, and the shipyards, particularly those in the United States, built new ships faster than the Germans could sink them.

The second great campaign was fought in the Pacific, where the Japanese started with a large fleet, mainly of very large boats, of which much was expected. Their overall performance, however, was disappointing, their big submarines being slow to dive, difficult to manoeuvre underwater and easy for Allied ASW forces to find. Their primary mission was to sink Allied warships and they certainly sank a number, including 2 carriers, 10 cruisers and 10 destroyers, but never enough to cause the Americans significant concern.

The United States' submarine force was based on the excellent "fleet" boats, which were large, capable, comfortable, and available in large numbers. They were ideally suited for conditions in the Pacific and by August 1945 had virtually stopped movements by Japanese surface shipping. A total of 53 U.S. submarines were lost during the war, 45 of them in action.

British submarines also fought a hard war, but of quite a different type, since Axis merchant shipping quickly disappeared and by 1942 there were very few such targets left. The British had, therefore, to concentrate on warships and sank six cruisers, 16 destroyers, 35 U-boats and many other smaller vessels.

The table shows the distribution of the world's submarine fleets at the start of World War II and makes it clear that, despite the attention paid to the German U-boat fleet, the largest submarine fleets were actually operated by the Soviet and Italian navies. The latter was by far the more effective, although the Soviets suffered from the perennial Russian maritime problem of having to operate four totally separate fleets, none of which was in a position to supprt another. Next came the United States, followed by France, with the British Royal Navy ranking fifth, only just ahead of Japan. Like the Soviets, however,

the British position was worse than the numbers suggest, since it had global commitments in defence of the Empire and colonies, which meant that its submarine fleet was spread very thinly.

World Submarine Fleets: September 1939			
Europe		United Kingdom	69
Denmark	11	USSR (approx)	150
Estonia	2	Yugoslavia	4
Finland	5		
France	77	**North America**	
Germany	65	United States	100
Greece	6		
Italy	107	**South America**	
Latvia	2	Argentina	3
Netherlands	24	Brazil	4
Norway	9	Chile	9
Poland	5	Peru	4
Portugal	4		
Romania	1	**Asia**	
Spain	9	Japan	65
Sweden	24	Siam	4
Turkey	9		

Below: Precursor of a massive fleet; Japanese No 69 built in the 1920s.

Daphne/
Havmanden-classes

Type: patrol.

Class	Daphne-class	Havmanden-class
Total built	2	4
Completed	1926-27	1938-42
Displacement surfaced submerged	308 tons 381 tons	320 tons 402 tons
Dimensions length beam draught	160ft 9in (49.0m) 17ft 1in (5.2m) 8ft 2in (2.5m)	157ft 6in (48.0m) 15ft 5in (4.7m) 9ft 2in (2.8m)
Propulsion main engines power electric motors power shafts	2 x Burmeister & Wain 2 x 600bhp 2 x Titan 2 x 200shp two	2 x Burmeister & Wain 2 x 600bhp 2 x Brown-Boveri 2 x 225shp two
Performance speed: surface submerged	13.4kt 6.8kt	15kt 8kt
Weapons TT location guns	63 x 18in (457mm) bow – 4, stern – 2 1 x 75mm gun 1 x 20mm AA cannon	5 x 18in (450mm) bow – 3, stern – 2 2 x 40mm AA 2 x 8mm MG
Complement	25	20

History: The Royal Danish Navy was one of the smallest to maintain its own submarine design and construction capabilities, having done so since 1915 when the Ægir-class of 5 boats was designed and built by the Royal Copenhagen Dockyard in 1915-16. That was followed by the Rota-class (C-class) three boats launched in 1918-20.

Building of the Daphne-class (D-class) started in 1924 and two were built; *Daphne*, completed in 1926 and *Dryaden* completed in 1927. This was a medium-sized design and rather surprisingly carried 18in (457mm) torpedo tubes. It was powered by diesel engines built by a Danish company, Burmeister & Wain. Both boats were scuttled with the rest of the Danish submarine fleet when the occupying German forces took control of the country on 29 August 1943. They were raised by the Germans but did not return to service and were scrapped in 1943.

Above: Two boats of the Havmanden-class; note cable cutters.

Above: Dryaden, a Daphné-class boat, built in the 1920s.

Despite the indifference of Danish politicians to defence matters, the Havmanden-class (H-class) of four submarines were completed between 1938 and 1940, while a fifth boat (known only as H-5) was cancelled. Two unusual features of this design were that they had three bow tubes and they were the last in any navy to be built with the outmoded 18in (457mm) tubes. Like the Daphne-class, all four were scuttled on 29 August 1943, but were later raised and scrapped.

Saukko-class

Type: inshore, patrol.
Total built: 1.
Completed: 1930
Displacement: surfaced 114 tons; submerged 142 tons.
Dimensions: length 107ft 10in (32.9m); beam 10ft 6in (3.2m); draught 9ft 6in (2.9m).
Propulsion: 1 x Germaniawerft diesel, 200bhp; 1 x electric motor, 120shp; one shaft.
Performance: surface – 10kt; submerged – 6.3kt; range surfaced 500nm at 8kt, submerged 50nm at 4kt.
Weapons: 2 x 18in (457mm) TT (bow); 9 x 176lb (80kg) mines; 1 x 12.7mm MG.
Complement: 15.

History: The Finnish Saukko is unique among the world's submarines in having been designed specifically to operate in a lake. Lake Ladoga (known as *Laatokka* to the Finns and *Ladozhskoye Ozero* to the Russians) is the largest lake in Europe, and is located northeast of St. Petersburg; it covers some 7,000 square miles (18,100sq km), and is approximately 130 miles (210km) long and 80 miles (130km) wide, with a maximum depth of 738ft (225m). Traditionally, the northern part of the lake belonged to the Grand Duchy of Finland which had been part of the Russian Empire since the Napoleonic Wars but regained her independence while the Russians were preoccupied with the revolution in 1917-18. A peace treaty was later signed between Finland and the Soviet Union (Treaty of Tartü, 14 October 1920),one of whose conditions was that neither side could operate

Vesikko-class

Type: coastal.
Total built: 1.
Completed: 1933.
Displacement: surfaced 250 tons; submerged 300 tons.
Dimensions: length 134ft 2in (40.9m); beam 13ft 6in (4.1m); draught 13ft 9in (4.2m).
Propulsion: 2 x M.W.M. diesels, 2 x 350bhp; 2 x electric motors, 2 x 180shp; battery 62 Tudor cells; two shafts.
Performance: surface – 13kt; submerged – 7kt; range surfaced 1,500nm at 13kt, submerged 50nm at 5kt; maximum operating diving depth 300ft (91m).
Weapons: 3 x 21in (533mm) TT (bow – 3); 6 x torpedoes;1 x 20mm cannon.
Complement: 30.

History: As early as 1930 German naval planners were considering the types of U-boat that would be needed for rapid construction in a future war and one of them, designated Project Lilliput, was a 200-250 ton boat which could be built rapidly and in large numbers when the time came. The Germans needed a foreign navy to order one and, having tried and failed with Estonia, they suggested to the Finnish Navy that such a boat would complement their planned submarine arm, although without, of course, letting on that it was merely a device for trialling a boat for the German Navy. The Finns insisted on waiting until they had trialled the *Vetehinen*, but then did place an order.

The new boat was built by Crichton-Vulcan at Abo, Finland, and was launched in 1932. It had three torpedo tubes, all in the bow, and was powered by two diesels from Motoren-Werke Mannheim (M.W.M.), which were already

Above: **Saukko*, the only submarine designed to operate in a lake.**

warships with a displacement exceeding 100 tonnes (98.4 tons) on Lake Ladoga.

I.v.S. produced a submarine design but the Finns did not place an order, possibly because they considered her to be too small to justify the establishment of a submarine arm. In 1929, however, the Finns placed an order for several sea-going boats and decided to include one of these smaller boats in their plans. Thus an order was placed for one boat to an improved design now designated Pu-110, which was built by Hietalahden Laivatelakka in Helsinfors and launched in July 1930. She was commissioned in late 1930 and named *Saukko*, being the smallest true submarine in any navy at the time.

Once built, it transpired that the displacement of *Saukko* was actually 116 tonnes surfaced and 144 tonnes submerged, so much in excess of the limit that the Finns decided not to annoy their far larger neighbour and Saukko never went to the lake, but she found plenty of employment in the Baltic, being constantly employed against Soviet forces between 1939 and 1944. She was stricken in 1947 and scrapped in 1953.

Right: The Finnish Vessikko was the prototype for Germany's Type IIA.

in production for the R-class motor-minesweepers. The Germans provided the full trials team and took the boat to Germany for its "designers' testing" which lasted some two years. Indeed, they even went so far as to prolong the trial period in order that the boat could be used to instruct officers attending the German Navy's first submarine engineering course since 1918. There were two results of this subterfuge, the first being that *Vesikko* was not commissioned into the Finnish Navy until 1936. The longer term outcome, however, was that the design for what was to become the new German Navy's Type IIA had been tried and tested and was ready as soon as Hitler gave the go-ahead for U-boat construction to restart.

Vesikko was employed in the Baltic throughout World War II and was stricken in 1947 when, in the peace treaty with Russia, Finland was banned from operating any submarines at all. However, the boat was retained as a memorial and remains on display in Finland.

Requin-class

Type: ocean-going attack/reconnaissance.
Total built: 9.
Completed: 1925-28.
Displacement: surfaced 947 tons; submerged 1,441 tons.
Dimensions: length 256ft 8in (78.25m); beam 22ft 5in (6.8m); draught 16ft 8in (5.1m).
Propulsion: 2 x Sulzer/Schneider diesels, 2 x 1,450bhp; 2 x electric motors, 2 x 900shp;
Performance: surface – 15kt; submerged – 9kt; range surfaced 6,400nm at 12kt, submerged 70nm at 5kt; maximum operating diving depth 250ft (80m).
Weapons: 10 x 21.7in (550mm) TT (bow – 4, stern – 2, external 2 x 2); 16 x torpedoes; 1 x 3.9in (100mm) gun, 2 x 8mm MG.
Complement: 51.

History: This was the French Navy's first post-World War I submarine programme and took advantage not only of the staff studies of the war but also of detailed physical examination of the 10 German U-boats handed over to France in 1920 as reparations. With this class three missions appeared which were to recur in the French Navy in the inter-war years: scouting for the battle fleet, long-range anti-shipping attacks, and colonial service.

These double-hulled boats were large by the standards of the time, and had a particularly heavy torpedo armament consisting of no fewer than 10 torpedo tubes and 16 torpedoes. There were four tubes in the bow, two in the stern, and two pairs in rotating mounts on the upper casing. The latter, which were to be fitted in most French submarines over the following 20 years, could be

600-tonnes type

Type: patrol (*sous-marins de moyenne patrouille*).

Class	Sirene-class	Ariane-class	Circe-class
Total built	4	4	4
Completed	1926-27	1926-2	1926-28
Displacement surfaced submerged	609 tons 757 tons	626 tons 787 tons	615 tons 776 tons
Dimensions length beam draught	209ft 11in (64.0m) 17ft 1in (5.2m) 14ft 1in (4.3m)	216 ft 6in (66.0m) 20ft 4in (6.2m) 13ft 6in (4.1m)	204ft 11in (62.5m) 20ft 4in (6.2m) 13ft 1in (4.0m)
Propulsion main engines power electric motors power shafts	2 x Sulzer 2 x 650bhp 2 2 x 500shp two	2 x Normand 2 x 625bhp 2 2 x 500shp two	2 x Schneider 2 x 625bhp 2 2 x 500shp two

Right: Narval, *one of the first submarines built by France after the war.*

rotated by mechanical linkages from inside the pressure hull, whether on the surface or submerged. In effect, they gave the beam-launching capability the British had sought in their fixed tubes (see E-class) but without the excessive beam, although they could not, of course, be reloaded at sea. Once in service the Requin-class proved to have poor handling characteristics and also suffered from the problem which afflicted so many submarines intended to cooperate with the battle fleet – a lack of speed. They also suffered from unreliable machinery and cramped bridges, both problems being addressed in major refits in the mid-1930s.

Narval and *Morse* were sunk by mines in 1940, and *Souffleur* was sunk by the British submarine HMS *Parthian* (25 June 1941). *Caiman*, having been scuttled and recovered, was finally sunk in a USAAF bombing raid on Toulon on 11 March 1944. Four were seized by the Germans on 8 December 1942 and were handed over to the Italians, who commissioned them as *FR-111* (ex-Phoque), *FR-113* (ex-Requin), *FR-114* (ex-Espadon) and *FR-115* (ex-Dauphin) and set about converting them to the transport role. The only one of these to be completed was *FR-111*, which was sunk by Allied aircraft while on a resupply run to the Italian island of Lampedusa (28 February 1943) while the other three were scuttled on 9 September 1943. *Marsouin* survived the war to be scrapped in 1946.

Performance			
speed: surface		14kt	
submerged		7.5kt	
range: surfaced		2,300nm/3kt	
submerged		75nm/5kt	
maximum			
diving depth		256ft (80m)	
Weapons			
TT		7 x 21.7in (550mm)	
location		bow – 1, external fixed, forward – 2, external fixed, aft – 2, external rotating – 2,	
torpedoes		8	
guns		1 x 3in (76mm)	
		2 x 8mm AA MG	
Complement	41	41	41

History: The French Navy tried a procurement experiment with the 600 tonne-class by issuing an operational requirement and a set of general specifications to three shipbuilders and leaving it to them to design and build four boats each. All three designs were considered to be reasonably satisfactory, being manoeuvrable both on the surface and when submerged, but with a curiously dispersed torpedo armament. This consisted of one internal tube in the bow and two fixed tubes on the upper casing, facing forward. There were also two fixed external tubes in the stern and a pair of tubes on a rotating, external mount. Thus, there were seven tubes with torpedoes immediately available to launch, but only one reload (for the bow tube). Armament was a single deck gun; this was 3in (76mm) in most boats, but 4in (102mm) in some.

All three designs were based on that of the German UB-III and each yard employed a well-known submarine designer as a consultant: AC de la Loire, Nantes (Sirene-class) – Simonot; Augustin-Normand (Ariane-class) – Fenaux; and Schneider (Circe-class) – Laubeuf. The double-hull, a feature inherited from the UB-III, resulted in cramped working conditions for the crew and slow diving characteristics, while although the machinery was

Katsonis/
Proteus classes

FRANCE (GREECE)

Type: medium-range, patrol.

History: These six submarines represented a major expansion of the Greek Navy's submarine arm, which since 1912 had consisted of just two small boats, *Delfin* and *Xiphias*. The first order was for two boats, Schneider-Laubeuf designs, based on that of the 600-ton Circe-class (see previous entry). These were fairly conventional designs, but with the unusual French combination of internal and external torpedo tubes which prevailed in the 1920s and 1930s. In this case, the Greek boats (*Katsonis, Papamicolis*) had four externally mounted tubes, two in the bows and two in the stern, which could not be reloaded at sea, and only two internal tubes in the bows for which just one reload was carried. The design differed from that of the French boats in having a rather large bridge tower, with the 3.9in (100mm) gun mounted on a rotating platform at its forward end, a design feature which appears to have originated with the British Royal Navy and which was intended to enable the gun-crew to get the weapon into action with a minimum of delay after surfacing.

The four-strong Proteus-class (*Glavkos, Nereus, Proteus, Triton*) were ordered about a year after the two Katsonis-class. These new boats were a Loire-Simonot design, and were slightly larger, which enabled a much more operationally effective armament to be carried, consisting of eight torpedo tubes, six in the bow and two in the stern, all mounted internally, with two

different in each of the types it was generally unreliable.

Ondine was sunk by a merchant ship in 1928 and *Nymphe* was paid off in 1938, but the remainder were refitted in 1937-38 and on the outbreak of World War II the 10 boats formed the largest single group of medium-range submarines in the French Navy. *Doris* was torpedoed and sunk by *U-9* (9 May 1940). Most of the remainder were scuttled at Toulon on 27 November 1942; a few of these were then raised, only to be bombed by the Allies. None survived the war.

**Below: Sirene*, the first of 12 French "600-tonne" types.*

**Above: French-built *Papamicolis; note high gun position.*

reloads. Also, the 3.9in gun mounting was brought down from the forward end of the bridge tower and mounted on the casing.

During World War II all six submarines escaped from Greece and

Class	Katsonis	Proteus
Total built	2	4
Completed	1927	1927-28
Displacement surfaced submerged	605 tons 778 tons	750 tons 960 tons
Dimensions length beam draught	204ft 9in (62.4m) 17ft 6in (5.3m) 11ft 0in (3.4m)	225ft 0in (68.6m) 18ft 10in (5.7m) 13ft 8in (4.2m)

thereafter operated under British direction. *Katsonis* was rammed and sunk in the Aegean by a German submarine-chaser (14 September 1943), but *Papamicolis* survived the war, only to be stricken in 1946. Three of the Proteus-class were war losses: two were sunk by Axis surface warships – *Proteus* (19 December 1940) and *Triton* (16 November 1942) – while *Glavkos* was sunk by bombs in Malta harbour (4 April 1942). *Nereus* survived, but was stricken immediately after the war.

1,500-tonnes type

FRANCE

Type: ocean-going (*sous-marins de grand patrouille*).
Total built: 31.Series 1 – 19; Series 2 – 6; Series 3 – 6.
Completed: Series 1 – 1928-31; Series 2 – 1931-35; Series 3 – 1934-37.
Displacement: surfaced 1,570 tons; submerged 2,084 tons.
Dimensions: length 302ft 10in (92.3m); beam 26ft 11in (8.2m); draught 15ft 5in (4.7m).
Propulsion: 2 x Schneider/Sulzer diesels, 2 x 3,00bhp; 2 x electric motors, 2 x 1,000shp; two shafts.
Performance: surface – 17kt; submerged – 10kt; range surfaced 10,000nm at 10kt, submerged 100nm at 5kt; maximum operating diving depth 250ft (76m).
Weapons: 9 x 21.7in (550mm) TT, 11 x torpedoes; 2 x 15.7in (400mm), 2 x torpedoes; 1 x 3.9in (100mm) gun, 2 x 13.2mm AA MG (1 x 2) (see text).
Complement: 61.
Specifications for Series 1, as built.

History: Like the American and British navies, the French Navy (*Marine*

Propulsion		
main engines	2 x Schneider-Carels	2 x Sulzer
power	2 x 650bhp	2 x 710bhp
electric motors	2	2
power	2 x 500shp	2 x 600shp
shafts	two	two
Performance		
speed: surface	14kt	14kt
submerged	9.5kt	9.5kt
range: surfaced	1,500nm/10kt	1,500nm/10kt
submerged	100nm/5kt	100nm/5kt
maximum		
divingdepth	2,760ft (850m)	270ft (85m)
Weapons		
TT	6 x 21in (533mm)	8 x 21in (533mm)
location	bow – 4, stern – 2	bow – 6, stern – 2
torpedoes	7	10
guns	1 x 3.9in (100mm)	1 x 3.9in (100mm)
	1 x 3pdr (76mm) AA	1 x 3pdr (76mm) AA
Complement	39	41

Above: 1,500-tonnes type submarine of the **Marine Nationale.**

Nationale) was fascinated by the idea of a "fleet submarine" (*sous-marin d'escadre*), which would be able to keep pace with the battle fleet, act as scouts and, if the opportunity arose, attack units of the enemy battle fleet. The project began in 1914, but became of greater importance in the 1920s when the most likely enemy was perceived as being Italy and the possibility of a clash between the two nations' battle fleets was something for which French naval planners had to prepare. As with the other navies, the target speed for the submarine was 20kt and the problem lay in obtaining sufficient power from the propulsion system; the British had used steam in their K-class (qv) but the French, despite their own long experience with steam submarines, decided to turn instead to the diesel. It was known that the German company M.A.N. had been planning a 3,000bhp diesel at the end of World War I and various French manufacturers were tasked with achieving similar power levels.

The outcome was the 1,500-tonnes-type, which was produced in three versions: Series 1 – Redoutable-class, 19 boats; Series 2 – L'Espoire-class, 6 boats; and Series 3 – Agosta-class (6 boats). The later two series had the same hull and weapons as Series 1, but differed in their power systems as the designers struggled to attain the magic figure of 20kt. Thus, in Series 1, two 3,000bhp diesels produced a speed of 17kt and in Series 2 this was increased to 3,600bhp and 19kt, while in Series 3 power output was 4,000bhp. Thus, the figure of 20kt was reached at last, although the French knew that stretching an engine to its limits reduced its overall life and increased the unreliability problem, so a peacetime limit of 75 per cent power was set, which reduced speed to a maximum of 15kt.

Armament comprised 11 torpedo tubes. There were four 21.7in

630-tonnes type FRANCE

Type: patrol (*sous-marins de deuxième classe*).

History: These 22 boats belonged to four distinct groups, the first three – Argonaute-, Diane- and Orion-classes – being further examples of the policy of issuing a specification to private yards and then allowing them to produce their own designs. The fourth was the Minerve-class, which was designed to the same specification by the official French Navy design bureau, S.T.C.N.; hence its alternative name, the Amirauté-type (admiralty-type). These were the outcome of a specification for a slightly larger and improved successor to the 600-tonnes type, and three yards were awarded contracts. Hulls and armament were essentially similar, but propulsion was different. The Argonaute-class was a Schneider-Laubeuf design and consisted of six boats, all built by Schneider, and powered by two-stroke Schneider-Carels diesels. The Diane-class was a Normand-Feneux design, powered by four-stroke Normand-Vickers diesels; nine boats were built at two different yards. The Orion-class consisted of just two boats; it was a Loire-Dubigeon design, powered by two-stroke Sulzer diesels; two were built at different yards.

Armament comprised six 21.7in (550mm) torpedo tubes, with three in the bows, one internal with a single reload, and two outside the pressure hull. There were a further two tubes in a trainable mounting on the upper deck, immediately abaft the tower. Finally, there was a second trainable mounting at the stern, which carried one 21in tube in the centre, flanked by two 15.7in (400mm) tubes.

(550mm) tubes forward, mounted internally, with another three 21.7in (550mm) tubes in a rotating mount on the upper deck immediately abaft the after gun position. As in other French classes, this could be trained from inside the boat, but could not be reloaded at sea. There was a second rotating mount right aft which contained four torpedo tubes, two for the heavyweight 20.7in (550mm) torpedoes, and two for the new 15.7in (400mm) torpedo. This had been developed because naval planners considered that a 550mm torpedo would provide an unnnecessary degree of overkill against small surface targets, although wartime experience would show that it was a most unreliable system and in 1943-44 surviving boats had their stern quadruple mount replaced by a triple 21.7in (550mm) mount.

Two boats, *Prométhée* and *Phénix*, were lost in pre-war accidents, leaving 29 at the outbreak of war, but their story is a sad one. Four were scuttled at Brest on 18 June 1940 and 10 were destroyed during Allied attacks on French colonial possessions under Vichy control. Seven were scuttled at Toulon on 27 November 1942, although some were later recovered, only to be destroyed by Allied bombing. *Sfax* was torpedoed in error by a German U-boat (19 December 1940) and *Protée* was sunk by German patrol boats in December 1943. The remainder survived the war and were broken up in the early 1950s.

A much improved, successor class was under construction at the start of the war. First-of-class *Roland Morillot* was ordered in 1934, followed by a second in 1937 and three more in 1938, with another 11 planned, but such was the slow pace of submarine construction that only three were laid down by the time of the German attack in June 1940 and all were destroyed in the ways.

The boats also included many minor improvements, including hydraulically operated (as opposed to electric) control surfaces, enhanced underwater stability, and a general tidying up of the exterior which resulted in an increase in underwater speed to 9kt.

The French Admiralty's own design, the Minerve-class, brought together the best points of the three earlier 630-tonnes designs. In addition, the armament was considerably improved. In the bows the number of tubes was increased from three to four, and all were internal. The stern trainable mounting was deleted and replaced by two internally mounted 21.7in (550mm) tubes. Finally, the midships trainable mounting was retained, but all tubes were of the lighter 14.7in (450mm) type. The Minerve-class was powered by four-stroke Normand-Vickers diesels, which had proved better than the two-stroke Sulzer and Schneider-Carels types.

All were in service at the time of the outbreak of war. In the Argonaute-

Below: Junon, *after post-war refit; the gun has been removed.*

Class	Argonaute-class	Diane-class	Orion-class	Minerve-class
Total built	5	9	2	6
Completed	1930-33	1930-33	1931	1935-39
Displacement surfaced submerged	630 tons 798 tons	571 tons 809 tons	558 tons 787 tons	662 tons 856 tons
Dimensions length beam draught	208ft 0in (63.4m) 21ft 0in (6.4m) 13ft 10in (42m)	211 ft 4in (64.4m) 20ft 4in (6.2m) 14ft 1in (4.3m)	219ft 0in(66.8m) 20ft 4in (6.2m) 14ft 5in (4.0m)	223ft 5in (68.1m) 18ft 5in (5.6m) 13ft 3in (4.0m)
Propulsion main engines power electric motors power shafts	2 x Schneider-Carels 2 x 650bhp 2 2 x 500shp two	2 x Normand 2 x 700bhp 2 2 x 500shp two	2 x Sulzer 2 x 700bhp 2 2 x 500shp two	2 x Normand 2 x 900bhp 2 2 x 615shp two

class, the nameship was sunk by depth charges (8 November 1942) and the remainder survived, only to be broken-up in 1946. In the Diana-class *La Sibylle* was believed to have been sunk in error by a German U-boat, four were scuttled and one beached itself during the Allied invasion of North Africa, and three survived, to be scrapped in 1946. The two boats of the Orion-class both joined the Free French Navy in Britain and were cannibalised for spares for *Junon* and *Minerve*, and then scrapped in 1943. In the Minerve-class, three were scuttled

Type IA-class   GERMANY

Type: ocean-going patrol.
Total built: 2.
Completed: 1937.
Displacement: surfaced 862 tons; submerged 983 tons.
Dimensions: length 237ft 6in (72.4m); beam 20ft 5in (6.2m); draught 14ft 1in (4.3m).
Propulsion: 2 x 8-cylinder, 4-stroke M.A.N. diesels, 2 x 1,400bhp; 2 x BBC electric motors, 2 x 500shp; battery 2 x 62 cells; two shafts.
Performance: surface – 17.8kt; submerged – 8.3kt; range surfaced 6,700nm at 12kt, submerged 78nm at 4kt; maximum operating diving depth 328ft (100m).
Weapons: 6 x 21in (533mm) TT (bow – 4, stern – 2), 14 x torpedoes; 1 x 105mm gun, 1 x 20mm AA cannon.
Complement: 43.

History: The decision to rebuild the U-boat arm was taken in late 1932 and the designs were designated *Motorenversuchsboote* (*M.W.B.* = experimental

Performance	
speed: surface	14kt
submerged	9kt
range: surfaced	4,000nm/10kt
submerged	85nm/5kt
maximum	
diving depth	256ft (80m)
Weapons	
TT	6 x 21.7in (550mm)
location	(see notes)
torpedoes	1 x 3in (76mm)
guns	1 x MG (Minerve-class – 2)
Complement	41

in November 1942, one was wrecked in September 1945, and two survived to be broken up in the early 1950s.

The Aurore-class was the culmination of the 600/630-tonne series, being a much improved version of the Minerve-class, and it was planned to build a total of 15, but the war intervened. Only *Aurore* had been completed by the time of France's capitulation in June 1940 and she was scuttled at Toulon.

La Creole was fitting out and was towed to the UK where she lay incomplete until 1946 when she was returned to France and completed. Four were captured incomplete by the Germans; three of these were given German naval numbers, but only one, *UF-2* (ex-*La Favorite*), was commissioned into the *Kriegsmarine* on 5 November 1940; she was decommissioned in June 1944 and scuttled at Gotenhafen in May 1945. Post-war, the five surviving boats were completed to a revised design and served until the 1960s when they were scrapped. The Aurore-class was larger than the Minerve-class, with a 1,170 ton submerged displacement, an overall length of 241ft 2in (73.5m) and nine 21.7in (550mm) torpedo tubes.

Above: Type IA-class** U-25 **sank six ships before being lost with all hands on 3 August 1940, possibly after hitting a mine.

motor boats).The larger of the two original designs, the Type I was based on the *E1* built for Spain and later sold to Turkey (see Gür-class). With a displacement of 983 tons, the Type I was considered large by the German

Navy, although it was modest compared to contemporary boats such as the British T-class (1,575 tons) and the U.S. Salmon-class (2,210 tons). Externally, the design showed evidence of German World War I practice, including the serrated cablecutter in the bows, the large bridge and the single 4.1in (105mm) gun, but there were major advances internally, including an all-welded pressure hull and 21in (533mm) torpedo tubes, thus adopting the *de facto* international standard for the first time in a U-boat.

U-25 and U-26 entered service in 1937 and were soon relegated to training duties, but they were reinstated as *frontboote* (operational boats) as soon as war broke out. U-25 carried out one successful Atlantic voyage, which included refuelling at supposedly neutral Cadiz; five merchant ships were sunk. She later took part in the invasion of Norway but was lost with all hands on 3 August 1940, possibly to a mine. U-26 also went into the Atlantic, but after sinking three merchant ships and damaging a fourth it was attacked by British ASW forces. She surfaced and, the crew having abandoned ship, the boat was scuttled; all 48 crew members were rescued.

Type II-class

GERMANY

Type: coastal patrol.

	Type IIA	Type IIB	Type IIC	Type IID
Total built	6	20	8	16
Completed	1936	1936-40	1938-39	1940
Displacement surfaced submerged	259 tons 301 tons	279 tons 329 tons	291 tons 341 tons	314 tons 364 tons
Dimensions length beam draught	134ft 2in (40.9m) 13ft 4in (4.1m) 12ft 6in (3.8m)	140 ft 1in (42.7m) 13ft 5in (4.1m) 12ft 9in (4.0m)	144ft 0in (43.9m) 13ft 5in (4.1m) 12ft 6in (3.8m)	144ft 4in (44.0m) 16ft 5in (5.0m) 12ft 9in (3.9m)
Propulsion main engines power electric motors power battery shafts	2 x M.W.M. 350bhp 2 x S.S.W. 2 x 180shp 62 cells two	2 x M.W.M. 350bhp 2 x S.S.W. 2 x 180shp 62 cells two	2 x M.W.M. 350bhp 2 x S.S.W. 2 x 205shp 62 cells two	2 x M.W.M. 350bhp 2 x S.S.W. 2 x 205shp 62 cells two

Above: U-26, second of two Type IAs commissioned in 1937.

Performance				
speed: surface	13kt	13kt	12kt	13kt
submerged	6.9kt	7kt	7kt	7.4kt
range: surfaced	2,000nm/8kt	3,900nm/8kt	4,200nm/8kt	3,200nm/12.7kt
submerged	35nm/4kt	35nm/4kt	35nm/4kt	56nm/4kt
maximum diving depth	328ft (100m)	328ft (100m)	328ft (100m)	256ft (80m)
Weapons				
TT		3 x 21in (533mm)		
location		bow		
torpedoes		6		
guns		1 x 20mm AA twin		
Complement		25		

History: The Type IIA was virtually identical to the Vesikko-class (qv) built for Finland and, although designated the second of the two new designs, the Type II was actually the first to be built. This was done in great secrecy and the programme was revealed only with the signing of the Anglo-German Naval Treaty. The Type IIA was a single hull boat, but had an all-welded hull (unlike the Vessiko-class which had a riveted hull) and was fitted internally to launch the latest G7a and G7e 21in (533mm) torpedoes. Work started on the Type IIB before the first Type IIA was launched, the main aim being to increase the range by adding three new frames in the hull and placing a new oil bunker beneath the control room. The Type IIC had a further two frames to improve facilities in the radio room and to accommodate a second periscope. The Type IID was generally similar to the Type IIC but had saddle tanks, which were used as self-compensating fuel tanks, thus increasing range yet again, and enabling these boats to operate around the Western coast of the British Isles. Kort nozzles (a shroud around the propellers) were also fitted and although they seem to have worked well enough they were not adopted on other U-boat classes. Two Type IIBs were being built for the Chinese Navy when war broke out and were immediately seized and incorporated into the German Navy.

These boats were nicknamed *Einbäume* (dug-out canoes) by their crews, from their small size and very heavy rolling on the surface. They were primarily intended to train the many crews needed for the resurrected U-boat arm, but had to be

Below: U-22, Type IIB, with 20mm mounted from 1943 .

Type VII

GERMANY

Type: ocean-going attack.

History: The Type VII is one of the most important designs in the history of the submarine, a total of 709 of all sub-types having been built between *U-27* (commissioned 12 August 1936) and *U-1308* (commissioned 17 January 1945). Although produced in such large numbers, and despite its great influence on the war at sea, the Type VII was by no means the best submarine of its era, nor was any aspect of its performance truly outstanding. Instead, it was an adequate compromise and its greatest attribute was that it could take the trade war well out into the Atlantic, having adequate range, armament and seaworthiness. It was also relatively easy to build and required a fairly small crew, although it should be noted that they lived in very cramped conditions, which became increasingly unpleasant as each voyage progressed.

Type VIIA. All Type VIIs followed the general pattern of the Type VIIA, a single-hull design with saddle-tanks,

Right: U-402, Type VIIC, before launch. Note saddle-tanks, twin rudders, canoe stern.

Above: Type IIBs were known as "dug-out canoes".

pressed into service in 1939-40 to overcome the desperate shortage of *frontboote* (operational boats). Six Type IIBs were transferred to the Black Sea in 1942, which involved them being dismantled and mounted on pontoons, enabling them to move by river and canal to Dresden in southern Germany. From there they went by road to Ingolstadt in Austria, where they were again loaded onto pontoons and moved down the Danube to Galati in Romania. Here they were reassembled and handed over to their crews, who took them on the final leg to Constanza on the Black Sea. It was an epic achievement by any standard.

Fifty Type IIs were built, of which 11 were lost in combat: aircraft – two, submarines – 2; mines – 2; surface ships – 5. Four were lost in training accidents, five were stricken in 1944, and five were scuttled in the Black Sea. That left 25 in service at the end of the war, of which 21 were scuttled in German waters and four went to the UK where they were sunk in Operation Deadlight.

Class	Type VIIA	Type VIIB	Type VIIC	Type VIIC/41
Total built	6	20	8	16
Completed	10	24	577	88
Displacement surfaced submerged	626 tons 745 tons	753 tons 857 tons	761 tons 865 tons	759 tons 860 tons
Dimensions length beam draught	211ft 7in (64.5m) 19ft 0in (5.8m) 14ft 4in (4.4m)	218ft 2in (66.5m) 20ft 3in (6.2m) 15ft 5in (4.7m)	220ft 1in (67.1m) 20ft 4in (6.2m) 15ft 8in (4.8m)	220ft 5in (67.2m) 20ft 4in (6.2m) 15ft 8in (4.8m)
Propulsion main engines power electric motors power battery shafts	2 2 x 1,160bhp 2 2 x 375shp 2 x 62 cells two	2 2 x 1,400bhp 2 2 x 375shp 2 x 62 cells two	2 2 x 1,400bhp 2 2 x 375shp 2 x 62 cells two	2 2 x 1,400bhp 2 2 x 375shp 2 x 62 cells two

Below: U-55, a Type VIIB, slightly longer than Type VIIA.

Performance				
speed: surface	16kt	17.2kt	17.2kt	13kt
submerged	8kt	8kt	7.6kt	7.4kt
range: surfaced	4,300nm/8kt	6,500nm/12kt	6,500nm/12kt	6,500nm/12kt
submerged	90nm/4kt	90nm/4kt	80nm/4kt	80nm/4kt
maximum				
diving depth	328ft (100m)	328ft (100m)	328ft (100m)	394ft (120m)
Weapons				
TT	5 x 21in (533mm)	5 x 21in (533mm)	5 x 21in (533mm)	5 x 21in (533mm)
location	bow – 4, stern – 1	bow – 4, stern – 1	bow – 4, stern – 1	bow – 4, stern – 1
torpedoes	11	14	14	14
guns	1 x 88mm	1 x 88mm	1 x 88mm	1 x 88mm
	1 x 20mm AA	1 x 20mm AA	1 x 20mm AA	1 x 20mm AA
Complement	44			

with six internal watertight compartments, and specially strengthened bulkheads at each end of the control room. There were five torpedo tubes, four in the bows and one, externally mounted, aft. Ten of these boats were built by AG Weser (6) and Germania (4), being commissioned between July 1936 and April 1937.

Type VIIB. The first Type VIIA was tested against the first Type IA (qv) and was the clear winner, although various improvements were suggested, which led to the Type VIIB. These included lengthening the hull by 6.6ft (2m), increasing the

capacity of the saddle tanks in order to give more fuel and thus greater range, and fitting superchargers to the engines. The single rudder was replaced by twin rudders, one behind each propeller, which not only improved manoeuverability but also enabled the stern torpedo tube to be resited within the pressure hull, a much more satisfactory arrangement. The torpedo load was also increased by three, a most important advance since many wartime patrols were to be ended due to running out of torpedoes.

Type VIIC. The VIIB solved most of the shortcomings of the VIIA, but simply did not have the space for new electronic devices coming into service, so the hull was lengthened yet again, the space inside the conning-tower was increased, and more fuel tanks were added. Other changes included a new diesel-oil filtration system, a new air compressor and an updated electrical control system. As there was no increase in engine power, the result was that the Type VIIC was slightly slower and had less range than the VIIB.

Type VIIC/41. Once combat experience began to be gained it became clear that the Type VIIC had a number of shortcomings and, in particular, that it did not have the speed and seakeeping ability to catch up with fleeing targets, while increased depth would enable the boats to escape from more ASW attacks. A major weight reduction programme pared some 11.5 tons off the weight, although 10 of these tons saved was immediately lost when it was decided to increase the thickness of the pressure hull, but this enabled the normal operating depth to be increased to 394ft (120m), a very significant operational gain. The seakeeping requirement was met by lengthening the bow by 5in (13cm) and widening the foredeck. These changes did not warrant a new sub-type designation, so the modified boat was termed the Type VIIC/41, the figures indicating that the decision to procure the modified boat had been made in 1941.

Others. There were several more projects which never reached production, including the Type VIIC/42 which would have had a longer hull, more powerful engines and a greater diameter pressure hull. The Type VIIC/43 was a Type VIIC/42 but with much heavier armament. Two types that did reach production were the Type VIID minelayer and the Type VIIF transport; the Type VIIE was

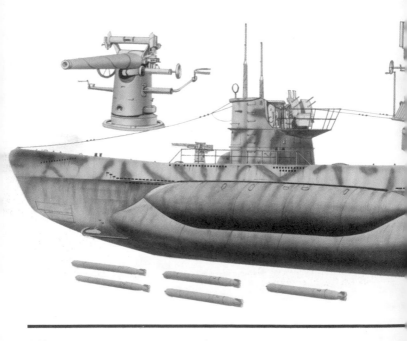

intended to test an experimental lightweight diesel, but never got beyond the drawing-board.

Conversions. Inevitably in a type produced in such vast numbers, there were numerous in-service conversions and modifications. One of the most serious threats facing the Type VIICs was air attack by the increasingly aggressive Allied air and naval forces, to which one answer was improved AA protection. Thus there were at least eight "bridge conversions" which mounted a variety of AA weapons on or around the bridge. Such additional platforms and weapons resulted in longer diving times and a loss in submerged speed and manoeuvrability. These bridge conversions were intended to improve individual U-boats' self-defence, but there were also *flak* U-boats, which were intended to provide an aggressive air defence umbrella for a group of U-boats (eg, when rendezvousing with a supply boat) and involved several extensive platforms for two quadruple 20mm mounts and a single 37mm. Two boats were converted and one was sent to sea but it quickly became apparent that the concept of "fighting it out on the surface" was flawed and work on five more ceased and the boats were returned to normal duties.

The Type VII was at the forefront of the U-boat battle in the North and central Atlantic, in the Mediterranean, and in the Arctic, and sank by far the greatest proportion of Allied shipping. *U-30* (Lemp) sank the liner *Athenia* on 3 September 1939, the first day of the war, in which 118 people, including 28 U.S. citizens, were killed. *U-48,* a Type VIIB, was the most successful submarine of World War II. Between September 1939 and June 1941 (when it was transferred to training duties) it undertook 13 operations, spending 291 days at sea under three captains, during which it sank 51 ships with a total tonnage of 310,407.

The Type VII remained in production until the final months of the war, but it had been gradually phased out in favour of the new *electroboote,* the Types XXI and XXIII. In retrospect, it is surprising that the Germans did not consider a radically modernised version of the Type VII, as the U.S. Navy did with its

Below: Type VIIC with naval 88mm gun and quad 20mm flak.

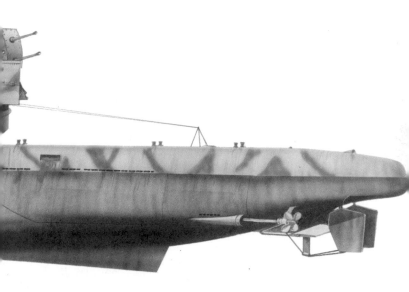

Guppy-series boats (qv) and the British with their modernised A- and T-classes (qqv). Both these navies showed how, by increasing battery power, deleting drag-creating protuberances and generally streamlining the hull, a much faster and more efficient boat could be produced at relatively small expense and with little technical risk. One particular shortcoming of the Garman design was its small size and as Admiral Dönitz sent his boats further across the Atlantic resupply of fuel, torpedoes and food became an increasingly severe problem; they left port literally stuffed solid, but resupply became inevitable and as this was a time-consuming process which could only be done on the surface they laid themselves open to attacks by Allied aircraft and ships.

No fewer than 437 Type VIIs were lost in action and a further number were lost in accidents or during Allied bombing of ports and harbours. At the end of the war a large number were scuttled, but even so there were a many surviving boats, of which a small number were transferred to Allied navies and the others were sunk in the British Operation Deadlight.

Right: Type VIIC returns to Narvik, Norway, after a series of attacks on Convoy PQ-17.

Type IX

GERMANY

Type: long-range attack.

History: The origin of the Type IX lay in a 1935 requirement for a long-range U-boat capable of fast transits to and from distant operational areas, with good endurance and a substantial load of weapons, fuel and supplies. The result was Germany's second most numerous class of U-boat, with 236 built in seven sub-types. Start point for the Type IX design was the Type IA (qv), which itself had been based on the World War I *U-81* design (qv). It was a fully double-hulled boat with a wide, flat upper deck, one of whose benefits was that it gave storage space for 10 torpedoes in watertight containers. There were four main variants.

Type IXA. The original version, of which eight were built in two four-boat batches.

Type IXB. This had fuel bunkerage increased from 154 to 165 tons, which increased range to 12,000nm. 14 were built.

Type IXC. Further evolutionary development with increased fuel bunkerage to 208 tons. A total of 54 were built.

Type IXC/40. A variant of the -C sub-type and by far the most numerous to go into service, the Type IXC/40 resulted from the designers managing to create yet further space for fuel bunkers, increasing the total to 214 tons and range to 11,400nm at 12kt. This led to orders for 163, but only 95 were laid down, of which 87 were actually commissioned.

Type IXD. Very long-range, with IXD1 maximised for speed and IXD2 for range. All IXDs had a longer pressure hull than earlier versions. IXD1 was built as a cargo boat with six fast diesels. Two were built but were unsuccessful, being

Above: **U-532, Type IXC, surrenders at Liverpool, England.**

Class	Type IXA/B*	Type IXC - C/40**	Type IXD2 -IXD/42***
Total built	22	141	29
Completed	1938-40	1940-44	1941-44
Displacement surfaced submerged	1,032 tons 1,153 tons	1,120 tons 1,232 tons	1,616 tons 1,804 tons
Dimensions length beam draught	251ft 0in (76.5m) 21ft40in (6.5m) 15ft 5in (4.7m)	252ft 0in (76.8m) 22ft 4in (6.8m) 15ft 5in (4.7m)	287ft 5in (87.6m) 24ft 7in (7.5m) 17ft 8in (5.4m)
Propulsion main engines power cruise engines power electric motors power battery shafts	2 x M.A.N. 2 x 2,200bhp 2 x S.S.W. 2 x 500shp 2 x 62 cells two	2 x M.A.N. 2 x 2,200bhp 2 x .S.S.W. 2 x 500shp 2 x 62 cells two	2 x M.A.N. 2 x 2,200bhp 2 x M.W.M. 2 x 580bhp 2 x M.W.M. 2 x 580shp 2 x 62 cells two

Below: Type IXC with 105mm deck gun forward, 37mm aft.

Performance speed: surface submerged range: surfaced submerged maximum diving depth	18.2kt 7.7kt 8,100nm/12kt 65nm/4kt 492ft (150m)	18.3kt 7.3kt 11,000nm/12kt 63nm/4kt 492ft (150m)	19.2kt 6.9kt 23,700nm/12kt 57nm/4kt 492ft (150m)
Weapons TT location torpedoes guns	6 x 21in (533mm) bow – 4, stern – 2 22 1 x 105mm 1 x 37mm 1 x 20mm AA	6 x 21in (533mm) bow – 4, stern – 2 22 1 x 105mm 1 x 37mm 1 x 20mm AA	6 x 21in (533mm) bow – 4, stern – 2 24 1 x 105mm 1 x 37mm 1 x 20mm AA
Aircraft	–	–	1 x Focke-Achgelis Fa-330
Complement	48	48	57

* Details are for Type IXA
** Details are for Type IXC
*** Details are for Type IXD2

converted to normal diesels. The Type IXD2 had the same hull as Type IXD1 but the propulsion system comprised two supercharged M.A.N. 9-cylinder, 4-stroke diesels, as in Type IXC, but with two additional M.W.M. 6-cylinder, 4-stroke unsupercharged diesels. The normal arrangement on the surface was to use the larger M.A.N. diesels to recharge the battery or for high-speed, and the smaller M.W.M. engines to power the boat in the cruise regime. Type IXD-42 incorporated minor changes from Type IXD2 but only one was completed before production switched to Type XXI. The Type IXD2 carried a single Focke-Achgelis Fa-330 rotary kite, which was stored in a cylinder on the bridge and was used to extend the observation range, particularly in the southern Atlantic and Indian Oceans, but it proved of very limited value.

Variations. Most of the later boats were fitted with *schnorchels* and some had extra radio masts. The Type IX's diving speed was slow by later war standards and in an effort to overcome this some Type IXC/40s had the forward section of the upper casing narrowed; this reduced the crash-dive time but also cut down the number of reload torpedoes that could be carried.

A total of 145 Type Is were lost at sea due to enemy action: aircraft – 74, surface ships – 58, submarines – five, mines – eight, and captured – one. A further five were lost at sea, one as a result of a collision with another U-boat and the other four from causes unknown. Five were passed to Japan, two as presents from Hitler and three taken over in Far Eastern ports when Germany surrendered. Six were stricken during the war and the remainder survived to be passed to the Allies; a few served in Allied navies but most were sunk in Operation Deadlight.

Type IXs had many achievements to their credit, one of the most remarkable being the Far Eastern cruise of *Kapitänleutnant* Lüdden in *U-188*, a Type IXC/40. Lüdden took his boat from France to Penang and Singapore and

---

Ay-class

GERMANY (TURKEY)

Type: ocean-going patrol.
Total built: 3.
Completed: 1938-39.
Displacement: surfaced 934 tons; submerged 1,210 tons.
Dimensions: length 262ft 6in (80.0m); beam 21ft 0in (6.4m); draught 14ft 0in (4.3m).
Propulsion: 2 x Burmesiter & Wain diesels, 2 x 1,750bhp; 2 x electric motors, 2 x 500bhp; two shafts.
Performance: surface – 20kt; submerged – 9kt; maximum operating diving depth 300ft (100m).
Weapons: 6 x 21in (533mm) TT (bow – 2; stern – 2); 1 x 3.9in (100mm) gun; 1 x 20mm AA cannon.
Complement: 44.

History: These three boats were part of a substantial modernisation. of the Turkish Navy which took place in the late 1930s, the other submarines involved including the German-built *Batiray* minelayer and the British-built Oruc Reis-class (qqv). The Ay-class was closely based on the German Navy's Type IXA, but with major modifications to comply with Turkish requirements, the most visually obvious being that the 3.9in (100mm) gun was mounted in a raised platform

Above: U-110, *Type IXB, sinks in the Atlantic, 10 May 1941.*

then back to France in a voyage lasting 354 days, during which time they were at sea for 297 days and covered 39,792 miles, of which 2,866 were submerged. During this voyage Lüdden sank eight merchant ships and damaged another, and sank seven dhows. He also made six successful high-seas rendezvous with other U-boats, each one highly hazardous, but survived all of them.

Another significant voyage was made by *Korvetten-Kapitän* Timm in command of *U-862*, a Type IXD2. Timm left Brest in June 1945 and arrived safely in Batavia, in the Dutch East Indies, in September 1944, during which voyage he sank five merchantmen (28,018grt). He and his men left Batavia on 17 November 1944 and headed south, sailing down the west coast of Australia and then eastwards, circumnavigating Australia and returning to Batavia on 15 February 1945. The only traces the Australians ever found of his presence were when he damaged one ship and two sank two others.

immediately forward of the bridge, as was the practice in contemporary British boats. *Atilay* was lost during a training exercise in July 1942 and the other two were scrapped in 1957.

Below: Ex-Turkish Batiray, *serving in German Navy as UA.*

Type XXI

Type: long-range attack *electroboot*.
Total built: 120.
Completed: 1944-45.
Displacement: surfaced 1,621 tons; submerged 1,819 tons.
Dimensions: length 251ft 7in (76.7m); beam 21ft 7in (6.6m); draught 20ft 9in (6.3m).
Propulsion: 2 x M.A.N. diesels, 2 x 2,200bhp; 2 x S.S.G. main electric motors, 2 x 2,500shp; 2 x S.S.W. "creep" electric motors, 2 x 323shp; battery 3 x 124 cells; two shafts.
Performance: surfaced – 15.7kt; submerged – 17.2kt; range surfaced 11,150nm at 12kt, submerged 285nm at 6kt; maximum operating diving depth 656ft (200m).
Weapons: 6 x 21in (533mm) TT (bow), 23 x torpedoes; 2 x twin 20mm AA cannon.
Complement: 57.

History: The Type XXI represented a major step forward in submarine technology but, although the concept and the design were brilliant, the actual story was by no means as successful as is often made out. Before the Type XXI the vessels were properly called submersibles, since they spent most of their time on the surface and submerged only for strictly limited periods, during which they were slow and relatively unmanoeuvrable. The Type XXI was, however, designed from the start as a submarine whose natural habitat was in the depths. Its design originated in late 1942 when the *Kriegsmarine* realised that the Allies were winning the war against the U-boats and that the balance could only be restored if the Type VIIs and IXs could be replaced by something greatly superior. Since the early 1930s Professor Walter, a distinguished engineer and inventor, had been working on a series of submarine projects with innovative hull shapes and powered by a revolutionary hydrogen-peroxide

Below: Type XXI had six bow torpedo tubes (no stern tubes), and carried 23 G7e torpedoes. Also carried two twin 20mm cannon for air defence. Note single rudder, twin propellers.

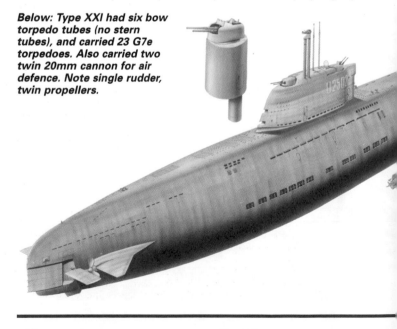

Above: **Wilhelm Bauer *(ex*-U-2540*), now a German museum.***

propulsion system. His most recent project was the Type XVIII and in May 1943 it was suggested that the best way to get a major new design into service quickly would be to modify this hull design, which showed excellent hydrodynamic properties, to take conventional diesel engines and batteries. This proposal was seized upon and in some areas progress was rapid. Admiral Dönitz approved the design on 19 June 1943 and the entire programme was given the go-ahead on 20 August. The first completed module was ready in December and the first boat was launched on 19 April 1944. Some 120 had been launched by the war's end, but the cold fact is that no more than a handful reached an operational state and just two Type XXIs carried out a combat patrol.

Everything about the Type XXI was new. It had a streamlined hull optimised for submerged operation, there were no deck guns and the two twin 20mm cannon were mounted in streamlined housings at each end of the bridge. On the bridge all extending devices such as the *schnorchel*, radar/radio masts and periscopes withdrew into the structure when not in use and the traditional open bridge was replaced by three small individual openings for the watchkeeper and lookouts.

Internally, the longer and better designed figure-of-eight pressure-hull gave much greater volume. Thus, the battery size was tripled (372 cells compared to the Type IX's 124), which in combination with the much more efficient hull design gave an underwater speed of 16kt and an underwater endurance of 72 hours at 5kt. Armament was greatly increased with six bow tubes for which 23 torpedoes were carried, but not so obvious was that there was a totally new rapid loading device, enabling the Type XXI to launch three full six-round salvoes in 20 minutes.

Allied with the revolutionary design was an equally ambitious plan for rapid construction in large numbers. The boat was assembled from 10 modules whose fabrication was dispersed over much of the Third Reich. This optimised the use of resources, reduced the time each hull would occupy space at the shipyards, and enabled groups of workers to accumulate considerable expertise in their particular area. Also, such wide dispersal would, it was thought, make the task of Allied bombers much more difficult. Finally, assembly of completely outfitted modules meant that it would no longer be necessary to install large, heavy items of equipment (eg, electrical cells, diesel engines) through soft patches. In theory, all this reduced the labour requirement per boat from 460,000 man-hours on a Type XB to some 300,000 on a Type XXI.

All did not go to plan, with transportation being one area that presented severe problems. Most movement was done using Germany's very efficient inland waterway system, but some works were up to six miles from the nearest canal or river and specially designed transporters were necessary to move sections from one to the other. Then, when the completed sections were moved long distances along the waterways, it was discovered that they would warp, with disastrous consequences when trying to align them with other sections, which necessitated them being fitted with complicated internal frames to ensure absolute rigidity.

There was immense pressure to get these boats into service; older men died from exhaustion and sections were despatched with parts missing in order to meet the rigidly imposed deadlines – such components then had to be added later, exacerbating the confusion. Allied bombing played a significant part, with many delays being caused by destruction, for example, at the M.A.N. and Siemens-Schukert works, and on the waterway systems. The bombing also had secondary effects such as lengthy power failures and workers taking time off to look after or rehouse their families.

All the completed Type XXIs worked up in the Baltic, where several were sunk by Allied aircraft. A number eventually sailed for the U-boat bases in Norway – with some being sunk en route – where deep-diving tests showed that yet further modifications were required, and this was done in local workshops. Two boats, *U-2511* and *U-3008*, carried out brief patrols before the war's end, but without scoring any successes. After the war, the French, Soviet, British and U.S. navies were all eager to test these boats and they undoubtedly learnt many lessons from them which were then incorporated into their own

Type XXIII   GERMANY

Type: coastal.
Total built: 62.
Completed: 1944-45.
Displacement: surfaced 234 tons; submerged 275 tons.
Dimensions: length 113ft 10in (34.7m); beam 9ft 10in (3.0m); draught 23ft 4in (7.7m).
Propulsion: 1 x M.W.M. 6-cylinder diesel, 630bhp; 1 x A.E.G. electrical motor, 580shp; 1 x "creep" motor, 35shp; battery 62 cells; one shaft.
Performance: surface – 9.7kt; submerged – 12.5kt; range surfaced 4,450nm at 12kt, submerged 285nm at 6kt).
Weapons: 2 x 21in (533mm) TT (bow), 2 x torpedoes.
Complement: 14.

History: The idea of a replacement coastal U-boat was mooted in 1942 and it was decided to produce a new design, using many of the ideas from the Type XXI, such as modular construction, streamlining, and high underwater performance. Admiral Dönitz approved the design in early 1943 but, as senior officers often do, he threw two spanners in the works by demanding that it be rail-transportable and that its torpedo tubes should be 23ft (7m)

Above: Type XXIs lying at Bergen, Norway, May 1945.

designs. Very few of the Type XXIs were put into service, however, except by the French and Soviet navies, and then only for a limited period. One sunken Type XXI was raised by the West German Navy in the 1950s and employed for 20 years as an experimental boat named *Wilhelm Bauer*. It is now preserved as a monument in Germany, the last of a remarkable breed.

Above: Type XXIII U-2325 at speed in the Baltic in 1945.

159

long, rather than the shorter 16.4ft (5m) tubes originally planned. The design was duly modified to meet the commander-in-chief's requirements, but every effort was made to use in-service components to ease production. It was decided that final assembly should be as near to the intended operational area as possible, which meant: Atlantic/North Sea – Hamburg; Mediterranean – Toulon and Genoa; and Black Sea – Nikolayev. A lot of effort was expended in preparing the foreign facilities, but by the time the project was ready for production Allied advances meant that none of the foreign yards was available, and the only yards involved were in Germany. Assembly of first-of-class *U-2321* started on 10 March 1944; it was launched on 17 April and commissioned on 12 June 1944.

The Type XXIII had an all-welded single hull, with no superstructure apart from the bridge and a small "hump" housing the diesel exhaust silencer. In line with Dönitz's requirements, the hull could be broken down into four sections, with the bridge making a fifth. In addition, the longer torpedo tubes were installed, as demanded by Dönitz, although this meant not only that no reloads could be carried, but also that the torpedoes were loaded by ballasting down the stern until the mouths of the tubes were above water-level, and then installing the torpedoes backwards from outside.

By the time war ended (8 May 1945) some 62 Type XXIIIs had been completed, of which 18 were stationed in Norway, the remainder in German ports. Ten boats carried out patrols which resulted in five Allied ships being sunk but without any loss to the U-boats, although seven Type XXIIIs were lost either in training or during transits between Germany and Norway.

Right: The Allies judged Type XXIIIs to be particularly dangerous.

Oberon/Oxley/Odin-classes GREAT BRITAIN
and Capitan O'Brien-class GREAT BRITAIN (CHILE)

Type: overseas patrol.

History: When the Anglo-Japanese friendship and cooperation treaty was ended in 1922, the British Admiralty was required to introduce a new type, the "overseas patrol" submarine, primarily for service in Far Eastern waters, in which the main advances over existing types were to be much greater endurance, increased diving depth and improved habitability. A prototype, HMS *Oberon*, was laid down in 1924, followed shortly afterwards by two boats for the Royal Australian Navy, *Otway* and *Oxley*, which were designed by Vickers and were marginally larger, had better lines and were thus faster, but with the same armament. Next came the Odin-class of six boats, which incorporated lessons learnt from experience with *Oberon*. Finally, in this "O-group" came three boats for the Chilean Navy: *Capitan O'Brien*, *Capitan Thompson* and *Almirante Simpson*. The design was generally similar to that of the Oxley-class and on the surface they were easily recognised by their huge bridge. These were the only boats in the group to mount the 4.7in (120mm) gun, which had originally been proposed for all the British O-class boats as well, but was not fitted due to a change in Admiralty policy.

Oberon had a vertical stem, but the remainder, including the Chilean boats, had a "ram" bow (ie, sloping back towards the upper casing), whose curve led directly into a net-cutter mounted on the foredeck. Two requirements, greater depth and increased fuel bunkerage, proved to be mutually incompatible. First,

Above: **Capitan O'Brien,** *built by Vickers for the Chilean Navy.*

the fuel oil was carried in external tanks, which "as built" were riveted, but the greater depth gave rise to oil leaks, creating a tell-tale track on the surface and these tanks had to be replaced by new welded tanks during refits. Second, the great amount of fuel needed made the boats very heavy for their size, with the result that they tended to dive very rapidly, which was frequently difficult to control.

All these class were armed with eight 21in (533mm) torpedo tubes, six in the bow and two in the stern. *Oberon* carried a total of 16 torpedoes, but all the others had 14. All mounted a single 4in (102mm) main gun, which was mounted on a trainable mount at the forward end of the bridge structure, which was characteristic of most British submarines of the time. This ever longer and higher bridge tower became so massive that it was easily visible when on the surface and caused considerable hydrodynamic drag when submerged.

Oberon was some 14 years old when World War II started and served until 1944 when she was stricken and scrapped. *Oxley* and *Otway* were delivered to the RAN in 1927, but defence cutbacks resulted in them being put into reserve in 1930 and transferred to the RN in 1931. *Triton*, a British T-class boat, accidentally torpedoed *Oxley* on 10 September 1939, making her the first British submarine casualty of the war, but *Otway* survived the war to be scrapped in 1945. In the Odin-class, four boats were wartime losses: *Odin*, *Orpheus* and *Oswald* were all sunk by Italian destroyers in 1940, while *Olympus* was sunk by a mine (8 May 1942). The remaining two sere stricken in 1946, *Osiris* being scrapped and *Otus* scuttled. The Chilean boats served until the late 1950s, when they were scrapped.

Class	Oberon	Oxley	Odin	Capitan O'Brien
Total built	1	2	6	3
Completed	1927	1927	1929-30	1929
Displacement surfaced submerged	1,598 tons 1,831 tons	1,354 tons 1,872 tons	1,475 tons 2,038 tons	1,540 tons 2,020 tons
Dimensions length beam draught	269ft 8in (82.2m) 28ft 0in (8.5m) 15ft 6in (4.7m)	275ft 0in (83.8m) 27ft 8in (8.4m) 15ft 9in (4.8m)	283ft 6in (86.4m) 29ft 11in (9.1m) 16ft 1in (4.9m)	260ft 0in (79.3m) 28ft 0in (8.5m) 13ft 6in (4.2m)
Propulsion main engines power electric motors power battery shafts	2 x Admiralty 2 x 1,350bhp 2 2 x 650shp 3 x 112 cells two	2 x Vickers 2 x 1,550bhp 2 2 x 675shp 3 x 112 cells two	2 x Admiralty 2 x 2,200bhp 2 2 x 660shp 3 x 112 cells two	2 x diesels 2 x 2, 375bhp 2 650shp 3 x 112 cells two
Performance speed: surface submerged range: surfaced submerged maximum diving depth	13.8kt 7.5kt 12,000nm/8kt 60nm/4kt 300ft (91.4m)	15kt 8.5kt 12,300nm/8kt 60nm/4kt 300ft (91.4m)	17.5kt 8kt 11,400nm/8kt 52nm/34kt 300ft (91.4m)	15kt 9kt 12,300nm/8kt 60nm/4kt 300ft (91.4m)
Weapons TT location torpedoes guns	8 x 21in (533mm) bow – 6, stern – 2 16 1 x 4in (102mm)	8 x 21in (533mm) bow – 6, stern – 2 14 1 x 4.in (102mm)	8 x 21in (533mm) bow – 6, stern – 2 14 1 x 4.0in (102mm)	8 x 21in (533mm) bow – 6, stern – 2 16 1 x 4.7in (120mm)
Complement	54	55	53	54

Above: One of the Chilean O'Brien-class at the Vickers yard.

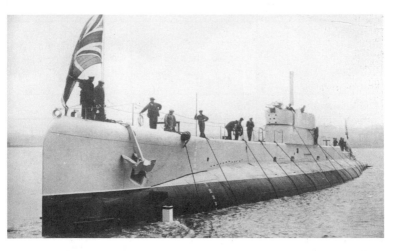

Above: Oberon, *the only one in the class with a vertical stem.*

Parthian/Rainbow-classes GREAT BRITAIN

Type: overseas patrol.

Class	Parthian	Rainbow
Total built	6	4
Completed	1928-31	1931-32
Displacement surfaced submerged	1,760 tons 2,040 tons	1,763 tons 2,030 tons
Dimensions length beam draught	289ft 2in (88.1m) 29ft 11in (9.1m) 15ft 11in (4.9m)	287ft 2in (87.5m) 29ft 11in (9.1m) 16ft 1in (4.9m)
Propulsion main engines power electric motors power battery shafts	2 x Admiralty 2 x 2,320bhp 2 2 x 817shp 3 x 112 cells two	2 x Admiralty 2 x 2,320bhp 2 2 x 835shp 3 x 112 cells two
Performance speed: surface submerged range: surfaced submerged maximum diving depth	17.5kt 8.6kt 7,050nm/9kt 62nm/4kt 300ft (91m)	17.5kt 8.8kt 7,050nm/9kt 70nm/4kt 300ft (91m)
Weapons TT location torpedoes guns	8 x 21in (533mm) bow – 6, stern – 2 14 1 x 4in (102mm)	8 x 21in (533mm) bow – 6, stern – 2 14 1 x 4.7in (120mm)
Complement	53	55

History: The P-class was designed as a lineal follow-on to the O-class, with six boats laid down in 1928 and launched in 1929. It was proposed to follow these with a further six boats in the R-class, but budgetary constraints reduced this to four, which were laid down in 1929 and launched in 1930. The O-class had not been totally satisfactory and unfortunately the shortcomings of that class were not resolved such that the P-class also proved less manoeuvrable than was required when submerged. There were minor differences with the previous class. The ram bow which had been such an obvious feature of the all the O-class (except *Oberon*) was discontinued and the P-class adopted the more conventional clipper bow, although not so sharply raked as in most foreign boats. In the P-class the main gun was at bridge level, but in the R-class it was located one deck level lower. In both classes the bridge was lower and the forward edge curved back to provide watchkeepers with some shelter.

A rearrangement of some of the internal spaces and equipment in the R-class enabled the pressure hull, and thus the overall length, to be shortened by some 2ft (0.61m). All boats had the standard battery fit of 336 cells, but one boat in each class (*Parthian* and *Rainbow*) had a new type of high capacity cell, the Exide HCSS 41/4750, which delivered 5,500 amperes/hour compared to 3,500 for cells in rest of the two classes. *Perseus* was fitted for a short period with an experimental 4.9in (125mm) gun, an unusual calibre for the Royal Navy.

One boat in this class was due to be named *Python* until it was observed that several RN ships with snake names had suffered disasters. *Serpent* was lost in 1890 with the loss of 173 lives, while both *Viper* and *Cobra* were wrecked within weeks of being commissioned in 1901, the latter breaking in two off the Yorkshire coast with the loss of 67 of her crew. As a result *Python* was renamed *Pandora*.

The loss rate in these classes was very high. In the P-class, the first to be lost was *Poseidon*, which was sunk in a peacetime collision off the China coast on 9 June 1931. During the war, two were lost to mines, *Perseus* (6 December 1941) and *Parthian* (10 August 1943), *Phoenix* was sunk on 16 July 1940 by an Italian MAS boat (equivalent to British MTB or U.S. PT-boat) and *Pandora* was bombed at Malta (1 April 1942). The sole survivor, *Proteus,* was scrapped in 1946. In the R-class, *Rainbow* was sunk in the Adriatic (15 October 1940), while two were lost to unknown causes, probably mines: *Regent* (18 April 1943) and *Regulus* (6 December 1940).

Above: Parthian-class patrol submarine, **Perseus.**

Thames-class

Type: fleet submarine.
Total built: 3.
Completed: 1932-35.
Displacement: surfaced 1,830 tons; submerged 2,680 tons.
Dimensions: length 345ft 0in (105.2m); beam 28ft 3in (8.6m); draught 15ft 8in (4.8m).
Propulsion: 2 x Admiralty supercharged diesels, 2 x 5,000bhp; 2 x electric motors, 2 x 1,250shp; 2 x Ricardo auxiliary engines, 2 x 400bhp; battery 2 x 112 cells; two shafts.
Performance: surface – 22.5kt; submerged – 10kt; range surfaced 13,200nm at 8kt, submerged 118nm at 4kt; maximum operating diving depth 200ft (60m).
Weapons: 6 x 21in (533mm) TT (bow), 12 x torpedoes; 1 x 4.7in (120mm), 2 x 0.303in MG.
Complement: 61.
Specifications are for Thames, as built.

History: The design for the Thames-class (sometimes known as the River-class) started as a replacement for the steam-driven K-class fleet submarines, but it was later decided to merge this role with that of the overseas patrol submarine (ie, O-/P-/R-classes). The first result was the Thames-class, large boats for their time, displacing 1,830 tons and with a design speed of 21kt, although 21.5kt was achieved on trials. Despite their large size, the high speed and long range could be achieved only at the expense of armament, which was not particularly heavy: six bow torpedo tubes (there were no stern tubes) and a

---

S-class

Type: short-range patrol.

Class	Swordfish	Shark	S-class War Programmes*
Total built	4	8	50
Completed	1932-33	1934-38	1942-45
Displacement surfaced submerged	730 tons 927 tons	761 tons 960 tons	715 tons 990 tons
Dimensions length beam draught	202ft 6in (61.7m) 24ft 11in (7.3m) 11ft 11in (3.6m)	208ft 8in (63.6m) 24ft 0in (7.3m) 11ft 10in (3.6m)	217ft 0in (66.1m) 23ft 9in (7.2m) 13ft 10in (4.2m)

* There were minor differences between batches. 1941 programme boats had 7 torpedo tubes, 1942 and 1943 programme boats had 6 (see notes).

History: The S-class was a replacement for the obsolete H-class (qv) and 63 boats were built in four groups, which were completed between 1932 and 1945. First came the Swordfish-class, followed by the Shark-class, which were

Above: **Severn***, one of the three-strong Thames-class.*

total of 12 torpedoes. *Thames* was armed with a 4.7in (120mm) gun, but this was later changed to 4in (102mm), and the other two had the smaller gun from the start, which saved 6 tons in topweight.

The maximum speed of 21kt (22.5kt in *Severn* and *Clyde*) was faster than any other European boat of the time, and exceeded only by a very few Japanese boats. Such a speed would have guaranteed a place with the battlefleet of the early 1920s, but by the time the Thames-class appeared in the mid-1930s capital ship speed had increased to some 30kt, and it was at last accepted that the concept of the fleet submarine could no longer be realised.

Thames was laid down in January 1931, followed by *Severn*, which was marginally larger, and then *Clyde* which was identical to *Severn*.

Propulsion			
main engines	2 x Admiralty	2 x Admiralty	2 x Admiralty
power	2 x 775bhp	2 x 775bhp	2 x 950bhp
electric motors	2	2	2
power	2 x 720shp	2 x 720shp	2 x 650shp
shafts	two	two	two
Performance			
speed: surface	13.8kt	15kt	14.8kt
submerged	10kt	10kt	9kt
range: surfaced	5,750nm/8kt	5,750nm/8kt	
submerged	.60nm/23kt	60nm/2kt.	
maximum			
diving depth	300ft (90m)	300ft (90m)	300ft (90m)
Weapons			
TT	6 x 21in (533mm)	6 x 21in (533mm)	7 x 21in (533mm)
location	bow	bow	bow – 6, stern – 1
torpedoes	12	12	13
guns	1 x 3in (76mm)	1 x 3in (76mm)	1 x 4in (102mm)
Complement	38	39	48

slightly larger and had greatly simplified internal arrangements; they were completed between 1933 and 1938. On the outbreak of war the War Emergency and 1941 programmes were rushed into production, comprising a series of 33 boats, which were a larger version of the Shark-class, with welded frames and other improvements, and also included a single, external stern torpedo tube. Finally came the 1942/43 programmes, which were virtually repeats of the War Emergency programme, but without the external torpedo tube (except in a few cases) and these were completed between 1943 and 1945.

All groups in the S-class were intended for short-range operations in enclosed waters such as the North Sea and Mediterranean, with a secondary role in training. They were double-hulled, saddle-tank boats and carried a relatively heavy armament of six torpedo tubes (all forward) with one reload per tube. One of the features of the initial Swordfish-class was a long additional casing ahead of the bridge, which housed a small boat and a disappearing mount for the 3in (76mm) gun. This casing proved heavy and the mount was over-complicated, so the greater part of the extension was removed, leaving a rump that was used as an ammunition store for the main gun, which was now mounted directly on the upper casing, as in virtually every other submarine. Like all other large classes, there were differences not only between the groups, but also minor variations between different boats in the same group.

All boats fought hard throughout the war, mainly in their planned operational areas of the North Sea and Mediterranean, and 18 were lost.

T-class

Type: patrol submarine.

History: The Oberon-, Parthian- and Rainbow-classes, while adequate, were never really successful and in the mid-1930s the British Admiralty decided to embark on the development of a replacement. A major design constraint was that the recently concluded London Naval Treaty stipulated that the permitted maximum submarine tonnage was 16,500, so the Admiralty decided on a displacement of 1,000 tons, which would enable 16 to be built. The displacement was some 400 tons less than the boats to be replaced and this limited the length, which in turn limited the size of the diesel engines, and as a result the surface speed was less. This apart, the resulting design was superior in almost every other respect, with more powerful armament, better handling both on the surface and when submerged, better habitability, and increased submerged speed. *Triton* and Group I had a unique armament with six internal torpedo tubes, two in the raised bow casing, and yet another two amidships, all 10 tubes launching their torpedoes ahead. This gave the boats a very impressive salvo, which was intended to provide a high probability of a hit at long ranges, although only the six internal tubes were reloadable. Underpinning all this was greatly simplified construction, thus reducing building time, and great attention to ease of operation and maintainability, which resulted in a technically very efficient and reliable submarine.

First-of-class was *Triton*, laid down at Vickers, Barrow, in August 1936, launched in October 1937 and commissioned in December 1938. She was followed by a further 21 boats, in which the dimensions and displacement were all reduced slightly, and which entered service between 1940 and 1941.

Of the 44 that survived, two were sunk in peacetime accidents, three were expended as targets, five were sold to friendly navies (Israel – 2, Portugal – 3), while the remainder were stricken between 1946 and 1960. A number of those that survived the war were converted to high-speed targets for ASW training, which involved streamlining the hull, casing and bridge tower, and fitting more powerful cells; as a result, submerged speeds of up to 17kt could be achieved for short periods.

Below: Scorcher, one of the S-class 1943 programme boats.

Above: A T-class Group II boat.

Class	Triton	Group I	Group II
Total built	1	21	31
Completed	1938-39	1941-43	1943-46
Displacement surfaced submerged	1,095 tons 1,585 tons	1,090 tons 1,575 tons	1,090 tons 1,575 tons
Dimensions length beam draught	277ft 6in (84.4m) 26ft 7in (8.1m) 15ft 0in (4.6m)	275ft 0in (83.8m) 26ft 6in (8.1m) 14ft 10in (4.5m)	273ft 6in (83.4m) 26ft 7in (8.1m) 14ft 10in (4.5m)
Propulsion main engines power electric motors power shafts	2 x Vickers 2 x 1,250bhp 2 2 x 725shp two	2 x Vickers 2 x 1,250bhp 2 2 x 725shp two	2 x Vickers 2 x 1,250bhp 2 2 x 725shp two

Experience of operating these new boats led to a requirement for more of a slightly modified design, which then became known as Group II. These boats had an all-welded hull with slightly modified lines, but the only changes of substance were to the armament. The Group I boats lacked the stern tubes which were carried by most contemporary submarines, so one tube was installed in the after casing, while the two forward launching tubes sited amidships were moved aft of the bridge tower and turned to face aft, angled out at about 20 degrees. Although primarily intended to provide an adequate salvo, this had a coincidental advantage in that when running on the surface or at periscope depth the forward-facing midships tubes created a substantial wave which had not only interfered with visibility, but also caused hydrodynamic drag and trim problems. The Group II boats were also fitted with a 20mm Oerlikon cannon on a platform at the after end of the bridge structure. A total of 40 Group II boats were ordered but the last seven were cancelled in favour of the even more advanced A-class (qv).

As always, there were many modifications. Once the addition of the stern tubes and the rearrangement of the midships tubes had been proved a success in the Group II boats, most Group I boats were modified to the same standard at their next refit. They were also given a 20mm Oerlikon. Later in the war many T-boats were required for service in the Far East and these had a number of ballast tanks converted into fuel tanks, increasing range to some 11,000nm at 8kt.

One tragic incident was the loss of *Thetis*, which sank in Liverpool Bay on 1 June 1939 while carrying not only her crew of 69 but also an additional 50 men from the shipyard and the Admiralty. A faulty indicator resulted in the boat being flooded and she sank. This tragedy apart, the T-boats operated with great success, although their heavy involvement in operations in every theatre brought with it the inevitable heavy losses. The T-class achieved particularly good results against enemy submarines, and they sank four German, six Italian and three Japanese boats. They also achieved some major successes against enemy surface warships, sinking one German and two Japanese

Performance			
speed: surface	15.3kt	15.3kt	15.3kt
submerged	9kt	9kt	9kt
range: surfaced	8,000nm/10kt	8,000nm/10kt	8,000nm/10kt
submerged	80nm/4kt	80nm/4kt	80nm/4kt
maximum			
diving depth	300ft (91m)	300ft (91m)	350ft (107m)
Weapons			
TT	10 x 21in (533mm)	10 x 21in (533mm)	11 x 21in (533mm)
location	bow – 6, external – 4	bow – 6, external – 4	bow – 6, external – 5
torpedoes	16	16	17
guns	1 x 4in (102mm)	1 x 4in (102mm)	1 x 4in (102mm)
	3 x 0.303in MG*	3 x 0.303in MG*	1 x 20mm AA
			3 x 0.303in MG
Complement	59	56	61

* Later replaced or supplemented by 1 x 20mm Oerlikon AA.

cruisers, and seriously damaging three others. In another success, *Thunderbolt* (which had originally been named *Thetis* and had been recovered and renamed after her sinking) carried some chariots (human torpedoes) which entered Palermo harbour and sank the almost completed cruiser, *Triano*. These successes were offset by 17 losses, plus another which was so badly damaged that it was consider irreparable.

The remaining 35 boats survived the war, of which *Truant* was wrecked in 1946 and *Truculent* was lost following a collision (12 January 1950). Six boats were transferred to foreign navies, three each to Israel and the Netherlands. Of the remainder, five riveted boats were given partial conversions, while five with welded hulls were given full conversions, equivalent to the U.S. Navy's Guppy programme, which extended their lives until 1965-60, while the others were broken up, some of them immediately after the war, although others lasted into the mid-1960s.

Below: **Truculent**, *lost in a collision in the Thames in 1950.*

U/V-class

Type: coastal.

Class	U-class Group I	U-class Group II	V-class
Total built	15	34	22
Completed	1938-39	1941-43	1943-46
Displacement surfaced submerged	630 tons 730 tons	648 tons 732 tons	660 tons 740 tons
Dimensions length beam draught	190ft 7in (58.1m) 15ft 9in (4.8m) 15ft 9in (4.8m)	195ft 6n (59.6m) 15ft 9in (4.8m) 15ft 10in (4.8m)	203ft 5in (62.0m) 15ft 9in (4.8m) 15ft 10in (4.8m)
Propulsion main engines power electric motors power battery shafts	2 x Paxman-Ricardo 615hp 2 2 x 825shp 2 x 112 cells two	2 x Paxman-Ricardo 615hp 2 2 x 825shp 2 x 112 cells two	2 x Paxman 615hp 2 2 x 825shp 2 x 112 cells two
Performance speed: surface submerged range: surfaced submerged maximum diving depth	11.5kt 9kt 4,050nm/10kt 23nm/8kt 200ft (61m)	11.5kt 9kt 4,050nm/10kt 23nm/8kt. 200ft (61m)	12.5kt 9kt 4,700nm/10kt 30nm/9kt 300ft (91m)
Weapons TT location torpedoes guns	6 x 21in (533mm) bow – 4, external – 2 8 3 x 0.303in MG (see notes)	4 x 21in (533mm) bow 8 1 x 3in (76mm) 3 x 0.303in MG	41 x 21in (533mm) bow 8 1 x 3in (76mm) 3 x 0.303in MG
Complement	27	33	33

History: The U-class had its origins in a 1936 Admiralty requirement for three small, unarmed submarines to be used as targets in anti-submarine warfare (ASW) training, which were to be easy and cheap to build, and to require a small crew. After the hulls had been laid down in February 1937 it was realised that they could also be suitable for short-range operational missions, so they were modified during construction to take six 21in (533mm) torpedo tubes, all in the bows, and with four inside the pressure hull, and two externally-mounted in a raised bow casing. The outcome of this somewhat piecemeal approach was an outstanding single-hulled design (the first since the R-class [qv]) which proved to have first-class handling, to be very manoeuvrable both on the surface and

Above. Norwegian **Ula** *in 1949, formerly HMS* **Varne.**

submerged, easy to produce and comparatively cheap to build, maintain and man. As a result 12 more were ordered, which were initially intended to be identical to the first three, but after four had been completed it was decided that the raised bow casing containing two external torpedo tubes was no longer required, so they were completed with just four tubes. These 15 boats constituted Group I and they were followed by 34 Group II boats, which were identical to the four-tube Group I boats except that the stern was extended by some 5ft (1.5m) in order to improve the flow of water over the propellers.

The first two boats to be completed, *Undine* and *Unity*, did not have a main gun and carried a 27-man crew, but from the third, *Ursula*, onwards, all boats mounted a 3in (76mm) gun, raising the crew to 33. As the gun was a retrospective modification there was no separate hatch for the gun crew and ammunition, which caused delays in getting into action on surfacing and prevented rapid crash-dives, one of the few shortcomings in this design.

It was decided in 1941 to develop a modified version of the U-class with similar characteristics and armament, but which would be even stronger, while being still easier and cheaper to build. This resulted in the V-class which were 7ft 11in (2.4m) longer (they are sometimes referred to as the "long-hull variant") and had a partly-welded pressure hull. It was slightly faster.

The U-class saw service mainly in the North and Mediterranean Seas, where they achieved some outstanding successes. Twenty were lost in the war and a number were supplied to Allied navies; the remainder were broken up in the late 1940s and early 1950s. The V-class entered service between 1943 and 1945 and there were no war losses. A number were passed to Allied navies (Denmark – 2, France – 2, Greece – 3 and Norway – 4) both during and after the war and the remainder served on with the Royal Navy, being progressively stricken between 1946 and 1961. One of this class, HMS *Venturer*, holds the unique distinction of being the only submarine ever to have sunk another submarine with both boats remaining submerged throughout the engagement when she sank *U-864*, a Type IXD2 off the Norwegian coast on 9 February 1945.

A brief note on names is required. The 15 Group I boats had names beginning with the letter "U." When Group II boats were launched it was Admiralty policy for new boats to be given a letter "P" (= patrol) followed by a number, but this was changed to names on the personal order of the Prime Minister, Winston Churchill. As a result, *P-44* became *United*, and so on, but those that had already been lost were never renamed and are thus recorded solely by their number – eg, *P-33*. One further complication is that the last five of the U-class Group II had names beginning with the letter "V" but were "short-hull" boats and not part of the "long-hulled V-class."

A-class

Type: long-range patrol.
Total built: 16.
Completed: 1945-48.
Displacement: surfaced 1,385 tons; submerged 1,620 tons.
Dimensions: length 279ft 3in (85.1m); beam 22ft 3in (6.8m); draught 17ft 1in (5.2m).
Propulsion: 2 x Vickers/Admiralty supercharged diesels, 2 x 2,150bhp; 2 x English Electric electric motors, 2 x 625shp; two shafts.
Performance: surface – 18.5kt; submerged – 8kt; range surfaced 10,500nm at 11kt, submerged 90nm at 3kt; maximum operating diving depth 350ft (107m).
Weapons: 10 x 21in (533mm) TT (bow – 6, stern – 4); 1 x 4in (102mm) gun, 1 x 20mm Oerlikon AA, 3 x 0.303in MG.
Complement: 61.

History: The great majority of British submarine production during World War II was either repeats or modifications of designs produced in the 1930s. The only exception (apart from the very small X-craft) was the A-class and even this was essentially an enlarged and greatly modified version of the T-class. The design was prepared in response to a requirement for boats for the war against Japan, for which the main requisites were very long range, heavy armament and plenty of reload torpedoes, and good habitability for long patrols in tropical conditions. The result was an excellent design, with an all-welded hull, simplified construction and a substantial armament of 10 torpedo tubes, six in the bow (two of which were external) and four aft (two external) and a total load of 20

Balilla/Calvi-classes and Humaita-class

Type: long-range cruiser.

Class	Balilla	Humaita	Calvi
Total built	4	1	3
Completed	1928-29	1929	1935-6
Displacement surfaced submerged	1,450 tons 1,904 tons	1,390 tons 1,884 tons	1,550 tons 2,060 tons
Dimensions length beam draught	282ft 09in (86.8m) 25ft 7in (7.8m) 15ft 3in (4.7m)	285ft 5in (87.0m) 25ft 7in (7.8m) 13ft 2in (4.0m)	276ft 7in (84.3m) 25ft 3in (7.7m) 17ft 1in (5.2m)

History: In the inter-war years the Italians had considerable colonial commitments on the east coast of Africa and the Balilla-class was designed to provide long-range patrol submarines for operations in the Indian Ocean

Above: A-class, HMS Affray, *lost on 17 April 1951.*

torpedoes. Range was 11,500nm at 11kt and an efficient air-conditioning system was installed for better crew comfort. Major efforts were made to reduce underwater noise levels and, after some initial problems with rolling, seakeeping was excellent. The class was also one of the first to be fitted with an air-warning radar antenna mounted on a hydraulic mast, which could be used while running at periscope depth. As built, the A-class did not have schnorkels; these were added after the war.

A total of 46 boats were ordered and the first to be launched was *Amphion* (31 August 1944); eight were launched and two completed before VJ-day, but none became operational in time to see combat. Meanwhile, the orders had been cut back and the total completed was only 16. One boat, *Affray*, was lost in a peacetime accident (17 April 1951). Of the remaining 15, all except one were given a Guppy-type conversion in the 1950s and then served into the 1970s.

Propulsion			
main engines	2 x Fiat	2 x Ansaldo	2 x Fiat
power	2 x 2,450bhp	2 x 2,450bhp	2 x 2,200bhp
cruise	1 x Fiat diesel	–	–
power	425bhp	–	–
electric motors	2 x Savigliano	2 x electric motors	2 x San Giorgio
power	2 x 1,100shp	2 x 450shp	2 x 900shp
shafts	two	two	two
Performance			
speed: surface	16kt	18.5kt	17kt
submerged	7kt	9.5kt	7.4kt
range: surfaced	12,000nm/7kt	12,000nm/7kt	11,400nm/8kt
submerged	110nm/3kt	110nm/3kt	80nm/4kt
maximum			
diving depth	288ft (90m)	288ft (90m)	288ft (90m)
Weapons			
TT	6 x 21in (533mm)	6 x 21in (533mm)	8 x 21in (533mm)
location	bow – 4, stern – 2	bow – 4 stern – 4	bow – 4, stern – 4
torpedoes	12	12	16
guns	1 x 4.7in (120mm)	1 x 4in (102mm)	2 x 4.7in (120mm)
	1 x 13mm AAMG	–	4 x 20mm AA
Mines	–	16	–
Complement	77	61	72

and Red Sea. This required a good endurance and surface speed, and a heavy torpedo armament with reloads. The resulting Balilla-class was based on detailed examination of *U-120*, a German U-117-class minelayer, which had been allocated to Italy at the end of the World War I and was a strongly-built, double-hulled design; the Balillas were also the largest submarines so far built for the Italian Navy.

The hull design was not as good as in later Italian submarines and the designed surface speed of 17.5kt and submerged speed of 8.9kt were never achieved in practice. There were six torpedo tubes, four in the bow, two in the stern, with one reload for each tube and one boat, *Antonio Sciesa*, also had a tube for four mines. The 4.7in (120mm) gun was originally built into the foot of the tower, but was later moved forward onto the open deck. One unusual feature was a 450bhp diesel which was intended for either very long-range cruising or for charging the battery when the main engines were being used for propulsion; this was never repeated in any successor classes.

The Calvi-class was an improved version of the Balilla-class, with a better hull form for increased stability, but less powerful machinery. Considerable extra space was gained by redesign, which enabled two more torpedo tubes and reloads to be carried aft. A second 4.7in (120mm) gun was also carried on the after deck.

The Brazilian Navy ordered a modified version of the Balilla-class, which was delivered in March 1929. The modifications were extensive and included siting the propulsion system well forward, eleminating diving planes, and the installation of a minelaying system which enabled 16 mines to be delivered.

All the Italian boats of both classes participated in the Spanish Civil War.

Pisani- and related classes

ITALY

Type: short-range patrol.

History: These 13 single-hull boats were designed by Bernadis for operations in the Mediterranean, the original Pisani-class being laid down in 1925-26 and launched in 1927-28. Once in service they proved to lack lateral stability and

Class	Pisani	Bandiera	Squalo	Fieramosca
Total built	4	4	4	1
Completed	1928	1930	1930-31	1930
Displacement surfaced submerged	866 tons 1,040 tons	925 tons 1,080 tons	920 tons 1,125 tons	1,530 tons 2,094 tons
Dimensions length beam draught	223ft 9in (68.2m) 20ft 0in (6.1m) 16ft 2in (4.9m)	212ft 9in (69.8m) 22ft 3in (7.3m) 16ft 0in (5.3m)	212ft 9in (69.8m) 22ft 0in (7.2m) 15ft 10in (5.2m)	275ft 6in (84.0m) 27ft 3in (8.3m) 16ft 9in (5.1m)

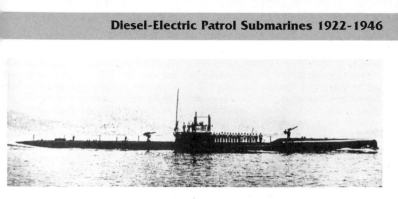

Above: **Balilla**, *launched in 1927, laid up in 1941.*

By the time World War II broke out the Balilla-class was somewhat dated, although *Enrico Toti* sank two British submarines, *Rainbow* (15 October 1940) and *Perseus* (1 December 1941). Two others were used as fuel storage tanks from April 1941, while *Toti* and *Sciesa* were used to transport supplies to North Africa. All three of the Calvi-class, *Calvi, Finzi* and *Tazzoli*, were employed in the Atlantic during the war, operating from the Italian base at Bordeaux, where *Tazzoli* became the most successful Italian submarine of the war, sinking 19 merchant ships (96,533grt). *Calvi* was sunk in the Atlantic (1942) and the other two were then modified for use as transport boats to the Far East, *Tazzoli* being lost on her first voyage to Singapore. *Finzi* was still at Bordeaux when Italy surrendered to the Germans and was taken over by the German Navy as *UIT-21*, but was destroyed in port on 25 August 1944.

Propulsion				
main engines	2 x Tosi	2 x Fiat or Tosi	2 x Fiat	2 x Tosi
power	2 x 1,500bhp	2 x 1,500bhp	2 x 1,500bhp	2 x 2,600bhp
electric motors	2 x C.G.E.	2 x Savigliano	2 x C.R.D.A.	2 x .Marelli
power	2 x 500shp	2 x 650shp	2 x 650shp	2 x 1,000 shp
shafts	two	two	two	two
Performance				
speed: surface	15kt	15kt	15.1kt	15kt
submerged	8.2kt	8kt	8kt	8kt
range: surfaced	4,230nm/9.3kt	4,750nm/8.5kt	5,650nm/8kt	5,300nm/8kt
submerged	70nm/4kt	60nm/4kt	100nm/3kt	90nm/3kt
maximum				
diving depth	288ft (90m)	288ft (90m)	288ft (90m)	288ft (90m)
Weapons				
TT	6 x 21in (533mm)	8 x 21in (533mm)	8 x 21in (533mm)	8 x 21in (533mm)
location	bow – 4, stern – 2	bow – 4, stern – 4	bow – 4, stern – 4	bow – 4, stern – 4
torpedoes	9	12	12	14
guns	1 x 4in (102mm)	1 x 4in (102mm)	1 x 4in (102m)	1 x 4.7in (120mm)
	2 x 13.2mm MG	2 x 13.2mm MG	2 x 13.2 AAMG	4 x 20mm AA
Complement	49	52	53	78

were fitted with external bulges, which resulted in a loss of speed of about 2kt on the surface and 1kt submerged. Next came the Bandiera-class, which not only also required additional bulges once in service, but also needed a raised bow to improve performance when steaming into a head sea. The Squalo-class was a virtual repeat of the Bandiera-class, but with additional bunkerage giving increased range; like the Bandieras they also need extra bulges and a raised bow. The sole Fieramosca-class boat was a much modified version of the Pisani design, and was originally intended to be a submarine cruiser, armed with nine torpedo tubes and a heavy gun (4.7in/120mm) and with a hangar for a small reconnaissance floatplane. At the time, similar concepts were being tested by other navies, but the Italian Navy changed its mind while the boat was under construction. As a result, the aircraft was cancelled, and the design of the submarine radically altered, with one torpedo tube and the hangar being deleted, and *Fieramosca* was completed as a normal patrol submarine.

By the outbreak of war the Pisani-class boats were old and had poor performance by contemporary standards, so after a few limited operations they were put to other uses, one becoming a floating oil tank and another a battery charger. Only one, *Vettor Pisani*, remained in service and was stricken in 1947.

The Bandiera-class were also inadequate for World War II operations and were used to transport supplies to North Africa; three were transferred to training duties in 1942, but *Samarosa* continued as a transport until it grounded and was then torpedoed by a British MTB (20 January 1943). The Squalo-class had a more active war, but with little success. *Tricheco* was sunk by the British submarine *Upholder* (18 March 1942), while *Narvalo* was scuttled to avoid capture by British ASW forces (14 January 1943) and *Deffino* was lost in an accident (23 March 1943). That left just one boat, *Squalo*, which survived the war and was broken up in 1948. *Fieramosca* was slow to dive and when she suffered a battery explosion in 1940 the opportunity was taken to lay her up.

In 1929, the Turkish Navy placed a large contract with Italy for the design and construction of four destroyers and two submarines. Both the latter were

Mameli/Settembrini/ Archimede-classes ITALY

Type: short-range patrol.

History: The Mamelli-class was designed by Cavallini and built by Tosi at Taranto. Like other Italian designs of the early/mid-1920s, they benefited greatly from the examination of their national share of the German U-boats which were

Class	Mamelli	Settembrini	Archimede
Total built	4	2	4
Completed	1928-29	1932	1934
Displacement surfaced submerged	830 tons 1,010 tons	953 tons 1,153 tons	985 tons 1,259 tons
Dimensions length beam draught	213ft 3in (64.6m) 21ft 4in (6.5m) 14ft 1in (4.3m)	226ft 8in (69.1m) 21ft 7in (6.6m) 14ft 7in (4.5m)	231ft 4in (70.5m) 22ft 6in (6.9m) 13ft 6in (4.1m)

Above: **Giovanni Bausan,** *one of the four-strong Pisani-class.*

laid down in February 1930, launched one year later and after the usual builder's trials arrived in Istanbul at the begining of November 1931. The two boats were different from each other, but both were designed by Bernadis and built by CNT, their designs being based on Italian boats. *Dumlupinar* was based on the Pisani-class, but with slightly different hull lines and a submerged displacement of 1,150 tons, and was powered by M.A.N. engines, which combined to give her an additional 2kt in surface speed. *Sakarya* was a little smaller, with a submerged displacement of 940 tons, her design being based on that of the Italian Navy's Argonauta-class. Like *Dumlupinar*, *Sakarya*, too, was powered by M.A.N. engines. Both were stricken about 1950.

Propulsion			
main engines	2 x Tosi	2 x Tosi	2 x Tosi
power	2 x 1,500bhp	2 x 1,500bhp	2 x 1,500bhp
electric motors	2 x C.G.E.	2 x Ansaldo	2 x Marelli
power	2 x 550shp	2 x 700shp	2 x 550shp
shafts	two	two	two
Performance			
speed: surface	15kt	17.5kt	17kt
submerged	7.5kt	7.7kt	8kt
range: surfaced	4,360nm/8kt	9,000nm/8kt	10,300nm/8kt
submerged	110nm/3kt	80nm/4kt	105nm/3kt
maximum			
diving depth	288ft (90m)	288ft (90m)	288ft (90m)
Weapons			
TT	6 x 21in (533mm)	8 x 21in (533mm)	8 x 21in (533mm)
location	bow – 4, stern – 2	bow – 4, stern – 4	bow – 4, stern – 4
torpedoes	10	12	16
guns	1 x 4in (102mm)	1 x 4in (102mm)	2 x 3.9in (100m)
	2 x 13.2mm MG	2 x 13.2mm MG	2 x 13.2mm MG
Complement	49	56	55

distributed to the victorious allies. They had partial double-hulls and were particularly strong, and although their normal diving depth was 288ft (90m) one boat reached 380ft (116m) during trials. As with so many Italian submarines of this period they proved to suffer from lateral instability and external bulges had to be added after completion, which reduced their speed, both on the surface and submerged. They mounted six 21in (533mm) torpedo tubes and reloads were provided only for the four bow tubes. The Settembrini-class, also designed by Cavallini and built by Tosi, were based on the Mamelli-class but with modifications to improve stability. The Archimede-class was a slightly enlarged version of the Settembrini-class, one specific improvement being the increase in torpedo load from 12 to 16.

The Mamelli-class took part in the Spanish Civil War and then spent World War II up to the Italian surrender in the Mediterranean where *Capponi* was sunk by the British submarine minelayer *Rorqual* (31 March 1941). In 1943 the three survivors were refitted with more powerful diesels, raising their surface speed to 17kt. After the surrender they were used in the Atlantic to train U.S. Navy ASW crews and all were scrapped in February 1948. The Settembrini-class spent most of the 1930s in the Red Sea and during the war they alternated between combat patrols, transporting supplies to North Africa and serving at the Submarine School. After the surrender they served as targets for U.S. Navy ASW crews, during which *Settembrini* was accidentally rammed and sunk by Buckley-class destroyer-escort USS *Frament* (DE-677) on 15 November 1922.

The Archimede-class were good boats and popular with their crews, and all four took part in the Spanish Civil War. During World War II, two of the boats were covertly sold to Spain, for which they served until scrapped in 1959. *Galileo* was lost on her first patrol, being forced to surface and then being captured, following which she was commissioned into the Royal Navy as HMS *X-2*. She was scrapped in 1946. The only other boat was *Ferraris* which operated in the Indian Ocean until 1941 when she transferred to the Atlantic, where she was sunk on 25 October 1941.

Argonauta/Sirena/Perla/ Adua/Acciaio-classes   ITALY

Type: short-range patrol.

History: This series of submarines was known after their designer as the "Bernardis 600-tonners". They were not particularly fast, but were strong and manoeuvrable. The first in the series, the Argonauta-class, were laid down in

Class	Argonauta	Sirena	Perla/Adua	Acciaio
Total built	7	12	10 + 17	13
Completed	1932	1933-34	1936-38	1942
Displacement surfaced submerged	650 tons 810 tons	679 tons 842 tons	696 tons 825 tons	715 tons 870 tons
Dimensions length beam draught	201ft 0in (61.5m) 18ft 6in (5.7m) 14ft 6in (4.6m)	197ft 6in (73.0m) 21ft 0in (6.5m) 15ft 0in (4.6m)	197ft 6in (60.2m) 21ft 0in (6.5m) 15ft 0in (4.6m)	197ft 0in (60.2m) 21ft 4in (6.4m) 14ft 9in (4.8m)

Above: **Tito Speri**, *the last of four in the Mameli-class.*

Propulsion				
main engines	2 x Fiat/Tosi	2 x Fiat /Tosi	2 x Fiat/C.R.D.A.	2 x Fiat/Tosi
power	2 x 750bhp	2 x 675bhp	2 x 700bhp	2 x 700bhp
electric motors	2 x C.R.D.A.	2 x C.R.D.A.	2 x C.R.D.A.	2 x C.R.D.A.
power	2 x 400shp	2 x 400shp	2 x 400shp	2 x 400shp
shafts	two	two	two	two
Performance				
speed: surface	14kt	14kt	14kt	14kt
submerged	8kt	7.5kt	7.5kt	7.3kt
range: surfaced	4,960nm/9.5kt	2,280nm/12kt	2,5000nm/12kt	5,000nm/8.5kt
submerged	110nm/3kt	72nm/4kt	740nm/4kt	80nm/3kt
maximum				
diving depth	256ft (80m)	256ft (80m)	256ft (80m)	256ft (80m)
Weapons				
TT	6 x 21in (533mm)	6 x 21in (533mm)	6 x 21in (533mm)	6 x 21in (533mm)*
location	bow – 4, stern – 2	bow – 4, stern – 2	bow – 4, stern – 2	bow – 4, stern – 2*
torpedoes	12	12	12	10*
guns	1 x 4in (102mm)	1 x 3.9in (100mm)	1 x 3.9in (100mm)	1 x 3.9in (100mm)
	2 x 13.2mm MG	2 x 13.2mm MG	4 x 13.2mm MG	4 x 13.2mm MG
Complement	44	45	45	48

* Some had 8 x 21in (533mm) TT, bow – 4, stern – 4

1929, the design being based on that of the Squalo-class (qv) but with detailed improvements, although it reverted to a long flat forecastle ending in a vertical stem, as opposed to the rather bulbous bow which had been found necessary in the Squalo-class. The Sirena-class (12 built) had detailed improvements but somewhat less engine power resulted in lower speed and a reduced range. However, it proved necessary to restore the Squalo-type bow once again.

Next came two groups which, although usually shown as separate classes, were virtually identical: 10 Perla-class (C.R.D.A., Monfalcone – 6, OTO, La Spezia – 4), and 17 Adua-class (C.R.D.A. – 4; OTO, Muggiano – 9; Tosi, Taranto – 4). There were minor differences between boats from the various yards; for example, the profile of the C.R.D.A. bridge was different from that of the OTO-built boats. Finally, came the Acciaio-class, the last in the 600-ton series, which was virtually identical to the Perla-class, but with minor increases in displacement, an increase in range, improvements in equipment and a reduction in the size of the bridge structure.

During the war the seven Argonautas were used exclusively in the Mediterranean, where *Serpente* sank the British destroyer *Hyperion* (December 1940) but six out of seven in the class were war losses. The only survivor was *Jalea*, scrapped in 1948. The same applied to the Sirena-clas; all were employed in the Mediterranean and just one survived.

The Perla-class took part in the Spanish Civil War, during which *Iride* and *Onice* were lent to the Nationalist Navy for a period of several months. On the outbreak of World War II *Perla* was in the Red Sea and after operating in the area sailed around Africa to Bordeaux and thence back to Italy. One of the most successful boats in the class was *Ambra* which sank the British cruiser *Bonaventure* (31 March 1941) and also delivered the assault craft which sank 20,000 tons of shipping in Algiers harbour in December 1942. There were five

Glauco/Marcello/ Marconi-classes ITALY

Type: long-range patrol.

History: In 1931 the Portuguese Navy ordered a number of submarines from abroad, including four from Italy, of which two were long-range, ocean-going patrol boats, to be designed by Bernadis and built by C.R.D.A., Monfalcone; they were to be named *Delfin* and *Espadarte*. Work was started on the boats

Class	Glauco	Marcello	Marconi
Total built	2	11	6
Completed	1935-36	1938-39	1940
Displacement surfaced submerged	1,055 tons 1,325 tons	1,060 tons 1,313 tons	1,195 tons 1,490 tons
Dimensions length beam draught	239ft 6in (73.0m) 23ft 6in (7.2m) 16ft 10in (5.1m)	236ft 6in (73.0m) 23ft 7in (7.2m) 16ft 8in (5.1m)	251ft 0in (76.5m) 22ft 4in (6.8m) 15ft 6in (4.7m)

Above: **Nichelio** *(Acciaio-class) surrenders in 1943.*

war losses. *Perla* was captured (9 July 1942) by the British who passed her to the Greek Navy, *Ambra* was scuttled and the remainder survived.

Propulsion			
main engines	2 x Fiat	2 x C.R.D.A./Fiat	2 x C.R.D.A.
power	2 x 1,500bhp	2 x 1,800bhp	2 x 1,800bhp
electric motors	2 x C.R.D.A.	2 x C.R.D.A.	2 x Marelli
power	2 x 600shp	2 x 550shp	2 x 750shp
shafts	two	two	two
Performance			
speed: surface	17kt	17.4kt	17.8kt
submerged	8kt	8kt	8.2kt
range: surfaced	9,760nm/8kt	7,500nm/9.4kt	10,500nm/8kt
submerged	110nm/3kt	120nm/3kt	110nm/34kt
maximum			
diving depth	288ft (90m)	328ft (100m)	288ft (90m)
Weapons			
TT	8 x 21in (533mm)	8 x 21in (533mm)	8 x 21in (533mm)
location	bow – 4, stern – 4	bow – 4, stern – 4	bow – 4, stern – 4
torpedoes	14	16	12
guns	2 x 3.9in (100mm)	2 x 3.9in (100mm)	1 x 3.9in (100mm)
	2 x 13.2mm MG	4 x 13.2mm MG	4 x 13.2mm MG
Complement	57	57	57

but Portugal then cancelled both Italian contracts. Fortunately for the builder, the design was so promising that the boats were ordered by the Italian Navy in

1932 as *Glauco* and *Otaria*. They were considered to be fast, strong, comfortable for the crew, and manoeuvrable both on the surface and when submerged. The Marcello-class, which followed on from the Glaucos, was almost identical and, with 11 built, was a surprisingly large class for the Italian Navy. Like the Glaucos, the Marcellos were considered to be very manoeuvrable, but were even faster, with one boat achieving 18.24kt on trials. The six-strong Marconi-class followed the same basic design, but the hull was lengthened, the beam reduced, the bunkers enlarged, and more powerful electric motors installed, while the bridge superstructure was reduced and the after gun removed. The result was an increase in speed, both on the surface and submerged, much greater range and better stability in a design that was considered the best of all the long-range submarines in the pre-war Royal Italian Navy.

Once World War II started, the two Glauco-class boats were employed for a short period in the North Atlantic, but *Glauco* had to be scuttled after being severely damaged by a British destroyer (27 June 1941). *Otaria* then undertook supply runs to North Africa and survived the war, to be stricken in 1948.

Of the Marcello-class, no fewer than nine were lost in the war, which included four sunk by enemy ASW forces, four lost due to causes unknown and one sunk by bombs while in harbour. The remaining two were fitted out as Far east transports in 1943, but *Barbarigo* was sunk in the Bay of Biscay, soon after starting the outward voyage. The other, *Capellini*, reached the Dutch East Indies, but on the Italian surrender in September 1943 the Japanese seized the crew and handed the boat to the Germans, who commissioned her as *UIT-24*. When Germany surrendered in May 1945 she was seized once again by the Japanese who renumbered her as *I-504*, but

Argo/Flutto (Series 1, 2)-classes ITALY

Type: medium-displacement patrol boats.

History: In the early 1930s the Portuguese Navy ordered four boats from Monfalcone-based C.R.D.A. (Cantieri Riuniti dell'Adriatico) and work had already begun when the order was cancelled. However, C.R.D.A. managed

Class	Argo	Flutto Series I	Flutto Series 2
Total built	2	9	3
Completed	1937	1942-43	1944
Displacement surfaced submerged	780 tons 1,000 tons	930 tons 1,093 tons	913 tons 1,113 tons
Dimensions length beam draught	207ft 4in (63.2m) 22ft 9in (6.9m) 14ft 7in (4.5m)	207ft 4in (63.2m) 22ft 11in (7.0m) 16ft 0in (4.9m)	210ft 7in (64.2m) 22ft 11in (7.0m) 16ft 2in (4.9m)

Above: **Glauco** *photographed in 1935.*

when, in their turn, the Japanese surrendered she was seized by the Americans who scuttled her on 15 April 1946.

Propulsion			
main engines	2 x Fiat	2 x Fiat	2 x Fiat
power	2 x 750bhp	2 x 1,200bhp	2 x 1,200bhp
electric motors	2 x C.R.D.A.	2 x C.R.D.A.	2 x CRDA/Marelli
power	2 x 400shp	2 x 400shp	2 x 400shp
shafts	two	two	two
Performance			
speed: surface	14kt	16kt	16kt
submerged	8kt	8kt	8kt
range: surfaced	5,300nm/14kt	5,400nm/8kt	5,400nm/8kt
submerged	100m/3kt	80nm/4kt	80nm/4kt
maximum			
diving depth	288ft (90m)	400ft (120m)	400ft (120m)
Weapons			
TT	6 x 21in (533mm)	6 x 21in (533mm)	6 x 21in (533mm)
location	bow – 4, stern – 2	bow – 4, stern – 2	bow – 4, stern – 2
torpedoes	10	12	12
guns	1 x 3.9in (100mm)	1 x 3.9in (100mm)	1 x 3.9in (100mm)
	4 x 13.2mm (4 x 1) MG	2 x 20mm (2 x 1) MG	4 x 13.2mm MG
Complement	46	50	50

to persuade the Italian Navy to take over the order, as a result of which the larger pair, *Delfim* and *Espadarte,* became the Italian *Glauco* and *Otaria* (see

Glauco-class), and the slightly smaller and less heavily armed pair became the Italian Argo-class (it should be noted that another three submarines, ordered by Portugal from Vickers, UK, were not cancelled and were delivered in 1936). Designed by Cavallini, the Argo-class boats were generally similar to the Italian Navy's 600-ton series, albeit slightly larger, and were of saddle-tank design. Once in service they were considered to be one of the best of the Italian Navy's medium-displacement boats, being of strong construction and possessing good range and excellent manoeuvrability.

The Italian Navy's high opinion of the Argo-class was reinforced by combat experience in 1940-41, as a result of which an improved design was ordered as the Flutto-class. These boats had marginally larger, but much stronger hulls, which led to a significant increase in maximum depth. More powerful diesels gave an increase of 2kt in surface speed and greater range, while a reduction in the size of the tower resulted in increased sub-surface manoeuvrability. The Flutto-class was also armed with two 20mm cannon, replacing the 13.2mm machine guns used in virtually all previous Italian submarines. A total of 12 were planned, but only nine were actually completed, two of them, *Grongo* and *Murena*, with large, deck-mounted cylinders for human torpedoes in place of their deck guns.

The initial order became the Series I. A further group was ordered; these being 3ft 3in (1m) longer to overcome some trim problems. Designated Flutto-class Series II, 24 were ordered, of which nine were actually laid down but only three were actually completed. It was planned to order a further 12, designated Flutto-class Series III; these would have been identical in all respects to the Series II, but none was ever laid down.

Neither of the two Argo-class survived the war: *Vellella* was sunk by

Brin/Liuzzi-classes   ITALY

Type: short-range patrol.

Class	Brin	Liuzzi
Total built	5	4
Completed	1938-39	1940
Displacement surfaced submerged	1,000 tons 1,245 tons	1,148 tons 1,460 tons
Dimensions length beam draught	237ft 8in (72.5m) 21ft 11in (6.7m) 14ft 11in (4.5m)	249ft 8in (76.1m) 22ft 11in (7.0m) 14ft 11in (4.6m)
Propulsion main engines power electric motors power shafts	2 x Tosi 2 x 1,700bhp 2 x Ansaldo 2 x 650shp two	2 x Tosi 2 x 1,750bhp 2 x Ansaldo 2 x 750shp two

Right: Flutto-class **Marea** *was given to Soviets in 1949.*

British submarine *Shakespeare* on 7 August 1943, and *Argo* was scuttled on the Italian surrender on 11 September 1943. Twelve Flutto Series I were laid down but three had not been completed by the time of the Italian surrender and the unfinished hulls were scrapped. Three of the nine boats completed were lost during the war, all to Allied surface warships: *Flutto* (11 July 1943), *Gorgo* (21 May 1943) and *Tritone* (19 January 1943). Four were scuttled in September 1943 but were raised by the Germans, repaired and recommissioned with "UIT" hull numbers: *Grongo* (UIT-20), Murena (UIT-16), Sparide (*UIT-15*) and *Nautilo* (UIT-19). All four were then sunk in Allied air raids. *UIT-19* (ex-*Nautilo*) was raised after the war by the Yugoslavs, refitted and recommissioned under its third flag as *Sava*.

Performance		
speed: surface	17.3kt	18kt
submerged	8kt	8kt
range: surfaced	9,000nm/7.8kt	13,000nm/8kt
submerged	90nm/4kt	110nm/4kt
maximum operational		
diving depth	288ft (90m)	288ft (90m)
Weapons		
TT	8 x 21in (533mm)	8 x 21in (533mm)
location	bow – 4, stern – 4	bow – 4, stern — 4
torpedoes	14 torpedoes	12 torpedoes
guns	1 x 3.9in (100mm)	1 x 3.9in (100mm)
	4 x 13.2mm MG	4 x 13.2mm MG
Complement	54	58

History: During the Spanish Civil War the Italian Navy, although supposedly neutral, provided a great deal of assistance to the Republican Navy, the most significant being the clandestine transfer in 1937 of two submarines – *Archimede* and *Torricelli* of the Archimede-class (see page 180) – which were immediately given Spanish names. In an attempt to conceal this from foreign intelligence two new submarines were built for the Italian Navy and given the names of the transferred boats. These two new boats, plus three others, were built to a modified Archimede-class design and named after the first to be completed, becoming the Brin-class. Compared with the Archimede-class, these had the same dimensions but the hull was much better shaped, resulting in a higher speed for the same installed power. Like the Foca-class minelayers, the Brin-class was built with its 3.9in (100mm) gun at the after end of the bridge, an arrangement somewhat lacking in tactical logic, and this was rectified in 1942 when the gun was moved to the foredeck.

The four-boat Liuzzi-class was designed and built by Tosi at Taranto, and was, in essence, a slightly enlarged and improved version of the Brin-class, the changes including further modifications to the hull-shape and mounting the main gun on the foredeck. Like many Italian designs of the period they had unnecessarily large bridge structures, which were modified and reduced in size in 1942. They were popular with their crews and were particularly fast, one boat achieving a surface speed of 17.9kt on trials.

On the outbreak of war four of the Brin-class were stationed in the Red Sea/Indian Ocean area and two – *Torricelli* and *Calvi* – were lost within days, the former being scuttled after a major battle in which she set fire to the British destroyer *Khartoum,* which subsequently sank. The two remaining boats, *Archimede* and *Guglielmotti,* continued to operate in the area until May 1941 when, in company with other Italian boats in the area, they sailed around Africa to Bordeaux, being refuelled en route by a German supply ship. On arrival, they joined the Italian squadron supporting the German U-boat campaign in the Atlantic. *Archimede* was lost off the coast of Brazil and *Guglielmotti* was sunk in the Mediterranean, leaving only *Brin*, which, following the Italian surrender, ended her days as a training ship for British ASW crews in Colombo, Ceylon.

At the start of the war the Liuzzi-class was in the Mediterranean, where *Liuzzi* herself was sunk by British destroyers (27 June 1940) and *Bagnolini* sank a British C-class cruiser (12 June 1940). The remaining three boats were then redeployed to Bordeaux and operated in the Atlantic, where *Tarantini* was sunk

Cagni-class ITALY

Type: long-range commerce raiders.
Total built: 4.
Completed: 1941.
Displacement: surfaced 1,708 tons; submerged 2,190 tons.
Dimensions: length 228ft 0in (87.9m); beam 25ft 6in (7.8m); draught 17ft 0in (5.7m).
Propulsion: 2 x C.R.D.A. diesels, 2 x 2,685bhp; 2 x C.R.D.A. electric motors, 2 x 900shp; two shafts.
Performance: surface – 16.5kt; submerged – 8.5kt; range surfaced 10,700nm at 12kt, submerged 107nm at 3.5kt; maximum operating diving depth 328ft (100m).
Weapons: 14 x 17.7in (450mm) TT (bow – 8, stern – 6), 36 x torpedoes; 2 x 3.9in (100mm), 4 x 13.2mm MG.
Complement: 78.

History: This class had an exceptional armament, which was the direct result of a very unusual decision by the Italian Naval Staff. The Cagni-class was designed to operate in distant waters against merchant shipping and the Naval Staff considered that the boats needed the heaviest possible torpedo battery to increase the probability of a hit and a large number of reloads to ease the resupply problems. Careful analysis indicated that the 18in (457mm) torpedo was perfectly adequate for destroying merchant shipping and by adopting this weapon the designers were able to mount eight tubes in the bows and six in the stern, and to carry a total of 36 torpedoes; no operational submarine has ever carried a greater load. It is highly unusual for new ships to incorporate an

Above: Torricelli *was built to replace a boat given surreptitiously to Spain. She was scuttled on 23 June 1940 following a short engagement with four British ships (the destroyers* Kandahar, Khartoum *and* Kingston, *and the sloop* Shoreham*) in the Red Sea.*

while returning from her first patrol. The final pair were both converted into transports and both were taken over by the Germans on the Italian surrender and given "UIT" numbers. *UIT-23* (ex-*Giulani*) was sunk while returning from Penang (February 1944) and *UIT-22* (ex-*Bagnolini*) was sunk in March 1944 while en route to the Far East.

Right: Ammiraglio Cagni, *nameship of a class of four.*

older, less powerful weapon system, but in this case the decision seems to have been fully justified. These boats also carried two 3.9in (100mm) guns and four 13.2mm machine guns in two twin mounts. The boats' large size made them relatively comfortable for the crew but, somewhat surprisingly, did not make them less manoeuvrable, and they were good seakeepers.

The four boats became operational in mid-1941 and were immediately pressed into service as transports, taking supplies to Axis forces in North Africa, in the course of which they moved a total of 2,370 tons of supplies during 15 voyages. Three boats – *Caracciolo*, *Millo* and *Saint Bon* – were sunk in the course of these activities; the first named was scuttled after being severely damaged, while the other two were both sunk by British submarine HMS *Upholder*. Only *Cagni* survived and she was sent to the Atlantic, departing from La Maddalena on 6 October 1942 and arriving at Bordeaux on 20 February 1943, having sailed out of the Mediterranean, then south as far as the Cape of Good Hope, before returning to France; she sank two merchant ships on the way, the longest voyage undertaken by any Italian submarine during World War II.

Japanese Attack Submarine Designations

During the period 1922-45 the Imperial Japanese Navy (IJN) employed a complicated system of designations for submarine classes. Originally each submarine was numbered in a single sequence in the order of launch but the system changed on 1 November 1924 when all submarines were divided into three groups, each given a letter prefix: large ocean-going boats (over 1,000 tons displacement) – I; coastal (500-1,000 tons) – Ro; and small (less than 500 tons) – Ha. Within these groups individual boats were allocated a new pennant number; thus No 51 became *I-52*, No 84 became *Ro-63*, No 17 became *Ha-8*, and so on. In addition to this, the system of class designations was changed, with each class being given a descriptor, such as "*kaigun-dai*" (= large navy design) which was then abbreviated, in this case to "KD." Successive classes of the same type were then numbered in sequence (KD1, KD2, etc) and minor variations indicated by letter suffixes (KD3a, KD3b, etc). The result was that a pennant number prefixed "I-" simply meant a long-range submarine and included attack boats, scouting boats, minelayers and aircraft-carrying submarines.

As a final complication, in May 1942 all surviving I-class boats had the number 100 added to their pennant numbers, *I-68* becoming *I-168*, and so on. This did not apply to the "Ro-" series boats, nor was it applied retrospectively to I-boats which had been lost prior to May 1942.

KD1/2/3-classes

JAPAN

Type: long-range patrol.

Class	KD1	KD2	KD3a/b
Total built	1	1	KD3a S 4, KD3b S 5
Completed	1924	1925	1927-31
Displacement surfaced submerged	1,500 tons 2,430 tons	1,500 tons 2,500 tons	1,800 tons 2,300 tons
Dimensions length beam draught	300ft 0in (91.4m) 28ft 10in (8.8m) 15ft 1in (4.6m)	330ft 10in (100.9m) 25ft 1in (7.6m) 16ft 10in (5.1m)	330ft 0in (100.6m) 26ft 2in (8.0m) 15ft 10in (4.8m)
Propulsion main engines power electric motors power shafts	4 x Sulzer 4 x 1,300bhp 4 4 x 500shp four	2 x Sulzer 2 x 3,400bhp 2 2 x 1,000shp two	2 x Kanpon 2 x 3,400bhp 2 2 x 1,400shp two

Abbreviated designator	Japanese meaning	Literal translation	Pennant prefix	Japanese class
C	*hei-gata*	C-model	I	1st
J	*jun(yo) sen (suikan)*	cruiser submarine	I	1st
K	*kai(gun)-chu*	Admiralty design, medium	Ro	2nd
KD	*kaigun-dai*	Admiralty design, large	I	1st
KS	*kai(gun)-sho*	Admiralty design, small	Ro	2nd
L	–	–	Ro	2nd
ST	*sen(suikan)-taka*	fast submarine	I	1st
STS	*sen(suikan) taka-sho*	small fast submarine	Ha	3rd

Performance			
speed: surfaced	20kt	22kt	20kt
submerged	10kt	10kt	8kt
range: surfaced	20,000nm/10kt	10,000nm/10kt	10,000nm/10kt
submerged	100nm/4kt	100nm/4kt	90nm/3kt
maximum diving depth	200ft (61m)	200ft (61m)	200ft (60m)
Weapons			
TT	8 x 21in (533mm)	8 x 21in (533mm)	8 x 21in (533mm)
location	bow	bow – 6, stern – 2	bow
torpedoes	24	16	16
guns	1 x 4.7in (120mm)	1 x 4.7in (120mm)	1 x 4.7in (120mm)
	1 x 3in (76mm)	1 x 3in (76mm)	
Complement	60	60	63

History: In the post-World War I era the Imperial Japanese Navy (IJN) was driven by two perceived imperatives: building more submarines to redress the imbalance of capital ships imposed by the Washington Naval Conference, and the requirement for such submarines to achieve trans-Pacific ranges. The KD1 and KD2 classes represented two early attempts in this area, the start of a series which would continue in production from 1921 to 1943. KD1 was based on British design practice, but with a very long range, and a heavy armament of eight torpedo tubes and two guns, one 4.7in (120mm) and one 3in (76mm). She had four propellers, each powered by a 1,300bhp Sulzer diesel, one of the very few submarines in any navy to be driven in this way, but enabling two diesels to be used for very long range cruising, and all four to be engaged to achieve maximum speed. Two complete power trains (diesel engine, electric motor, shafts and propeller) were removed in 1932 and no further four-shaft submarines were built. The 3in gun was also removed in the 1932 refit.

The KD2-class also consisted of one boat, *I-52* (ex- *No 51*) similar in size and identically armed to the KD1-class, but the design was based on that of the German *U-139*, which had been given to Japan as post World War I reparations. Despite having only half the power, maximum speed was a remarkable 22kt, some 2kt faster than the KD1, but surface range was reduced by some 50 per cent.

It was planned to build five more of the KD2-class, but the order was cancelled in favour of the KD3a, which was the first totally Japanese-designed long-range cruiser submarine, although the design incorporated lessons learnt with the KD2 and (to a lesser extent) KD1 designs. Four were built: *I-53* (ex-No 64), *I-54* (ex-No 77), *I-55* (ex-No 78) and *I-58* (the last-named did not have a previous number as it was ordered after the introduction of the new system). These were followed by the five-strong KD3b-class, which was virtually identical to the KD3a, differing only in the shape of the bow and stern, which resulted in a 6in (127mm) increase in overall length. The shape of the bridge tower was also altered, giving a sloping leading edge.

I-51 (KD1-class) served as an operational boat from 1924 to 1930, but was then employed as a training boat until 1939, being stricken in 1941. *I-52* (KD2-class) served long enough to be renumbered *I-152* in May 1942, but was then put into reserve and cannibalised for spares.

Of the KD3a/b-classes, *I-63* was lost in peacetime, when she collided with *I-60* in the Bungo Strait on 2 February 1939, which resulted in 81 deaths. Most boats in both groups were transferred to the training role in March 1942 and all

KD4/5/6/7-classes JAPAN

Type: long-range patrol boats.

Class	KD4/5	KD6a/b	KD7
Total built	KD4 – 3, KD5 – 3	KD6a – 6, KD6b – 2	10
Completed	1930	1934-38	1943
Displacement surfaced submerged	1,720 tons 2,330 tons	1,785 tons 2,440 tons	1,833 tons 2,603 tons
Dimensions length beam draught	310ft 6in (94.6m) 25ft 7in (7.8m) 15ft 10in (4.8m)	342ft 6in (104.7m) 26ft 11in (8.2m) 15ft 0in (4.6m)	346ft 2in (105.5m) 27ft 1in (8.3m) 15ft 1in (4.6m)
Propulsion main engines power electric motors power shafts	2 x M.A.N. 2 x 3,000bhp 2 2 x 900shp two	2 x Kanpon 2 x 4,500bhp 2 2 x 900shp two	2 x Kanpon 2 x 4,000bhp 2 2 x 900shp two

Above: **I-58** *lies outboard of* **I-53** *at the war's end.*

were renumbered by the addition of "1" before their old numbers on 20 May 1942. One wartime loss, *I-60* was sunk by British destroyer *Jupiter* on 17 January 1942. Four of the KD3a-class were laid up in reserve in early 1944, but one KD3a and three KD3bs were converted into *Kaiten* carriers in early 1945; all four survived the war and were scuttled in 1946.

Performance			
speed: surface	20kt	23kt	23.1kt
submerged	8.5kt	8.2kt	8kt
range: surfaced	10,800nm/10kt	14,000nm/10kt	8,000nm/16kt
submerged	60nm/3kt	65nm/3kt	50nm/5kt
maximum diving depth	230ft (70m)	250ft (76m)	260ft (80m)
Weapons			
TT	6 x 21in (533mm)	6 x 21in (533mm)	6 x 21in (533mm)
location	bow – 4, stern – 2	bow	bow
torpedoes	14	14	12
guns	1 x 4.7in (120mm)	1 x 3.9in (100mm)	1 x 5.0in (127mm)
	1 x 0.303in MG	1 x 13.2mm AA	2 x 25mm AA
Complement	58	60-84	88

History: The *kaidai* series continued with a number of further classes, each of which represented a small improvement on its predecessor. The KD4-class (three units) was some 10ft 8in (3.3m) shorter than the KD3b and mounted six instead of eight torpedo tubes (four tubes in the bows and two in the stern) and also had an increase in range. Next came the KD5-class (three units), which were very similar to the KD4 but were armed with one 3.9in (100mm) in place of the KD3b's 4.7in (120mm), although the secondary weapon was a 13.2mm machine gun in place of the earlier, and much lighter) 0.303in (7.7mm) weapon. The KD6a boats (six units) were larger versions of the KD4; in effect, the designers returned to the size of the KD3b, the extra size being used for increased bunkerage, thus increasing range to 14,000nm at 10kt. These were among the first Japanese submarines to be powered by the all-Japanese diesel engine designed by the Naval Technical Bureau (*kansei honbu*) and which was generally known by that bureau's acronym of "Kanpon." The KD6b-class (two units) were virtually identical to KD6a. Finally, came the KD7-class (10 boats) in which, once again, the great majority of the changes were very small, except for the armament. The original intention was for each boat not to have a medium calibre main gun, but to mount four 25mm cannon in two twin mounts. However, the weapon was new and suffered from production problems, and only half the number required were available. As a result, a 4.7in (102mm) main gun was retained and a single twin 20mm mount was installed at the after end of the bridge. It should also be noted that the torpedo load was reduced from 14 to 12. Endurance of these long-range cruisers was 75 days.

Those boats that survived into 1942-43 were relegated to the training role or converted to transports to carry men and supplies to the Japanese-occupied outposts. Most of the latter received only minimal conversion for this new role, but *I-171* (ex-*I-71*) was refitted to carry *Daihatsu* amphibious landing craft on its deck. Of these, those that remained in service in mid-1944 were then converted into *kaiten* carriers.

There were three KD4s, of which *I-61* was lost in a pre-war collision with a Japanese gunboat (2 October 1941), *I-164* (ex-*I-64*) was sunk by submarine USS *Triton* (17

Right: I-70. The KD6a-class had long range and high speed.

J1-class

Type: long-range cruiser.
Total built: 4.
Completed: 1929.
Displacement: surfaced 2,135 tons; submerged 2,791tons.
Dimensions: length 319ft 11in (97.5m); beam 30ft 3in (9.22m); draught 16ft 5in (5.0m).
Propulsion: 2 x M.A.N diesels, 2 x 3,000bhp; 2 x electric motors, 2 x 1,300shp; two shafts.
Performance: surface – 18kt; submerged – 8kt; range surfaced 24,400nm at 10kt, submerged 60nm at 3kt; maximum operating diving depth 260ft (80m).
Weapons: 6 x 21in (533mm) TT (bow – 4, stern – 2), 20 torpedoes; 2 x 5.5in (140mm) guns; 1 x 0.303in (7.7mm) MG.
Complement: 92.

History: These four boats were the first to be designated *junsen* (= cruiser) by the IJN and also the first to wear I-series pennants, being numbered *I-1* to *I-4*, respectively. The programme came under strong German influence, the design being based on that of the proposed U-142-class and powered by the latest M.A.N. diesels obtained from Germany. More than that, however, a prominent submarine designer/engineer, Dr. Ing. Techel, who had worked at the Krupp-owned Germaniawerft throughout the late war, was brought to Japan to advise during the final phase of the design process and the first months of construction (December 1924 to April 1925). They were double-hulled boats and were designed for a surface range of 24,000nm at 10kt, which was satisfactorily demonstrated during an early trial, although, like all boats of that

Above: Unknown KD7-class submarine under attack, 1944.

May 1942) and *I-162* (ex-*I-62*) survived the war. There were also three KD5s: *I-67* was lost in a pre-war accident (29 August 1940) and the other two, *I-165* (ex-*I-65*) and *I-66* (ex- *I-66*), were lost in the war. There were eight KD6a/b boats, not one of which survived the war: three were sunk by surface warships; two were sunk by submarines; one was sunk by carrier-borne aircraft; one was lost when it was accidentally flooded during an air raid; and one was lost on operations, cause unknown.

Above: I-3 *(J1-class); note the two 5.5in (140mm) guns.*

era, submerged range was very poor, in this case 60nm at 3kt.

    I-3 was sunk by the U.S. *PT-59* (10 December 1942) and *I-4* by USS *Seadragon* (20 December 1942), and the two remaining boats were then converted for use as transports, with the after gun removed, torpedo-carrying capacity reduced, and fittings installed on the upper casing for carrying *daihatsu* landing craft. *I-1* was damaged by two New Zealand ships and scuttled (29 January 1943) and *I-2* was sunk by a U.S. destroyer (7 April 1944).

    The J1 design was continued, but with facilities for carrying a small amphibious aircraft

C1/C2/C3-classes

Type: long-range attack boats.

History: Designed in the mid-1930s and launched in 1938-39, the C1-class were specialised long-range attack boats, their design being developed from that of the KD6-class (qv). They were generally similar in size and capability to the A1-class and B1-class, but without the aircraft facilities. Instead, the C1-class was fitted to carry one Type A midget submarine on the after casing. The C2-class, laid down in 1942 and completed in 1944, was a repeat of the C1-class, with some modern equipment, with slightly less powerful diesels (5,500bhp each, as opposed to 6,200bhp), but without

Class	C1/C2	C3
Total built	C1 – 5, C2 – 3	3
Completed	1941-44	1944
Displacement surfaced submerged	2,554 tons 3,561 tons	2,564 tons 3,644 tons
Dimensions length beam draught	358ft 7in (109.3m) 29ft 10in (9.1m) 17ft 7in (5.4m)	356ft 7in (108.7m) 30ft 6in (9.3m) 16ft 10in (5.1m)
Propulsion main engines power electric motors power shafts	2 x diesels 2 x 6,200bhp 2 2 x 1,000shp two	2 x diesels 2 x 2,350bhp 2 2 x 600shp two
Performance speed: surface submerged range: surfaced submerged maximum diving depth	23.6kt 8kt 14,000nm/16kt 60nm/3kt 330ft (100m)	17.7kt 6.5kt 21,000nm/16kt 105nm/3kt 330ft (100m)
Weapons TT location torpedoes guns	8 x 21in (533mm) bow 20 1 x 5.5in (140mm) 2 x 25mm AA	6 x 21in (533mm) bow 19 2 x 5.5in (140mm) 2 x 25mm AA
Complement	101	101

the fittings for the midget submarines. Next in this series was the C3-class, which had the same hull as the C2-class, but the main difference was that they had much less powerful main machinery (2,350bhp per engine) which gave a dramatic 50 per cent increase in range, albeit with a reduction in speed from 23.6kt to 17.7kt.

All the C1-class took part in the Pearl Harbor operation, in which they carried their midget submarines, but every one of them was subsequently sunk during the Pacific War by U.S. forces: *I-22* in 1942, *I-18*, *I-20* and *I-24* in 1943. *I-16* was converted into a transport submarine in 1943, and was sunk while carrying out a resupply operation in 1944.

The C2-class did not join the fleet until 1944 and *I-47* and *I-48* were immediately converted to suicide-submarine carriers, first for four *kaiten* and later for six. Two were sunk in the war, *I-46* (27 October 1944) and *I-48* (23 January 1945), but *I-47* survived, to be scuttled in 1946. Similar fates befell the C3-class, with two war losses, one of them *I-55* in the Pacific (28 July 1944), while the other was sunk in the Atlantic, while sailing as a transport to Brest. The third, *I-53* was scuttled in 1946.

Plans to build 17 more C3-class and 25 of a modified C4-class were both still-born.

***Below:** **I-22**, along with the other four C1-class boats, took part in the attack on Pearl Harbor. She was sunk on either 5 October or 4 November 1942.*

No 71/ST-classes

Type: experimental fast attack.

Class	No 71	ST
Total built	1	6
Completed	1938	1945
Displacement surfaced submerged	213 tons 240 tons	1,291 tons 1,450 tons
Dimensions length beam draught	140ft 5in (42.8m) 10ft 10in (3.3m) 10ft 2in (3.1m)	259ft 2in (79.0m) 19ft 0in (5.8m) 17ft 11in (5.5m)
Propulsion main engines power electric motors power shafts	1 x diesel 1 x 1,200bhp 1 1 x 1,800shp one	2 x diesel 2 x 1,325bhp 2 2 x 2,500shp two
Performance speed: surface submerged range: surfaced submerged maximum diving depth	18kt 25kt 3,830nm/12.5kt 33nm/7kt 280ft (85m)	15.8kt 19kt 5,800nm/14kt 135nm/3kt 360ft (110m)
Weapons TT location torpedoes guns	3 x 18in (457mm) bow 3 –	4 x 21in (533mm) bow 10 2 x 25mm AA
Complement	11	31

History: The German high-speed submarine programme which culminated in the development of the Types XXI and XXIII "*electroboats*" is well-known, but the equally daring Japanese programme has been largely overlooked by historians. As allies during World War II, there was a certain amount of exchange of information between Japan and Germany; in particular, the Japanese Naval Attaché in Berlin obtained a great deal of information about the German Type XXI and Type XXIII U-boats from late 1943 onwards. The Japanese high-speed submarine programme, however, started with experimental *No 71,* which was laid down in December 1937 and launched in August 1938 and was thus well ahead of the German programme. Given the name *No 71* for security reasons, the only boat in the programme was intended solely as what would be described in modern terms a "technology

Above: **No 71, *fastest submarine since the British R-class.***

demonstrator." Despite its experimetnal status, the design incorporated three 18in (457mm) torpedo tubes, a calibre which had not been used by the IJN for many years. *No 71's* hull design appears modern, even by today's standards, with its exceptionally clean lines broken only by the sail (itself of very streamlined design) and two small platforms, which were presumably necessary for ship-handling in port, and may well have been detachable. There was a single propeller with cruciform after controls, and no forward hydroplanes. *No 71* carried out a series of intensive tests over the period 1938-40 and was then scrapped, but her value was derived from the lessons learned, which were then incorporated into two operational classes: the ST- and STS-classes.

The first of the ST-class was launched in 1944 and with a length of 259ft 2in (79.0m) and submerged displacement of 1,450 tons it was of a similar size to the German Type XXI. The STS was armed with four 21in (533mm) torpedo tubes and there were two deck-mounted 25mm AA cannon on fully disappearing mounts. There was a long, very clean, all-welded hull but, as with the German Type XXI programme, the Japanese naval staff insisted on twin propellers with twin diesels and electric motors. Surface speed was nearly 16kt, but this was not so important as the submerged speed, which was designed as 19kt, although only 17kt was achieved in practice; this was, however, considerably in excess of any other contemporary submarine except for the German Types XXI and XXIII. The STS design was optimised for rapid mass-production although, in the event, only three were completed out of a planned 100.

The hulls were very careful streamlined with an absolute minimum of drag-inducing protrusions, and items such as cleats and capstans were retractable. The other element necessary for high underwater speed was greater battery power, but while the German solution was to use more cells the Japanese opted instead for a new type of battery, which had a much higher capacity but at the price of a short life. As in other navies, the designers wanted to do away with forward hydroplanes, which were considered unnecessary, but the submariners insisted on them being fitted. They were needed for low-speed control and to avoid broaching during the period immediately following the launch of a torpedo. The STS also had a Japanese-designed schnorkel, which was raised vertically to a height of about 10ft (3m).

A total of 100 STs were planned in the initial order, but just three were completed before the surrender; two of which went to the USA while the third was scuttled in Japanese waters in 1946. Another three were near completion and were broken up on the stocks.

One of the most surprising aspects of this story is that throughout the 1920s and 1930s the Japanese produced a series of boats which, apart from sheer size and aircraft-carrying capability, did very little to extend the boundaries of submarine technology. Their streamlined programme, however, was revolutionary and there is no doubt that the Japanese should

Below: **No 71** *predated the German Walter boats by four years.*

L4-class

JAPAN

Type: coastal (second class).
Total built: 9.
Completed: 1923-27.
Displacement: surfaced 996 tons; submerged 1,322 tons.
Dimensions: length 256ft 0in (76.2m); beam 24ft 3in (7.4m); draught 12ft 4in (3.8m).
Propulsion: 2 x Vickers diesels, 2 x 1,200bhp; 2 x electric motors, 2 x 800shp; two shafts.
Performance: surface – 16kt; submerged – 8kt; range surfaced 7,000nm at 10kt, submerged 85nm at 4kt; maximum operating diving depth 200ft (61m).
Weapons: 6 x 21in (533mm) TT (bow), 10 x torpedoes; 1 x 3in 76mm) gun; 1 x MG.
Complement: 60.

History: Japan built a series of medium submarines based on the British L-class (qv), starting with the L1-class, two of which were built by Mitsubishi to Vickers' plans in 1919-20. These were virtually identical to the British-built L-class, with six 18in (457mm) torpedo tubes, four in the bows and two in the beam. The IJN quickly established that these beam tubes had little practical value and the next four boats – the L-2-class – were simply L1s with only four torpedo tubes, all in the bows. These were followed by three L3-class, which were virtual repeats of the L2-class and then by the L4-class, which were the last submarines to be built for the IJN based on British plans. These were externally very similar to the L3s but with

have given higher priority to this programme. However, in the early years of the war their entire attention was devoted to attacking the Americans as far across the Pacific as possible. The STS did not fit in with this plan as it was a relatively short-range boat; nevertheless, it was a remarkable achievement.

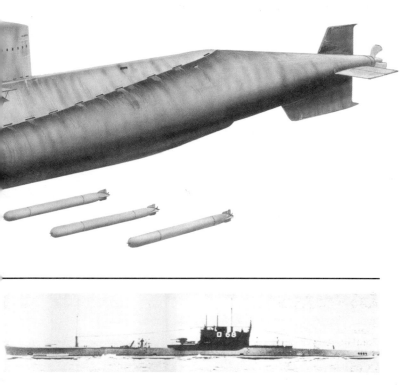

Above: Ro-68, *one of many medium submarines in the IJN.*

significant internal improvements and two major changes in armament. The most important of these was that there were now six torpedo tubes, all in the bows, and the calibre was increased to 21in (533mm), giving a major increase in offensive capability. Also, a 3in (76mm) gun was mounted forward of the bridge tower. The change to the new numbering system took place during the construction of the L4-class, with the result that the first four were launched as Nos *59, 72, 73* and *74* and the remaining five as *Ro-64* to *Ro-68*; following the change the first four were renumbered as *Ro-60* to *Ro-63*.

All nine boats were still in service on the outbreak of war, but two were soon lost: *Ro-66* sunk after colliding with *Ro-62* (17 December 1941) and *Ro-60* was shipwrecked (29 December 1941). The remainder were relegated to training duties in mid-1942, but *Ro-61* was sunk by U.S. ships and aircraft (31 August 1942), and *Ro-65* dived onto a reef while under air attack (4 November 1942). *Ro-64* was in service as a training boat when sunk by a mine (12 April 1945) with the loss of 50 crew plus 30 trainees. The remaining boats surrendered in August 1945 and were then scrapped.

STS-class

Type: high performance, coastal defence.
Total built: 10.
Completed: 1945.
Displacement: surfaced 320 tons; submerged 440 tons.
Dimensions: length 173ft 11in (53.0m); beam 13ft 1in (4.0m); draught 11ft 3in (3.4m).
Propulsion: 1 x diesel, 1 x 400bhp; 1 x electric motor, 1 x 1,250shp; one shaft.
Performance: surface – 10.5kt; submerged – 13kt; range surfaced 3,000nm at 10kt, submerged 100nm at 2kt; maximum operating diving depth 500ft (152m).
Weapons: 2 x 21in (533mm) TT (bow); 1 x 7.7mm MG.
Complement: 22.

History: The STS (*sensuikan*) *taka-sho* = small fast submarine) were the second outcome of the *No 71* experimental programme (qv), and were directly comparable with the German Type XXIII. The Japanese boats were designed specifically for homeland defence against the inexorable advance of the U.S. forces. They were designed for simple, mass production, using prefabricated, all-welded, highly streamlined hulls and a single propeller. Items such as bollards were retractable, but they were fitted with both a search radar and a Japanese-developed schnorkel. Range was

K-XI/O-9-classes

Type: East Indies, patrol; European waters, patrol.

Class	K-XI	O-9
Total built	3	3
Completed	1925	1931-32
Displacement surfaced submerged	670 tons 815 tons	515 tons 647 tons
Dimensions length beam draught	218ft 10in (66.9m) 20ft 2in (6.2m) 12ft 2in (3.7m)	179ft 6in (54.7m) 18ft 8in (5.7m) 11ft 6in (2.5m)
Propulsion main engines power electric motors power battery shafts	2 x M.A.N. diesels 2 x 1,200bhp 2 2 x 360shp 132 cells two	2 x Sulzer 2 x 450bhp 2 2 x 305shp 120 cells two

some 3,000nm at 10kt and endurance was about 15 days. Like other 3rd class boats, they were numbered in the "Ha-" series.

The first was not laid down until March 1945 and the production plans were very ambitious, calling for 13 to be completed every month. However, as with the Germans, the planners were living in a fantasy world, and just 10 were completed before the end of the war, all of which were still working up when the war ended, and not one was employed operationally. All completed boats and the incomplete boats on the ways were captured by the Americans.

Below: Like the Type XXI, not one STS became operational.

Performance		
speed: surface	15kt	12kt
submerged	8kt	8kt
range: surfaced	3.500nm/12kt	3,500nm/8kt
submerged	13nm/8kt	11nm/7.5kt
maximum		
diving depth	200ft (60m)	280ft (85m)
Weapons		
TT	2 x 21in (533mm)	2 x 21in (533mm)
location	bow	bow
TT	4 x 17.7in (450mm)	3 x 17.7in (450mm)
location	bow – 2, stern – 2	bow – 2, stern – 1
torpedoes	4 x 21in; 8 x 17.7in	4 x 21in, 6 x 17.7in
guns	1 x 3.4in (88mm) AA	1 x 3.4in (88mm) AA
	1 x 12.7mm AAMG	1 x 12.7mm AAMG
Complement	31	29

History: Starting in the early 1900s, the Dutch system was that submarines for use in European waters were paid for out of the naval budget, whereas those intended for use in the East Indies were paid for by the Colonial Ministry. The former were designated "*Onderzeeboot*" (undersea boat = submarine) followed by an Arabic numeral, and the latter "*Koloniën*" (colonial) , followed by a Roman numeral. This system continued throughout the 1920s, the first post-Wolrd War I boats being the K-XI-class, which was a development of the K-VIII-class (qv), but the torpedo armament consisted of a mix of two calibres. In the bow there were four tubes, two of them 21in (533mm) with one reload for each tube, the first time that tubes of this calibre had been fitted into Dutch submarines. The bow torpedo room also contained two 17.7in (450mm) tubes, with two reloads for each tube. This mix of two calibres was a most unusual arrangement, which must have casued logistic difficulties in supplying two different types of torpedo and practical complications within the boat, especially over settings and fire control arrangements. The remaining two tubes were aft, but in this case were both 17.7in plus two reloads.

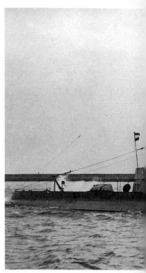

The O-9-class was developed from the K-XI design, but was slightly smaller and slower, although range was still the same. The O-9-class also retained the mix of 21in and 17.7in in the forward torpedo room, but there was only one tube aft.

At the outbreak of war the three O-9-class were all in Dutch waters; *0-11* was captured by the Germans and eventually scuttled as a blockship, while *O-9* and *O-10* escaped to Britain, where they operated with the British Royal Navy until stricken in 1944. The three K-XI-class boats were in Far Eastern waters at the time of the Japanese attack; *K-XII* was sunk in

K-XIV/O-12-classes   NETHERLANDS

Type: East Indies, patrol; European waters, patrol.

Class	K-XIV	O-12
Total built	5	3
Completed	1933-34	1931-32
Displacement surfaced submerged	771 tons 1,008 tons	568 tons 715 tons
Dimensions length beam draught	242ft 9in (74.0m) 25ft 0in (7.6m) 12ft 10in (3.9m)	198ft 6in (60.5m) 18ft 4in (5.6m) 11ft 10in (3.6m)
Propulsion main engines power electric motors power battery shafts	2 x M.A.N. diesels 2 x 1,600bhp 2 x W. Schmitt motors 2 x 50360shp 120 cells two	2 x Sulzer/M.A.N. 2 x 900bhp 2 2 x 310shp 192 cells two

a Japanese air attack, while the other two went to Australia where they operated as part of the Allied naval force until 1944 when they were stricken.

Below: K-XI, a class of fhree boats developed from the K-VIII.

Performance		
speed: surface	17kt	15kt
submerged	9kt	8kt
range: surfaced	3.500nm/11kt	3,500nm/10kt
submerged	26nm/8.5kt	12nm/8kt
maximum		
diving depth	260ft (80m)	280ft (85m)
Weapons		
TT	8 x 21in (533mm)	5 x 21in (533mm)
location	bow – 4, stern – 2, rotating – 2	bow – 4, stern – 1
torpedoes	14	10
guns	1 x 3.4in (88mm) AA	2 x 40mm AA
	2 x 40mm AA	1 x 12.7mm MG
Complement	38	31

History: Starting in the early 1900s, the Dutch system was that submarines for use in European waters were paid for out of the naval budget, whereas those intended for use in the East Indies were paid for by the Colonial Ministry. The former were designated "*Onderzeeboot*" (undersea boat = submarine) followed by an Arabic numeral, and the latter "*Koloniën*" (colonial), followed by a Roman numeral. This system continued throughout the 1920s, the first post-Wolrd War I boats being the K-XI-class, which was a development of the K-VIII-class (qv), but the torpedo armament consisted of a mix of two calibres. In the bow there were four tubes, two of them 21in

(533mm) with one reload for each tube, the first time that tubes of this calibre had been fitted into Dutch submarines. The bow torpedo room also contained two 17.7in (450mm) tubes, with two reloads for each tube. This mix of two calibres was a most unusual arrangement, which must have casued logistic difficulties in supplying two different types of torpedo and practical complications within the boat, especially over settings and fire control arrangements. The remaining two tubes were aft, but in this case were both 17.7in plus two reloads.

The O-9-class was developed from the K-XI design, but was slightly smaller and slower, although range was still the same. The O-9-class also retained the mix of 21in and 17.7in in the forward torpedo room, but there was only one tube aft.

At the outbreak of war the three O-9-class were all in Dutch waters; *O-11* was captured by the Germans and eventually scuttled as a blockship, while *O-9* and *O-10* escaped to Britain, where they operated with the British Royal Navy until stricken in 1944. The three K-XI-class boats were in Far Eastern waters at the time of the Japanese attack; *K-XII* was sunk in a Japanese air attack, while the other two went to Australia where they operated as part of the Allied naval force until 1944 when they were stricken.

Above right: O-12-class O-13, seen in 1931. She was sunk in error in the North Sea by the Polish submarine Wilk shortly after escaping to Britain in 1940.

Right: K-XIV class K-XVI, which sank the Japanese destroyer Sagiri, 24 December 1941, but was sunk a day later by IJN submarine I-66 off Kunching.

O-16/O-21-classes · NETHERLANDS

Type: European waters, patrol; ocean patrol.

Class	O-16	O-21
Total built	1	7
Completed	1936	1940-41
Displacement surfaced submerged	896 tons 1,170 tons	990 tons 1,205 tons
Dimensions length beam draught	251ft 0in (76.5m) 21ft 9in (6.6m) 13ft 3in (4.0m)	255ft 0in (77.7m) 22ft 3in (6.8m) 13ft 1in (4.0m)
Propulsion main engines power electric motors power battery shafts	2 x M.A.N. diesels 2 x 1,600bhp 2 x W. Schmitt motors 2 x 500shp 2 x 96 cells two	2 x Sulzer diesels 2 x 2,600bhp 2 2 x 500shp 2 x 96 cells two

Performance		
speed: surface	18kt	19.5kt
submerged	9kt	9kt
range: surfaced	10,000nm/12kt	10,000nm/12kt
submerged	26nm/8.5kt	28NM/8.5KT
maximum		
diving depth	262ft (80m)	328ft (100m)
Weapons		
TT	8 x 21in (533mm)	8 x 21in (533mm)
location	bow – 4, stern – 2, rotating – 2	bow – 4, stern – 4
torpedoes	14	14
guns	1 x 3.4in (88mm) AA	1 x 3.4in (88mm) AA
	2 x 40mm AA	1 x 12.7mm MG
Complement	38	39

History: The sole O-16-class boat was the last Dutch submarine to be designed specifically for employment in European waters, and was slightly larger than the preceding O-12-class. The torpedo armament was increased from five to eight tubes, the latter including a twin-tube rotating mounting inside the upper casing, as first installed in the K-XIV-class. The O-21-class was the first Dutch submarine design to be intended for use in any theatre and proved to be outstanding design. In 1940 was one of the best general-purpose boats in any navy. It was generally similar to the O-19-class but, since it did not carry mines, was slightly smaller. The hull was fabricated from high yield (HY-52) steel giving the boats an excellent dividng depth for the time of 328ft (100m). As with all Dutch submarines of the era, they were very well equipped, and included a schnorkel.

O-16 was, in fact, in the Far East at the time of the Japanese attack, but was sunk when she blundered into a British-laid minefield off Singapore island (16 December 1941). Five of the O-21-class had been launched at the time of the German invasion, four of which managed to reach the UK. *O-25*, which was fitting out, was scuttled by the Dutch but raised by the Germans, refitted and commissioned in 1942 as *UD-3*. A further two hulls (*O-26* and *O-27*) were completed by the Germans and commissioned as *UD-4* and *UD-5*. The Germans made various modifications, including the removal of the external rotating torpedo mounting, replacing the 40mm weapons with German 20mm AA, and replacing the bridge tower with a German-pattern device. *UD-3* and *UD-4* were scutled in May 1945, but *UD-5* was returned to the Dutch who commissioned her under her original number of *O-27*.

Orzel-class

NETHERLANDS (POLAND)

Type: ocean-going patrol.
Total built: 2.
Completed: 1939.
Displacement: surfaced 1,473 tons; submerged 1,650 tons.
Dimensions: length 275ft 7in (84.0m); beam 22ft 0in (6.7m); draught 13ft 8in (4.2m).
Propulsion: 2 x Sulzer diesels, 2 x 2,370bhp; 2 x Brown-Boveri electric motors, 2 x 550shp; battery 100 cells; two shafts.
Performance: surface – 20kt; submerged – 9kt; range surfaced 7,000nm at 10kt, submerged 100nm at 5kt; maximum operating diving depth 260ft (80m).
Weapons: 12 x 21.7in (550mm) TT (bow – 4, stern – 4, rotating mount – 4); 20 x torpedoes; 1 x 4.1in (105mm) Bofors gun, 2 x 40mm Bofors AA, 2 x 13.2mm MG.
Complement: 60.

History: With the prospect of war with Germany growing ever nearer, the Polish Navy was forced to expand, and national feeling was so strong that the cost of the first of a new class of submarine was raised by popular subscription. The selected design was from RDM in The Netherlands and was an adaptation of the impressive O-19-class but without the minelaying capability. It was a double-hull design and equipment came from all over Europe: the boats were powered by Sulzer diesels from Switzerland and Brown-Boveri electric motors from Germany, and both the 4.1in (105mm) and 40mm guns were from the Swedish company, Bofors. The torpedo tubes were French and were 21.7in (550mm) calibre, which was not used before outside the French Navy. Indeed,

The four boats which reached England had to be put into dockyard hands for completion, but were then all put into service, under British command, but with Dutch crews. *O-22* was sunk by a German minesweeper (8 November 1940) but the other three – and the returned *O-27* – served on until the 1950s.

Below: O-21-class O-24 survived the war, to be stricken in 1956.

Right: Polish Orzel-class comprised two boats built in the Netherlands.

the tubes in the two Polish boats were fitted with liners to enable international standard 21in (533mm) torpedoes to be launched, and from 1939 onwards only such torpedoes were embarked. The main gun was located at the foot of the forward edge of the bridge tower behind a large gunshield, an arrangement which enjoyed a brief vogue in the late 1930s.

Both boats had unusual careers. First-of-class *Orzel* was operating in the Baltic on 15 September 1939 when she was forced to put into the Lithuanian port of Talinn, where, to everyone's surprise, the authorities interned both the boat and her crew. They escaped three days later and managed to reach Scotland, where *Orzel* came under the operational control of Britain's Royal Navy. Unfortunately, this boat and her brave crew were lost, cause unknown, on a North Sea patrol in June 1940. Second-of-class *Sep* was still undergoing builder's trials when her captain and crew seized control and sailed her to Gdynia. Once war broke out and Polish defeat was inevitable she was sailed to Sweden where she was interned for the duration of hostilities. She was returned to Poland in October 1945 and served on until 1970.

B-class

Type: coastal patrol.
Total built: 6.
Completed: 1926-30.
Displacement: surfaced 420 tons; submerged 545 tons.
Dimensions: length 167ft 4in (51.0m); beam 17ft 6in (5.3m); draught 11ft 6in (3.5m).
Propulsion: 2 x Sulzer diesels, 2 x 450bhp; 2 x electric motors, 2 x 350shp; two shafts.
Performance: surface – 14.8kt; submerged – 11kt; maximum operating diving depth 164ft (50m).
Weapons: 4 x 18.0in (456mm) TT (bow – 2, stern – 2), 1 x 3in (76mm) gun.
Complement: 23.

History: Like its Nordic neighbours Denmark and Sweden, Norway maintained a small flotilla of submarines, which were constructed in its own yards, although design was sometimes put out to contract. In the case of the B-class, the design was prepared by the Electric Boat Co. of Groton, Connecticut, USA, in 1915, but due to World War I (in which Norway was neutral) construction could not be started for several years and the first-of-class was not launched until August 1922, followed by three more in 1923 to 1924. After that there was a five year gap until the last two boats were launched. Construction took place at the Royal Norwegian Navy's Marinens Hovdewerft (= admiralty yard) at Horten. The boats were very conventional, but were one of the last designs to mount 18in (457mm) torpedo tubes, with two forward and two aft.

Series I-class

Type: medium-range patrol.
Total built: 6.
Completed: 1929-30.
Displacement: surfaced 933 tons; submerged 1,354 tons.
Dimensions: length 249ft 4in (76.0m); beam 21ft 4in (6.5m); draught 12ft 6in (3.8m).
Propulsion: 2 x diesels, 2 x 1,300bhp; 2 x electric motors, 2 x 800shp; two shafts.
Performance: surface – 14kt; submerged – 9kt; range surfaced 7,000nm at 9kt, submerged 105nm at 4kt; maximum operating diving depth 246ft (75m).
Weapons: 8 x 21in (533mm) TT (bow – 6, stern – 2) 14 x torpedoes; 1 x 4in (102mm) gun; 1 x 45mm gun; 1 x 0.30in MG; 8 x mines.
Complement: 53.

History: The six boats of the D-class were the first attempt following the Bolshevik Revolution to rebuild the Soviet submarine fleet, the design being based on that of the Bars-class of 1915-16 (qv). The class was originally called the D-class and the boats were given individual names, that of the first-of-class being *Dekabrist*; but they were later simply numbered from *D-1* to *D-6*. Once *D-1* commenced sea-trials in 1930 it was found that there were many problems, some due to shortcomings in the basic design, others to the slip-shod standards in Soviet industry. There was a lack of stability, particularly a tendency to list when surfacing, which was eventually cured, but there was a much more dangerous tendency for the quick-dive tank to flood suddenly at depth. The design and construction of the battery tank also left a lot to be

Above: B-3, *launched on 25 January 1924, was scuttled in May 1940 when the Germans invaded Norway.*

All six boats were still in service when the Germans invaded Norway in 1940. *B-1* escaped to England, where it served as a target boat for ASW training until stricken in 1944, while *B-3* was scuttled. The other four were captured by the Germans: the fate of *B-2* and *B-4* is not known, but *B-5* and *B-6* were commissioned into the German Navy as *UC-1* and *UC-2*, but served for only a short while before being stricken and broken up.

Above: Soviet Series I-class submarine Yakobinec (D-6).

desired, and installation, maintenance and removal of the electric storage cells were always very difficult processes. The boats were refitted on several ocasions, the last in 1940 and were subject to many modifications.

The first loss was *D-1*, which disappeared without trace while on a training exercise in November 1940; no cause was ever established but it may have been due to the flooding problem mentioned earlier. *D-3* was mined (July 1942), *D-4* was sunk by German surface warships (December 1943) and *D-6* was damaged at sea in an air attack, but returned to port only to be destroyed by bombers in dry dock. The two remaining boats were stricken in the 1950s.

Series III/V/Vbis/Vbis2/ X/Xbis-class

Type: coastal patrol.

Series	III	V	Vbis/Vbis[2]	X/Xbis
Total built	4	19	21	53
Completed	1931-32	1933-34	1935	1936-37
Displacement surfaced submerged	578 tons 704 tons	589 tons 708 tons	607 tons 749 tons	590 tons 708 tons
Dimensions length beam draught	187ft 0in (57.0m) 20ft 4in (6.2m) 12ft 5in (3.8m)	191ft 11in (58.5m) 20ft 4in (6.2m) 14ft 1in (4.3m)	192ft 9in (58.8m) 20ft 4in (6.2m) 14ft 1in (4.3m)	192ft 9in (58.8m) 20ft 4in (6.2m) 14ft 1in (4.3m)
Propulsion main engines power electric motors power battery shafts	2 x diesels 2 x 685bhp 2 2 x 400shp 2 x 56 cells two	2 x diesels 2 x 800bhp 2 2 x 400shp 2 x 56 cells two	2 x diesels 2 x 685bhp 2 2 x 400shp 2 x 56 cells two	2 x diesels 2 x 800bhp 2 2 x 400shp 2 x 56 cells two
Performance speed: surface submerged range: surfaced submerged maximum diving depth	12.5kt 8.5kt 3,250nm/8kt 110nm/2kt 295ft (90m)	14kt 8kt 6,700nm/8kt 100nm/2kt 295ft (90m)	14kt 8kt 6,700nm/8kt 100nm/2kt 295ft (90m)	15kt 8.7kt 6,140nm/7kt 122nm/2kt 295ft (90m)
Weapons TT location torpedoes guns	6 x 21in (533mm) bow – 4, stern – 2 10 1 x 45mm 2 x 0.3in MG	6 x 21in (533mm) bow – 4, stern – 2 10 2 x 45mm 1 x 0.3in MG	6 x 21in (533mm) bow – 4,stern – 2 10 2 x 45mm AA –	6 x 21in (533mm) bow – 4 stern – 2 10 2 x 45mm AA 1 x 0.3in MG
Complement	35	40	40	40

History: The Schulka-class of medium submarines was built in very large numbers and was the subject of steady development through three major types – Series III, Series V (three sub-types) and Series X (two sub-types). This was the first original submarine design produced in the USSR and remained in constant production, incorporating a steady stream of improvements, from 1929 to 1948. At the time of its entry into service in the mid-1930s the Series V was only marginally smaller than the contemporary German Type VIIA,

Above: **Kambala *(Shch-203) of the Series Vbis.***

although the Soviet boat's performance and capabilities were far less.

First to appear was the Series III, three of which were approved as part of the First Five Year Plan, but with a fourth paid for by popular subscription. They were double-hull boats with saddle tanks covering some two-thirds of the pressure hull, which was sub-divided into six watertight compartments. Power was provided by two 8-cylinder, 685bhp Soviet-made diesels, giving a maximum surface speed of 13kt; endurance was 20 days. Thus, they had poor range, low endurance and to add to all this were particularly noisy.

Many of the shortcomings of the first four boats were addressed in the much more numerous Series V, which had a longer hull, sub-divided into seven compartments, and more powerful engines, while rearrangement and extension of the bunkers increased fuel capacity from 25 to 58 tons. There were two minor variations in this group, the Series Vbis and Vbis2 (originally to have been designated the Series VIII) which had a slightly longer hull, but reverted to the earlier, less powerful engines. The Series X was generally similar to the earlier boats, but with more powerful engines, while some at least had a sloping forward edge to the bridge tower. By this time endurance had doubled to 40 days and the Series X boats were no longer coastal boats, but had an ocean-going capability. In the Series Xbis the major improvements were concerned with enabling production to be both easier and quicker.

The construction programme was complicated and reflects the difficulties created by the vast geographical spread of the USSR. Thus, boats for the Black Sea Fleet were built in the 61-Kommunar and Marti Yards in Nikolayev in the Crimea, and those for the Baltic Fleet by the Marti, Ordzhonikidze and Zhdanov yards in Leningrad. The Marti and Ordzhonikidze yards also fabricated parts which were then shipped to the Far East for assembly by the Dalzavod yard and service with the Pacific Fleet.

It appears that the numbering system was originally intended to be based on the yards; for example, the Dalzavod yard built *Shch-101* to *-112* (Series V), *Shch-113* to *-121* (Series Vbis), *Shch-122* to *-125* (Series Vbis2), *Shch-126* to *-130* (Series X) and *Shch-135* to *-138* (Series Xbis). However, the apparent logic of the sequence was marred when *Shch-131* to *-134*, and *Shch-139* to *-141* were built at other yards. Further complications were caused by renumbering.

All the boats served in the Great Patriotic War and some were quite successful. *Shch-307* sank the German *U-144* in the Baltic (9 August 1941) while *Shch-211* sank the German tanker *Peles* in the Black Sea (15 August 1941). Thirty-three boats were lost during the war and the remainder served on until the 1950s except for 11 Series Xbis which survived into the 1960s.

Series VI/XII-class

Type: coastal patrol.

Series	VI/VIbis	XII/XIIbis
Total built	VI - 30, VIbis - 20	XII - 4; XIIbis - 45
Completed	1933-37	1938-43
Displacement surfaced submerged	160 tons 200 tons	206 tons 218 tons
Dimensions length beam draught	124ft 0in (37.8m) 10ft 3in (3.1m) 8ft 6in (2.6m)	146ft 0in (44.5m) 10ft 10in (3.3m) 10ft 1in (3.1m)
Propulsion main engines power electric motors power shafts	1 x diesel 1 x 685bhp 1 x PG60 motor 1 x 240shp one	1 x diesel 1 x 800bhp 1 1 x 400shp one

History: The original Series VI was a response to a naval staff requirement for a small submarine for employment in defending harbours and the coastline. The official Russian type designation was *maliye lodki*, usually abbreviated to *malodki* (= small submarine) and the actual design was based on that of the AG-class (qv) which had been very successful in the Imperial Russian Navy. The Series VI boats were built at the Gorky Shipyard on the Volga river and then transported by rail on specially constructed railcars to the Black Sea where they ran trials. They were then replaced on the railcars and transported to Vladivostock for service with the Pacific Fleet. They were single-hull boats and were the first Soviet boats to use welding, but this was confined to the bridge tower and casing. One of the major design constraints was that the dry weight of the boats could not exceed 120 tons, since this was the maximum capacity of the railcars.

The original Series VI boats had a number of shortcomings, mainly their very limited armament – just two torpedoes – restricted range (1,600nm at 8.5kt on the surface and 55nm at 3.5kt submerged), and a poorly designed hull. The latter was partially overcome in the Series VIbis which had a much better hull, and the 20 boats were built by more exeprience shipyards at Leningrad and Nikolayev.

The other problems had not been resolved and this led to the Series XII which was longer, with a stronger hull, more powerful engines and two reload torpedoes. The outcome was a far more satisfactory boat, with much greater range, a deeper operating depth and much improved internal

Performance		
speed: surface	13kt	14kt
submerged	6kt	8kt
range: surfaced	1,600nm/8.3kt	3,440nm/9kt
submerged	55nm/2.5kt	107nm/3kt
maximum		
diving depth	200ft (60m)	246ft (75m)
Weapons		
TT	2 x 21in (533mm)	2 x 21in (533mm)
location	bow	bow
torpedoes	2	4
guns	1 x 45mm AA	1 x 45mm AA
Complement	16	20

equipment. Only four were built since construction then switched to the Series XIIbis, which had a better designed bridge tower and increased fuel bunkerage. A total of 45 were completed between 1937 and 1941. One Series XII and one Series XIIbis were converted to take a Special Purpose Regenerating Power Unit (ie, an air-independent propulsion system); this is described in the Quebec-class entry in the AIP section.

There were no war losses among the Series VI boats, but losses in the other groups were: Series VIbis – 8, Series XII – 2; Series XIIbis – 26. The survivors served on into the 1950s and were then scrapped, except for a small number which were passed to friendly navies: Bulgaria – three Series XIIbis; China – one Series VI, one Series XIIbis, North Korea – one Series Vibis. A further development was the larger Series XV built between 1940 and 1947.

Below: M-35, a coastal submarine of Series XIIbis.

Series IX/IXbis/XVI-class SOVIET UNION

Type: coastal patrol.

Series	IX	IXbis/XVI
Total built	3	IXbis - 39; XVIbis - 6
Completed	1936	1937-40
Displacement surfaced submerged	840 tons 1,070tons	856 tons 1,090 tons
Dimensions length beam draught	255ft 1in (77.8m) 21ft 0in (6.4m) 13t 3in (4.0m)	255ft 1in (44.5m) 21ft 0in (6.4m) 13ft 4in (4.1m)
Propulsion main engines power electric motors power shafts	2 x diesel 2 x 2,000bhp 2 2 x 550shp two	2 x diesel 2 x 2,000bhp 2 2 x 550shp two
Performance speed: surface submerged range: surfaced submerged maximum diving depth	19.5kt 9kt 9,800nm/10kt 148nm/3kt 328ft (100m)	18.9kt 8.8kt 9,800nm/10kt 148nm/3kt 328ft (100m)
Weapons TT location torpedoes guns	6 x 21in (533mm) bow – 4; stern – 2 12 1 x 3.9in (100mm) 1 x 45mm AA	6 x 21in (533mm) bow – 4; stern – 2 12 1 x 3.9in (100mm) 1 x 45mm AA 1 x 0.3in MG
Complement	46	45

History: The Soviet Navy was not satisfied with the design of the Series VI (Pravda-class) and requested *Ingenieurskantoor voor Scheepsbouw* (I.v.S.), the German submarine design office located in the Hague, to produce a design for a medium-displacement, ocean-going submarine. The result was the Series IX, an excellent design which was produced at the same time that I.v.S. was working on the *Gür* for the Turkish Navy and the Type IA for the German Navy; the three bear marked resemblances to each other, as well as to the German

Above: S-102, Stalinetz-class, returns to her Arctic base.

Type VII, which was developed later. The Series IX was a single-hull with a saddle tank and an armament of six torpedo tubes and a deck gun located at the foot of the forward edge of the bridge tower, behind a large gunshield. It was slightly larger than the *Gür* and Type IA, with a more powerful propulsion system. Soviet designers then refined the design, resulting in the Series IXbis, one of the major changes being to move the gun (whose shield not only caused considerable hydrodynamic drag but also made the gun very difficult to work) forward to an open mount, which then also enabled the shape of the bridge tower to be refined. The design was improved yet further with the Series XVI, which was constructed of tougher steel, with an all-welded hull, and the deck gun was moved to a new position abaft the tower. These boats were also known as the S-class, some sources claiming that this stood for *srednaya* (= medium), others that it meant *Stalinetz*, after the dictator who took a great interest in naval matters.

The original Series IX comprised just three boats, all built at the Ordzhonikidze Yard under German supervision. This was followed by an order for 44 Series IXbis, which included four paid for by public subscription, although five of these boats were not completed due to the German invasion. The Series XVI, which were idnetical in all major respects to the Series IXbis, were completed in 1947-49.

The Series IX boats fought in all theaters and proved themselves to be the best all-round boats in the Soviet Navy. All three Series IX were lost in the war; one was blown up to prevent its capture, one was mined and one was sunk. Of the 39 Series IXbis completed, 13 were lost in the war to variety of causes; the surviviving boats served on into the 1950s-60s, but four were transferred to China in 1955. The six Series XVI were built after the war and all served into the 1960s, when they were scrapped; none was transferred to foreign navies.

Below: Series IX was designed by German-run bureau I.v.S.

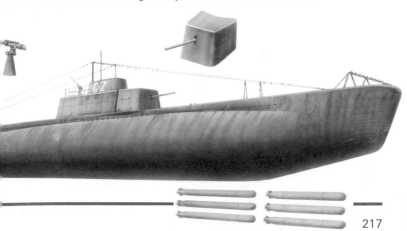

Series XIV

Type: ocean-going patrol.
Total built: 11.
Completed: 1940-42.
Displacement: surfaced 1,498 tons; submerged 2,095 tons.
Dimensions: length 320ft 4in (97.7m); beam 24ft 3in (7.4m); draught 14ft 10in (4.5m).
Propulsion: 2 x diesel, 2 x 4,200bhp; 2 x electric motors, 2 x 1,200shp; battery 4 x 60 cells; two shafts.
Performance: surface – 21kt; submerged – 10kt; range surfaced 14,000nm at 9kt, submerged 160nm at 3kt; maximum operating diving depth 263ft (80m).
Weapons: 10 x 21in (533mm) TT (bow – 6, stern – 2, rotating mount – 2), 24 x torpedoes; 2 x 3.9in (100mm) guns, 2 x 45mm cannon; 20 x mines.
Complement: 60.

History: Despite the failure of the Series IV (Pravda-class) the Soviet naval high command persisted with its goal of a "big navy", one element of which was a large, ocean-going *kreyser* (= cruiser). The next step was the Series XIV, a totally new, double-hulled design, with a range of some 14,000nm at 9kt and a submerged displacement of 2,095 tons, which was considerably larger than any submarine operated by the British Royal Navy and in the same league as the German Type XB and U.S. Gato-class. The armament was particularly heavy, comprising 10 torpedo tubes (six in the bow, two in the stern and two on a rotating mount in the after casing) with a total of no fewer than 24 torpedoes. There were also two 3.9in (100mm) guns, one at each end of the bridge tower,

C/D-classes

Type: ocean-going patrol.

Class	C	D
Total built	6	3
Completed	1928-30	1947-54 (see notes)
Displacement surfaced submerged	916 tons 1,290 tons	1,065 tons 1,480 tons
Dimensions length beam draught	247ft 0in (75.3m) 20ft 10in (6.3m) 13ft 6in (4.1m)	275ft 6in (84.0m) 21ft 9in (6.6m) 13ft 2in (4.0m)
Propulsion main engines power electric motors power shafts	2 x Vickers diesels 2 x 1,000bhp 2 2 x 375shp two	2 x Sulzer diesels 2 x 2,500bhp 2 2 x 675shp two

Above: Series XIV boat returns to port after a war-time patrol.

and two 45mm AA guns in single mounts. In addition, while not minelayers as such, the boats had internal chutes and a mine-room carrying 20 mines.

Eleven boats were completed between 1940 and 1942, leaving one incomplete hull on the slips. There was a post-war plan to complete this boat, but this did not come to fruition and the boat was scrapped, still incomplete, in about 1949. During the war six boats operated in the Arctic, but plans to transfer the remaining five from the Baltic were thwarted by the German invasion. Five were lost in the war and the remainder served on until the mid-1950s, when they were scrapped.

Performance		
speed: surface	16kt	20.5kt
submerged	8.5kt	9.5kt
range: surfaced	6,800nm/10kt	9.000nm/12kt
submerged	125nm/4.5kt	
maximum		
diving depth	262ft (80m)	300ft (90m)
Weapons		
TT	6 x 21in (533mm)	6 x 21in (533mm)
location	bow – 4, stern – 2	bow – 4, stern – 2
torpedoes	10	..
guns	1 x 75mm AA	1 x 4.7in (120mm)
		4 x 37mm AA
Complement	40	60

History: The C-class was an Electric Boat Co. design built under licence in Spain, and was, in essence, a development of the B-class (qv), the main change being an increase from four to six torpedo tubes and the adoption of the international standard 21in (533mm) torpedo tubes. A total of six were built, being launched between 1927 and 1929.

The D-class was an entirely new design, intended for long-range oceanic patrols. The torpedo armament of six tubes was not particularly heavy for the size and role of the submarines, although the 4.7in (120mm) gun was of larger calibre than usual. A combination of the Spanish Civil War and World War II meant that construction was particularly protracted: *D-1* was laid down in 1933, launched in 1944 and completed in 1947, while *D-2*, laid down in 1934 and launched in 1944, but did not join the fleet until 1951. *D-3* was not even laid down until 1945, and was completed in 1952.

The C-class all became involved in the Spanish Civil War, in the course of which four were lost, two of them in December 1936, *C-3* being sunk by an Italian submarine (21 December), while *C-5* simply disappeared, cause and date unknown. The other two were lost as a result of air attacks: *C-6* was so badly damaged that she had to be scuttled (20 October 1937), while *C-1* was sunk by bombs and although recovered was never repaired. The other two, *C-2* and *C-4*, survived because they spent most of the conflict undergoing refits in France and were handed over to the victorious Nationalists in March 1939; *C-4* was lost in a peacetime accident (June 1946) and *C-2* was stricken in 1952.

Because of their long construction time, the D-class boats were essentially out-of-date before they were first commissioned and had realtively short service lives. *D-1* was stricken in the late 1960s and the other two followed in 1971.

Right: The C-class was a Holland-type Electric Boat Co. design built in Spain. This is C-2, *which, while under refit in France, was surrendered to the Nationalists in 1939 during the Spanish Civil War, and was stricken in 1952.*

Draken/Sjölejonet/
U-1-classes

SWEDEN

Type: coastal patrol.

History: Sweden continued its policy, established in the early years of the 20th century, of maintaining domestic submarine design and construction capabilities by ordering successive classes to be built in small numbers. Thus, three Bävern-class

Classes	Draken	Sjölejonet U-1	
Total built	3	9	9
Completed	1927-31	1937-42	1942-45
Displacement surfaced submerged	667 tons 850 tons	580 tons 760 tons	367 tons 450 tons
Dimensions length beam draught	216ft 10in (66.1m) 21ft 0in (6.4m) 10ft 10in (3.3m)	210ft 8in (64.2m) 21ft 0in (6.4m) 11ft 2in (3.4m)	162ft 9in (49.6m) 15ft 5in (4.7m) 12ft 6in (3.8m)

Propulsion			
main engines	2 x Götawerken	2 x M.A.N.	1 x M.A.N.
power	2 x 960bhp	2 x 1,050bhp	1 x 1,350bhp
electric motors	2	2	2
power	2 x 500shp	2 x 500shp	2 x 500shp
shafts	two	two	two
Performance			
speed: surface	13.8kt	16.2kt	13.8kt
submerged	8.3kt	10kt	7.5kt
Weapons			
TT	4 x 21in (533mm)	6 x 21in (533mm)	4 x 21in (533mm)
location	bow – 3, stern – 1	bow – 3, stern – 1, rotating mount – 2	bow – 3, stern – 1
guns	1 x 4.1in (105mm)	2 x 40mm Bofors	1 x 20mm AA
	1 x 25mm AA	–	–
Complement	35	38	26

attack submarines were built in the early 1920s, followed by a single Valen-class minelayer, which led to the Draken-class, launched at the Karlskrona Navy Yard between 1926 and 1930. These were double-hulled boats, armed with four torpedo tubes, three in the bows and one, internally mounted, in the stern.

Next came the Delfinen-class minelayers and then, with the probability of a European war clearly evident, by far the largest group of patrol submarines yet built for the Sweish Navy: the nine-strong Sjölejonet-class. These were slightly smaller than the the Draken-class but with a heavier armament, comprising three bow and one stern tubes, all internally mounted, and two external tubes in a rotating mount located on the upper casing abaft the bridge tower. They all served for some 18-23 years, and were stricken between 1959 and 1964.

For some years the size of the patrol submarines had been steadily increasing, so that the Sjölejonet-class were 210ft 8in (64.2m) long and displaced 760 tons, but this trend was reversed by the next group, known simply as the U-1-class, which was only 162ft 9in (49.6m) long and displaced 367 tons. These were commissioned between June 1943 and early 1945 and helped in the task of maintaining Sweden's neutrality. Armament was four torpedo tubes, with three in ther bows and one mounted externally in a fixed mount at the stern. The propulsion system was an unusual combination of a single diesel engine and two electric motors. *U-1* and *U-2* were stricken in 1960 followed by *U-3* in 1964 but the remaining six boats were taken in hand between 1960 and 1964 and converted to ASW submarines.

Right: Sjölejonet, *one of nine built between 1936 and 1941.*

Barracuda-class   UNITED STATES

Type: fleet.
Total built: 3.
Completed: 1924-26.
Displacement: surfaced 2,000 tons; submerged 2,620 tons.
Dimensions: length 334ft 6in (102.0m); beam 27ft 7in (8.4m); draught 15ft 2in (4.6m).
Propulsion: 2 x Busch-Sulzer diesels, 2 x 2,250bhp; 2 x M.A.N. auxiliary engines, 2 x 1,000bhp; 2 x Elliott electric motors, 2 x 1,200shp; battery 2 x 60 Exide cells; two shafts.
Performance: surface – 18.7kt; submerged – 9kt; range surfaced 6,000nm at 11kt, submerged 10hr at 5kt; maximum operating diving depth 200ft (61mm).
Weapons: 6 x 21in (533mm) TT (bow – 4, stern – 2); 12 x torpedoes; 1 x 5in (127mm) gun.
Complement: 88.

History: The three-strong Barracuda-class was part of a group of nine known as the "V-boats": Barracuda-class *V-1*, *V-2*, *V-3*; Argonaut-class (minelayer) *V-4*; Narwhal-class *V-5*, *V-6*; Dolphin-class *V-7*; and Cachalot-class *V-8*, *V-9*. (The boats were known by these numbers until 1931, when all submarines were given names, but this did not interfere with their hull numbers in the overall U.S. Navy system: thus, *V-1* was also SS-163.)

The Barracuda-class was the first to be built after World War I and the boats were large by contemporary standards, their size being dictated by the need to be capable of 20kt surface speed to meet the perceived need

Above: Nameship **Barracuda** *(SS-163), which was broken up in 1945.*

in many navies in the 1920s for a "fleet submarine". But, as with all the others, the Barracuda-class failed to meet this goal, in this case by a margin of just over 1kt. Armament was not heavy for the size of the boat: six torpedo tubes, all in the bows, with a 5in (127mm) gun, as built, although this was replaced by a 3in (76mm) gun in 1928.

The Barracuda-class was not a real success and all three boats were put into reserve in the late 1930s. They were reactivated for training, and at one time there was a plan to convert them into transports, but this never came to fruition. All three were stricken in March 1945.

Narwhal-class

Type: fleet.
Total built: 2.
Completed: 1930.
Displacement: surfaced 2,730 tons; submerged 3,900 tons.
Dimensions: length 371ft 0in (112.1m); beam 33ft 3in (10.1m); draught 16ft 11in (5.24.6m).
Propulsion: 2 x M.A.N. main diesels, 2 x 2,350bhp; 2 x M.A.N. auxiliary engines; 2 x 450bhp; 2 x Westinghouse electric motors, 2 x 800shp; battery 2 x 120 Exide cells; two shafts.
Performance: surface – 17.4kt; submerged – 8kt; range surfaced 18,000nm at 10kt, submerged 10hr at 5kt; maximum operating diving depth 300ft (91mm).
Weapons: 6 x 21in (533mm) TT (bow – 4, stern – 2); 40 x torpedoes; 2 x 6in (152mm) gun.
Complement: 89.

History: These two boats were essentially the same as the *Argonaut* (see Special-Role, Minelayer section) but with the minelaying facilities deleted and the space used to provide an extremely heavy armament of 40 torpedoes, with six in the tubes, 20 reloads carried internally, and a further 14 externally in storage containers inset under the gun deck. Gun armament comprised two 6in (152mm) guns and the rounds were so heavy that special access trunks and power hoists were required to bring them up from the magazines.

Like the Barracuda-class, these were not a great success. They were very large (they were several feet longer than today's Los Angeles-class SSNs),

---

Dolphin-class

Type: patrol.
Total built: 1.
Completed: 1932.
Displacement: surfaced 1,618 tons; submerged 2,240 tons.
Dimensions: length 319ft 3in (97.3m); beam 27ft 11in (8.5m); draught 13ft 1in (4,0m).
Propulsion: 2 x M.A.N. main diesels, 2 x 1,750bhp; 2 x M.A.N. auxiliary engines; 2 x 450bhp; 2 x Electro-Dynamic electric motors, 2 x 875shp; battery 2 x 120 Exide cells; two shafts.
Performance: surface – 17kt, submerged – 8kt; range surfaced 16,000nm at 7kt, submerged 10hr at 5kt; maximum operating diving depth 250ft (76m).
Weapons: 6 x 21in (533mm) TT (bow – 4, stern – 2), 18 x torpedoes; 1 x 4in (102mm) gun.
Complement: 63.

History: By the standards of the day the Barracuda- and Narwhal-classes were huge and this led to a reassessment of the requirement. The most likely operational scenario appeared to be that U.S. Navy submarines would have to operate on their own at some 3,000nm from their base on patrols lasting up to 90 days, which made the range, torpedo battery, reliability and crew conditions the most valuable attributes, while high surface speed was of lesser significance. Sheer size was also of reduced importance, both because this would improve handling and also, at a time of financial stringency, it would reduce both building and running costs. The first outcome of this new policy was a 2,215-ton boat initially designated *V-7*, but later named *Dolphin* (SS-169).

Right: Nautilus; *note large size, 6in (152mm) gun.*

which made them difficult to manoeuvre, especially when submerged, while the size combined with their extensive flat decks and the large gun platform made them slow to dive. The sheer size also made it easy to detect them, both on the surface and when submerged. Their design speed on the surface was over 17kt, but they were unable to make more than 14kt in practice.

Nautilus was modified in early 1941 to take a large stock of aviation fuel for refuelling seaplanes, but when war came it was found that this had little operational relevance. Both ships were refitted in 1941-42, being modernised and given new main engines as well as a further four external torpedo tubes. These measures were meant to make them more effective patrol submarines, but when they returned to the fleet they were actually used as transports, mainly for personnel, their large size enabling them to accommodate 120 troops for short periods. They took part in the landings on Makin Island in 1942 and on Addu Atoll in 1943. Both boats were scrapped in 1946.

Above: Dolphin, first of the medium-sized, long-range boats.

In the design phase, Dolphin was termed a "cruiser submarine" but in size, layout and general appearance she was, in effect, the first of the fleet type that would lead to the outstanding Gato/Balao-classes; indeed, Dolphin's measurements are virtually identical to those of the later boats. Dolphin was armed with six torpedo tubes, four in the bow and two in the stern, and, as built, carried a total of 18 torpedoes, all internally, but external stowage for a further three was added in 1933. The single 4in (102mm) gun was located on the after deck and was served through a door in the bridge tower, rather than having a separate access trunk.

Dolphin was a front-line submarine throughout the 1930s and carried out three wartime patrols. During the second she developed a serious oil leak which led to her being referred to as a "death-trap" and after one further patrol she was relegated to training duties. She was scrapped in 1946.

Cachalot-class

Type: patrol.
Total built: 2.
Completed: 1933-34.
Displacement: surfaced 1,120 tons; submerged 1,650 tons.
Dimensions: length 271ft 1in (82.9m); beam 24ft 9in (7.5m); draught 14ft 0in (4.3m).
Propulsion: 2 x M.A.N. main diesels, 2 x 1,535bhp; 2 x M.A.N. auxiliary engines; 2 x 450bhp; 2 x Westinghouse electric motors, 2 x 800shp; battery 2 x 120 Exide cells; two shafts.
Performance: surface – 17kt, submerged – 8kt; range surfaced 11,000nm at 10kt, submerged 10hr at 5kt; maximum operating diving depth 250ft (76m).
Weapons: 6 x 21in (533mm) TT (bow – 4, stern – 2); 16 x torpedoes; 1 x 4in (102mm) gun.
Complement: 45.

History: The Cachalot-class was the last in the "V-boat" series, and there were a number of separate influences all pressing for a smaller design. There was a vocal group calling for smaller designs for tactical and budgetary reasons, while the recently concluded London Naval Conference had imposed a limit on total submarine tonnage, so that smaller boats would mean greater overall numbers. The outcome was a double-hulled design that was smaller than any of the other V-boats and which was heavily influenced by the German *U-135*. The boat also included two new M.A.N. engines, procured direct from Germany, which offered greater power for considerably less space. Another measure was to reduce the main gun to 3in (76mm) caliber, which caused some derision in the Submarine Force which was

Porpoise/Shark/Perch-classes

Type: fleet.

History: These were the first "all-electric" submarines, in which the shafts were turned only by the electric motors, which could either be powered by the batteries or the diesel-generators; ie, there was no direct drive from the main engines to the propellers. Such a system offered several advantages, but in particular it got away from the vibration problems associated with direct drive from the diesels to the shafts, and it also broke the hold of M.A.N. licenses. Thus, there were four Winton

Class	Porpoise	Shark	Perch
Total built	2	2	6
Completed	1935	1936	1936-37
Displacement surfaced submerged	1,316 tons 1,934 tons	1,316 tons 1,968 tons	1,330 tons 1,997 tons
Dimensions length beam draught	301ft (91.8m) 24ft 11in (7.6m) 14ft 1in (4.3m)	298ft 1n (90.8m) 25ft 1in (7.6m) 15ft 1in (4.6m)	300ft 7in (91.6m) 25ft 1in (7.7m) 15ft 2in (4.6m)

Right: **Cuttlefish**, *first submarine built by Electric Boat since 1924.*

more used to 6in (152mm) and 5in (127mm) guns. A significant event, unrelated to the design, was the decision to allocate construction of one of these two boats, *Cuttlefish* (SS-171), to the Electric Boat Company at Groton, Connecticut. This company had not built any submarines for the U.S. Navy since *S-47* (SS-158), which was launched in 1924, and the company's most recent work had been the four R-class (qv) built for Peru. The company was allowed to develop its own ideas for the interior layout of their boat, which resulted in some major advances, especially where crew comfort was involved. Another innovation was the installation of the first Torpedo Data Computer (TDC), a mechanically operated analogue computer, which proved to be a major advance over all previous U.S. systems, and far ahead of anything in any foreign navy at the time.

Once again, the overall result was not particularly satisfactory. The boats proved difficult to maintain, while the M.A.N. engines suffered from such excessive and incurable vibration that they had to be replaced by General Motors engines of a type which was not actually optimised for submarine installation, but proved, nevertheless, to be a great improvement. When war came both boats carried out three operational patrols and were then transferred to training duties. They were stricken and scrapped immediately after the end of the war.

Propulsion			
main engines	4 x Winton	4 x Winton	4 x Winton
power	4 x 1,300bhp	4 x 1,300bhp	4 x 1,300bhp
electric motors	4 x Elliott	4 x Elliott	8 x General Electric
power	4 x 1,075shp	4 x 1,075shp	8 x 538shp
battery	2 x 120 Exide	2 x 120 Exide	2 x 120 cells
shafts	two	two	two
Performance			
speed: surface	18kt	18kt	18.8kt
submerged	8kt	8kt	8kt
range: surfaced	11,000nm/10kt	11,000nm/10kt	11,000nm/10kt
submerged	10hr/5kt	10hr/5kt	10hr/5kt
maximum			
diving depth	250ft (76m)	250ft (76m)	250ft (76m)
Weapons			
TT	6 x 21in (533mm)	6 x 21in (533mm)	6 x 21in (533mm)
location	bow – 4, stern – 2	bow – 4, stern – 2	bow – 4, stern – 2
torpedoes	16	16	16
guns	1 x 3in (76mm)	1 x 3in (76mm)	1 x 3in (76mm)
	2 x 0.5in MG	2 x 0.5in MG	2 x 0.5in MG
	4 x 0.3in MG	4 x 0.3in MG	4 x 0.3in MG
Complement	50	50	50

diesels, all of which could be brought on line for maximum speed or, for cruising, three could power the motors while the fourth recharged the cells, and they also had sufficient electrical power to drive the air-conditioning system that was installed in U.S. submarines for the first time. Even the U.S.-sourced diesels had problems, however, and the first type fitted suffered repeated breakdowns and had to be replaced by a lower-powered model.

As built, torpedo armament was the standard four bow tubes and two in the stern, with a total of 16 torpedoes. The officers of the Submarine Force deemed this to be insufficient in combat and most boats were fitted with an additional two bow tubes early in the war; these were externally mounted, bringing the bow salvo up to six and total carried to 18.

The Porpoise- and Shark-classes were Navy Department designs, but financed by the 1933 National Recovery Act, with the first two being built by Portsmouth

Salmon/Sargo/Seadragon/ Tambor-classes

UNITED STATES

Type: fleet.

History: These four very similar classes represent the final development of the U.S. Navy's fleet submarine to peacetime standards. The Salmon-class marked the addition of two more torpedo tubes aft, which necessitated an enlargement of the hull, and the bridge tower was a different design. A new type of "composite drive"

Class	Salmon	Sargo/Seadragon	Tambor
Total built	6	10	12
Completed	1938	1939-40	1940-41
Displacement surfaced submerged	1,449 tons 2,210 tons	1,450 tons 2,350 tons	1,475 tons 2,370 tons
Dimensions length beam draught	308ft 0in (93.9m) 26ft 2in (8.0m) 15ft 7in (4.8m)	310ft 6n (94.6m) 27ft 1in (8.3m) 16ft 8in (5.1m)	307ft 3in (93.6m) 27ft 3in (8.3m) 15ft 0in (4.1m)

Navy Yard and having riveted hulls. The second pair was built by the Electric Boat Company and, while having the same measurements and armament, had many differences, one of the most important being that they were the first U.S. submarines with all-welded hulls. (Note that despite their names starting with "S" they were P-class boats.) The Perch-class were virtually repeat Sharks.

All 10 boats served in the war. The two Porpoise-class boats were relegated to training duties in 1942 and survived, following which they became docksisde trainers until being broken up in 1957. Of the Shark-class, *Shark* (SS-174) was lost in February 1942, cause unknown, while *Tarpon* (SS-175) sank while under tow to the breakers in August 1957. Of the Perch-class, three were war losses and three survived to be broken up, one in 1947, the other two in 1957.

Below: Porpoise, (SS-172), first of the 10-strong P-class.

Propulsion			
main engines	4 x H.O.R.*	4 x H.O.R.*	4 x General Motors
power	2 x 1,535bhp	4 x 1,535bhp	4 x 1,535bhp
electric motors	4 x Elliott	4 x General Electric	4 x General Electric
power	4 x 667shp	4 x 685shp	4 x 1,375shp
battery	2 x 126 Gould	2 x 126 Exide	2 x 126 Exide
shafts	two	two	two
Performance			
speed: surface	17kt	20kt	20.8kt
submerged	8.75kt	8.75kt	8.75kt
range: surfaced	11,000nm/10kt	11,000nm/10kt	11,000nm/10kt
submerged	48hr/2kt	48hr/2kt	48hr/2kt
maximum diving depth	250ft (76m)	250ft (76m)	250ft (76m)
Weapons			
TT	8 x 21in (533mm)	8 x 21in (533mm)	10 x 21in (533mm)
location	bow – 4, stern – 4	bow – 4, stern – 4	bow – 6, stern – 4
torpedoes	20	20	24
guns	1 x 3in (76mm)	1 x 3in (76mm)	1 x 3in (76mm)
	2 x 0.5in MG	2 x 0.5in MG	2 x 0.5in MG
	2 x 0.3in MG	2 x 0.3in MG	
Complement	55	55	60

* Hooven, Owens, Rentschler

was introduced in which one diesel engine and two electric motors were connected to each shaft, while two more diesel engines were used to recharge the batteries, an arrangement which proved to be physically cramped, but worked well in war. Three boats were built in Navy yards and were powered by a new model of General Motors diesels which proved very satisfactory, but the three built by Electric Boat were powered by Hooven, Owens, Rentschler (H.O.R.) engines, which proved troublesome and had to be replaced by General Motors engines during wartime refits. The Sargo-class was very similar, except for certain internal rearrangements and a hull lengthened by 2 ft 6in (0.8m) to improve crew conditions. Also introduced was a new type of high-capacity cell (Exide VLA47B) which remained in use for many years and was always known as the "Sargo battery". The Seadragon-class (four boats) was virtually identical to the Sargo-class except that, in a last minute change, propulsion was once again all-electric. The Tambor-class consisted of 12 boats (although the last six had names beginning with the letter "G") in which the forward torpedo battery was increased to six tubes and the total torpedoes carried to 24, but these were otherwise identical to those of the earlier groups.

These were the latest boats in commission at the time of the Japanese attack on Pearl Harbor and all fought a very hard war. *Stingray* (SS-186) carried out 16 combat patrols, the highest number by any U.S. submarine in World War II. Nameship of its class *Salmon* (SS-182) survived one of the heaviest depthcharge attacks on record and was forced so deep that the pressure hull wrinkled around some of the frames; she and her crew survived but the damage was so severe that she never went on another operation. Four boats were stricken and broken-up in 1946, while *Seal* (SS-183) survived until 1956. *Skipjack* (SS-184) achieved the dubious distinction of being sunk as a target twice, first at Bikini (July 1946), but she was then raised and sunk as an aircraft target on 11 August 1948.

Of the Sargo-class, *Squalus* (SS-192) was lost on sea trials due to the failure of

Gato/Balao/Tench-classes   UNITED STATES

Type: fleet submarine.

History: At the time of the Japanese attack on Pearl Harbor on 7 December 1941 there was just one Gato-class boat in commission: *Drum* (SS-228). By the war's end almost four years later 221 Gatos and their very closely related Balao- and Tench-classes had been built in a great feat of engineering and production, and the boats' crews had played a major role in bringing Japan to defeat. The Gatos were the outcome of the steady development which could be traced back in a direct line to the *Dolphin* (SS-169) of 1932. These three classes were always referred to as "fleet" boats but they were never meant to operate with the main battlefleet as the name implied; instead they conducted very long range, independent missions in the western Pacific, their high surface speed being used to get them rapidly to their patrol areas and back again.

The design was essentially the same as that of the Tambor-class, the only change of any significance being that an extra watertight bulkhead was installed to sub-divide the somewhat large engine room; this required the hull to be lengthened by 5ft (1.5m). The hull was of all-welded construction and this, combined with increased strengthening, enabled the new boats to be cleared to operate at 300ft (91m). Armament and general performance remained the same as the Tambor-class. As soon as war was declared the design was frozen for mass-production and 77 were completed, of which 20 were lost in combat.

The Gato-class was followed into production by the Balao-class, which was virtually identical except that the hull was made from high tensile rather than the earlier mild steel, which increased operational diving depth to 400ft (122m). The total number of orders placed was 256, but there were many cancellations

the main induction valve, and 26 men were lost; the boat was then raised, refitted, renamed *Sailfish* (also SS-192) and put into service. There were two war losses: *Sculpin*, (SS-191) was sunk by Japanese destroyers (19 November 1943), with 48 men rescued to become prisoners-of-war, of whom just 12 survived to be released in August 1945. The other war loss was *Swordfish* (SS-193) which was lost with all hands in January 1945. The remainder were stricken after the war.

The Seadragon-class boat *Sealion* (SS-195) was in refit at Cavite in the Philippines when the Japanese attacked, and was so badly damaged in an air attack that she had to be scuttled (10 December 1941). *Seawolf* (SS-197) was sunk by U.S. destroyer-escort (30 October 1944) and the other two were scrapped in 1948. Seven of the 12 Tambor-class were lost in the war; the others were either expended as targets or stricken between 1948 and 1960. The Tambor-class lost seven of its number, more than 50 per cent, but one of those that survived, *Tautog* (SS-199), not only shot down a Japanese aircraft during the attack on Pearl Harbor, but then went on to achieve the highest score in terms of ships sunk – 26 – of any U.S. submarine.

Below: **Tuna *(SS-203) of the Tambor-class.***

Above: **Tinosa *(SS-283) returns wearing many "kill" flags.***

Class	Gato	Balao	Tench
Total built	77	119	25
Completed	1941-43	1943-45**	1944-45**
Displacement surfaced submerged	1,526 tons 2,410 tons	1,525 tons 2,415 tons	1,570 tons 2,415 tons
Dimensions length beam draught	311ft 9in (95.0m) 27ft 3in (8.3m) 15ft 3in (4.7m)	311ft 9in (95.0m) 27ft 3in (8.3m) 15ft 3in (4.7m)	311ft 8in (95.0m) 27ft 3in (8.3m) 15ft 0in (4.1m)
Propulsion main engines* power electric motors* power battery* shafts	4 x General Motors 2 x 1,535bhp 4 x General Electric 4 x 1,375shp 2 x 126 Exide cells two	4 x General Motors 4 x 1,535bhp 4 x General Electric 4 x 1,375shp 2 x 126 Exide two	4 x Fairbanks, Morse 4 x 1, 600bhp 2 x General Electric 2 x 2,700shp 2 x 126 Gould cells two
Performance speed: surface submerged range: surfaced submerged maximum diving depth	20.25kt 8.75kt 11,000nm/10kt 48hr/2kt 300ft (91m)	20.25kt 8.75kt 11,000nm/10kt 48hr/2kt 400ft (122m)	20.25kt 8.75kt 11,000nm/10kt 48hr/2kt 400ft (122m)
Weapons TT location torpedoes guns	10 x 21in (533mm) bow – 6, stern – 4 24 1 x 3in (76mm) 2 x 0.5in MG 2 x 0.3in MG	10 x 21in (533mm) bow – 4, stern – 4 24 1 x 3in (76mm) 2 x 0.5in MG 2 x 0.3in MG	10 x 21in (533mm) bow – 6, stern – 4 28 1 x 3in (76mm) 2 x 0.5in MG
Complement	81 (wartime)		

* Various different makes of diesel, electric motors and batteries were installed.

** A few more were completed after the war; see next section.

and only 119 were actually completed. There were nine war losses, the low number being due to the fact that the Balaos entered service late in the war.

Externally, the Tench-class was virtually indistinguishable from the Balao-class, but there were many internal differences. Combat experience resulted in a major rearrangement of the ballast and fuel tanks to make them less vulnerable to damage, while further rearrangements of living and storage space forward resulted in a further four torpedoes being shipped.

Although these are generally recorded as three separate classes, the differences, apart from the stronger steel introduced in the Balao-class, were minimal, and, in any case, many changes were retrofitted into older boats as they entered refit. As in other navies, gun armament varied widely between boats and local commanders and commanding officers often added or removed

Above: Gato-class Perch (SS-313), here seen post-war.

weapons according to their perceived requirements. The original Gatos, for example, were built with a platform suitable for a 5.5in (140mm) gun, but were actually completed with the standard 3in (76mm) gun. However, Rear-Admiral Lockwood, the Commander Submarines Pacific (COMSUBPAC), soon ensured that as many 4in (102mm) and 5in (127mm) guns were mounted as he could lay his hands on.

A few Gatos operated in the Atlantic for a short period in 1943, during which one was lost and another sank a U-boat, but that apart they spent their entire war in the Pacific, where they bore the lion's share of the submarine war against the Japanese. They were capable of very long patrols and their main task was to carry out offensive action in enemy sea lanes, although they were also used to lay mines, run supplies to Philippine guerrillas, reconnoitre landing beaches, pick up downed U.S. aircrew, and even carry out shore bombardments. Their primary targets were enemy merchant ships, the highest tonnage sunk being by *Flasher* (SS-249) with 100,231grt, although *Barb* (SS-220), *Rasher* (SS-269) and *Silversides* (SS-236) were close behind with over 90,000grt each.

When the war ended there were large numbers of these boats in service with more under construction. Further orders were immediately cancelled but Gatos, Balaos and Tenches proved not only to have long lives but also to be very adaptable, providing the U.S. Navy with its main body of submarines well into the 1960s, while some remained in service with foreign navies right up to the end of the 20th century (see Guppy-class).

Below: Gato (SS-212), as she appeared in August 1942.

Above: Mingo *(SS-261) after post-war transfer to Japan.*

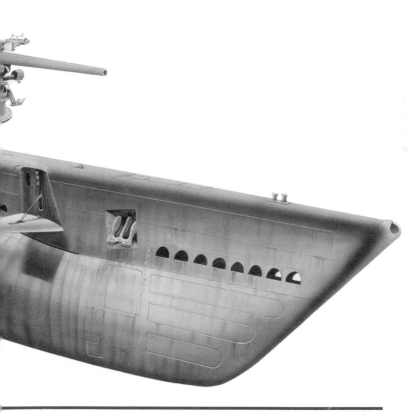

Diesel-Electric Patrol Submarines 1947-2002

During the 1950s it appeared that the days of the diesel-electric submarine were numbered and that all future boats in the major navies would be nuclear-powered; indeed, some of the smaller European navies, such as the Royal Netherlands Navy, also seriously considered nuclear propulsion. However, matters have not worked out that way and at the start of the 21st century there are large and growing numbers of diesel-electric submarines in service around the world, with the number of navies operating such boats gradually increasing, although the production capability clearly exceeds the present requirements by a considerable margin. Even the advent of non-nuclear air-independent propulsion systems has not seriously affected the position, since for the foreseeable future such systems will be in addition to and not replacements for diesel-electric propulsion.

The influence of even a very small number of such boats has been demonstrated on numerous occasions as they have exerted strategic and operational effects out of all proportion to their numbers. Thus, just one Argentine submarine was at sea in the 1982 Falklands War, but it caused extreme concern in the British task force, which had no choice but to deploy a sizable ASW force to keep it away from its two vital aircraft carriers. Similarly, the three Russian Kilo-class boats purchased by Iran have changed the naval strategic equation in the Gulf, and the three Swedish Sjöormen-class boats purchased by Singapore have had a similar impact in South-East Asian waters.

The position today is that among the designers and builders of submarines for export, the position of Germany is almost unassailable and in every international competition the German entry is the one to beat.

China

As it has done throughout its history, China has taken a very long-term view and has slowly built up a large diesel-electric submarine fleet, together with the appropriate design and construction capabilities. Its diesel-electric submarine designs have been developed from Russian-supplied boats, and it has achieved a few export orders, notably four to Egypt in the 1980s. It continues to build its

own designs in small numbers and has also recently purchased four Kilo-class boats from Russia.

France
Germany's main competitor as an exporter is France, which still designs and builds diesel-electric boats, even though the French Navy itself does not intend to buy any more. Currently, three Agosta 90s are building for Pakistan and two Scorpénes for Chile, while France is also actively competing for other orders, especially from Malaysia and Saudi Arabia.

Germany
The present influence of German designers cannot be underestimated. There are five different versions of the Type 209 on offer, with 53 in service around the world with 13 navies. Other German submarines in service are two TR-1700s in Argentina, three Dolfin-class in Israel and six Ula-class in Norway, and there are firm orders for four Type 212 for Germany and two for Italy, with a further three Type 214 on order for Greece. One reason for the German advantage is a readiness to help potential customers establish their own submarine-building facilities, with particular success having been achieved in Turkey.

Great Britain
The last diesel-electric boat to be completed was HMS *Unicorn* in 1993, although refitting the four Upholders for delivery to Canada brought some more work to the yard. It appears unlikely, however, that the UK will build any further diesel-electric boats, concentrating instead on SSNs for the Royal Navy.

Italy
Italy was once among the great designers and builders of submarines. The last

Below: Soviet Tango-class is inspected by a NATO helicopter.

Italian-designed submarine was completed in 1995. In the 1990s Italcantieri offered to sell two reconditioned Toti-class boats to the United Arab Emirates (UAE), which would have been followed by an order for new builds, but it was not taken up. At home, the Italian Navy spent a long time considering an indigenous design for its next class, but has now ordered two German-designed Type 212As, with an option on two more, although these will be built in Italy.

Japan
The JMSDF has one of the largest and certainly the most modern diesel-electric fleets in the world. It has followed a careful policy of construction by two yards which have built a succession of evolutionary designs, with new boats being commissioned at a rate of one per year. This has ensured an up-to-date fleet, coupled with a steady and predictable flow of work in the shipyards, and it is probably fortunate for the submarine-exporting countries that Japanese industry is prevented by law from exporting warlike material.

North Korea
The North Koreans have built small numbers of Romeos and have also designed and built their own coastal submarines, all for employment in the decades-old confrontation with South Korea.

Netherlands
The most recent Dutch-built submarine to be completed was the final Walrus-class boat in 1993, but the Dutch company RDM has been very active in trying to obtain foreign orders. In 1995 RDM bought the two recently retired Zwaardvis-class boats from the Dutch Navy and has attempted to sell a rebuilt version to Egypt, Malaysia and a number of other customers. It also has a new design, the Moray-class, which has also been offered to Egypt and Malaysia, but again with no takers, so far. The most likely customer for the Moray-class is Egypt, but with the boats actually being built by Ingalls in the United States, which would not only enable the deal to be paid for by U.S. offshore procurement funds but would also help Ingalls to reacquire a diesel-electric building expertise.

Russia
Russia still operates a small number of Kilos and has exported to several countries, including 10 to India and four to China. It is also trying to secure an order from South Korea for two refitted Russian Navy boats, together with two new construction boats, but without success, so far. Russian designer Rubin has also offered a new design, the Amur, for export, but it has not yet attracted any orders.

Spain
The Spanish yard IZAR is currently assembling two French-designed Scorpéne-class boats for Chile which, the company hopes, will lead to a contract for a Daphne-replacement for the Spanish Navy.

Sweden
Like Japan, but on a much smaller scale, Sweden produces a steady stream of its own designs for the Royal Swedish Navy and this domestic requirement will continue. For many years the Swedish policy of neutrality precluded exports, but this was relaxed to enable Kockums to achieve a major success with the Collins-class for Australia, although the project has since hit snags. Sweden has also sold four elderly submarines to Singapore which gives it a possible advantage for a future order when these need to be replaced. Sweden is also the leader in the Nordic project for a new submarine for the Danish, Norwegian and Swedish navies.

Taiwan

In early 2001, the United States promised Taiwan a large package of naval equipment, including eight new diesel-electric submarines for delivery starting in 2010. This is an extremely large contract which has excited considerable international interest, primarily because the USA, as described below, has no design or manufacturing base for diesel-electric boats. The proposal has also aroused extreme indignation from Beijing which is bringing very strong pressure on any country considering involvement in the deal, as it did with the Netherlands over the Hai Lung-class order, and both Germany and the Netherlands were very quick in disassociating themselves from the deal.

United States

The world's greatest naval power, the United States has had an all-nuclear submarine fleet since the 1980s, which has meant that it is unable to supply diesel-electric boats to allies. There can be no doubt that the technical and industrial might of the USA could design and build a new class of diesel-electric submarine if it wished to do so, but such a project would be extremely expensive. However, the prospect of an order for eight boats for Taiwan could be the spur that encourages a return to this field.

Building Facilities

When negotiating a submarine purchase, some countries have insisted that the contract must include assistance in establishing a domestic submarine construction facility; such countries have included Argentina, Australia, Brazil, India, Turkey, Greece, South Korea and Pakistan. This involves very considerable work in establishing the industrial base, and in transferring technical know-how in both submarine technology and advanced industrial techniques. This inevitably causes additional expense and usually results in major delays in the programme. In most cases the initial order is met, but the problems arise when new work must be obtained to keep the yard and workers employed and the indigenous navy has no requirement for further boats for at least a decade.

Below: German export Type 209 submarine for India.

Collins-class

AUSTRALIA

Type: patrol.
Total built: 6.
Completed: 1996-2001.
Displacement: surfaced 3,051 tons; submerged 3,353 tons.
Dimensions: length 253ft 10in (77.4m); beam 25ft 7in (7.8m); draught 23ft 0in (7.0m).
Propulsion: 3 x Garden-Island Hedemora B210 diesel generator sets, 3 x 2,000bhp; 1 x Jeumont-Schneider electric motor, 1 x 7,000shp; 1 x emergency propulsor, 100shp; one shaft.
Performance: surface – 10.5kt; submerged – 21kt; range surfaced 11,500nm at 10kt, submerged 480nm at 4kt.
Weapons: 6 x 21in (533mm) TT (bow); 23 x Harpoon SSM/Mk 48 torpedoes.
Complement: 42.

History: The Royal Australian Navy (RAN) operated a small number of submarines for many years, always British-built, but the six Oberon-class (qv) acquired in the 1970s proved to be the last of that particular line. Planning for a successor began in the early 1980s, the basic assumptions being that it would be a totally new design, tailored to meet RAN operational requirements, and most importantly, would be built in Australian yards using as many Australian materials and components as possible. A hard-fought international competition then took place which was eventually won by the Australian Submarine Corporation, a consortium composed (at that time) of Swedish submarine designers and builders, Kockums; the partially government-owned Australian Industrial Development Co (AIDC); and two Australian companies, Wormald International Ltd. and CBI Constructors Pty. The contract was placed on 18 May 1987 for what was then the largest and most complex defence project ever undertaken in Australia.

Kockums has designed and built a series of submarines for the Royal Swedish Navy, of which the largest is the current Gotland-class (qv), with a displacement of 1,494 tons and length of 198ft 9in (60.6m). The Collins-class is however, not only a totally new design but is also considerably larger, displacing 3,353 tons and with a length of 253ft 10in (77.4m). It is armed with six 21in (533mm) torpedo tubes for which it carries 23 weapons, a mix of Mk 48 torpedoes and UGM-84C Harpoon missiles. It is also fitted with a comprehensive range of the latest sensors and electronic equipment, and the entire system is controlled by a purpose-built fire-control system. Propulsion is by means of three Australian-built Hedemora diesel-generators and a single water-cooled 5,250kW electric motor driving a seven-bladed skewback propeller. From the second boat onwards the hull is totally covered in anechoic tiles.

The project has encountered problems, not only with the minor sub systems as is inevitable in any new project, but also with a number of major systems and components, the most important being the combat direction system. As a result, a great deal of remedial work has had to be done, at considerable extra cost and with consequent delays to the boats' entry into service, all of which has led to the project becoming embroiled in controversy. There have been numerous reviews, all trying to establish what went wrong why, and how to put it right, one of the most important being the McIntosh/Prescott Report to the Australian Minister for Defence dated 20 June 1999. All the problems are being addressed and progressively solved, including the most challenging of them all, software integration, and the Collins-class will undoubtedly become one of the most successful diesel-electric submarines in the first two decades of the 21st century, but it has been a salutary, expensive

Above: Collins-class **Farncomb** *(S-72) prior to her launch in December 1995. Four of the six boats are based at HMAS Stirling in Western Australia, and the other two at HMAS Platypus.*

and often painful experience.

In the early stages of the project the RAN had an option on two more boats and it was planned not only that these would be fitted with an air-independent propulsion (AIP) system but also that the first six boats would then be backfitted with the same AIP system. A number of AIP systems were examined, but in view of the problems experienced with the design the option on hulls #7 and #8 has been cancelled, and plans for AIP postponed indefinitely.

Below: Collins – biggest industrial project in Australian history.

Ming-class

Type: patrol.
Total built: 19.
Completed: 1975-onward.
Displacement: surfaced 1,584 tons; submerged 2,113 tons.
Dimensions: length 249ft 3in (76.0m); beam 24ft 10in (7.6m); draught 16ft 8in (5.1m).
Propulsion: 2 x Type 6E390ZC diesels, 2 x 2,600bhp; 2 x electric motors, 2 x 1,750shp; two shafts.
Performance: surface – 15kt, schnorkel – 10kt, submerged – 18kt; range schnorkel 8,000nm at 8kt, submerged 330nm at 4kt; maximum operating diving depth 984ft (300m).
Weapons: 8 x 21in (533mm) TT (bow – 6, stern – 2), 16 x torpedoes.
Complement: 55.

History: After it came into existence in 1949 the submarine arm of the People's Liberation Army Navy (PLAN) depended initially upon boats supplied from the Soviet Union, but a construction facility was established and copies of Soviet boats were then built under licence. Large numbers of Romeo-class boats were built as the PLAN's Project 033, but production eventually switched to the Project 035, known in the West as the Ming-class, with the first being launched in 1975. Production has continued at a slow rate since and at least 17 are now in service.

The Ming is based on the Romeo design but has a fuller hull, which is 2ft 0in (0.6m) shorter but 3ft 0in (0.9m) broader in the beam. Armament is eight

Delfinen-class

Type: coastal.
Total built: 4.
Completed: 1960-64.
Displacement: surfaced 595 tons; submerged 643 tons.
Dimensions: length 177ft 2in (54.0m); beam 15ft 5in (4.7m); draught 13ft 1in (4.0m).
Propulsion: 2 x Burmeister & Wain diesels, 2 x 600bhp; 2 x Brown-Boveri electric motors, 2 x 600shp; two shafts.
Performance: surface – 15kt; submerged – 15kt; range surfaced 4,000nm at 8kt; maximum operating diving depth 300ft (91m).
Weapons: 4 x 21in (533mm) TT (bow), 8 x torpedoes.
Complement: 33.

History: The Delfinen-class were the first submarines to be designed and built in Denmark after World War II. They were contemporary with the French Arethuse-class (qv) and similar in operational concept and size, although the Danish boats have twin propellers as opposed to the French boat's one. One of the four boats was paid for by U.S. Offshore Funds. Although the Danes have maintained a submarine construction capability, the Delfinen-class was the last to be designed by the Royal Copenhagen Dockyard and the next class, the Narvhalen-class, was a German design, built under licence. There was considerable hesitation about ordering a replacement for the Delfinen-class and eventually the Danes opted for purchasing a number of surplus Kobben-class boats from Norway and the Delfinens were stricken in 1983 (one), 1984 (one) and 1989 (two). Under present plans Denmark intends to remain part of the

Above: Ming-class, a Chinese improved-Romeo design.

torpedo tubes, of which two are in the stern, making this one of the very few modern submarines with stern tubes. A total of 16 torpedoes are carried, with reloads only for the bow tubes. The Ming is fitted with Chinese-designed diesels, which are a little more powerful than those installed in the Romeos. The Ming has been offered for export, but as of 2002 no foreign navy had taken up the offer.

Above: **Springgaren,** *of the Danish Delfinen-class.*

Viking consortium with Sweden and Norway to develop a common future submarine for all three navies.

La Créole-class

Type: patrol.
Total built: 5.
Completed: 1949-54.
Displacement: surfaced 970 tons; submerged 1,250 tons.
Dimensions: length 241ft 0in (73.5m); beam 21ft 0in (6.5m); draught 14ft 0in (4.2m).
Propulsion: 2 x Sulzer diesels, 2 x 1,500bhp; 2 x electric motors, 2 x 700shp; two shafts.
Performance: surface – 15.5kt, submerged 9.3kt; range surfaced 8,800nm at 10kt; maximum operating diving depth 330ft (100m).
Weapons: 10 x 21.7in (550mm) TT (bow – 4, amidships – 4, stern – 2); 1 x 3.5in (88mm) gun (first three only), 1 x 20mm AA.
Complement: 62.

History: When the French signed the Armistice in 1940 there were five half-built Aurore-class submarines lying in various French shipyards and one, *La Créole*, which had been towed semi-complete to England. After the war *La Créole*, still incomplete, was towed back to France and together with two of her sisters, *L'Africaine* and *L'Astrée*, was completed, entering service in 1949. The design was modernised to a certain extent, with a larger bridge tower and a surface armament of a single German 88mm gun (naval version) forward and a twin 20mm mounting aft. The number of torpedo tubes was also increased from 9 to 10, with 4 in the bows, 2 in the stern and 4 external tubes, 2 forward and 2 aft. Another two boats, *L'Artémis* and *L'Andromede*, were given a more

Narval-class

Type: patrol.
Total built: 6.
Completed: 1957-60.
Displacement: surfaced 1,635 tons; submerged 1,910 tons.
Dimensions: length 257ft 0in (78.4m); beam 26ft 0in (7.8m); draught 17ft 0in (5.2m).
Propulsion: 2 x Schneider diesels, 2 x 2,200bhp; 2 x electric motors, 2 x 2,500shp; two shafts.
Performance: surface – 16kt, submerged – 18kt; range surfaced 15,000nm at 8kt; maximum operating diving depth 656ft (200m).
Weapons: 8 x 21.7in (550mm) TT (bow – 6, stern [external] – 2), 14 x torpedoes.
Complement: 63.

History: In 1947 the French Navy issued its first post-war operational requirement for a submarine, whose capabilities were to include a submerged speed in excess of 16kt and a snorkelling range of 15,000nm. France had been allocated one of the German Type XXIs – *U-2518* – which had been commissioned into the *Marine Nationale* as the *Roland Morillot*, and this had a heavy influence on the design of the new boat, with the Narval-class bearing many similarities to the Type XXI. The French boats were, however, slightly larger, had marginally better performance, and, being free of wartime shortages and bombing attacks which had plagued the German programme, were much better built. They were armed with eight torpedo tubes of the unique French 21.7in (550mm) calibre, with six tubes in the bow and two, externally mounted,

Above: La Créole, *unfinished in 1940, was completed in 1949.*

substantial conversion with a large, streamlined fin and a schnorkel, similar to that in the U.S. Guppies (qv), while *L'Artémis* was also given the first of a new type of fire control equipment. *La Créole* was given a schnorkel in a subsequent refit. All were stricken and scrapped in the 1960s.

Above: Narval, *a design that was based on the German Type XXI.*

in the stern; there were six reloads for the bow tubes, none for the stern..

Six boats were built, *Narval, Marsouin, Dauphin, Requin, Espadon* and *Morse*, with the last two being completed in 1960. As built, Schneider two-stroke, seven-cylinder diesels were installed, but these were not totally satisfactory and were replaced by three SEMT-Pielstick 12-cylinder diesels in mid-life refits which took place between 1965 and 1970. The six boats served with the French Navy's Atlantic Squadron until the mid-1980s, when all but one were stricken and scrapped. The exception was *Dauphin*, which was used to test the bow section for the new Améthyste-class SSNs, the new structure increasing its length by 9ft 2in (2.8m); with this installed she continued in service until 1992 when she, too, was scrapped.

Arethuse-class

Type: attack *(sous-marins de chasse)*.
Total built: 4.
Completed: 1958-60.
Displacement: surfaced 869 tons; submerged 1,043 tons.
Dimensions: length 163ft 0in (49.7m); beam 19ft 0in (5.8m); draught 13ft 0in (4.0m).
Propulsion: 2 x SEMT-Pielstick diesels, 2 x 530bhp; 1 x electric motor, 1,300shp; one shaft.
Performance: surface – 12.5kt, submerged – 16kt.
Weapons: 4 x 21.7in (550mm) TT (bow), 8 x torpedoes.
Complement: 39.

History: The Arethuse-class were designed to meet an operational requirement for a *sous-marin de chasse*, a concept known in other navies as an "attack", "ASW" or "hunter-killer" submarine (see also U.S. Navy Barracuda-class). They were intended for service in the Mediterranean, where their mission was to prevent hostile submarines from attacking the considerable traffic expected in wartime between France's (then) North African colonies and Metropolitan France, particularly troop convoys. They were required to be particularly quiet and were, therefore, fitted with electric drive and one propeller, in which the single electric motor was driven either by the battery when submerged or by the twin diesel-generator sets when on the surface; ie, the diesels were not coupled to the shaft. All four boats – *Arethuse, Argonaute, Amazone* and *Ariane* – spent their entire operational careers in the Mediterranean. They were stricken between 1979 and 1982.

Daphné-class

Type: patrol.
Total built: 25.
Completed: 1964-70.
Displacement: surfaced 869 tons; submerged 1,043 tons.
Dimensions: length 190ft 0in (57.8m); beam 22ft 0in (6.8m); draught 17ft 0in (5.3m).
Propulsion: 2 x SEMT-Pielstick diesel-generator sets, 2 x 650bhp; 2 x electric motors, 2 x 800shp; two shafts.
Performance: surface – 13.5kt, submerged – 16kt; range surfaced 4,500nm at 5kt.
Weapons: 12 x 21.7in (550mm) TT (bow – 4, stern – 4, external – 4), 12 x torpedoes.
Complement: 45.

History: Following World War II the French Navy had some 14 different types of submarine in service, ranging in size from ocean-going to midgets, some of them 20 years old. It was, therefore, very necessary both to modernise and to standardise, and for the medium-sized boat they selected a new design, which was essentially a scaled-up version of the Arethuse-class. The new Daphné-class was the result of careful attention being paid to silent operation, with the hull shape subjected to extensive tank testing and all mooring equipment made retractable. Microphones were fitted around the hull which enabled crew members inside to monitor ambient noise levels and to regulate speed or manoeuvre accordingly. Armament was 12 21.7in (550mm) torpedo tubes, eight of them in the bows in two vertical rows of four, internally mounted, but

Above: Arethuse, designed for Mediterranean attack missions.

Above: Pakistan's Daphné-class Ghazi, built in France, bought from Portugal in December 1975

without reloads. The remaining four tubes were aft, all externally mounted in the casing, with two launching directly over the stern and two mounted further forward and launching at an angle of about 30 degrees.

The Daphné-class was an immediate success and 11 entered service with the French Navy between 1964 and 1970. A further 10 were built in France for sale to foreign navies – South Africa (3); Pakistan (3); and Portugal (4) – while four were built in Spain with French technical help. Pakistan subsequently increased its fleet to four by purchasing one of the Daphnés from Portugal. One of these Pakistani boats, *Hangor,* sank the Indian Navy frigate, *Khukri,* during the 1971 war.

The class suffered a series of disasters in French service, starting with the inexplicable disappearance of *Minerve* in the Mediterranean in 1968. This was followed by the equally mysterious disappearance of *Eurydice* in 1970. These tragic losses were nearly followed by a third in 1971 when *Flore's* schnorkel sprang a leak but an alert captain reacted promptly and saved his boat. Modifications were quickly implemented and there were no more incidents; equally, there were no further overseas sales.

All the navies involved carried out mid-life updates to their boats. The French boats were stricken in between 1988 and 1998, while the Spanish boats

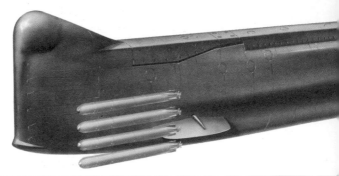

Agosta (S-70/A-90B)-class FRANCE

Type: attack.
Total built: 10.
Completed: 1977-2005.
Displacement: surfaced 1,510 tons; submerged 1,760 tons.
Dimensions: length 221ft 9in (67.6m); beam 22ft 4in (6.8m); draught 17ft 8in (5.4m).
Propulsion: 2 x SEMT-Pielstick diesel-generator sets, 2 x 850kW; 1 x electric motor, 3,500kW; 1 x creep motor, 23hp; battery 320 cells; one shaft.
Performance: surface – 12.5kt, schnorkel – 10.5kt, submerged – 20.5kt; range schnorkel 8,500nm at 9kt, submerged 280nm at 3kt; maximum operating diving depth 984ft (300m).
Weapons: 4 x 21.7in (550mm) TT (bow), 20 x SM-39 Exocet/torpedoes.
Complement: 54.
Specifications are for Agosta S-70, as built.

History: The Agosta-class (S-70) is an ocean-going design, which was authorised in the French Navy's 1970-75 programme, with the four boats for the French Navy entering service in 1977 (two) and 1978 (two). This was followed by two export orders. The Spanish order was for four, which were built under licence by Bazan (now IZAR) at Cartagena and entered service in 1983 (two), 1985 (one) and 1986 (one). The other order was for two for South Africa to be built in France, but construction was well in hand in 1977 when the order had to be cancelled because of the United Nations arms embargo. Work continued at a slower pace for a time, but Pakistan then took up the order in November 1978 and the boats entered service in 1979 and 1980.

will remain in service until at least 2003. The others will remain in service with the Pakistani, Portuguese and South African navies for a few years after that, meaning that the Daphné design will have been in service for at least 40 years, no mean record for a submarine.

Above: The Daphné-class was sold to three foreign navies.

Right: Two Agosta-class, last diesel-electric boats for the French Navy.

The French then continued marketing the design for some years but without success until 1994 when a further contract was signed with Pakistan for three boats designated Agosta A-90B and known in Pakistan as the Khalid-class. The A-90B has virtually identical measurements to the S-70, but the hull is fabricated from HLES-80 steel (equivalent to the U.S. HY-100), published figures giving an operating depth of 1,050ft (320m), although it is probably rather more. The A-90B also has entirely new internal equipment, including an integrated weapon/fire control system and greater automation, which enable the crew to be reduced from 54 to 36. The first boat was built entirely in France and delivered in September 1999, while sections for the second were fabricated in France and sent to Pakistan for assembly, fitting out and completion in 2002/03. The third boat is to be built entirely in Pakistan for an estimated completion in 2006, but is to a modified design, incorporating the French-designed air-independent propulsion system MESMA.

Hai-class (ex-Type XXIII) GERMANY

Type: coastal.
Total built: 2.
Completed: 1957.
Displacement: surfaced 234 tons; submerged 275 tons.
Dimensions: length 118ft 6n (36.1m); beam 9ft 9in (3.0m); draught 12ft 3in (3.7m).
Propulsion: 1 x Mercedes-Benz diesel, 635bhp; 1 x electric motor, 580shp; 1 x "creep" motor, 35shp; battery 62 cells; one shaft.
Performance: surface – 9.7kt, submerged – 12.5kt; range surfaced 1,350nm at 9k, submerged 285nm at 6kt.
Weapons: 2 x 21in (533mm) TT (bow), 2 x torpedoes.
Complement: 17.

Type 201/205-classes GERMANY

Type: short-range patrol.

Type	201	205
Total built	3	10
Completed	1962	1962-69
Displacement surfaced submerged	395 tons 433 tons	419 tons 455 tons
Dimensions length beam draught	142ft 9in (43.5m) 15ft 0in (4.6m) 13ft 0in (4.0m)	144ft 5in (44.0m) 15ft 0in (4.6m) 13ft 0in (4.0m)
Propulsion diesel generators power electric motors power shafts	2 x Mercedes-Benz 2 x 600bhp 1 1 x 1,500shp one	

History: These two boats were built during World War II as Type XXIII and commissioned in 1945 as *U-2365* and *U-2367*, but both were sunk prior to the German surrender, the former in a bomb attack (8 May 1945) and the latter after a collision (5 May 1945). The new Federal German Navy, the *Bundesmarine,* was formed in 1955 and in 1956 these two boats were raised and completely rebuilt as *Hai* (UW-20) and *Hecht* (UW-21). The original M.W.M. diesel was replaced by a modern Mercedes-Benz unit and a new, larger bridge tower was fitted. Propulsion was totally electric, with the diesels being used only to recharge the battery, and all propulsion being by the electric motor. They were employed as training boats for the new navy submarine crews. *Hai* foundered in the North Sea (14 September 1966) and *Hecht* was scrapped in 1969.

Left: Two Type XXIIIs were raised in the 1950s.

Above right: The newly rebuilt Hai *leaves the dock.*

Performance	
speed: surface	10kt
submerged	17.5kt
range: schnorkel	3,950nm/4kt
submerged	228nm/4kt
maximum	
diving depth	492ft (150m)
Weapons	
TT	8 x 21in (533mm)
location	bow
torpedoes	8
Complement	21

History: The Type 201 was designed by the German submarine design bureau *Ingenieurkontor Lübeck* (IKL) as West Germany's first post-war class for employment primarily in the Baltic. It was decided that the hull should be constructed of austenitic (non-magnetic) steel and the order for 12 was placed in March 1959, with the first, *U-1* (S-180), launched in October 1961, followed by *U-2* and *U-3* in early 1962. Unfortunately, the project hit a major problem as it transpired that the water of the Baltic had a highly corrosive effect on the particular type of non-magnetic steel then in use; the effect was so rapid and so severe that *U-1* and *U-2* had to be taken out of commission within months. *U-3* was also completed but was loaned to Norway as a training boat, since Norwegian waters had no effect on the steel.

Construction of the next five boats, *U-4* to *U-8*, was already well in hand and had to be allowed to continue, but their exteriors were completely covered in a thin film of tin, which meant that severe constraints had to be placed on their operational performance. Meanwhile, construction of the remaining boats, *U-9* to *U-12*, was postponed until a totally new, non-corrosive, non-magnetic steel had been developed and they were then completed to the same design but with the new hull. Finally, *U-1* and *U-2* were returned to the yard, where their old hulls were removed and replaced by the new material. *U-3* was never rebuilt.

After all this, there were some minor differences between the boats; *U-11* and *U-12* had different rudders from the rest, while there were four different varieties of bridge. *U-4* to *U-8* spent their entire service from 1963 to the mid-1970s with the training organisation, after which they were scrapped. The remainder served on into the 1990s, except for *U-11* and *U-12* which were still in service in 2002 having been extensively modified as the Type 205A and 205B, respectively. *U-11* will be stricken in 2003 but *U-12* will remain in service until 2006.

There was also a Type 202, a very small (137 tons submerged displacement) coastal submarine. Two were completed in 1966, but after extensive trials it was decided that they were far too small and

Type 206-class and Gal-class

Type: patrol.
Total built: 18.
Completed: 1972-74.
Displacement: surfaced 456 tons; submerged 500 tons.
Dimensions: length 159ft 6in (48.6m); beam 15ft 0in (4.6m); draught 14ft 0in (4.3m).
Propulsion: 2 x Mercedes-Benz diesel generators, 2 x 600bhp; 1 x electric motor, 1,500shp; batteries 3 x 92 cells; one shaft.
Performance: surface – 10kt, submerged – 17.5kt; range surfaced 3,950nm at 4kt, submerged 200nm at 5kt; maximum operating diving depth 492ft (150m).
Weapons: 8 x 21in (533mm) TT (bow), 16 x torpedoes.
Complement: 21.
Specifications are for Type 206, as built.

History: Designed, like all post-war German submarines, by the IKL design bureau, the order for the first 12 (*U-13* to *U-24*) Type 206 was placed in 1969, followed by the order for *U-25* to *U-30* in 1970. The boats were launched between 1971 and 1974, with production being shared between Rheinstahl-Nordeseewerke, Emden (10), and Howaldtswerke, Kiel (8). The design was little changed from the Type 201/205, except that there was a new rounded bow housing the sonar dome.

Right: **U-30*, fitted with a strap-on mine "girdle".*

the type was not put into production. The two completed boats were scrapped in the early 1970s.

Below: U-1 after conversion to test an air-independent system.

Improvements include better manoeuverability, greater silencing, and the ability to launch wire-guided torpedoes. They can carry up to 24 mines internally in lieu of torpedoes, but can be fitted with a strap-on mine "girdle" carrying a total of 24 mines without reducing the number of torpedoes. Twelve boats were upgraded to Type 206A standard, which included updated electronics, new periscopes and improved crew accommodation.

Five of the six unconverted Type 206 boats were to have been sold to Indonesia and matters proceeded to the point where, while still in German waters, they were manned by Indonesian crews and flying the Indonesian flag, but the sale was then cancelled and the boats handed back to the Germans in 1998. All six Type 206s were then scrapped. Disposal of the Type 206As started with one in 2002, and will continue with one in 2004 and two in 2005, but the details for the remainder have yet to be announced.

Three of a modified version of the Type 206 were built for the Israeli Navy as the Gal-class, although, for political reasons, the boats had to be built by the British shipyard, Vickers, Barrow. The most obvious external difference was the larger sail which was intended to accommodate an anti-helicopter missile system, although this was never actually installed. They were regularly updated, with Sub-Harpoon being installed in 1983, making them by far the smallest

Type 207-class (Kobben-class)

GERMANY (NORWAY)

Type: coastal patrol.
Total built: 15.
Completed: 1964-67.
Displacement: surfaced 370 tons; submerged 530 tons.
Dimensions: length 149 ft 0in (45.4m); beam 15ft 0in (4.6m); draught 14ft 0in (4.3m).
Propulsion: 2 x Maybach diesel generators, 2 x 600bhp; 1 x electric motor, 1,200shp; batteries 3 x 92 cells; one shaft.
Performance: surface – 10kt, submerged – 17kt; range schnorkel 5,000nm at 8kt, submerged 141nm at 6kt; maximum operating diving depth 623ft (190m).
Weapons: 8 x 21`in (533mm) TT (bow), 8 x torpedoes.
Complement: 18.
Specifications for Type 207, as built

History: After World War II the Royal Norwegian Navy used five British U- class boats, supplemented in 1950 by three German Type VIICs and one Type XXIII supplied from stocks held by the British. When it was decided to obtain more modern boats, the Norwegians turned to Germany and in 1959 ordered 15 boats from Nordeseewerke, Emden, with half the funding provided by the United States. The design was based on that of the German Type 207, but with a strengthened hull to allow deeper diving in the waters off the Norwegian coasts. One boat, *Svenner* (S-309), was 3ft 3in (1m) longer than the others,

submarines to carry this weapon. Updated sensors and fire control equipment were fitted in 1994/95, but they were all stricken in 1999. At one stage a sale to Ecuador was under serious consideration, but fell through.

Above: **U-16***, an early Type 206.*

Above: **Kobben***, one of the Type 207s built for Norway.*

since it is used for officer training and mounts a second periscope.

Six boats were modernised in 1989-91, being lengthened by 6ft 7in (2m), given new MTU diesel engines, and fitted with new electronics and a modernised fire control system. In 2002 four of these remained in service, but are likely to be progressively retired, with the last going in 2006. Of the unmodernised boats, one was transferred to the U.S. Navy in 1991, four were stricken and scrapped and four were transferred to Denmark between 1989 and 1991. (Only three were purchased by Denmark, but one was lost on tow during delivery, and was replaced by the Norwegians.)

Type 209-class

Type (Example)	Type 209/1100 (Greece)	Type 209/1200 (S. Korea)	Type 209/1300 (Venezuela)	Type 209/1400 (Turkey)	Type 209/1500 (India)
Displacement surfaced submerged	1,100 tons 1,207 tons	1,100 tons 1,285 tons	1,265 tons 1,295 tons	1,464 tons 1,586 tons	1,660 tons 1,850 tons
Dimensions length beam draught	177ft 6in (54.1m) 20ft 3in (6.2m) 19ft 5in (5.9m)	184ft 0in (56.1m) 20ft 4in (6.2m) 17ft 11in (5.5m)	200ft 10in (61.2m) 20ft 8in (6.3m) 18ft 0in (5.5m)	203ft 5in (62.0m) 20ft 4in (6.2m) 18ft 0in (5.5m)	211ft 3in (64.4m) 21ft 3in (6.5m) 19ft 8in (6.0m)
Propulsion diesels power electric motors power battery shafts	4 x M.T.U. 4 x 550bhp 1 x Siemens 5,000shp 4 x 120 cells one	4 x M.T.U. 4 x 800bhp 1 x Siemens 5,000shp 4 x 120 cells one	4 x M.T.U. 4 x 600bhp 1 x Siemens 4,600shp 4 x 120 cells one	4 x M.T.U. 4 x 800bhp 1 x Siemens 5,000shp 4 x 120 cells one	4 x M.T.U. 4 x 800bhp 2 x Siemens 4,600shp 4 x 132 cell one
Performance speed: surface submerged range: schnorkel submerged maximum diving depth	11.5kt 22kt 8,600nm/4kt 230nm/8kt 820ft (250m)	10kt 22kt 6,000nm/8kt 230nm/8kt 820ft (250m)	11kt 21.5kt 8,200nm/8kt 400nm/4kt 820ft (250m)	11kt 21.5kt 8,200nm/8kt 400nm/4kt 1,050ft (320m)	11kt 22kt 13,000nm/10kt 8,000nm/8kt 853ft (260m)
Weapons TT location torpedoes/ missiles	8 bow 14	8 bow 14	8 bow 14	8 bow 14	8 bow 14
Complement	31	34	32	30	40

History: The German Type 209 is one of the most important diesel-electric submarines in the world. Fifty-one are in service with 13 navies and construction has taken place in Germany and in five other countries under licence: Argentina, Brazil, India, South Korea and Turkey. In 2002, firm orders were in place for a further 12 and others are in the pipeline. The Type 209 first came onto the market in the mid-1960s, at a time when several smaller navies wanted to purchase submarines for the first time, while many existing operators were starting to look for replacements for their second-hand U.S. and British World War II submarines, both because they were getting old and because they required high levels of crewing: 86 men for a Guppy III, for example. At the time only a few new Western submarine designs were available, and all were large, expensive to buy and to operate, and designed for Cold War operations, with few concessions to export requirements. Export submarines were available from the USSR, but no Western and few Latin American or Asian customers wanted to deal with the Soviets while the Cold War lasted. Thus, the Type 209 provided a good solution: a powerful weapons system at a reasonable price, and with almost a century of German submarine experience behind it; above all, it was designed specifically for export, but actively backed, especially where training was concerned, by the *Bundesmarine.*

The Type 209 is a single-hull design with two main ballast tanks, and forward and after trim tanks. Forward and after ends are free-flooding, as is the sail.. There is an electric drive system, with four M.T.U. diesels and four A.E.G. generators. The original engine was the MTU 493-V12, but recent boats and refits are using the MTU 396-V8, which has lower specific fuel consumption, reduced noise levels and greater time between overhauls. Most versions have four 120-cell batteries delivering 11,500 ampere-hours and weighing some 257 tons, driving a single A.E.G. electric motor, the exception being the Indian Type 209/1500 which has four 132-cell batteries and two motors. Earlier Type 209s had a five-bladed propeller, but the latest versions have a large-diameter, seven-bladed, skew-back propeller whose slow rate of revolution allied to the low propeller load results in a highly efficient propulsion system. The hull is constructed of HY 80 steel, but could be constructed of non-magnetic steel if a customer wished, although this would be a very expensive option and no nation has yet requested it. Cruising range is some 400nm between two snorting periods, based on a speed of 4 kt and 80 per cent battery discharge, and the total cruising range is more than 12,000nm at 4kt submerged. Provisions are carried for 50-day patrols.

Two air-independent propulsion (AIP) options are now on offer, both of which would require a plug-in section some 19ft 8in (6m) long to be inserted immediately abaft the sail. The systems use either fuel cells or closed-cycle diesels, both with liquid oxygen for the reaction process.

There are five basic models, the Types 209/1100, /1200, /1300, /1400 and /1500, the second figure denoting the submerged displacement. In essence,

Below: **Atilay,** *Type 209/1400 for Turkey.*

TYPE 209 - ORDERS/DELIVERIES

| Type | Country | Orders | | Entered | In Service |
		Number	Total	Service	2002
209/1100	Greece	4	4	1971-72	4
209/1200	Argentina*	2		1974	1
	Colombia	2		1975	2
	Greece	4		1979-80	4
	Korea, South**	9		1993-?	8
	Peru	6		1974-83	6
	Turkey	6	29	1976-90	6
209/1300	Ecuador	2		1977-78	2
	Indonesia	2		1981	2
	Venezuela	2	6	1976-77	2
209/1400	Brazil	5		1989- 2003	4
	Chile	2		1984	2
	South Africa	3		2005-07	0
	Turkey	8	18	1994-2006	4
209/1500	India	6	6	1986-2005	4
	TOTAL		63		51

* 1 stricken in 1997.

** Last one may not be completed.

the extra size is obtained by stretching the pressure hull to enable extra fuel or additional sensors to be carried, or, in the case of the Indian Type 1500, a Gabler rescue sphere, the only such system installed in any Western submarine.

Argentina

Argentina ordered two Type 209/1200s in 1968, which were built in four sections by Howaldtswerke (HDW) at Kiel, Germany, and shipped to Argentina for assembly in Buenos Aires at the Rio Santiago Navy Yard. On the outbreak

Above: **San Luis**, *a Type 209/1200 of the Argentine Navy.*

of the Falklands (Malvinas) War in 1982 both immediately went to sea to counter the British task force, although *Salta* returned due to a mechanical problem and then remained in harbour for the rest of the conflict. *San Luis* carried out two attacks, launching torpedoes on both occasions, but scored no hits; the reason for the failure of the torpedoes has never been established, at least in public. Despite the lack of actual hits, the campaign by *San Luis* caused the British task force a serious problem and remains an excellent example of the influence that can be exercised by even one quiet submarine. *Salta* underwent a mid-life modernisation 1988-95 and was fitted with new engines, weapons and electrical systems. *San Luis* was stricken in 1997.

Brazil

The order for Type 209/1400 Mod. 3 boats (Tupi-class), signed in 1984, was Brazil's first ever order from a German shipyard. The original plan was to purchase six boats, of which one would be built in Germany and the remaining five in Brazil. Following lengthy delays the total to be built in Brazil was reduced to three in 1992 and the last of these (and fourth in total) was completed in 1999. An order for another boat was, however, reinstated in 1994 and this boat, *Tikuna* (S-34), will be completed in 2003. This will be to a greatly improved design, being 2ft 9in (0.85m) longer and fitted with new diesels, a different electric motor and more modern command-and-control, electronic and sensor equipment. All Brazilian Type 209/1400s carry eight reload torpedoes for their tubes, for a total of 16, whereas all other Type 209s can accommodate only six reloads. A plan to build a Brazilian-designed diesel-electric successor to the Tupi-class was cancelled in 1993 and work is now proceeding on a nuclear-powered design.

Chile

The Chilean Navy ordered two Type 209/1400s in 1980, which were delivered in 1984. These submarines are of standard IKL design except that both have the sail and associated masts raised by 19.7in (50cm) to cope with the high waves encountered off the Chilean coast. While many other Type 209 users return their submarines to Germany for refitting by HKW, the Chilean Navy uses its own ASMAR navy yard, at Talcahuano, and both these boats have undergone 10-month refits there, *Thompson* completing in late 1990 and *Simpson* in 1991. At one stage the Chilean Navy planned to buy two more Type 209s but this was cancelled, following which serious consideration was given to the purchase of the four redundant British Upholder-class submarines (qv), but this came to nought. An order was placed in 1997 for two French-designed Scorpéne-class boats, with one being built by DCN, Cherbourg, the other by IZAR, Cartagena (formerly Bazan), for delivery in 2004/2005.

Colombia
The two Colombian Type 209/1200s were ordered in 1971 and delivered in 1975, and are virtually identical to the Greek Glavkos-class. Both were refitted by HDW, Kiel, in 1990-91, which included a complete replacement of the main batteries. The Colombian Navy has a requirement for two more submarines and has shown an interest in more new Type 209s as well as the two Type 1700s (qv) offered for sale by Argentina, but funding has never been available.

Ecuador
Ecuador ordered two Type 209/1300s in 1974, which were delivered in 1977/78. Both underwent major refits at HDW in Germany in 1983-84 and a local refit in 1993-94. The Chilean ASMAR yard has made a bid to carry out their next refit, but this has yet to be accepted.

Greece
The Hellenic Navy was the first customer for the Type 209; the initial order for four Type 209/1100s was placed in the mid-1960s and they were delivered in 1971-72. They underwent a major modernisation in the 1990s, bringing them up to the same standard as the German Navy's Type 206s and extending their lives well beyond the nominal 30-year point, which was reached in 2001-2002. The Hellenic Navy took delivery of a further four Type 209/1200s in 1979-80, a lengthened version of the Type 209/1100 with additional fuel bunkerage. The modernisation of the Type 209/1100s having been completed, the Type 209/1200s are now undergoing the same process. The Hellenic Navy has ordered three of the new Type 214 for delivery from 2009 onwards.

India
The Indian contract was signed in December 1981 and covered the construction in Germany of two Type 209/1500 submarines; the supply of `packages' for the building of two more boats at Mazagon, Bombay; training specialists for the design and construction of the Mazagon pair; logistic services during the trials and early part of the commissions; and consultation services in Bombay. The two German-built boats were laid down in 1982 and arrived in India in 1987. The third boat was laid down in Mazagon in June 1984, but work was delayed by assembly problems due to faulty welding, a problem by no means unique to the Mazagon yard. A plan to build two more was cancelled on several occasions, but finally given the go-ahead in 1999, with delivery scheduled for 2004/05. The Type 209/1500 is the largest variant of the German design and one unusual feature is the IKL-designed, integrated escape sphere, which can carry the full crew of 40 men. The sphere sits just forward of the sail, has an oxygen supply for eight hours, and can withstand pressures at least as great as those that can be withstood by the submarine's pressure hull.

Indonesia
These two submarines were ordered in 1977 and delivered in 1981. They underwent major refits at HDW during 1986-89, a process the Indonesian Navy considered to take too long and to be too expensive. As a result the next refits in the mid/late 1990s were carried out in Indonesia. Indonesia has been seeking more submarines for years, one possibility being two more Type 209s, while the Netherlands is known to have offered the two redundant Zwaardvis-class submarines.

Republic of Korea (RoK)
The ROK ordered three Type 209/1200 boats in late 1987, the first being built at Kiel and handed over in October 1992 and the other two assembled by Daewoofrom material packages transported from Germany; these were

commissioned in 1994-95. A second batch of three was ordered in October 1989 and a third batch, also of three, in January 1994. The first batch of Korean Type 209/1200 are very similar to those built for the Turkish Navy, with a heavy dependence on Atlas Elektronik sensors and STN torpedoes, but there has been a progressively greater Korean content in each boat as it is built.

Peru

The Peruvian boats were ordered in pairs: SS 35 and SS 36 in 1973; SS 31 and SS 32 in 1976; and SS 33 and SS 34 in 1977. All have undergone a mid-life modernisation refit.

Turkey

The Turkish Navy operated a sizeable force of ex-U.S. Navy World War II submarines for some years and then decided in the late 1960s to purchase modern submarines and selected the Type 209/1200, not least because HDW were ready to help establish a shipyard in Turkey. The first three of the first order were built at HDW, Kiel, with Turkish technicians and artificers under training, and the boats were delivered in 1975-78. The next three were then built at Gölcük Navy Yard with technical help form HDW, these boats being delivered rather more slowly, with one each in 1981, 1985 and 1990. These will all be modernised in the current decade. The initial order was for 12 Type 209/1200s but was stopped at six because the Turkish Navy decided to build six of the larger Type 209/1400. The order for first two was signed in November 1987 and the option on a further pair was taken up in 1993, all built at the Gölcük Navy Yard with assistance from HDW. However, the total order is now for eight. These boats, the Preveze-class, are 8ft 6in (2.6m) longer than the earlier class, have more advanced electronics, and can launch both Sub-Harpoon missiles and Tigerfish Mk 24 Mod 2 torpedoes, giving them considerably more hitting power.

Venezuela

The Venezuelan Navy originally planned to procure four submarines, but financial considerations limited this to two, which were delivered in 1976/77. Both were refitted at HDW, Kiel, in the early 1980s and again in the early 1990s. The latter included slightly lengthening the hull to accommodate a new sonar dome, raising the forward casing and installing new engines, fire-control, sonar and attack periscopes.

Below: **Nanggala**, *Type 209/1300 of the Indonesian Navy.*

Type 210 (Ula-class) GERMANY (NORWAY)

Type: patrol.
Total built: 6.
Completed: 1989-92.
Displacement: surfaced 1,040 tons; submerged 1,150 tons.
Dimensions: length 193ft 7in (59.0m); beam 17ft 8in (5.4m); draught 15ft 1in (4.6m).
Propulsion: 2 x M.T.U. diesels, 2 x 1,260bhp; 1 x Siemens electric motor, 6,000shp; one shaft.
Performance: surface – 11kt, submerged – 23kt; range schnorkel 5,000nm at 8kt; maximum operating diving depth 820ft (250m).
Weapons: 8 x 21in (533mm) TT (bow), 14 x torpedoes.
Complement: 20.

History: When it was decided to replace half the Kobben-class the result was the most expensive project ever undertaken by the Royal Norwegian Navy (RNorN). Designated the Ula-class (known in Germany as the Type 210) the contract for six boats was signed on 30 September 1982; there was an option for two more, but this was not taken up. The first hull was manufactured in Germany, while the remainder were made by Kvaerner Brug in Norway and then transported to Kiel, Germany. The equipment was truly international: American navigation system (Rockwell-Collins); British radar (Kelvin Hughes Type 1007) and EW suite (Racal Sea Lion); French conformal arrays (Thomson-Sintra); German sonar (STN Atlas DBQS-21F), torpedoes (AEG DM 2A3 Seeal); Italian periscopes (Riva-Calzoni); and Norwegian fire-control system (Norsk

Dolfin-class (IKL Type 800) GERMANY (ISRAEL)

Type: patrol.
Total built: 3.
Completed: 1999-2000.
Displacement: surfaced 1,565 tons; submerged 1,720 tons.
Dimensions: length 187ft 8in (57.3m); beam 24ft 3in (7.4m); draught 20ft 3in (6.2m).
Propulsion: 3 x M.T.U. diesels, 3 x 800bhp; 3 x generator sets, 3 x 313kW; 2 x Siemens motors, 2,850shp; battery 2 x 216 cells; one shaft.
Performance: surface – 11kt, submerged – 20kt; range surfaced 14,000nm at 4kt, schnorkel 8,000nm at 8kt, submerged 420nm at 8kt; maximum operating diving depth 1,150ft (350m).
Weapons: 10 x 21in (533mm) TT (bow), 16 x torpedoes/Sub-Harpoon/Triton (see notes).
Complement: 30.

History: The Israeli Navy sought additional submarines for many years and in mid-1988 Ingalls Shipbuilding in the USA became prime contractor for two IKL-designed submarines; sections were to be fabricated in Germany and then shipped to the United States for assembly, fitting out and trials. The boats would have used a U.S. command system and be funded by the U.S. Government under the FMS (Federal Military Sales) programme, but the project was cancelled in November 1990 due to pressures on U.S. defence funds. The

Above: **Ula***, nameship of a class of six Norwegian Type 210s.*

Forsvarsteknologie).

The programme seems to have suffered more than its fair share of problems. *Ula* (S-300) was hit by its own practice torpedo on trials; *Uredd* (S-305) hit a jetty while coming alongside and in a separate incident had a fire in the control room; and *Uthaug* (S-304) collided with an uncharted rock while submerged, and ran aground later the same day while returning to port on the surface.

The RNorN plans to purchase four submarines of a new design to replace the remaining four Type 207s, possibly in the 2010-2015 time frame. To this end it has joined with Denmark and Sweden in the Nordic submarine project.

Above: The Dolfin-class was built in Germany for Israel.

contract was resurrected following the April 1991 Gulf War, but this time with German Government funding for two submarines with an option on a third. That option was taken up in 1994, but this time with funding shared equally between Germany and Israel. The first hull was launched in April 1996, followed by the second in 1997 and the third in 1998. The Dolphin-class is generally similar to the German Type 212 in design but with the forward hydroplanes atop the forward hull rather than on the sail, as in other modern German-designed submarines. Another specifically Israeli feature is the incorporation of a `wet and dry' compartment for special forces swimmers. These boats will be used for interdiction, surveillance and special forces' operations.

Type TR-1700

Type: ocean-going patrol.
Total built: 2.
Completed: 1984-85.
Displacement: surfaced 2,116 tons; submerged 2,264 tons.
Dimensions: length 216ft 6in (66.0m); beam 23ft 11in (7.3m); draught 21ft 4in (6.5m).
Propulsion: 4 x M.T.U. diesels, 2 x 1,680bhp; 4 x alternator sets, 4 x 1.1MW; 1 x electric motor, 8,970shp; one shaft.
Performance: surface – 15kt, schnorkel – 15kt, submerged – 25kt; range surfaced 12,000nm at 8kt, submerged 4,650nm at 6kt; maximum operating diving depth 984ft (300m).
Weapons: 6 x 21in (533mm) TT (bow), 22 x torpedoes.
Complement: 26.

History: These two boats remain the largest submarines built in Germany since the end of World War II and are the fastest known diesel-electric submarines in the world, with a burst speed of 26kt. The original contract, signed in November 1977, was for six submarines: two TR-1400s and four of the larger TR-1700, but the order for the two TR-1400s was subsequently changed to two more TR-1700s. The first two boats were built at Emden, Germany, and delivered on time, but the remaining four were to be built in Argentina by Astilleros Domecq Garcia in Buenos Aires, and this element of the contract hit endless problems, and by early 1996 *Santa Fé* (S-43) was 52 per cent complete, *Santiago del Estero* (S-44) just 30 per cent complete, and no work had been done on either for at least 12 months. Both hulls were offered for sale and at one point a plan was considered whereby they would be sent to Thyssen Nordseewerke for completion and resale to a third party (possibly Taiwan), which would have rid the Argentine Navy of a financial and public relations embarrassment and also cleared the yard for privatisation. The third hull had been laid down, but that was about all and nothing had been done on the fourth. In the event all plans came to nought and not one of the four Argentine-built boats was ever completed, the parts being used instead to keep the two German-built boats going.

Below: Designed and built by Thyssen, only two TR-1700s were built, both for Argentina.

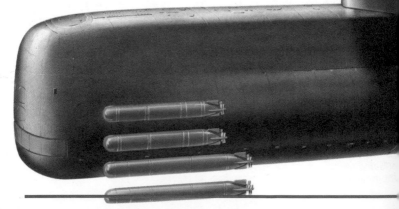

Above: Santa Cruz *departs for Argentina in December 1984.*

T-class Conversion/ Streamline

GREAT BRITAIN

Type: ocean-going patrol.
Total converted: 8.
Converted: 1949-56.
Displacement: surfaced 1,535 tons; submerged 1,734 tons.
Dimensions: length 293ft 6in (89.5m); beam 26ft 7in (8.1m); draught 16ft 0in (4.9m).
Propulsion: 2 x Admiralty Standard Range supercharged diesels, 4 x 700bhp; 4 x Laurence Scott electric motors, 4 x 1,500shp; battery 4 x 112 cells; two shafts.
Performance: surface – 14kt, schnorkel – 9.4kt, submerged – 15.4kt; maximum operating diving depth 350ft (107m).
Weapons: 6 x 21in (533mm) TT (bow), 12 x torpedoes.
Complement: 68.
Specifications are for Tabard group, as converted.

History: In the late 1940s, the British Royal Navy, as with the U.S. Navy, decided to modernise a number of its World War II boats in order to provide some modern operational boats quickly. They were also needed to provide fast-moving targets for its surface ASW warships. Eight of the all-welded T-class boats were selected and their pressure hulls were cut in two and a plug inserted, which varied in length between 12ft (3.7m) in three, 14ft (4.3m) in one and 20ft (6.1m) in the remainder. The original diesels were retained, but the plug enabled an extra pair of electric

A-class Conversion

GREAT BRITAIN

Type: ocean-going patrol.
Total converted: 14.
Converted: 1955-60.
Displacement: surfaced 1,443 tons; submerged 1,620 tons.
Dimensions: length 279ft 90in (85.3m); beam 22ft 3in (6.8m); draught 18ft 1in (5.5m).
Propulsion: 4 x Admiralty Standard Range supercharged diesels, 4 x 1,075bhp; 2 x electric motors, 2 x 625shp; two shafts.
Performance: surface – 19kt, schnorkel – 11kt, submerged – 15kt; range surfaced 11,000nm at 11kt, submerged 114nm at 3kt; maximum operating diving depth 500ft (152m).
Weapons: 6 x 21in (533mm) TT (bow – 4, stern – 2), 16 x torpedoes; 1 x 4in (102mm) gun (see notes).
Complement: 63.

History: The A-class boats were built specifically for the World War II Pacific campaign but were completed too late to see war service. As a result, the British Royal Navy found itself in the late 1940s with 16 virtually new submarines on its hands. They were well-built, but according to pre-Type XXI standards of propulsion and streamlining. The early boats were not completed with schnorkels; this new device was fitted in boats from *Alliance*, the ninth boat, onwards, and retrofitted in the others during their first refit, but many more improvements were clearly needed, although pressure of events and shortage of funds kept these boats in service in their original state for some years. Following the success of the T-class conversion, however, the A-class

Right: **Tireless, T-class partial modernisation with new sail.**

motors to be installed together with a fourth battery of 112 cells, and propulsion was changed from direct to diesel-electric drive. The Admiralty-pattern diesels were provided with a supercharger and a schnorkel was installed.

Externally, the gun was removed, the bow and stern were reshaped, and all external pro-tuberances were either removed or made retractable. A large streamlined sail was installed, which incorporated the bridge in two (*Tabard* and *Trump*) while in others there was a small bridge constructed low in front of the fin. Armament was reduced to six tubes, all in the bow, with 12 torpedoes carried (mines could be carried as an alternative). Other equipment was updated or replaced. The result was a thoroughly serviceable boat with its underwater speed actually doubled. Two were transferred to Israel in 1964-65, but one was lost on its delivery voyage and was replaced by a third boat in 1968. The remaining British boats were stricken and broken up in the early 1970s.

As with the U.S. Navy's Fleet Schnorkels, five riveted T-class boats were given a partial modernisation, which consisted of removing the gun and some external fittings and installing a higher, more streamlined sail and a schnorkel.

Right: **Amphion, one of 14 A-class given a thorough rebuild 1955-60.**

were taken in hand and 14 were thoroughly modernised between 1955 and 1960 (the only boats not converted were *Affray*, lost on 16 April 1951, and *Aurochs* which in 1964 was found to be in a bad state of repair and not worth converting). The work did not involve length-ening the pressure hull, nor were the propulsion machinery and batteries changed, but the hull was reshaped fore and aft, and all external fittings streamlined, made retractable or removed. A fully streamlined sail was fitted, at 26ft 6in (8.0m) the highest installed in any RN submarine to date. The external torpedo tubes were removed, but the mounting for the 4in (102mm) gun was left in place so that the gun could be mounted, if required. This proved to be a perceptive measure, since there were a number of British campaigns, particularly in Asia, where the weapon came in very useful for challenging small vessels. The various measures had a good but not dramatic effect: the submerged speed increased by some 2kt.

Porpoise/
Oberon-classes

Type: ocean-going patrol.
Total built: 22.
Completed: 1958-67.
Displacement: surfaced 1,975 tons; submerged 2,303 tons.
Dimensions: length 290ft 3in (88.5m); beam 26ft 6in (8.1m); draught 18ft 3in (5.6m).
Propulsion: 2 x Admiralty Standard Range diesels, 2 x 1,840bhp; 2 x English Electric electric motors, 2 x 3,000shp; battery 448 cells; two shafts.
Performance: surface – 12kt, submerged – 17kt; range surfaced 9,000nm at 12kt, schnorkel 11,000nm at 8kt; maximum operating diving depth 656ft (200m).
Weapons: 8 x 21in (533mm) TT (bow – 6, stern – 2), 18 x torpedoes.
Complement: 71.
Specifications for Porpoise-class, as built.

History: The first British submarines to be designed after World War II were the hydrogen-peroxide-powered experimental submarines, *Explorer* and *Excalibur* (qv), but the first operational diesei-electric boats were the Porpoise-class. Orders for eight boats were placed in 1951, although the first-of-class was not actually laid down until 1955 and was not completed until 1958. The design incorporated the lessons learnt from the war, plus those derived from detailed examination of the captured German boats, such as the Type XXI, as well as post-war experience with the T-class conversions and observation of U.S. Navy

Above: Oberon-class SSK in Australian service.

programmes. The hull was of a very clean design and this, coupled with the very powerful batteries, gave a submerged speed of 17kt and also ensured that when travelling at slow speed they were very quiet. They were stricken between 1977 and 1990, not because they had reached the end of their service lives, but due to RN financial and manpower cuts.

After the eight Porpoise-class came the Oberon-class, whose dimensions,

Below: Oberons were the most successful second generation SSKs in any navy and the last British submarines to be exported.

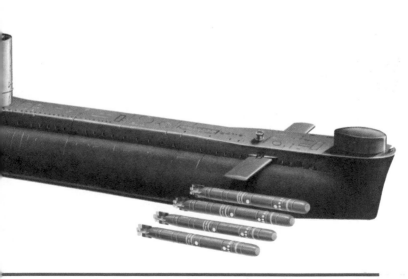

displacement and propulsive machinery were identical to that in the Porpoise-class, but there were important developments in weaponry, sonar and construction. The all-welded pressure-hull was the same as on the Porpoise-class, but fabricated from a higher quality steel which increased the diving depth to a reported 1,000ft (305m). The superstructure was made of steel only in the first-of-class; in the second boat, *Orpheus*, it was made of aluminium, while in the remainder it was made of glass-reinforced plastic (GRP), the first time such a material had been used in a large scale in a RN warship. The sonar outfit was also considerably improved and the class was able to launch Mk 24 homing torpedoes.

A grand total of 27 Oberons were built, with 13 being delivered to the RN in 1960-67. One of those building for the RN was bought on the stocks by the Royal Canadian Navy (RCN) and a replacement boat was then added to the RN's order. A total of 14 were exported: Australia – six (Oxley-class, 1968-78); Brazil – three (Humaita-class, 1973-78); Canada – three (Ojibwa-class, 1965-68); Chile – two (Hyatt-class, 1976).

The RN boats were upgraded several times during their service, and boats from the class took part in both the Falklands (1982) and Gulf (1991) Wars, as well as playing a very energetic role in Cold War operations. The RN cut its SSK force in 1991, as a result of which these Oberons went out of service early. Five were scrapped in 1991-92, while a number were bought by UK-based civil companies in order to refit them and sell them abroad; in the event no sales were achieved.

Right: Sealion, *a Porpoise-class SSK.*

Upholder/
Victoria-class
GREAT BRITAIN (CANADA)

Type: attack.
Total built: 4.
Completed: 1990-93.
Displacement: surfaced 2,185 tons; submerged 2,400 tons.
Dimensions: length 230ft 7in (70.3m); beam 24ft 11in (7.6m); draught 18ft 0in (5.5m).
Propulsion: 2 x Paxman Valenta diesel generators, 2 x 2,035bhp; 2 x alternators; 1 x electric motor, 5,400shp; battery 2 x 240 cells; one shaft.
Performance: surface – 12kt, schnorkel – 919kt, submerged – 20kt; range schnorkel 8,000nm at 8kt, submerged 270nm at 3kt; maximum operating diving depth over 820ft (250m).
Weapons: 6 x 21in (533mm) TT (bow), 18 x torpedoes.
Complement: 44.

History: The Upholder-class was originally conceived as a hunter-killer for the British Royal Navy, their Cold War mission being to lie in wait for Soviet submarines seeking to pass through the Greenland-Iceland-UK gaps. They were intended to be replacements for the Porpoise/Oberon-classes, the last of which had been launched in 1967, but they were commissioned just as the Cold War came to an end. The British government quickly concluded that the RN could no longer afford to maintain fleets of both nuclear and conventionally powered submarines, and so the four Upholder-class were taken out of service,

Above: Victoria, *first of four British Upholders sold to Canada.*

despite the large amount of money expended first on designing and building these four boats and then on resolving various problems once they were in service. They were then offered for sale to various countries, including Australia, Chile and South Africa, while Taiwan made an unsolicited bid which was rejected under pressure from China. No purchaser could be found until 1998 when they were acquired by Canada on an eight-year lease, at the end of which they will be purchased for a nominal £1 sterling.

The Upholder-class are among the most sophisticated and capable diesel-electric submarines ever built, with an unusually short and fat tear-drop hull with a beam:length ratio of 1:9, giving three deck levels inside. The pressure hull has a single skin constructed of NQ-1 high-tensile steel and is covered in elastomeric acoustic tiles. Curiously, this class was not fitted with the British-developed pump-jet propulsor installed in all SSNs since the early 1980s, having, instead, a more conventional seven-bladed, skewback propeller. On entry into service it was discovered that there were problems with the torpedo discharge system, which required dockyard work on the first three boats, while the last boat's tubes were rectified before commissioning.

The four boats underwent a substantial refit in preparation for their transfer to Canada, and the first boat, renamed HMCS *Victoria*, was delivered in May 2000.

Enrico Toti-class   ITALY

Type: coastal hunter/killer.
Total built: 4.
Completed: 1968-69.
Displacement: surfaced 535 tons; submerged 591 tons.
Dimensions: length 151ft 6in (46.2m); beam 15ft 5in (4.7m); draught 13ft 1in (4.0m).
Propulsion: 2 x diesels, 2 x 1,100bhp; 1 x electric motor, 2,200shp; one shaft.
Performance: surface – 9.7kt, submerged – 14kt; range surfaced 3,000nm at 5kt; maximum operating diving depth 680ft (300m).
Weapons: 4 x 21in (533mm) TT (bow), 8 x torpedoes.
Complement: 26.

History: The Italian Navy's post-war submarine fleet initially consisted of a bewildering array of pre-war and wartime designs, most of which were in poor condition. Many were scrapped in 1947 and the remainder were lost in 1948 as a result of the Peace Treaty, except for two passed to the USSR and two which remained in Italian hands disguised as "battery chargers". The ban on submarines expired in 1952 and the two "battery chargers" were returned to commission as operational boats. The Italian Navy also acquired a number of boats from the U.S. Navy: Guppy IB – 2; Guppy II – 2; Fleet Schnorkel – 3; and Tang-class – 2. Although these were all sound designs they were somewhat large for Mediterranean operations, and were also very manpower intensive.

The first new-build boats were the Toti-class, for which the operational requirement changed several times, with the design recast accordingly, until it was finally settled upon as a coastal hunter/killer for employment under NATO

Above: The Upholder-class was built to block the GIUK gap.

Right: The Italian Navy's Toti-class was designed to be fast and agile.

command in the central Mediterranean and Adriatic. As a result, their size was kept to a minimum and long range was not a requirement. The Totis were small and highly manoeuvrable, with a "teardrop" hull, diesel-electric drive, and a single propeller. Like other hunter-killers of the time, they mounted an active sonar in a large dome on the bows and a passive sonar aft. The design was offered for export but never won any orders. The four boats joined the fleet in 1968-69 and were stricken in 1991-93.

Nazario Sauro-class

Type: ocean-going patrol.

Class	Sauro	Pelosi	Longobardo
Total built	4	2	2
Completed	1980-82	1988-89	1993-95
Displacement surfaced submerged	1,4565 tons 1,641 tons	1,476 tons 1,662 tons	1,653 tons 1,826 tons
Dimensions length beam draught	209ft 7in (63.9m) 22ft 5in (6.8m) 18ft 9in (5.7m)	211ft 2in (64.4m) 22ft 5in (6.8m) 18ft 7in (5.7m)	217ft 8in (66.4m) 22ft 5in (6.8m) 19ft 8in (6.0m)
Propulsion diesel power electric motors power battery shafts	3 x GMT 3 x 1,070bhp 1 x Marelli 1 x 3,650shp 2 x 148 cells one	3 x GMT 3 x 1,070bhp 1 x Marelli 1 x 3,650shp 2 x 148 cells one	3 x GMT 3 x 1,070bhp 1 x ABBI 1 x 4,270shp 2 x 148 cells one
Performance speed: surface submerged range: surfaced schnorkel submerged maximum diving depth	12kt 20kt 7,000nm/8kt 2,500nm/12kt 250nm/4kt 984ft (300m)	11kt 19kt 6,150nm/11kt 2,500nm/12kt 250nm/4kt 984ft (300m)	12kt 20kt 7,000nm/8kt 2,500nm/124kt 250nm/4kt 984ft (300m)
Weapons TT location torpedoes	6 x 21in (533mm) bow 12	6 x 21in (533mm) bow 12	6 x 21in (533mm) bow 12
Complement	49	50	50

History: The Nazario Sauro-class of four submarines was built by Italcantieri's Monfalcone yard, the only Italian post-war submarine builder. The hull, made of HY-80 steel, is tear-drop shaped with cruciform after control surfaces and a seven-bladed propeller. The forward hydroplanes are mounted American-style on the fin. There are six torpedo tubes and a total of 12 torpedoes, which seems a little inadequate for such a large boat intended for 45-day patrols; the French Agosta-class, for example, of equivalent size, carried a total of 20. The Italian boats were given a mid-life update from 1990 inwards which included new cells, improved habitability and a new fire control system.

At one time it was proposed to replace the Sauros by a totally new design

Above: Sauro-class submarine, **Carlo Fecia di Cossato.**

with the title of "Submarine for the 90s" (S90) but this fell through and an improved version of the Sauro was built instead. Completed in 1988-89, the two boats of the Salvatore Pelosi-class were slightly longer and fitted to launch Sub-Harpoon, but otherwise were a little advance on the Sauros. Faced with a need to keep the yard occupied and with the S90 design still not finalised, two more boats were built, completing in 1993 and 1995, respectively. The Primo Longobardo-class was again marginally longer, giving an increase in fuel bunkerage, but otherwise showed no real advance.

The four Sauro-class boats continue in service, but one is used almost solely for trials. The two Pelosi-class boats underwent a mid-life refit in 2000-2001 and the Longobardo-class will be refitted in due course. The replacement for all these boats will not be the Italian S90, as originally planned, but will be a licence-built version of the German Type 212, the first of which is due in service in 2005.

Below: **Nazario Sauro**, *first of a class of eight SSKs.*

Oyashio-class

Type: patrol.
Total built: 1.
Completed: 1960.
Displacement: surfaced 1,139 tons; submerged 1,420 tons.
Dimensions: length 258ft 6in (78.8m); beam 22ft 11in (7.0m); draught 15ft 0in (4.6m).
Propulsion: 2 x diesels, 2 x 1,350bhp; 2 x electric motors, 2 x 2,980shp; battery 4 x 120 cells; two shafts.
Performance: surface – 13kt, submerged – 19kt; range surfaced 10,000nm at 10kt.
Weapons: 4 x 21in (533mm) TT (bow).
Complement: 65.

History: Following the end of World War II all Japanese submarines were destroyed, the great majority by scuttling, but a few by scrapping. The first submarine to serve in the newly created Japanese Maritime Self-Defense Force (JMSDF) was a U.S. Navy Gato-class boat, formerly USS *Mingo* (SS-261), renamed *Kuroshio* (SS-510), which was transferred in 1955 under the U.S. Mutual Defense Aid Pact (MDAP). She did not have any form of modernisation prior to transfer (ie, not a Guppy boat) and was used almost entirely as a training boat until stricken in 1966.

The first submarine to be built for the JMSDF was *Oyashio* (SS-511) which was laid down in 1957, launched in 1959 and commissioned in 1960. She had a "long/narrow" hull, similar to many boats being built at that time, and although

---

Hayashio/Natsushio-classes

Hayashio
Type: coastal hunter/killer.
Total built: 2.
Completed: 1962.
Displacement: surfaced 650 tons; submerged 800 tons.
Dimensions: length 193ft 6in (59.0m); beam 13ft 6in (4.3m).
Propulsion: 2 x diesels, 2 x 675bhp; 2 x electric motors, 2 x 850shp; two shafts.
Performance: surface – 12kt, submerged – 15kt.
Weapons: 3 x 21in (533mm) TT (bow). 6 x torpedoes.
Complement: 43.

Natsushio
Type: coastal hunter/killer.
Total built: 2.
Completed: 1963-64.
Displacement: surfaced 690 tons; submerged 850 tons.
Dimensions: length 200ft 1in (61.0m); beam 21ft 2in (6.5m); draught 13ft 6in (4.1m).
Propulsion: 2 x diesels, 2 x 675bhp; 2 x electric motors, 2 x 850shp; two shafts.
Performance: surface – 12kt, submerged – 15kt.
Weapons: 6 x 21in (533mm) TT (bow). 12 x torpedoes.
Complement: 43.

History: These two closely related classes appeared in the early 1960s and were modelled on the U.S. Navy's Barracuda-class (qv), thus starting a Cold War

Above: Oyashio, *first post-war Japanese-built submarine.*

obviously incorporating the latest equipment she bore a more than passing resemblance to the Japanese World War II ST-class (qv). For example, lengths were ST – 259ft (78.9m), *Oyashio* – 258ft (78.6m), while submerged displacements were ST – 1,450 tons and *Oyashio* – 1,420 tons. The physical resemblance was also very strong, with an uncluttered exterior and upper casing, a tall sail, and a vertically deployed schnorkel. *Oyashio* served as a front-line boat for some years and was then transferred to a training role in 1975 and scrapped in 1976.

Above: Hayashio, *as completed, at sea in the 1960s.*

trend in which Japanese naval developments reflected U.S. advances. These hunter/killers were intended to sit off a maritime choke point and acquire Soviet targets using the powerful bow-mounted sonar, whereupon they would attack. Japan's first post-war submarine, *Oyushio* (SS-511) (qv), had a traditional long, narrow hull, but these two classes had a shorter hull in which the beam was proportionally greater, starting a gradual Japanese evolution towards the "Albacore hull." Another change was that in Japanese submarines up to the end of World War II the crew's living conditions had received a very low priority, but beginning with this class matters started to improve and air-conditioning was introduced. Attention was also paid to manoeuvrability and joystick-control was used for the first time. The two Hayashio-class boats were stricken in 1979, but the one year younger Natsushio-class went the previous year.

Uzushio/Yushiuo/ Harushio-classes

JAPAN

Type: ocean-going patrol.

Class	Uzushio	Yuushio	Harushio
Total built	7	10	7
Completed	1971-78	1980-89	1990-97
Displacement surfaced submerged	1,850 tons 3,600 tons	2,200 tons 2,450 tons	2,450 tons 2,750 tons
Dimensions length beam draught	236ft 3in (72.0m) 32ft 6in (9.9m) 24ft 7in (7.5m)	250ft 0in (76.2m) 32ft 6in (9.9m) 24ft 7in (7.5m)	253ft 11in (77.4m) 32ft 10in (10.0m) 25ft 4in (7.7m)
Propulsion diesel power electric motors power Battery shafts	2 x Kawasaki/MAN 2 x 1,800bhp 2 2 x 3,600shp n.k. one	2 x Mitsubishi-M.A.N. 2 x 1,700bhp 2 x Fuji 2 x 3,600sgp 2 x 480 Nihon cells one	2 x Kawasaki 2 x 1,700bhp 2 2 x 3,600shp 2 x 480 Yuasa cells one
Performance speed: surface submerged maximum diving depth	12kt 20kt 656ft (200m)	13kt 20kt 1,300ft (400m)	12kt 20kt –
Weapons TT location torpedoes	6 x 21in (533mm) amidships 20	6 x 21in (533mm) amidships 20	6 x 21in (533mm) amidships 20
Complement	80	77	75

History: JMSDF policy has been one of steady progress, with a series of classes, none of which has been a revolutionary advance on its predecessor, but resulting in a series of what have been among the very best diesel-electric submarines of their era. All have featured an Alabcore-type hull and forward hydroplanes mounted midway up a large sail, and until the current Oyashio-class had a very large sonar array in the bow, which displaced the six torpedo tubes to the midships position, as in U.S. Navy SSNs. The tubes are used to launch Japanese-designed torpedoes (Type 72, Type 80 or Type 89) and from the Yuushio-class onwards, UGM-84 Sub-Harpoon; all classes are fitted with six tubes and carry a total of 20 torpedoes/missiles. Production has been shared equally between two Kobe-based shipyards, Mitsubishi and Kawasaki, with

Above: **Isoshio***, third of the JMSDF's Uzushio-class.*

boats being commissioned at a rate of one per year, almost invariably in the month of March.

The seven-strong Uzushio-class (SS-566 to SS-572) were the first JMSDF boats to have Albacore-style tear-drop hulls and were generally similar to, but slightly larger than, the U.S. Navy's Barbel-class. The hull was constructed of NS-63 steel which gave a maximum operating depth of 660ft (200m) and the boat was fitted with an automatic steering system. The first two boats were stricken in 1987-88, but the other five were converted to auxiliary and training submarines (ATSS) between 1989 and 1993 as the Harushio-class boats came into service. These, too, were then stricken at a yearly rate from 1992 onwards.

Next came 10 Yuushio-class (SS-573 to SS-582), which were slightly larger, much better equipped and made of NS-80 steel, giving a deeper diving capability. They mounted a Japanese ZQQ-4 or -5 sonar in the bows, modified versions of the U.S. Navy's AN/BQS-4 sonar and certain boats were fitted to take Sub-Harpoon. After the ZQR-1 towed array had been trialled in *Nadashio* (SS-577) it was fitted in all the remainder. First-of-class *Yuushio* (SS-573) became a training boat in 1996, followed by the remaining boats at a rate of one per year as the Oyashio-class came into service.

Third in this group came the Harushio-class (SS-583 to SS-589), completed between 1990 and 1997 as replacements for the Uzushio-class.. They have improved noise reduction and all have been fitted with the ZQR-1 towed array while building. The pressure hull is built of NS-110 steel, allowing a further increase in operating depth. Last-of-class *Asashio* (SS-589) incorporated a number of changes, including increased automation which allowed a reduction in crew numbers and was the first Japanese boat to be built with anechoic tiles.

Below: **Yushio** *shows the classic "tear-drop" hull.*

Oyashio-class

Type: ocean-going patrol.
Total built: 10.
Completed: 1996-2005.
Displacement: surfaced 2,750 tons; submerged 3,600 tons.
Dimensions: length 268ft 0in (81.7m); beam 33ft 9in (10.3m); draught 24ft 3in (7.4m).
Propulsion: 2 x Kawasaki diesels, 2 x 1,700bhp; 2 x electric motors, 7,750shp; one shaft.
Performance: surface – 12kt, submerged – 20kt; maximum operating diving depth at least 1,300ft (400m).
Weapons: 6 x 21in (533mm) TT (bow), 20 x torpedoes/missiles.
Complement: 69.

History: The latest Oyashio-class breaks with the 30-year custom of progressive enhancements to a basic design by introducing a totally new design, with a new shape of pressure hull, which is made of a new and even stronger steel (but of undisclosed specifications) and is coated in anechoic tiles. There is a rather higher upper casing than in previous classes, possibly to create storage space for the towed array, aft of the sail. The torpedo tubes have been restored to their traditional position in the bows and are mounted high in the hull

---

Sang-O-class

Type: coastal/special forces.
Total built: 22.
Completed: ca. 1980-?
Displacement: surfaced 275 tons; submerged 360 tons.
Dimensions: length 111ft 7in (34.0m); beam 12ft 6in (3.8m); draught 10ft 6in (3.2m).
Propulsion: 1 x diesel generator set, 300bhp (est), electric motor, 200shp (est); one shaft.
Performance: surface – 7.2kt, submerged – 4kt; range surfaced 1,500nm, schnorkel 2,700nm/8kt; maximum operating depth 492ft (150m).
Weapons: 4 x 21in (533mm) TT (bow), 4 x torpedoes.
Complement: 14.
Specifications for torpedo-armed version; see notes for special forces version.

History: The North Korean Navy obtained four Whiskey-class submarines from the Soviet Union in the 1960s and then received a number of Chinese-built Whiskeys and Romeos in the 1970s. Several submarine building facilities were then established at Mayang Do in North Korea and some 18 Romeos were completed between 1976 and 1996. North Korea has only one enemy – South Korea – and has long pursued a policy of infiltrating special forces into its southern neighbour's territory, and one method has been by submarine. A number of M100-D mini-subs (also known as the Una-class) were bought from Yugoslavia in the 1980s and the North Koreans developed this design into a rather more effective vessel, known in the West as the "Yugo-class", and some 40 were built at one of their own shipyards. The next stage was to design a completely new type, based on experience gained with the Romeo- and Yugo-classes; this has been designated by U.S. Intelligence agencies as the Sang-O (= shark) class, and 22 have been built. There are two versions. One is torpedo-armed, with four bow-mounted 21in (533mm) tubes and no reloads, while the other is a swimmer delivery vehicle with a lock-out chamber and

Above: Latest JMSDF SSK Oyashio *at sea.*

with a chin-mounted sonar array below. The sail is of a different shape and is further back along the hull, indicating that the control room is now further aft than in previous classes. First-of-class *Oyashio* (SS-590) cost $US534,000,000 at 1993 prices. These are undoubtedly among the very finest diesel-electric submarines in existence.

Above: **Sang-O** *grounded off South Korean coast in 1996.*

accommodation for up to 15 special forces troops in the torpedo space. This special forces version can also carry 16 mines.

In a spectacular failure, one of these boats ran aground on the South Korean coast on 17 September 1996. There had been 26 aboard and all appear to have got ashore. The South Koreans quickly captured one man and found the bodies of 11 others who had committed suicide, but it took them over six weeks to deal with the remainder, killing 13 of them – just one man escaped. The North Koreans insisted that it had been a training mission and that the boat had suffered an engine fault which resulted in it drifting on to the southern shore, a story which nobody believed.

Dolfijn-class

Type: ocean-going patrol.
Total built: 4.
Completed: 1960-66.
Displacement: surfaced 1,494 tons; submerged 1,826 tons.
Dimensions: length 260ft 10in (79.5m); beam 25ft 7in (7.8m); draught 15ft 9in (4.8m).
Propulsion: 2 x M.A.N. diesels, 2 x 1,250bhp; 2 x Smit electric motors, 2 x 2,100shp; battery 2 x 168 Chloride cells; two shafts.
Performance: surface – 14.5kt, submerged – 17kt; maximum operating diving depth 985ft (300m).
Weapons: 8 x 21in (533mm) TT (bow – 4, stern – 4), 22 x torpedoes.
Complement: 67.
Specifications are for Dolfijn-class, as built.

History: These four boats were built to a unique design by M. F. Gunning, in which three separate but interconnected pressure hulls were enclosed within an outer hull. The uppermost (and largest) hull contained the control centre, the torpedo tubes (four at each end), storage spaces and the crew accommodation. Below were two parallel hulls, slightly shorter and of smaller diameter, each containing one complete power train, consisting of machinery, batteries and stores. The advantage of this arrangement was that it combined great strength with compactness, and made the best possible use of the steel then available.

This was, however, somewhat offset by the cramped conditions in the lower hulls, with machinery maintenance at sea being particularly difficult.

These Dutch boats had an exceptional diving depth for their day and were very highly regarded by other NATO navies, although the high cost of construction and the availability of higher-strength steels meant that the design was not repeated. However, Gunning's basic concept of multiple hulls, developed in the 1940s, seems to have reappeared in the Soviet Typhoon-class SSBNs in the 1970s (qv).

The first two boats, *Dolfijn* and *Zeehond,* were laid down in 1954 and completed in 1960-61, but laying down the second pair was delayed by several years while consideration was given as to whether to install nuclear power-plants. In the end this was not done and *Potvis* and *Tonijn* were laid down in 1962 and completed in 1965-66, and differed from the first two in being shorter (78.3m) and having Swedish Varta cells.

All four boats served as part of the Netherlands' contribution to NATO for many years. Three boats were stricken at the end of their operational lives: *Dolfijn* – 1985, *Tonijn* – 1991 and *Potvis* – 1992. *Zeehond* was to have been retired in 1987, but her life was extended for three years due to a fire in *Walrus* (qv), after which she was purchased by her builders, RDM, and used as a test-bed for a new AIP system.

Below: Dutch submarine Dolfijn *had three pressure hulls.*

Zwaardvis/
Hai Lung-classes

NETHERLANDS/TAIWAN

Zvaardvis
Type: ocean-going patrol.
Total built: 2.
Completed: 1972.
Displacement: surfaced 2,408 tons; submerged 2,640 tons.
Dimensions: length 219ft 0in (66.9m); beam 28ft 0in (8.4m); draught 23ft 0in (7.1m).
Propulsion: 3 x Werkspoor diesels, 3 x 1,400bhp; 1 x Holec electric motor, 5,100shp; battery 2 x 196 cells; one shaft.
Performance: surface – 13kt, submerged – 20kt; range schnorkel 10,000nm at 9kt; maximum operating diving depth 722ft (220m).
Weapons: 6 x 21in (533mm) TT (bow), 20 torpedoes.
Complement: 67.

Hai Lung
Type: ocean-going patrol
Total built: 2.
Completed: 1987-88.
Displacement: surfaced 2,376 tons; submerged 2,660 tons.
Dimensions: length 219ft 7in (66.9m); beam 27ft 7in (8.4m); draught 22ft 0in (6.7m).
Propulsion: 3 x Bronswerk/Stork-Werkspoor diesels, 3 x 1,350bhp; 1 x Holec

---

Walrus-class

NETHERLANDS

Type: ocean-going patrol.
Total built: 4.
Completed: 1990-94.
Displacement: surfaced 2,465 tons; submerged 2,800 tons.
Dimensions: length 222ft 1in (67.7m); beam 27ft 6in (8.4m); draught 22ft 11in (7.0m).
Propulsion: 3 x SEMT-Pielstick diesels, 3 x 2,300bhp; 1 x Holec electric motor, 5,430shp; battery 3 x 140 cells; one shaft.
Performance: surface – 13kt, submerged – 21kt; range schnorkel 10,000nm at 9kt; maximum operating diving depth 984ft (300m).
Weapons: 4 x 21in (533mm) TT (bow), 20 torpedoes.
Complement: 52.
Specifications for first pair, as built.

History: This is, in effect, an improved version of the Zwaardvis-class, with similar dimensions and general appearance, the only noticeable external difference being the use of X-configured stern hydroplanes. The pressure hull is built from Marel steel, giving a 50 per cent increase in operating depth over the Zwaardvis. The first two, *Walrus* and *Zeeleeuw*, were ordered in 1978-79, but the project did not get off to a good start. First, construction was delayed by a decision to replace the planned diesels by different and more powerful models, which required the hull to be lengthened. Then, when *Walrus* was conducting builder's trials in August 1986 she was so severely damaged by fire that she had to be taken back into dock and completely rebuilt, being relaunched in September 1989. Meanwhile, a second pair

Right: **Hai Lung***, one of two exported to Taiwan, to the fury of Communist China.*

electric motor, 5,100shp; battery 2 x 196 cells; one shaft.
Performance: surface – 12kt, submerged – 20kt; range schnorkel 10,000nm at 9kt; maximum operating diving depth 787ft (240m).
Weapons: 6 x 21in (533mm) TT (bow), 20 torpedoes.
Complement: 79.

History: The design of the Zwaardvis-class was closely based on that of the U.S. Navy's Barbel-class (qv), the last diesel-electric boats to be built for the United States. The Dutch boats were laid down in 1966 and completed in 1972, and are of single-hull construction with three main internal divisions. Forward are the sonars, torpedo tubes and torpedo-handling room and aft are the machinery spaces, housing three diesel-generator sets, mounted on a false deck, a large Holec electric motor and the single shaft. In the centre is the control centre, with the crew accommodation below, and the batteries below that. Virtually all equipment is of Dutch design and manufacture. Two were supplied to the Republic of China in 1987/88 as the Hai Lung-class.

Right: The Dutch Walrus-class is widely considered to be one of the finest SSK designs of the 20th century.

(*Dolfijn* and *Bruinvis*) were ordered in 1984-85 and completed in 1993-94, but plans to order a fifth and sixth were cancelled by the Dutch Parliament in 1988.

These boats enjoy a high reputation for efficiency and effectiveness and are among the finest diesel-electric boats yet built. They have a particularly comprehensive outfit of sensors and are fitted to launch Sub-Harpoon, although no missiles have been purchased. Assuming they have a 30-year life they will be due for replacement in the 2020s, but there is no talk, as yet, of a project for a successor.

Whiskey-class

Type: ocean-going patrol.
Total built: 236.
Completed: 1951-58.
Displacement: surfaced 1,080 tons; submerged 1,350 tons.
Dimensions: length 249ft 3in (76.0m); beam 21ft 3in (6.5m); draught 16ft 1in (4.9m).
Propulsion: 2 x Type 37D diesels, 2 x 2,000bhp; 2 x electric motors, 2 x 1,350shp; 2 x creep motors, 2 x 50shp; two shafts.
Performance: surface – 18.5kt, schnorkel – 7kt, submerged – 13.1kt; range surfaced 8,500nm at 10kt, submerged 335nm at 2kt; maximum operating diving depth 560ft (170mm).
Weapons: 6 x 21in (533mm) TT (bow – 4, stern – 2), 12 x torpedoes; 2 x 25mm AA (1 x 2).
Complement: 54.
Specifications for Whiskey I, as built.

History: In 1943 the Soviet Naval Staff issued a requirement for a new submarine to replace the widely-used S- and Shch-classes (qqv), which resulted in Project 608, essentially a modernised version of the S-class with various modifications resulting from wartime experience, together with a sonar which was reverse-engineered from a set supplied by their British ally. Then, in September 1944, the Soviet Navy recovered *U-250,* a German Type VIIC which had been sunk in the Gulf of Finland several weeks previously, and detailed examination showed that Soviet designs had slipped well behind those of their enemy (the salvage team also recovered an Enigma machine, a Zaunkönig torpedo and many secret documents – no mean haul). Project 608 was immediately cancelled so that the design could be reworked to incorporate the lessons of the Type VIIC. Later the design was altered yet again to include some of the lessons of the Type XXIs captured at the end of the war. The outcome was a larger design, finalised in 1948 as Project 613, which would become known to NATO as the Whiskey-class, but was by no means the Type XXI-clone as often suggested in the West.

The first-of-class was launched in 1951 and by the time production ended

in 1958 four yards had produced a total of 215 for the Soviet Navy (Baltic – 19, Gork'iy – 113, Komsomolsk – 11, and Nikolayev – 72) and a further 21 were assembled in China from parts supplied by the Soviet Union. A total of 39 operational boats were transferred from the Soviet Navy to foreign navies (Albania – 4; Bulgaria – 2; China – 5; Egypt – 7; Indonesia – 12; North Korea – 4; Poland – 5). These were followed by four non-operational boats: battery charging hulks (to Cuba – 1, Syria – 1) and for cannibalisation (to Indonesia – 2).

The Whiskey was a double-hulled boat with twin propellers, each shaft having its own diesel engine, electric motor and creep motor, and for the first time in a Soviet submarine all these were mounted on shock absorbers. Armament comprised six torpedo tubes, four in the bow and two in the stern with an outfit of 12 torpedoes. The five major variants identified by Western naval intelligence concerned the guns. Whiskey I was the original version with a single 25mm AA mount on a platform before the bridge tower, while Whiskey II had an additional twin 57mm mounted at deck level immediately abaft the tower, the only version to mount this particular weapon. Whiskey III had no gun armament but retained the platforms and Whiskey IV had the forward 25mm gun but no 57mm; it was also the first to be fitted with a schnorkel. The final version, Whiskey V, was streamlined and had no guns at all, the platforms being removed; a total of 60 boats were upgraded to this standard in mid-life modernisation refits, but the programme was ended when more modern new-build submarines began to join the fleet. The Soviet Navy's Whiskey fleet began to run down in the 1970s, with unmodernized boats being scrapped, and by 1982 only 60 remained, reducing to 18 in 1992 and the last were scrapped the following year.

There were a number of conversions. One boat was converted to serve as a missile test platform – Whiskey Single-Cylinder – and was followed by six operational boats armed with two SS-N-3 – Whiskey Twin-Cylinder (qv) – and a further six with four missiles – Whiskey Long Bin (qv). Four were converted as radar pickets – Whiskey Canvas Bag – while other boats were employed on tasks which required little modification, such as two for fishery research.

Below: The Whiskeys were sturdy and reliable work-horses.

Romeo-class (Project 633)

Type: ocean-going patrol.
Total built: 112.
Completed: 1958-95.
Displacement: surfaced 1,330 tons; submerged 1,700 tons.
Dimensions: length 252ft 8in (77.0m); beam 22ft 0in (6.7m); draught 16ft 1in (4.9m).
Propulsion: 2 x diesels, 2 x 2,000bhp; 2 x electric motors, 2 x 1,350shp; 2 x creep motors, 2 x 50shp; battery 2 x 112 cells; two shafts.
Performance: surface – 15.5kt, submerged – 13kt; range surfaced 16,000nm at 10kt, schnorkel 7,000nm at 5kt; maximum operating diving depth 984ft (300m).
Weapons: 8 x 21in (533mm) TT (bow – 6, stern – 2), 14 x torpedoes.
Complement: 56.

History: The Soviet Navy's requirement for a new class of submarine was issued in the early 1950s and designated Project 633 (NATO = Romeo-class). It was to be an improved version of the Project 613 (Whiskey-class), powered by the Kreislauf AIP system (see Quebec-class), but when that system proved impracticable the design was modified for normal diesel-electric drive. It was a double-hull design, divided into seven internal compartments, and although deck fittings for a gun were included no such weapon was ever mounted. An important change from the Whiskey-class was the addition of two more torpedo tubes in the bows. The new sonar outfit was a major advance on that installed in Project 613, paralelling that being installed on the new Project 641 (Foxtrot class) ocean-going submarines and offering greatly improved target acquisition and localisation capabilities. Derived from the World War II German GHG/Balkon system and installed in a bow "onion", the MG-10 Feniks-M system offered a reasonable submarine detection capability. Directly above this was the MG-200 Arktika-M active scanning sonar that supplied target data to the new Leningrad fire-control system. A sonar intercept system was installed in the sail structure. Finally, a small underwater telephone was installed on top of the MG-200 set to give the bow "rhino-horn" characteristic of this class.

The early 1950s were a period of great ambition in the Soviet Navy and at one point it was planned to build no fewer than 560 Romeos, but in 1955 President Kruschev issued orders that the production of all non-nuclear submarines should cease. The Soviet Naval Staff fought this decision, arguing that nuclear submarines were very expensive and, in any case, diesel-electric boats were much better in littoral waters. However, the Project 641 (Foxtrot-class) was already on the drawing boards and there was clear duplication between the two, so it was decided to end production of the Romeo in 1962 with the 21st unit. With hindsight this appears to have been the wrong decision, since the Romeo was a quieter and generally more effective design, but the decision could not be reversed. A total of 15 of these were transferred to friendly navies and those that remained in the Soviet Navy were used mainly for research or as auxiliaries. All had been stricken by 1987.

Meanwhile, it was decided to help China establish its own submarine building capability and since there was no longer a Soviet requirement the production drawings and tooling were transferred to the PRC, where the type was built in large

Above: A Chinese-built copy of the Soviet Romeo-class design.

numbers. The PRC seems to have concentrated its efforts on simply producing Romeos in large numbers; there have been minor upgrades in equipment but no significant improvements to the design, except for the Ming-class (qv). Egypt, however, modernised its four Chinese-built Romeos from 1992 onwards, with many U.S. systems being installed and the boats being given the ability to launch Sub-Harpoon. The North Koreans also built 12 Romeos, of which they have lost two.

In summary, a total of 112 Romeos were built: Russia – 21 (entered service in 1958-62); China – 72 (in service 1960-84); North Korea – 19 (in service 1973-95). The Soviet Navy transferred a number from its own stocks: Algeria – 2; Bulgaria – 4; Egypt – 6; Syria – 3. China built eight specifically for export: Egypt – 4; North Korea – 4. North Korea built 12, of which two were lost in 1985. By 2002 some 84 remained in service: Bulgaria – 1; China – 64 (many in reserve); North Korea – 19.

Below: The Romeo's hull-shape was very little different from that of the German Type XXI of 1944-45.

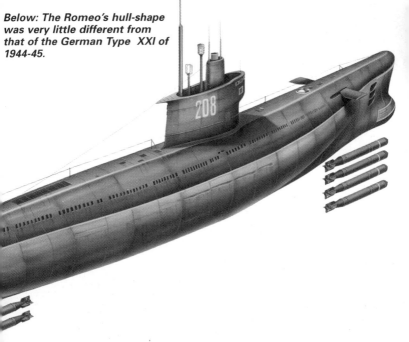

Zulu-class (Project 611)

RUSSIA

Type: ocean-going patrol.
Total built: 26.
Completed: 1958-95.
Displacement: surfaced 1,900 tons; submerged 2,350 tons.
Dimensions: length 295ft 3in (90.0m); beam 24ft 7in (7.5m); draught 19ft 8in (6.0m).
Propulsion: 3 x diesels, 3 x 2,000bhp; 3 x electric motors, 3 x 1,750shp; battery 4 x 112 cells; three shafts.
Performance: surface – 18kt, submerged 16kt; range schnorkel 9,500nm at 8kt, submerged 480nm at 4kt; maximum operating diving depth 655ft (200m).
Weapons: 10 x 21in (533mm) TT (bow – 6, stern – 4), 22 x torpedoes; 2 x 57mm guns (1 x 2); 2 x 25mm AA.
Complement: 70.
Specifications for Zulu I, as built.

History: Project 611 (NATO = Zulu) was the lineal successor to the pre-war K-class (qv) and was also the large displacement design prepared in parallel to that of Project 613 (Whiskey-class). Design work started in 1943, but it quickly became clear that the original specifications would result in a boat that was obsolete before it entered service, so the requirement was altered three times, in 1944, 1946 and, finally, in 1947, with the actual design being finalized in 1949 and the first-of-class launched in 1952.

The boat was of conventional double-hull construction, but had an unusual machinery arrangement, with three shafts, each driven by a 2,000bhp diesel or a 1,750shp electric motor. The three-shaft arrangement had some theoretical advantages, principally in that when running on the surface the two wing engines could be used to propel the submarine while the centre engine was used to recharge the batteries. In addition, when the boat was submerged the extra propeller, in combination with the large 448-cell battery, could be used either to raise maximum speed or to extend the range. However, the latter proved unrealisable because the three propellers and their shafts caused considerable vibration when running at specific speeds, the noticeable flexing giving rise to very real fears of structural failure, which resulted in orders banning the use of particular revolutions to prevent the harmonics. Independent

Above: A Soviet Navy Zulu IV-class diesel-electric boat.

of this it also transpired that there were inherent weaknesses in the hull, which prevented the Zulus from descending below about 164ft (50m). As a result, only very limited construction occurred, ending with the 26th unit and a major redesign took place, leading to the Foxtrot-class (qv).

As built, the Zulus had two 57mm and two 25mm guns, but these were removed starting in 1956, while schnorkels, which had not initially been fitted, were installed. NATO identified four different versions of the basic class: Zulu I, as in the specifications above, while Zulu II, III and IV had no deck guns, but did have a schnorkel and differed from each other in minor details only. However, one Zulu was converted as a missile test-bed, and five were subsequently converted to become the first operational SSBs (see Zulu V). In view of the restrictions placed on them, Zulus saw little operational service and most were used for trials and experimental work. Most were scrapped in the early 1980s.

Below: The Zulu was designed in parallel to the Whiskey.

Foxtrot-class (Project 641)

Type: ocean-going patrol.
Total built: 62.
Completed: 1961-83.
Displacement: surfaced 1,957 tons; submerged 2,484 tons.
Dimensions: length 299ft 6in (91.3m); beam 24ft 7in (7.5m); draught 19ft 8in (6.0m).
Propulsion: 3 x 2D-42 diesels, 3 x 2,000bhp; 3 x electric motors, 3 x 1,750shp; battery 4 x 112 cells; three shafts.
Performance: surface – 16.6kt, submerged – 15.9kt; range surfaced 20,000nm at 8kt; submerged 380nm at 2kt; maximum operating diving depth 820ft (250m).
Weapons: 10 x 21in (533mm) TT (bow – 6, stern – 4), 22 x torpedoes.
Complement: 75.

History: The problems with Project 611 (Zulu-class) (see previous entry) caused the Soviet naval staff to issue an urgent new requirement for a replacement, which would fulfil the mission set for that project but without the crippling problems. The result was the Project 641 (NATO = Foxtrot-class) which was essentially a major redesign of the Zulu-class. The Foxtrots had a double hull, with the pressure hull having especially heavy framing to overcome the earlier problems. The power-train was a virtual repeat of that for the Zulu-class, retaining the triple-shaft arrangement, but with a greatly revised stern which combined a new profile with much stronger framing in an effort fo overcome the vibration problems. Surface power was originally provided by three 2D-42 diesels (each 2,000bhp) but these were replaced in later production versions by three Type 40-D diesels (each 1,740bhp), this version being designated Project 641K; performance was little affected by the reduction in horsepower. Although these measures largely overcame the hull vibration problems, the triple propellers still suffered from acoustic interference, enabling NATO submarines to detect them with ease.

   This new class never had gun mounts and a schnorkel was

Above: Foxtrot; note the three sonars – one is in the forward edge of the sail, one atop the bows and the third is a long array around the bows.

Above: An export Foxtrot, operated by the Cuban Navy.

installed from the start. The Foxtrot introduced a new generation of sensors, including a large passive sonar array (Feniks; NATO = Trout Cheek) in the upper bow which was covered by a prominent silver dielectric cover. A prominent dome atop the bow casing housed the Herkules (NATO = Piker Jaw) active sonar, and some boats had a further small cylindrical dome atop this housing an underwater telephone system. As usually happened with the Soviet Navy the original grandiose plans for some 160 were reduced to 60, which were built between 1958 and 1984. Production in the later years was for export: Cuba – 3 (1979084), India – 8 (1968- 75), and Libya – 6 (1976-83). In addition, two were supplied to Poland in 1987/88 from Soviet Navy stocks.

Several missile-armed versions of the Foxtrot were planned but never came to fruition. One of these, however, the Project 641A armed with four SS-N-3 Shaddock missiles, eventually led to the Project 651 (NATO = Juliett-class) SSG, whose hull, in turn, was used as the basis for the Project 641BUKI (NATO = Tango-class) attack submarine (qv). The Foxtrots gave excellent service to the Soviet Navy and in their heyday were to be found in every ocean in the world. They were stricken from the 1980s onwards.

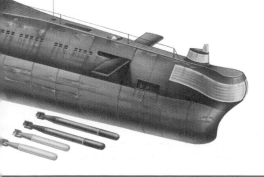

Tango-class (Project 641BUKI)

RUSSIA

Type: ocean-going ASW .
Total built: 18.
Completed: 1972-81.
Displacement: surfaced 2,700 tons; submerged 3,556 tons.
Dimensions: length 295ft 11in (90.2m); beam 20ft 2in (8.6m); draught 18ft 8in (5.7m).
Propulsion: 3 x Type 2D-42 diesels, 3 x 1,825bhp; 3 x PG-102 electric motors, 3 x 1,750shp; 2 x creep motors, 2 x 140shp; battery 4 x 112 cells; three shafts.
Performance: surface – 13kt, submerged – 16kt; range surfaced 20,000nm at 11kt, schnorkel 14,000nm at 7kt, submerged 450nm at 2.5kt; maximum operating diving depth 984ft (300m).
Weapons: 6 x 21in (533mm) TT (bow), 24 x torpedoes/SS-N-15 missiles.
Complement: 75.

History: As described in the previous entry, a planned version of the Foxtrot-class, Project 614A, led to the Juliett-class missile submarine (qv). However, Juliett-class production was ended early, as a result of which there were a number of surplus hulls. Thus, when an urgent requirement arose for a specialised ASW submarine it was decided to combine these hulls with normal Foxtrot-class components to produce a new type, designated Project 641BUKI (NATO = Tango-class), the number indicating that it was seen as a variation of the Foxtrot design, while the suffix "I" indicates a high priority design. The first-of-class *B- 380* was delivered on 20 May 1973 and appeared at the July 1973 Sebastopol naval review in the Black Sea, although for many years the only known operational deployments were with the Northern Fleet; however, some boats later deployed in the Baltic. The Tangos were among the first Soviet boats to be coated with anechoic tiles and, like many such boats in all navies, were frequently to be seen with missing tiles.

Below: The Tango-class caused much alarm in the West as the purpose for a new "long-thin" diesel-electric boat was unclear. It was later learnt that the mission was "bastion defence" protecting Soviet SSBNs from attack by U.S. forces.

Above: A Tango beats its way into a head sea, its patrol ended.

The Tangos were conceived to meet a requirement for "bastion defence"; ie, protecting Soviet SSBNs, particularly the Delta-class, from U.S. and British SSNs. The crew had a higher proportion of officers than is common – 17 officers compared to 8 in a Foxtrot – which suggests that the systems were considerably more complex than usual. There was an unusual rise in the hull forward of the sail, suggesting a need for greater volume forward for the weapons and their reloading system. No Tangos were exported and the first three boats were stricken in 1995, followed by a further two in 1996, and the remainder have become progressively unserviceable through lack of maintenance and shortage of manpower. As of 2002, nine remained, but all were in reserve. The Tango's main claim to fame is that it is the largest diesel-electric patrol boat ever to enter service.

Kilo-class

Type: ocean-going patrol.

Class	Kilo (Project 877)	Improved Kilo (Project 636)
Total built	12	9
Completed	1980	1987-88
Displacement surfaced submerged	2,325 tons 3,076 tons	2,350 tons 2,126 tons
Dimensions length beam draught	238ft 2in (72.6m) 32ft 6in (9.9m) 21ft 7in (6.6m)	242ft 1in (73.8m) 32ft 6in (9.9m) 21ft 7in (6.6m)
Propulsion diesel power electric motors power creep motors power battery shafts	2 x Type 4-2D 2 x 1,825bhp 1 5,900shp 2 x MT-186 2 x 204shp 2 x 120 cells one	2 x Type 4-2AA-42M 2 x 1,825bhp 1 5,500shp 2 x MT-186 2 x 204shp 2 x 120 cells one
Performance speed: surface submerged range: schnorkel submerged maximum diving depth	10kt 17kt 6,000nm/7kt 400nm/3kt 984ft (300m)	12kt 20kt 7,500nm/7kt 400nm/3kt 984ft (300m)
Weapons TT location torpedoes SAM	6 x 21in (533mm) bow 18 x torpedoes/SS-N-16 1 x Fasta-4	6 x 21in (533mm) bow 18 x torpedoes/SS-N-16 1 x Fasta-4
Complement	53	52

History: The first Type 877, launched in 1980, was built specifically for trials by the Soviet Navy, resulting in many modifications and improvements, which were then incorporated into the second and subsequent boats. The overall design is relatively short and fat, with a single main propeller, but retains the traditional Russian double-hull, which not only enhances survivability but also provides valuable space outside the pressure-hull for equipment such as steering gear and high-pressure air bottles. All Type 877 variants have a common pressure-hull 169ft 11in (51.8m) long and a common outer hull 238ft 2in (72.6m) long, with the large, well-shaped bow giving good hydrodynamic and acoustic performance, as well as being the optimum shape

*Above: Indian Navy **Sindhuratna**, an export Kilo-class SSK.*

for the sonar; it also enables six torpedo tubes to be installed. There were five versions, the first being the sole prototype (Type 877). Next came Type 877M, which incorporated the lessons learnt from testing the prototype; 14 were built for the Russian Navy. The export variant of this model was the Type 877EM, which was supplied to: Algeria (2), China (2), India (9), Poland (1) and Romania (1). The Type 877MK was the -M model with a much improved command system, which was supplied to the Russian Navy (7), while the Type 877EMK was the export version, of which the Russian Navy had two (for training foreign crews), and three went to Iran (1992-97).

The improved Type 636 appeared in the mid-1980s, one of the primary differences being greater noise reduction, which included mounting the electric motor on a flexibly mounted raft; halving the shaft speed (from 500 to 250 rpm); redesigning many auxiliary systems; revising the bow profile to reduce flow noise yet further; and removing all noise-producing equipment from the forward compartment. Much greater use was made of automation and new, more powerful and more fuel-efficient diesel engines were also installed, together with more powerful electric motors. The exterior of the hull is totally coated in anechoic tiles made from rubber with a classified additive. Eight have been built so far, six for the Russian Navy and two for the Chinese Navy.

The Types 877 and 636 share two unusual features. First, they have two small, auxiliary propellers, each driven by a 75kW electric motor, which are housed in two 13ft (4m) long tunnels in the stern casing, both of which have hydraulically operated entrance and exit doors. These propel the submarine at some 3kt in a "get-you-home" role, but are also used for mooring and when traversing restricted waterways. The other unusual feature is a portable SAM launcher. An automatic SAM system would have been too heavy, so a manually operated launcher is used from a well in the sail between the snorkel and the radio antenna masts. The SAM crew consists of two men: a launcher operator and a loader who extracts new rounds from the missile container.

Below: Kilo was the first Soviet diesel-electric design to have an "Albacore" tear-drop hull.

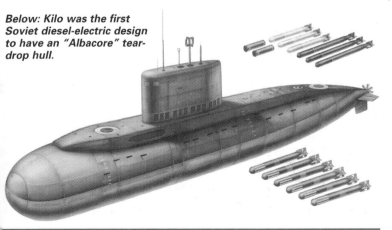

Hajen-class

Type: Baltic patrol.
Total built: 6.
Completed: 1957-60.
Displacement: surfaced 720 tons; submerged 900 tons.
Dimensions: length 216ft 6in (66.0m); beam 16ft 8in (5.1m); draught 16ft 5in (5.0m).
Propulsion: 2 x Pielstick diesels, 2 x 830bhp; 2 x ASEA electric motors; two shafts.
Performance: surface – 16kt, submerged – 20kt.
Weapons: 4 x 21in (533mm) TT (bow), 8 x torpedoes.
Complement: 44.

History: These were Sweden's first post-World War II submarines and were built after a 10-year gap following the completion of the last of the U-1-class in 1944, the main reason for this gap being the German Type XXI. The Royal Swedish Navy knew that its submarine designs had been outdated at a stroke by the German Type XXI and XXIII, but since their country had been neutral in the war it was not privy to the design information available to the victorious Allies. However, by a fortunate stroke of fate, a German crew had scuttled *U-3503*, a Type XXI boat, off the entrance to Gøteborg on 8 May 1945, following which they had surrendered and been interned. The Swedish Navy recovered the hulk in 1946 and subjected it to the most detailed examination before scrapping it. The Swedes took their time in studying the lessons, as a result of which the first of the new Hajen-class was not laid down until 1953.

Draken-class

Type: Baltic patrol.
Total built: 6.
Completed: 1961-62.
Displacement: surfaced 835 tons; submerged 950 tons.
Dimensions: length 226ft 6in (69.3m); beam 16ft 9in (5.3m); draught 17ft 5in (5.3m).
Propulsion: 2 x Pielstick diesels, 2 x 800bhp; 2 x ASEA electric motors, 2 x 840kW; one shaft.
Performance: surface – 17kt, submerged – 22kt.
Weapons: 4 x 21in (533mm) TT (bow), 12 x torpedoes.
Complement: 36.

History: The second post-World War II class for the Royal Swedish Navy, the Draken-class was essentially an improved version of the Hajen-class. It retained the long, thin hull and careful streamlining of the German Type XXI, the major difference being the replacement of the small, fast-rotating twin propellers by a single, much slower-revving design. This not only gave higher speed, but also considerably reduced the submarine's acoustic signature.

The normal practice for the RSwedN at this time was to build one new class of six boats every decade, with each class serving for 20 years and receiving a major modernisation at approximately the 10-year point. There was, however, an interruption in this very logical process, caused partly by the very rapid developments in both submarine and anti-submarine technology from the 1950s onwards and also by the ever-escalating cost of defence equipment. Thus, it would have been normal practice for the entire Draken-class to serve

Above: **Bavern** *emerges from its solid rock shelter.*

Although somewhat smaller than the Type XXI, these 720-ton vessels were the largest built so far for the RSwedN and their long, smooth hull and careful streamlining, especially of the fin, and high battery power resulted in a very effective design. They had twin, fast-rotating propellers, giving a maximum underwater speed of 16kt, although they were somewhat noisy by later standards. They were armed with four torpedo tubes, all in the bow, and were the first Swedish submarines for some 40 years not to have any guns. They were designed for fast diving and were the first Swedish submarines to be fitted with schnorkels. All six boats were stricken in 1980.

Above: **Draken-class** Nordkaparen *amidst the Baltic ice.*

on to approximately 1980, but this did not happen. All six boats were modernised in 1970-71, but only *Draken* and *Gripen* were stricken in 1981 in accordance with previous practice, when they were replaced by the three-strong Näcken-class. The other four, however – *Vargen, Delfinen, Nordkaparen* and *Springaren* – were given a major rebuild in 1981-83 and then served on until striking in 1988 (thus serving for some 26 years), when they were replaced by the four-strong Västergotland-class. At one stage in the mid-1980s two of the rebuilt-Draken class were offered to the Royal Malaysian Navy for the initial training of a submarine arm prior to an order for new-build boats, but the plan fell through.

Sjöormen (A-11)-class

SWEDEN

Type: Baltic patrol.
Total built: 5.
Completed: 1968-69.
Displacement: surfaced 1,125 tons; submerged 1,400 tons.
Dimensions: length 165ft 7in (50.5m); beam 20ft 0in (6.1m); draught 19ft 0in (5.1m).
Propulsion: 2 x Hedemora-Pielstick diesels, 2 x 525bhp; 1 x ASEA electric motor, 1,500 hp; one shaft.
Performance: surface – 12kt, submerged – 20kt; maximum operating diving depth 492ft (150m).
Weapons: 4 x 21in (533mm) TT (bow), 8 x torpedoes; 2 x (400mm) TT (bow), 4 x torpedoes.
Complement: 23.

History: The Sjöormen-class was designed in the early 1960s, with five boats entering service between 1967 and 1969, where they replaced the Abboren (rebuilt U-1)- class. This was the first of a succession of Swedish designs to break away from conventional practice, its principal novelty being a "tear-drop" hull, although it would be incorrect to describe it as an "Albacore-hull" since it is quite different in shape to that revolutionary U.S. submarine. The Sjöormen's control surfaces were also of a totally new layout for Swedish submarines, with X-planes aft and sail-mounted forward hydroplanes. Finally, the design also introduced the unique Swedish torpedo layout, with a row of four 21in (533mm) tubes above and the two shorter 15.7in (400mm) tubes below, with reloads for

Näcken (A14)-class

SWEDEN

Type: Baltic patrol.
Total built: 3.
Completed: 1980-81.
Displacement: surfaced 1,050 tons; submerged 1,145 tons.
Dimensions: length 162ft 5in (49.5m); beam 18ft 8in (5.7m); draught 18ft 0in (5.5m).
Propulsion: 1 x M.T.U diesel, 2,100bhp; 1 x Jeumont-Schneider electric motor, 1,150kW; one shaft
Performance: surface – 20kt, submerged – 25kt; maximum operating diving depth 984ft (300m).
Weapons: 6 x 21in (533mm) TT (bow), 8 x torpedoes; 2 x 15.7in (400mm) TT (bow) 4 x torpedoes.
Complement: 19.

History: As usual in Sweden, laying down the first of the next submarine class followed closely on completion of the previous class and in this case the Näcken design followed on from the last of the Sjöormen-class as a replacement for three of the six-strong Draken-class. The first-of-class *Näcken* was laid down in November 1972 and the three boats entered service in 1980/81. Following construction of the Sjöormen-class the RSwedN re-examined the design using computer analysis and arrived at a rather different result with a longer, parallel-sided hull with a high beam-to-length ratio, and a very angular sail located further aft. There is a large bow-mounted sonar and the main accommodation space is abaft the control room with machinery spaces right aft. Unlike most other submarines, there is just one combined search and

Right: The design of the Sjöormen-class began to show a definite Swedish style.

all tubes positioned on an automated loading rack immediately behind. The sail in this class is set far forward on the hull, indicating that the control-room is also far forward.

All five boats were modernised in 1984-85, among the main changes being the installation of a new combat data/fire-control system, and a new sonar suite. *Sjölejonet* and *Sjöhunden* then received a "mid-life" update in 1992-94, which included yet another new sonar suite, and the same electronic system as that installed in the Näcken-class during their latest refits. This extended the operational lives of these two boats into the late 1990s.

All five boats have been sold to the Singapore Navy. *Sjöhunden* was transferred in 1995 to serve as a training boat, and was followed by *Sjöormen*, *Sjöljonet* and *Sjölhästen* which were fully refurbished as operational boats before being transferred in 1999-2001. The fifth boat, *Sjöbjornen*, was retained in Swedish waters and is serving as a source of spares.

Above: Näcken, *seen here after lengthening as an AIP test-bed.*

attack periscope. Arma-ment is very heavy for the size of the hull, with six 21in (533mm) tubes and eight torpedoes, with a further two 15.7in (450mm) tubes and four torpedoes below.

Näcken was converted into a hybrid-powered submarine in 1987-88, being lengthened by 19ft 8in (6.0m) so that two Stirling closed-cycle engines, two LOX (liquid oxygen) tanks and the necessary control systems could be installed. The Stirling engines are used for submerged patrols at low speed, with low use of battery power. LOX provides the combustible air and the exhaust products dissolve in water.

Västergotland (A17)-class SWEDEN

Type: Baltic patrol.
Total built: 4.
Completed: 1987-90.
Displacement: surfaced 1,070 tons; submerged 1,143 tons.
Dimensions: length 159ft 2in (48.5m); beam 20ft 0in (6.1m); draught 18ft 4in (5.6m).
Propulsion: 2 x Hedemora diesels, 2 x 1,300bhp; 2 x Jeumont-Schneider generator sets, 2 x 760kW; 1 x ASEA electric motor, 1,800shp; one shaft.
Performance: surface – 11kt, submerged – 20kt; maximum operating diving depth 984ft (300m).
Weapons: 6 x 21in (533mm) TT (bow), 12 x torpedoes; 3 x 15.7in (400mm) TT, 6 x torpedoes.
Complement: 20.

History: The design contract for the replacement of the last three of the Draken-class was awarded to Kockums in April 1978 and the construction contract in December 1981. As had now become the practice, the bow and stern sections were built by Karlskronavarvet and then shipped to Malmö where Kockums built the centre section and was responsible for final assembly and trials. The four Västergotland-class boats are of single-hull design, with a computer-controlled indexed (ie, X-configured) rudder/after hydroplane. The hull comprises two compartments separated by a watertight bulkhead, and there is an escape chamber for the crew situated aft of the sail, which is designed to mate with the RSwedN's URF-class rescue submersible. The hull is covered with a coating of anechoic tiles. There are nine bow torpedo tubes, six 21in (533mm) and three 15.7in (400mm), together with one reload per tube, one of the heaviest batteries ever installed in a submarine of this relatively small size. At one stage the RSwedN considered installing four vertical launch tubes in the sail for RBS-17 anti-ship missiles (a version of the Saab RBS-15 surface-skimmer), but this did not take place, mainly because the missiles were not considered to be cost-effective in the context of submarine operations in the Baltic. Another proposal was to retrofit these submarines with Sterling engines, but this, too, has been dropped..

Two of these boats, *Södermanland* and *Östergötland*, are currently being rebuilt and given a 32ft 10in (10m) extension to enable them to accommodate two Sterling Mk 3 closed-cycle engines and the associated tanks and controls, and will return to service in 2004. At that point the other two boats,

Guppy I-class Conversions UNITED STATES

Type: ocean-going patrol.
Total converted: 2.
Completed: 1947.
Displacement: surfaced 1,900 tons; submerged 2,400 tons.
Dimensions: length 307ft 6in (93.7m); beam 27ft 4in (8.3m).
Propulsion: 4 x main diesel generators, 4 x 1,350bhp; 2 x electric motors, 2 x 1,370shp; battery 4 x 126 cell; two shafts.
Performance: surface – 17.8kt, submerged – 18.2kt; range surfaced 11,000nm at 8kt; maximum operating diving depth 400ft (122m).

Right: **Västergotland, *seen here at "launch", shows the typically Swedish hull contours.***

Västergotland and *Hälsingland,* will be stricken, leaving the RSwedN with an entirely Sterling-powered sub-marine fleet. (The latest Götland-class is described in the AIP section.)

Above. This class has a heavy bow battery of six 21in (533mm) and three 15.7in (400mm) torpedo tubes.

Weapons: 10 x 21in (533mm) TT (bow – 6, stern – 4), 28 x torpedoes.
Complement: 79.
Specifications for Guppy I, as converted.

History: At the end of World War II the U.S. Navy possessed a huge fleet of submarines, almost all of them war-built Gato-, Balao- and Tench-classes. Pre-war boats were immediately scrapped, together with a number of the older Gatos, while most boats still under construction were broken up on the ways, apart from four, on which work was suspended against possible future use.

Some boats were converted for specialised roles such as radar pickets, hunter-killers, amphibious transports, oilers and missile launchers, while others were used in various types of research, but most were given a GUPPY (Greater Underwater Propulsion Program) upgrade, which included streamlining the hull and superstructure, removing unnecessary protuberances, increasing battery power and fitting a schnorkel. These measures resulted in greater range, much increased underwater speeds and increased tactical effectiveness. There were six Guppy conversions, plus the fleet schnorkel.

Guppy I.
Two boats were converted in 1945-47 to provide high-speed underwater targets for U.S. ASW forces to train against, with external streamlining, particularly of the sail, and extra batteries; this enabled them to achieve just under 18kt submerged, a 100 per cent increase in speed. They also had some internal reorganisation and, where necessary, equipment was updated, but they were not fitted with a schnorkel. The specifications for the two boats concerned are given above. Both were later converted for a second time, on this occasion to Guppy II.

Guppy IA.
The Guppy II programme (see next entry) proved rather expensive, so a less elaborate conversion was evolved, designated Guppy IA. This still included streamlining and a schnorkel, but did not include a fourth 126-cell battery, instead of which the boats were given three batteries of a new type of cell; this was known as the "Sargo II battery". The internal rearrangement was also less elaborate than in the Guppy II conversion. This Guppy IA conversion was applied to 10 Balao- and Tench-class boats and took place in 1951-52.

Guppy IB.
If Guppy IA was an austere version of Guppy II, then Guppy IB was an austere

Guppy II-class Conversions

UNITED STATES

Type: ocean-going patrol.
Total converted: 24.
Completed: 1949-51.
Displacement: surfaced 2,040 tons; submerged 2,400 tons.
Dimensions: length 307ft 0in (93.6m); beam 27ft 4in (8.3m).
Propulsion: 3 x main generator diesels, 3 x 1,350bhp; 2 x electric motors, 2 x 1,370shp; battery 4 x 126 cell; two shafts.
Performance: surface – 18kt, submerged – 16kt; range surfaced 11,000nm at 8kt; maximum operating diving depth 400ft (122m).
Weapons: 10 x 21in (533mm) TT (bow – 6, stern – 4), 28 x torpedoes.
Complement: 85.
Specifications for Guppy II, as converted.

History: Learning from the Guppy I programme, the U.S. Navy embarked on an even more ambitious conversion in which 24 boats were converted to Guppy II standard in 1948-51. This involved 17 serving Balao- and Tench-class boats, five unfinished hulls on which work had been suspended at the end of the war, and the two Guppy Is. The work involved similar additional batteries and the streamlining of the sail and hull as in Guppy I, but differed in including a schnorkel. By this time the boats, large as they were, had become overcrowded and considerable internal reorganisation was required to fit everything in.

version of Guppy IA. This conversion was devised for four boats transferred abroad in the early 1950s, two to the Netherlands and two to Italy.

Below: Guppy IB; **Italian** *da Vinci,* **ex-USS** *Dace (SS-247).*

Above: **Thornback** *(SS-418), a Guppy IIA conversion.*

Guppy IIA.

A further 16 Balao and Tench boats were converted to a generally similar standard to the Guppy II, but with less drastic internal reorganisation. Both Guppy IIs and IIAs were badly overcrowded and after several years' service one engine and one generator were removed. This reduced performance, but this was more than offset by the gains in space and ease of maintenance.

Guppy III-class Conversions

UNITED STATES

Type: ocean-going patrol.
Total converted: 9.
Completed: 1959-63.
Displacement: surfaced 1,975 tons; submerged 2,870 tons.
Dimensions: length 322ft 0in (98.1m); beam 27ft 4in (8.3m).
Propulsion: 4 x main generator diesels, 4 x 1,350bhp; 2 x electric motors, 2 x 1,370shp; battery 4 x 126 cells; two shafts.
Performance: surface – 17kt, submerged – 14kt; range surfaced 11,000nm at 8kt; maximum operating diving depth 400ft (122m).
Weapons: 10 x 21in (533mm) TT (bow – 6, stern – 4), 28 x torpedoes.
Complement: 95.
Specifications for Guppy III, as converted.

History: Nine Guppy IIs were given an even more drastic conversion in 1959-62 as part of the Fleet Rehabilitation And Modernization (FRAM) programme, the need in this particular case being to maintain the effectiveness of the submarine fleet until sufficient SSNs were in service. The greatest single element of the work involved cutting the pressure-hull in two at a point where the forward battery compartment joined the control room and inserting a 15ft (4.6m) "plug" to provide much-needed additional volume for the crew, the ever-growing amount of electronic equipment, and extra torpedoes. The sail was extended and inside it the conning tower was also lengthened to accommodate

Below: Brazilian **Guanabara,** *a Balao-class Guppy II.*

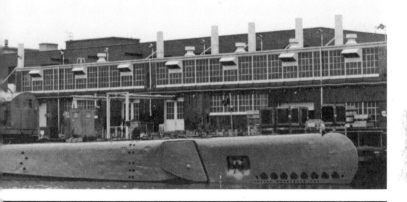

Above: Guppy III **Cobbler** *(SS-344); note sonar domes.*

additional equipment. Externally, these conversions were instantly recognisable by the three large fins covering the hydrophones of the PUFFS passive sound-ranging equipment, and by the very high sail.

Originally it was intended that all the Guppy IIs would have been brought up to this standard, but financial constraints compelled a reduction to just nine. The work was completed between 1959 and 1963 but the boats remained in service for only a few years and most were transferred to foreign navies in 1973: Brazil – 2; Greece – 1; Italy – 2; Turkey – 2. The

Fleet Schnorkel
Conversions

UNITED STATES

Type: ocean-going patrol.
Total converted: 19.
Completed: 1947-52.
Displacement: surfaced 2,040 tons; submerged 2,400 tons.
Dimensions: length 312ft 0in (95.1m); beam 27ft 4in (8.3m).
Propulsion: 4 x main diesel generators, 4 x 1,350bhp; 2 x electric motors, 2 x 1,370shp; battery 4 x 126 cell; two shafts.
Performance: surface – 17.8kt, submerged – 18.2kt; range surfaced 11,000nm at 8kt; maximum operating diving depth 400ft (122m).
Weapons: 10 x 21in (533mm) TT (bow – 6, stern – 4), 28 x torpedoes.
Complement: 83.

History: Even the "austere" Guppy IA and IIA conversions proved too expensive to be applied to the entire fleet of the U.S. Navy's diesel-electric boats, so an even more limited programme was instituted, the main purpose of which was to install the schnorkel in as many boats as possible. Two different types of schnorkel had been developed during the war by the Germans and Japanese, and had entered service on a number of their submarines from early 1944 onwards. A much improved version was developed by the U.S. Navy as a matter of urgency in the immediate post war years. The first fleet boat to be fitted being USS *Irex* (SS-482) in 1947. In essence this conversion simply involved a higher, semi-streamlined sail containing the periscopes and the schnorkel mast, while no effort was made to remove the guns or other protuberances on the upper casing. Following successful testing, the schnorkel was approved for service and was installed in all Guppy boats from the Guppy II onwards.

last of these Guppy IIIs to retire from active service with the U.S. Navy was USS *Tiru* (SS-416), which was also the last of the Gato-/Balao-/Tench-classes which had served the Navy so well.

Below: Greek Guppy III, **Katsonis,** *with sonar domes removed.*

Above: **Sabalo** *(SS-302); "Fleet Schnorkel" limited conversion.*

The "fleet schnorkel" was a very limited conversion, carried out in the course of routine refits and involved the installation of a schnorkel together with some streamlining, the removal of guns, and, in some later cases, the installation of a GRP sail. By no means all the boats classified as "fleet schnorkels" were identical and there were a variety of sail profiles and upper casing work. Internally, apart from the ducting and controls associated with the schnorkel, very few alterations were made. All were converted in 1951-52 and over the following 20 years considerable differences developed between them. Some remained as they had been when they left the yards in the 1950s but others were given the very tall streamlined GRP sail of the Guppy III, while three (*Piper, Sterlet* and *Sea Owl*) retained the original sail but were given very large bow sonar domes. All had been stricken from the U.S. Navy by 1970, and some were then transferred to foreign navies. Some other boats which were transferred to foreign navies in the 1950s were given the equivalent of a fleet schnorkel refit prior to being handed over.

Barracuda-class

Type: hunter/killer.
Total built: 3.
Completed: 1951-52.
Displacement: surfaced 765 tons; submerged 1,160 tons.
Dimensions: length 196ft 1in (59.8m); beam 24ft 7in (7.5m); draught 14ft 5in (4.4m).
Propulsion: 2 x General motors diesels, 2 x 525bhp; 2 x General Motors electric motors; two shafts.
Performance: surface – 13kt, submerged – 8.5kt.
Weapons: 4 x 21in (533mm) TT (bow – 2, stern – 2).
Complement: 37.

History: An operational concept was developed in the late 1940s for a mass-produced hunter/killer submarine (also known as an "SSK"), which would position itself off enemy bases or in maritime choke-points just before a war started and then ambush enemy submarines as they sailed for their war stations. The operational requirement for the submarine to fulfil such a mission stressed quietness; a long-range, passive sonar; low cost; and ease of manufacture in large numbers. High speed and deep diving capabilities were not required and thus the "thin-skinned" Gatos were particularly suitable, and a total of seven of these were converted to the SSK role in 1951-53. A purpose-built design was also developed, being known originally as the K-class and later as the Barracuda-class.

  The Barracudas were smaller than contemporary U.S. Navy submarines

Tang/Darter-class

Type: attack.
Total built: 7.
Completed: 1951-56.
Displacement: surfaced 1,560 tons; submerged 2,260 tons.
Dimensions: length 269ft 2in (82.0m); beam 27ft 2in (8.3m); draught 17ft 0in (5.2m).
Propulsion: 3 x Fairbanks-Morse Type 3 diesels, 3 x 1,500bhp; 2 x electric motors, 2 x 1,800shp; two shafts (see notes).
Performance: surface – 15.5kt; submerged – 18.3kt.
Weapons: 8 x 21in (553mm) TT (bow – 6, stern – 2).
Complement: 83.
Specifications are for Tang-class, as built.

History: The Tang-class was the U.S. Navy's first post-war, totally new attack submarine design and thus equivalent to the Soviet Whiskey- and the British Porpoise-classes (qqv). Like those other two classes the design assimilated the lessons of the war and took account of the examination of captured Type XXI boats. They thus had a long, thin and carefully streamlined hull, and high power batteries. To reduce the size of the submarine a totally new design of diesel engine was selected; made by General Motors. The new design was, however, a failure, proving to be mechanically unreliable and very difficult to maintain, and on several occasions Tang-class boats had to be towed across the Atlantic for repairs in the United States. The problem was so severe that a major and very expensive programme had to be set in train to replace these troublesome engines with a lightweight Fairbanks-Morse model; this required the hull to be

Above: Barracuda *(SST-3), here seen as a training boat.*

with a massive dome in the bows for the BQR-4 sonar. They served in this role only until 1959 when the mission was recognised as impracticable; the bow sonar was removed from all three, whereupon two were reclassified as attack submarines, while the third became a training boat.

These boats are an example of how even the highly logical U.S. Navy designation system occasionally becomes muddled. The boats were originally not given names but numbers with a "K" prefix: *K-1* (SSK-1), *K-2* (SSK-2) and *K-3* (SSK-3). Then, in December 1955, two of them were given names and hull numbers in the usual "SS-" series; thus, *K-2* (SSK-2) became *Bass* (SS-551) and *K-3* (SSK-3) became *Bonita* (SS-552). The former *K-1* (SSK-1), however, retained its original number until July 1959 when it became *Barracuda* (SST-3) (SST = training submarine), but although it was reclassified yet again as an attack submarine in 1972 it was never given a hull number in the full U.S. Navy series. *Bass* and *Bonita* were scrapped in 1967 but *Barracuda* survived until 1974.

Above: USS Darter *(SS-576), a lengthened version of the Tang.*

lengthened by 9ft (2.7m) and even then only three engines could be installed. The last two boats, *Gudgeon* (SS-567) and *Harder* (SS-568) were lengthened and re-engined while still under construction, but the other four *Tang* (SS-563), *Trigger* (SS-564), *Wahoo* (SS-565) and *Trout* (SS-566) had to be returned to the builder's yards for a major reconstruction in the late 1950s. In a further rebuild in the late 1960s the boats were again lengthened, this time by 18ft (5.5m) to enable them to accommodate the PUFFS sonar system and to provide more room for the crew. These boats were instantly recognisable by the characteristic three fin-shaped domes on the upper casing.

Darter (SS-576) was essentially a repeat of the lengthened/re-engined version of the Tang-class, with improved control systems. Only one was built.

Abtao-class

Type: patrol.
Total built: 4.
Completed: 1954-57.
Displacement: surfaced 825 tons; submerged 1,400 tons.
Dimensions: length 243ft 0in (74.1m); beam 22ft 0in (6.7m); draught 14ft 0in (4.3m).
Propulsion: 2 x General Motors diesels, 2 x 1,200bhp; 2 x electric motors, 2 x 1,200shp; two shafts.
Performance: surface – 16kt, submerged – 10kt; range surfaced 5,000nm at 10kt.
Weapons: 6 x 21in (533mm) TT (bow – 4, stern – 2); 1 x 5in (127mm) gun.
Complement: 40.

History: This class had three claims to fame. The first was that they were the only submarines in the world to retain a deck-gun to the very last year of the 20th century, some 40 years longer than any other navy; second, they were direct descendants of one of the most unpopular classes ever to have served in the U.S. Navy; and, third, they were the last submarines to be built in a United States shipyard for an export customer. In the late 1940s the Peruvian Navy sought new submarines which were smaller than the surplus "fleet submarines" then becoming available, but would incorporate recent advances, such as streamlining and extra battery power.

The Electric Boat Company based the design on the Mackerel-class, two of which had been built for the U.S. Navy in the late 1930s as a smaller and more economical alternative to the "fleet submarines". *Mackerel* (SS-204) and *Marlin*

Barbel-class

Type: patrol.
Total built: 3.
Completed: 1959.
Displacement: surfaced 2,146 tons; submerged 2,894 tons.
Dimensions: length 219ft 2in (66.8m); beam 29ft 0in (8.8m); draught 20ft 8in (6.3m).
Propulsion: 3 x Fairbanks-Morse diesels, 3 x 1,600bhp; 1 x Westinghouse electric motor, 3,150shp; one shaft.
Performance: surface – 15kt, submerged – 21kt.
Weapons: 6 x 21in (533mm) TT (bow).
Complement: 83.

History: These were the last three diesel-electric submarines to be built for the U.S. Navy, all three being launched in 1958 and completed in 1959. Their design was derived from the lessons learnt with *Albacore* (AGSS-569), which demonstrated the many advantages of the short, fat hull, technically known as a "body-of-revolution" but popularly described as a "tear-drop" shape, and also showed the superiority of the single- over the double-propeller propulsion system. The latter arrangement made it impossible to mount torpedo tubes firing astern. The Barbel design was based on that of the Albacore and as built the boats had bow diving planes, although this was changed during their service to sail-mounted planes. Unlike other U.S. Navy submarines of the period they were not fitted with the PUFFS sonar system, possibly because the three fin-shaped domes would have caused too much hydrodynamic drag.

Bonefish (SS-582) suffered a serious fire at sea on 24 March 1988, resulting

Right: Tiburon, *re-named* Abtao *in 1957, first of four boats built in the USA for Peru.*

(SS-205) proved too small and of little value and were deeply dis-liked within the Sub-marine Force, as a result of which they were relegated to training tasks until the war's end, when they were quickly scrapped. Despite this unpromising background, the basic design proved suitable and the hull and sail were streamlined as requested. To the considerable surprise of the Electric Boat Company, however, the Peruvians also insisted on a gun, and a 127mm (5in) "wet mount" was duly fitted on the after casing.

The four submarines were regularly upgraded during their service, with major refits at Electric Boat in 1965 for two boats and in 1968 for the other two. This work included replacing the original stepped sail by a tall type modelled on that of the Guppy III and removing the deck gun on two of the boats. In 1981 new batteries were shipped and the engineering and electrical systems modernised. and Eledone sonar fitted. *Angamos* (S-43) was stricken in 1990, followed by *Iquique* (S 44) in 1993, but the remaining pair (which happened to be the two retaining the gun) served on until 1999, when both were scrapped. The boats were originally named *Tiburon, Atun, Lobo* and *Merlin*, but these were changed during their service to *Abtao, Angamos, Dos de Mayo* and *Iquique.*

Above: Barbel was the U.S .Navy's last diesel-electric boat class.

in three fatalities and causing so much damage that she was stricken and scrapped. The other two, *Barbel* (SS-580) and *Blueback* (SS-581), lasted only two years longer, being stricken in 1990, the last of a very long line of diesel-electric submarines that had served the U.S. Navy so well over a period of 80 years.

Air-Independent Propulsion (AIP) Submarines

S ince the very earliest submarines, designers have tried to find a system for submerged propulsion which is independent of the atmosphere. Initially, this power was provided by the crew themselves, either using their arms to turn a crank or their legs to operate a treadle, but such human power was clearly inadequate, even in the CSS *Hunley* which employed eight brawny crewmen. One of the earliest mechanical systems was invented by the Englishman, George Garrett, who attempted to harness the power of latent steam so that one propulsion plant sufficed for both surface and submerged propulsion; it was ingenious and the world's first air-independent propulsion (AIP) system, but was never made to work properly. Other 19th century designers used compressed-air or electricity from accumulators, both of which were clean and economical, but were very short-ranged and required a return to harbour for recharging; they were, therefore, only suitable for boats involved in harbour or coastal defence.

For many years, the combination of a battery for submerged power and internal-combustion engines – kerosene, gasoline or diesel – for surface power and recharging the battery reigned supreme. In the late 1930s, however, engineers in Russia and Germany started to examine the use of closed-cycle engines for submerged propulsion. The German Professor Walter was particularly active, producing a host of designs based on the use of hydrogen-peroxide, but although numerous prototypes were produced none of his designs ever saw operational service. Nevertheless, after World War II the American, British and Soviet navies examined his ideas very closely, but hydrogen-peroxide proved difficult to use and

the advent of nuclear propulsion proved a far more cost-effective and much less dangerous alternative for the larger navies.

For several more decades the smaller navies were forced to rely on diesel-electric propulsion, but the subject of "air-independent propulsion" began to be re-examined from the 1970s onwards, particularly in Germany, France, Sweden and the USSR. At first it was thought that an AIP system could be found which would totally replace the electric-storage battery for submerged propulsion, but this proved impossible and all present AIP plants provide a relatively low-power cruise capability, but a battery is still needed for high- speed operations.

The known current AIP programmes involve various nations and a number of different technologies. Fuel-cell projects are being pursued by Germany and Italy for their Type 212 submarines, while Russia is working on a different type of fuel-cell for installation in both new and existing boats. The Stirling system continues to be developed, with Japan also showing a close interest. A group of British, Dutch and German firms are cooperating in the development of the Spectre closed-circuit diesel (CCD) system, while France and Spain are cooperating on the MESMA system. Finally, Canada is also known to have an AIP project. So, for the next few years, the fuel-cell and the Stirling engine will be the main systems and both appear to be equally promising, but AIP is an area where rapid technological development, possibly even major breakthroughs, can be expected.

Below: Germany's "Ex-U1," one of many AIP test-beds.

Drzewiecki Man-powered Submarines

RUSSIA

Type: air-independent human power.

History: Although these would today be classified as "minisubs", the Drzewiecki submersibles are significant as one of the few successful man-powered designs. A Pole, Stefan Drzewiecki (1844-1942), was one of those extraordinary men who turn their minds to a bewildering variety of areas: an early invention was a distance-measuring device for Parisian horse-drawn taxis, another an automatic plotter which marked a ship's track on a chart, while he later became involved in aeronautics and a specialist in propeller design. In 1877 during the Russo-Turkish War he turned his mind to submarines and designed a craft – Drzewiecki No 1 – which had a crew of just one man, who sat under a small conning-tower and was assisted by a periscope and other innovations. He powered the boat using his feet to operate a treadle which drove the single propeller. The towed mines were to be attached to the target ship by the operator who remained in his craft. Trials were successful but the war ended and the Russian Navy lost interest, although the army ordered an improved version, the Type II, and then placed a production order for 50 of the improved Type III. Two Type IIIs were converted to electrical propulsion in

Hunley

CONFEDERATE STATES OF AMERICA

Type: air-independent human power.
Total built: 1.
Completed: 1863.
Displacement: not known.
Dimensions: length 39ft 6in (12.0m); beam 3ft 10in (1.2m); height of hull 4ft 3in (1.3m).
Propulsion: 8-man; manual; one shaft.
Performance (estimated): surface – ca 3-5kt; submerged – 2-3kt.
Weapons: 1 x spar torpedo.
Complement: 9.

History: Named after its designer/builder, the Confederate submarine *H.L. Hunley* carried out the first successful underwater attack in history when it sank USS *Housatonic* (17 February 1864). The hull was fabricated from a steam boiler with a very sharp bow, and entry was by two watertight hatches, the forward also serving as the conning tower for the captain. Amidships, a vertical tube extended some 4ft (1.2m) above the hull to serve as a primitive schnorkel when travelling awash, with a stop-cock that could be shut prior to diving. There were ballast tanks at each end of the boat with sea-cocks open to the outside; the tanks were filled by opening the cocks and emptied by means of a manually operated pump; depth was assessed by means of a simple mercury tube. The craft was steered by the captain, using levers to control the midships diving-planes and a wheel to control the rudder. The inside was painted white and lighting was by means of one or more candles. There was a single shrouded propeller attached to a long

Class	Type I	Type II	Type III
Completed	1877	1879	1878-81
Number in class	1	1	50
Displacement	n.k.	ca 2.5 tons	ca 2.5 tons
Dimensions length beam draught	15ft (4.5m) 5ft (1.5m) 5ft (1.5m)	20ft (6.1m) 5ft (1.5m) 3ft 6in (1.0m)	20ft (6.1m) 5ft (1.5m) 3ft 6in (1.0m)
Propulsion	1 x shaft treadle	2 x shaft treadle	1 x shaft treadle
Performance	ca 1.5kt	2kt	2-3kt
Weapons	2 mines	2 mines	2 mines
Complement	1	4	4

1884 and another to gasoline-propulsion in 1905.

crank, which was turned by the crew of eight men.

The weapon was a "spar torpedo", with a fused copper cylinder containing 143lb (65kg) of explosive mounted at the end of a 17ft (5.2m) long iron tube mounted some 4in (10cm) above the foot of the bow. The concept was that the submarine would approach at such a speed that barbs would be lodged in the target's wooden hull, whereupon the charge was detonated by a lanyard operated by the captain. A 4,000lb (1,814kg) cast-iron keel was fitted, which ensured that the craft remained upright and which could be released from the inside in an emergency.

The *Hunley* sank three times during training, with the loss of 23 men, each time due to water lapping over the forward hatch, whose cover was open while running awash. She was raised and recommissioned on each occasion. Vast amounts of money were offered to her fourth crew for the attack on *Housatonic*. But it appears that she was too close to the explosion and was dragged down by her victim. She has now been raised.

Below: **Hunley** *was powered by eight men turning a crank.*

Nordenfelt-class   SWEDEN/UNITED KINGDOM

Type: air-independent steam-power.
Total built: Nordenfelt I – 1; Nordenfelt II – 2.
Completed: Nordenfelt I – 1885; Nordenfelt II – 1886-87.
Displacement: surfaced 100 tons; submerged 160 tons.
Dimensions: length 100ft 0in (30.5m); beam 12ft 2in (3.7m).
Propulsion: Lamm steam-compound engine, 250ihp; one steam accumulator for underwater propulsion; one shaft.
Performance: surface – 8kt; submerged – 4.5kt, 14nm/4kt; maximum operational depth 50ft (15m).
Weapons: 2 x 14in (356mm) external TT (bow) (2 torpedoes); 2 x Nordenfelt MGs
Complement: 7.
Specifications are for Nordenfelt II, as built.

History: Later steam-powered submarines used steam for surface propulsion only and relied on a battery for underwater propulsion, but it was first used in a singular manner. These three submarines were the result of cooperation between the Swedish armaments manufacturer, Thorsten Nordenfelt, and an eccentric British clergyman, Reverend George Garrett, who had been responsible for *Resurgam*, a steam-powered experimental submarine. Their first boat, *Nordenfelt I*, was built in Sweden in 1885 and sold to Greece, while the two slightly larger *Nordenfelt IIs* were built in England and sold to Turkey in 1886.

The power system was ingenious. The boats were powered on the surface by a steam engine, using steam from a boiler in the normal way, but with some steam being fed into a special accumulator tank, where it passed through a heat-exchanger, heating the water in that tank before being pumped back into the boiler. On submerging, the super-heated water in the accumulator was fed back into the main boiler, where it flashed into steam and drove the over-size pistons. The system worked after a fashion but had drawbacks, not least of

Le Plongeur   FRANCE

Type: air-independent compressed-air power.
Total built: 1.
Completed: 1863
Displacement: surfaced 420 tons; submerged 435 tons.
Dimensions: length 146ft 0in (44.5m); beam 19ft 8in (6.0m); draught 9ft 2in (2.8m).
Propulsion: 4-cylinder compressed-air engine, 80hp; one shaft.
Performance (estimated): surface – 4.1kt, 7.5nm/2.4kt; submerged – ca 4kt, 5.7nm/3.8kt.
Weapons: 1 x spar torpedo.
Complement: 13.

History: This was by far the largest and one of the most imaginative 19th century submarine designs, and the first to find an alternative to manpower for submerged propulsion. *Plongeur*, designed by Captain Bourgois of the French Navy in cooperation with engineer Charles Brun, was powered by an engine driven by compressed-air. The air was carried in 23 containers, with a total capacity of 4,520cu ft (128m³) at 171psi (12kg/cm²), which had to be recharged in port. This enabled the 85hp engine to propel the submarine at some 4kt, both

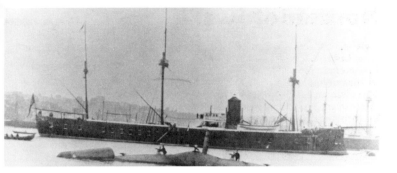

Above: Nordenfelt's boats were powered by latent steam.

which was that steam had to be raised three days prior to sailing in order to heat the accumulator effectively.

The boats operated by a system of positive buoyancy to ensure that they returned to the surface. To submerge, water was allowed into the main ballast tank until the boat was just under the surface when two vertical propellers on the craft's bottom were engaged to drive the boat downwards. The propellers had to be constantly driven to maintain depth, but to surface, particularly if something had gone wrong, the propellers were stopped and the boat automatically returned to the surface.

None of the three boats became operational. They were allowed to rust away, although during World War I the Germans found the rusting hulks of the *Nordenfelt IIs* in a shed in Constantinople (Istanbul) and attempted to make them usable. A further design, *Nordenfelt IV*, was built, also in England. This was much larger, displacing 245 tons, and had a more powerful propulsion system, but still using the latent steam principle. It was bought by the Russian Navy but sank off the Danish coast on its delivery voyage.

on the surface and when submerged, but range was very low.

Unfortunately, the one insoluble problem in the design was stability, the outcome of a combination of her long, flat hull-shape and an intricate system of internal piping which was intended to maintain balance by moving water from one end of the boat to the other. This system reacted slowly and then tended to over-compensate, resulting in a series of underwater lurches, which was extremely un-nerving for the crew. Various remedies, such as enlarged after hydroplanes and a vertical propeller, were tried but without success.

Among the successful ideas was the first use of compressed-air to drive water out of the ballast tanks, which had previously been done by pumps, an idea later adopted by every submarine designer in the world. Another unusual idea was the ship's boat which sat, upside down, in a recess on the hull, and was held in place with bolts, but with an air overpressure to prevent water leakage through the bolt-holes. The weapon was a spar torpedo and, as always with this weapon, the problem was to make it powerful enough to damage the target but without damaging the attacking boat. *Plongeur* was a fascinating design, particularly for 1863, and had great potential, but was dropped by the French Navy because of its stability problems.

Aleksandrowski

Type: air-independent compressed-air power.
Total built: 1.
Completed: 1865.
Displacement: 355 tons.
Dimensions: length 110ft 0in (33.5m); beam 13ft (4.0m); draught 12ft (3.8m).
Propulsion: 2 x compressed-air engines; two shafts.
Performance (estimated): surface – 1.5kt; maximum operational depth 30ft (9m).
Weapons: 2 x mines.
Complement: 22.

Pochtovy

RUSSIA

Type: air-independent diesel/compressed-oxygen.
Total built: 1.
Completed: 1908.
Displacement: surfaced 134 tons; submerged 146 tons.
Dimensions: length 113ft 0in (34.4m); beam 10ft (3.0m); draught 9ft 3in (2.8m).
Propulsion: 2 x gasoline engines, 260hp; two shafts.
Performance (estimated): surface – 10.5kt; submerged – 6.2kt.
Weapons: 4 x Drzewiecki torpedo drop-collars.
Complement: 22.

History: This was a fascinating design, another product of the remarkable brain of Stefan Drzewiecki. His main aim was to power the submarine by a single internal-combustion engine for both surfaced and submerged propulsion, with a supply of compressed-oxygen held in 45 air bottles ($350ft^3/9.91m^3$) at a pressure of 2,500psi ($0.2kg/m^2$), which was fed to the engine when submerged. Exhaust gases were ejected under pressure from a perforated pipe located under the keel. Unfortunately, Drzewiecki was unable to find a suitable diesel and had to use two gasoline engines instead. The system seems to have worked reasonably well, giving a submerged range on one engine of 28 miles (44.8km). The main disadvantages, which appear to have been considered insuperable, were the very heavy condensation when submerged, and the very prominent bubble-wake on the surface, which gave away the submarine's position without the need for any acoustic devices. As a result, the idea was dropped, although as with the French *Plongeur* (qv) further development of a very interesting idea might well have paid considerable dividends.

Drzewiecki was a Polish scientist and one of those men whose interests covered an immense range of topics. Thus, he made considerable contributions in fields such as aeronautics, gliding, ship and submarine design, and the theory and manufacture of propellers for both ships and aircraft. Although he did not pursue his idea of feeding compressed-air to an internal combustion engine, this basic concept is used in several of today's AIP submarines.

Right: **Pochtovy, a 1908 attempt at a true AIP submarine, which involved feeding compressed oxygen to a gasoline engine; with more work and money the idea might have been made to be practicable.**

History: I. F. Alexandrowski was the second submarine designer to try to use compressed-air, his design being ordered in 1863 and completed in 1865. The boat was quite sophisticated for the period, with a chamber in the bow which divers could enter and leave underwater, and a sail. The submarine stored 220cu ft (6.2m^3) of air at a pressure of 1,500psi (0.11kg/m^3) which was sufficient for an operating radius of 2.5nm. She appears not to have lived up to expectations and was then used for diving trials, attaining 60ft (18m) without apparent difficulty, but was later crushed at 100ft (30m).

Gymnôte/Gustave Zédé/ Morse-classes

FRANCE

Type: air-independent all-electrical power.

Class	Gynmôte	Gustave Zédé	Morse
Completed	1888	1893	1899-1901
Total built	1	1	3
Displacement: surfaced submerged	30 tons 31 tons	266 tons 272 tons	143 tons 149 tons
Dimensions: length beam draught	58ft 5in (17.8m) 5ft 11in (1.8m) 5ft 6in (1.7m)	159ft 1in (48.5m) 10ft 6in (3.2m) 10ft 79in (3.2m)	119ft 9in (36.5m) 9ft (2.7m) 9ft 3in (2.8m)

History: These three designs represent the French attempt to produce an effective all-electric submarine, which seemed to hold considerable promise in the 1890s. The first, *Gymnôte*, designed by Gustave Zédé, was a very small, single-hulled craft, with one electric motor powered by a battery of 204 cells. As built, it was difficult to control, but the addition of three hydroplanes per side cured this and it proved a most successful design, making some 2,000 dives during its 10-year operational life. Next came *Gustave Zéd*é (originally named *Sirène*, but renamed after the early death of *Gymnôte*'s designer), which was much larger and constructed of bronze, but also suffered from control problems, which were cured in the same way, with hydroplanes. This boat was also a success and recorded over 2,500 dives. Finally came the Morse-class, which was intended to combine the best points of both *Gymnôte* and *Gustave Zéd*é. The second and third boats of this class (*Algerien* and *Français*) were

Propulsion:			
battery	204 cells	720 cells	n.k.
electric motor	1 (33.4shp)	1 (208shp)	1 (284shp)
shaft	one	one	one
Performance:			
surface	7.3kt, 65nm/5kt	9.2kt, 220nm/6kt	7.3kt, 90nm/4kt
submerged	4.3kt, 25nm/4kt	6.5kt, 105nm/5kt	5.5kt
Weapons:			
TT	2x14in (356mm)	1 x 17.7in (450mm)	
Torpedoes	2	3	
Complement	5	19	13

Specifications for Morse-class are for first-of-class, as built.

slightly larger, with a submerged displacement of 160 tons and with the armament of three 17.7in (450mm) torpedoes rearranged into one bow tube and two externally mounted Drzewiecki drop-collars.

Another class of all-electric boats was built: the three-strong Farfadet-class, displacing 202 tons and powered by a single electric motor. Launched in 1901-03, they had short lives, two being stricken in 1906, one in 1907 and the last in 1913.

All these boats performed well but the all-electric concept suffered an inherent disadvantage, in that the boat always had to return to port to recharge its battery, which was operationally unsound. All had been scrapped by 1908-09.

Below: **Gustav Zédé**, *one of several all-electric drive designs.*

Isaac Peral

Type: air-independent all-electrical power.
Total built: 1.
Completed: 1890.
Displacement: surfaced 77 tons; submerged 85 tons.
Dimensions: length 72ft 2in (22.0m); beam 9ft 5in (2.9m); draught 9ft 3in (2.8m).
Propulsion: 2 x electric motors, 2 x 30HP; two shafts.
Performance (estimated): surface – 7.8kt, 400nm/3kt; submerged – 3kt.
Weapons: 1 x 14in (356mm) TT (bow) (3 torpedoes).
Complement: 10.

History: Although the original Spanish submarine, *Ictineo,* was launched in 1859 and underwent trials in 1860-61, the *Peral* is generally acknowledged to be the first successful design. It was the idea of a serving naval officer and electrical specialist, Lt. Isaac Peral (1851-95), and was commissioned in 1890. The boat was extremely well streamlined and was powered by two electric motors, driving one propeller each, with vertical movement controlled by ballast tanks and two small propellers, one under the bow, the other under the stern. The boat was fitted with a small conning-tower and a periscope, and was probably the first to use chemicals to re-oxygenate the crew's air supply when submerged. Armament comprised a single tube in the bow, with three Schwarzkopf torpedoes carried. The submarine was powered by two electric motors driven by a battery of 613 cells. The boat performed very successfully and earned its designer a jewelled sword from the Queen of Spain, but Peral,

---

Type XVIIB

Type: air-independent Walter system power.
Total built: 3.
Completed: 1944-45.
Displacement: surfaced 307 tons; submerged 332 tons.
Dimensions: length 136ft 2in (41.5m); beam 10ft 10in (3.3m); draught 14ft 1in (4.3m).
Propulsion: 1 x Deutz diesel, 210hp; 1 x Walter turbine, 2,500hp; 1 x electric motor, 77shp; one shaft.
Performance: surface – 8.5kt, 3,000nm/8kt; submerged – 21.5kt, 150nm/20kt.
Weapons: 2 x 21in (533mm short) TT (bow) (4 torpedoes).
Complement: 19.

History: Professor Helmut Walter was a gifted engineer and inventor who, although few of his submarine designs were built and none became operational, nevertheless played an important role in Germany's U-boat development in World War II. His concepts covered both the design of the submarine and their propulsion and the key to his ideas was the use of hydrogen-peroxide (H_2O_2), which was stored in external plastic bags, with the normal pressure of sea-water being used to force the fuel into the boat, where it served as the oxidant in a closed-cycle diesel operation. His first boat, the four-man *V-80*, had a submerged speed of 26.5kt and this was followed by the much larger *V-300* and then four boats using the Walter principles but designed by B+V (*U-792/-793*) and Germania (*U-794/-795*). These had all been experimental, but in January 1943 an order was placed for 24 Type XVIIs which were intended to be fully operational, split into 12 Type XVIIBs built by B+V and

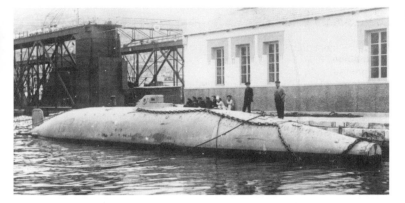

Above: **Isaac Peral** *had all-electric power, using 613 cells.*

like so many inventors, appears to have made enemies and eventually resigned from the navy, dying a disappointed man in 1895. Fortunately, his submarine survives and is on public display in Cartagena, Spain. Although never used in combat, this was a very impressive design and its designer deserved a better fate.

A Portuguese-designed, all-electric submarine was launched in 1892. Named *Plongeur*, it underwent some tests and survived until 1910, but does not seem to have aroused much enthusiasm in the Portuguese Navy.

Above: **Walter's** *U-1407* *used hydrogen-peroxide propulsion.*

12 Type XVIIGs by Germania. The order was later cut-back to six Type XVIIBs of which only three were actually Completed: *U-1405* – December 1944, *U-1406* – February 1945, and *U -1407* – March 1945. All were scuttled on 5 May 1945, but were raised by the Allies, following which *U-1406* went to the USA and *U-1407* to the UK, where it was commissioned as HMS *Meteorite*. The U.S. Navy's sole use of hydrogen-peroxide was in the X-1, whose design was based on that of the British wartime X-craft, but with a Walter-type propulsion system. She suffered a major internal explosion in February 1958, but was rebuilt with diesel engines and then served until 1973. Walter was undoubtedly a brilliant man, but his designs tended to bring too many novel ideas together, resulting in protracted development programmes.

Explorer-class

GREAT BRITAIN

Type: air-independent Walter system power.
Total built: 2.
Completed: 1956-58.
Displacement: surfaced 980 tons; submerged 1,076 tons.
Dimensions: length 225ft 0in (68.7m); beam 15ft 8in (4.8m); draught 18ft 2in (5.5m).
Propulsion: 1 x Vickers hydrogen-peroxide turbine, 15,000bhp; 1 x electric motor, 400shp; two shafts.
Performance: surface – 27kt; submerged – 18kt.
Complement: 41-49.

History: Having raised *U-1407*, the Royal Navy took it to the UK where it was commissioned as HMS *Meteorite* and subjected to extended trials. They also took Professor Walter and key members of his team to England where he spent several years at Vickers, Barrow. It was believed that the Russians were continuing work on hydrogen-peroxide (true) and this, combined with the need for high-speed targets for ASW forces, led to the development of these two unarmed boats. The hydrogen-peroxide was stored in internal open-topped plastic tanks, and proved very difficult to work with, since, if it came into contact with any dirt, dust or metal there would be an immediate and violent reaction, producing vast amounts of steam which could cause the submarine to blow apart. (Indeed, a small leak of hydrogen-peroxide in a torpedo aboard the S-class submarine, HMS *Sidon*, in 1955 caused an explosion, not involving the warheads, which resulted in 12 deaths. The Royal Navy then ceased all work on

Type 212/Type 214

GERMANY

Type: air-independent fuel-cell power.
Total on order: Type 212 – 6; Type 214 – 3.
Completed: Type 212 – due 2003-2006; Type 214 – due 2009-2012.
Displacement: surfaced 1,450 tons; submerged 1,840 tons.
Dimensions: length 184ft 8in (56.3m); beam 22ft 4in (6.8m); draught 23ft 0in (7.0m).
Propulsion: 1 x MTU 8V183 SE83 diesel, 1,040kW; 1 x Siemens Permasyn motor, 2.8mW (3,821hp); 9 x Siemens Polymer Electrolytic Membrane fuel cells; one shaft.
Performance: surface – 12kt, 8,000nm/8kt; submerged – batteries 20kt, fuel cells 8kt, 420nm/8kt.
Complement: 27.
Specifications are for Type 212 (Germany) as being built.

History: German submarine companies have developed a new AIP system, using fuel cells, which was successfully trialed in *ex-U-1* in 1988-89. Following completion of the Type 206 (qv) programme in the mid-1970s, there was a long gap in submarine construction for the German Navy until 1998 when work started on the first Type 212. This is very much larger than the Type 206 – with a submerged displacement of 1,850 tons compared to 520 tons – but the most important difference is the propulsion system, which has three elements: a diesel engine for surface propulsion and charging the battery; the lead-acid battery for high-speed underwater propulsion; and the fuel cell for underwater cruise.

The pressure hull is constructed of austenitic (non-magnetic) steel and has a safety factor of two between the maximum operating depth and calculated

Above: HMS Explorer, known to her crew as "Exploder".

such a dangerous substance.) The sailors' attitude to these two boats is summed up in their nicknames – *Exploder* and *Excrutiator* – and there were no regrets when the boats were scrapped and the use of hydrogen-peroxide in submarine propulsion systems consigned to history, except in certain types of Russian torpedoes.

collapse. The pressure hull is a hybrid shape with large diameter forward and smaller diameter after sections, connected by a short, conical section. The fuel cell plant is housed in the conical section, with the liquid oxygen (LOX) and hydrogen storage tanks grouped around the after hull, inside the free-flooding outer casing. *Ex-U-1* had 16 fuel cells using liquid electrolyte, each generating 25kW of power, but the Type 212's production system consists of nine PEM (polymer electrolyte membrane) fuel cells, using solid polymer technology, each providing some 30-50kW power. This enables the boat to cruise submerged for 420nm at 8kt, and much further at lower speeds, while it can attain 20kt submerged, using its silver hydride battery.

Unlike all earlier German submarines, the Type 212 has two innovations in order to achieve greater manoeuvrability: the forward hydroplanes have been moved from the lower bows to the sail, and the after control surfaces are an "X" configuration. A further innovation is that after long use of "swim-out" torpedo launches, the Type 212 uses a hydraulic water-ram system, which is claimed to give low-noise discharge, even of heavyweight torpedoes, an absence of swell or bubbles, high discharge velocity, and no restrictions on submarine operation up to 12 knots. Mines can be carried internally in place of torpedoes (three ground or two anchored mines per tube) but there is also a specially developed mine "girdle" carrying 24 mines; this reduces speed and endurance, but enables a full load of torpedoes to be carried and it can be jettisoned at any time.

Even before the first boat has been launched two foreign orders have been placed: two by Italy for two Type 212As (with an option on two more), while the Greek Navy has ordered three of an improved version, the Type 214. This has a 213ft (65m) hull and a displacement of 1,700 tons, with diving depth ncreased to 1,300ft (400m). There will be eight torpedo tubes, of which four will also be able to launch guided missiles, such as UGM-84 Sub-Harpoon. Over-all mission endurance is 84 days, with up to 14 days at a time being spent submerged.

Right: When dived Germany's Type 212 will be powered by fuel cells giving a 14-day submerged endurance at a speed of about 4 knots.

Quebec-class (Project 615)   RUSSIA

Type: air-independent Kreislauf system power.
Total built: 30.
Completed: 1955-58.
Displacement: surfaced 460 tons; submerged 540 tons.
Dimensions: length 183ft 9in (56.0m); beam 16ft 5in (5.1m); draught 12ft 6in (3.8m).
Propulsion: Kreislauf system; 1 x Type 32D diesel, 900bhp; 2 x Type M-50P diesels, each 700bhp; 1 x creep electric motor, 100shp; three shafts.
Performance: surface – 18kt, 2,750nm at cruising speed; submerged – 16kt.
Weapons: 4 x 21in (533mm) TT (bow) (8 x torpedoes); 2 x 25mm AA.
Complement: 30.

History: In the 1930s the Soviet Navy built the M-class "coastal defence submarines" which needed high submerged speed, but not the extended endurance of ocean-going boats. Two of these were powered by experimental closed-cycle systems, the first of which used liquid-oxygen (LOX) as the oxidant, with the exhaust passing overboard. In the next version the exhaust was passed through a cooler filled with lime to leach-out the carbon dioxide and then enriched with oxygen (from the LOX) before returning it to the engine. Work was suspended during World War II, but afterwards development restarted and the propulsion system was installed in the Project 615 (NATO = Quebec) submarines, of which 30 were completed in the 1950s. The Western Allies had examined Professor Walter's closed-cycles systems in the post-war years and the first assumption by NATO was that the Quebecs were powered by a development of the Walter system, but this was incorrect (the Soviets did

build one Walter boat, Project 617, NATO = Whale, but it suffered an explosion and was scrapped). The Russian system did not use the scarce and expensive but energy-rich hydrogen-peroxide of the Walter system. Nevertheless, even LOX has severe operational limitations and can be stored for only a limited period, so in the mid-1950s a further development (Project 637) appeared in which the exhaust was passed through a filter/enricher consisting of granules containing both a carbon dioxide (CO_2) absorbent and bonded oxygen; this combined the process of leaching-out the CO_2 and adding oxygen. One Quebec-class boat was fitted with this system in 1959, but the success of nuclear propulsion made the programme redundant and it was ended in 1960.

The Kreislauf system installed in the majority of the Quebec-class was very dangerous, the boats being known to their crews as "cigarette lighters", and numerous boats suffered accidents, usually involving fires.

Below: Quebec-class used the Kreislauf propulsion system.

Gotland (Type A-19)-class SWEDEN

Type: air-independent Stirling system power.
Total built: 3.
Completed: 1996-97.
Displacement: surfaced 1,384 tons; submerged 1,494 tons.
Dimensions: length 196ft 11in (60.6m); beam 20ft 4in (6.1m); draught 18ft 5in (5.6m).
Propulsion: 2 x Hedemora V12A/15-Ub diesels, 2 x 1,300bhp; 1 x ASEA electric motor, 1,800shp; 2 x Stirling V4-275R Mk II engines, 2 x 75kW; one shaft.
Performance: surface – 11kt; submerged – battery 20kt, AIP 5kt.
Weapons: 4 x 21in (533mm) TT (bow) (12 x torpedoes); 2 x 15.7in (400mm) TT (4 torpedoes); 22 x mines in external belt (optional).
Complement: 23.

History: The research contract for a new class to replace the Sjöormen-class (qv) in the mid-1990s was awarded to Kockums in 1986. The operational requirement included stealthy signature, high shock tolerance, long submerged endurance, and substantial weapons load. The outcome was a design which was essentially a progressive development of the Västergotland-class, but with the addition of a section containing two Stirling engines, which had already been trialed in the Modified Näcken. The production order was placed in March

1990 and all three boats entered service in September 1999. Plans for a further two have been cancelled.

The Kockums V4-275R Mk2 engine has four 275cc cylinders in a V layout, operates at a constant 2,000rpm and uses the Sterling principle to convert heat into mechanical work through a thermodynamic process. The engine uses standard diesel fuel from the boat's normal fuel tanks and liquid oxygen (LOX), which is stored in cryogenic tanks in the lower level of the AIP section (ie, within the pressure hull). These are combined in a ratio of 4 parts diesel fuel to 1 part LOX and are burnt inside a circular combustion unit, with the resultant heat being passed through a heat exchanger to the working gas (helium) which expands over each piston when heated and contracts below each piston when cooled, thus driving the piston up and down, and rotating the crankshaft. The exhaust gas passes through a cooler which reduces its temperature from 800deg C to about 25deg C and then through an absorber, where it is mixed with seawater, cooling it even further; it is then expelled, without bubbling, into the surrounding seawater.

The next Swedish submarine project is the Viking-class, a joint project with Norway and Denmark, which will start to enter service in about 2010.

Below: Sweden's Gotland-class uses the Stirling engine.

Steam-powered Submarines

By the late 19th century steam technology was well understood and for some years submarine designers tried to harness it for use in submarines. The first such system was in many ways the most imaginative, since it endeavoured to use steam for submerged as well as surface propulsion, thus providing a truly air-independent capability, but this Nordenfelt-Garrett system, while used in three different designs, never worked properly.

Some designers then turned to using steam to provide sufficient power for high speed on the surface, combined with charging the batteries for submerged use. Steam, however, suffered from two major drawbacks. First, it took a long time to raise sufficient steam, both when leaving harbour and after surfacing at sea, and it also took time to damp-down the plant prior to submerging; French steam-powered submarines, for example, were reckoned to take 15 minutes to submerge. One way around this was used in the British K-class, which had an additional diesel engine to propel the submarine, albeit at a relatively slow speed, while the steam system was being started or stopped.

Secondly, the steam plant required many more penetrations through the

pressure hull for funnels, intakes, and vents, each of which was a source of potential disaster, the danger being enhanced because all were only a short distance above the waterline. One K-class captain made a personal inspection to see that every opening was closed prior to diving, which certainly ensured his men's safety but would scarcely have been practicable in action.

By the early 1930s the last K-boat had been retired and the era of steam propulsion appeared over. However, there was a brief resurgence of interest in the late 1940s when the U.S. Navy, which had never used steam propulsion before, investigated the use of a pressure-fired boiler for a steam turbine to produce very high surface speeds for radar picket submarines, but the plan was dropped. Then, however, came the final triumph of steam, since in nuclear propulsion it is steam that is the agent which carries the power from the nuclear plant to the turbines.

Below: K-class – most notorious of steam-powered submarines.

Narval/Sirène

FRANCE

Total built: Narval 1; Sirène 4.
Completed: Narval – 1899; Sirène – 1901.
Displacement: surfaced 157 tons; submerged 213 tons.
Dimensions: length 106ft 7in (32.5m); beam 12t 10in (3.9m); draught 8ft 2in (2.5m).
Propulsion: triple-expansion steam engine, one boiler, 250ihp; one electric motor, 100shp; one shaft.
Performance: surface – 9.8kt, 600nm/8kt; submerged – 6kt; range 55nm/3.8kt.
Weapons: 4 x 17.7in (450mm) Drzewiecki drop-collars (4 torpedoes).
Complement: 13.
Specifications are for Saran-class (see text), as built.

History: *Narval* was among the first steam-electric submarines and won an 1896 design competition for a boat with ranges of 100nm on the surface and 10nm submerged. Operationally, the design was a submersible torpedo-boat which spent most of its time on the surface, but which could submerge when necessary. The oil-fired tubular boilers drove a triple-expansion steam engine for surface propulsion and battery charging, although it took 20 minutes (later reduced to 12) to blow-off steam before diving. Other innovations were the double-hull design with the ballast tanks between the hulls, a pattern followed by many successors to this day.

The Saran-class was the production version, slightly shorter, with an 11 ton increase in displacement and marginally more powerful engine. Major efforts were made to reduce the diving time, but it still took 6-9 minutes, although this

---

Pluviôse/Archimède-classes

FRANCE

Total built: Pluviôse – 18; Archimède – 1.
Completed: Pluviôse – 1908-11; Archimède – 1909.
Displacement: surfaced 398 tons; submerged 550 tons.
Dimensions: length 167ft 4in (51.1m); beam 16ft 4in (4.9m); draught 16ft 3in (3.0m).
Propulsion: reciprocating steam engine, two boilers, 700ihp; two electric motors, 450shp; two shafts.
Performance: surface – 12kt, 1,500nm/9kt; submerged – 8kt, 50nm/5kt.
Weapons: 1 x 4 x 17.7in (450mm) TT (bow); 2 x Drzewiecki drop-collars (2 torpedoes), 4 x cradles (4 torpedoes).
Complement: 24.
Specifications are for Pluviôse-class, as built.

History: Built to a design by the famous French naval architect, Laubeuf, these were numerically the largest class of steam-powered submarines ever built. They were powered by reciprocating steam engines and, while they took time to blow off steam, lower the funnel and seal the vents, they were good seaboats and served throughout World War I. Six were lost: three sank in collisions with merchant ships, one collided with a battleship, and two were destroyed by Austro-Hungarian surface warships.

Archimède was an improved version of the Pluviôse-class, somewhat longer (197ft/60.5m overall) and with considerably more powerful machinery – 1,700ihp compared to 700ihp. The design was considered a great success and the boat sank four enemy transports during the war. It was stricken in 1919.

The steam propulsion system was found adequate in the Mediterranean

Above: French Narval, *one of the first steam-electric boats.*

was not too serious a disadvantage in the early 20th century. Although the choice of steam seems perverse by modern standards, it should be remembered that at the time these boats were being built the alternative for surface propulsion and battery-charging was either gasoline engines, which were very dangerous, or kerosene engines which were smelly and emitted a dense cloud of white smoke. *Narval* was stricken in 1909, but the four Saran-class boats all survived World War I, to be stricken in 1919.

and in French coastal waters, but some of this class were sent into the North Sea during the war, where their low freeboard was a disadvantage, while the funnel and its associated watertight valve system were always vulnerable.

Below: No fewer than 18 of the Pluviôse-class were built.

Gustave Zédé/
Dupuy de Lôme

FRANCE

Total built: Gustave Zédé – 1 (see notes); Dupuy de Lôme – 2.
Completed: Gustave Zédé - 1913; Dupuy de Lôme - 1915-16.
Displacement: surfaced 833 tons; submerged 1,287 tons.
Dimensions: length 246ft 1in (75.0m); beam 21ft 0in (6.4m); draught 11ft 10in (3.6m).
Propulsion: Delaunay-Belleville 3-cylinder reciprocating steam engines plus two du Temple boilers, 3,500ihp; two electric motors, 1,640shp; two shafts.
Performance: surface – 17kt, 2,350nm/10kt; submerged – 11kt, 120nm/5kt.
Weapons: 6 x 17.7in (450mm) TT (bow – 2; inboard 4) (8 torpedoes); 2 x external cradles (2 torpedoes).
Complement: 43..
Specifications are for Dupuy de Lôme, as built.

History: Although separate classes, the specifications and histories of these two groups of two boats each are so similar are treated together. *Gustave Zédé*, was the lead-ship of a two-ship class, but while she was powered by a steam unit, the other boat, *Néréide*, was powered by Schneider-Carels diesels (see diesel-electric section). *Gustave Zédé* was powered by Delaunay-Belleville units identical to those in the Dupuy de Lôme-class, as shown above; the latter class was marginally longer, 246ft (75.0m) compared to 242ft 9in (74.0m), and had a slightly greater displacement, 1,287 tons versus 1,098 tons, but their

Swordfish

GREAT BRITAIN

Total built: 1.
Completed: 1916.
Displacement: surfaced 932 tons; submerged 1,105 tons.
Dimensions: length 231ft 4in (70.5m); beam 22ft 11in (7.0m); draught 14ft 11in (4.5m).
Propulsion: Parsons geared impulse reaction steam turbines, one Yarrow boiler, 4,000ihp; 2 x electric motors, 1,400shp; 2 batteries, each of 64 cells; two shafts.
Performance: surface – 18kt, 3,000nm at 8.5kt; submerged – 10kt.
Weapons: 2 x 21in (533mm) TT (bow) (2 x torpedoes); 4 x 18in (457mm) TT (beam) (8 x torpedoes); 2 x 3in (76mm) guns.
Complement: 42.

History: One of the requirements set by the Admiralty's Submarine Committee in 1912 was for an "overseas" submarine with a 1,000-ton displacement and a surface speed of 20kt. The Italian designer Cesare Laurenti submitted a bid, which was initially rejected in favour of *Nautilus* (qv) but was later accepted, and an order was placed with Scott for a modified version. The power required for such a high speed could be produced only by steam propulsion and *Swordfish* became the Royal Navy's first steam-powered submarine, being powered by Parsons geared turbines, although even with these an absolute maximum of 18kt was all that could be achieved. The funnel was raised and lowered electrically, as was the watertight cover, an operation which took about 1.5 minutes, although blowing-off steam took considerably longer. As with all steam-

armaments were identical. After World War I, however, all three were fitted with diesels removed from surrendered German U-boats, and in the same refit enlarged bunkers were installed together with new bridges and ventilation systems. Guns were also mounted, usually one 75mm gun.

The official performance figures for both classes include a submerged speed of 11kt and radius of 120nm at 5kt for the Dupuy de Lôme-class and slightly more for the Gustave Zédé-class, both of which are difficult to believe.

Below: **Sané** *(de Lôme-class), as completed in 1916.*

powered submarines there was considerable heat and condensation below, resulting in frequent short-circuits at the main switchboard and several injuries. The boat was also unstable when surfacing and submerging, rolling to such an extent as to alarm the crew. Various Italian features, particularly with regard to safety, impressed the British, but overall the design was a failure and after lengthy trials she was converted into a surface patrol boat, at which she also failed to excel.

Below: **Swordfish**, *the first British steam-powered submarine.*

K/K-26-classes

Total built: K – 17; K26-class – 1.
Completed: K – 1917-18 ; K-26 class – 1923.
Displacement: surfaced 1,980 tons; submerged 2,566 tons.
Dimensions: length 339ft 0in (103.4m); beam 26ft 7in (8.1m); draught 17ft 0in (5.2m).
Propulsion: Brown-Curtis or Parsons geared steam turbines, two Yarrow boilers, 10,500bhp; 1 x "E-class" auxiliary diesel, 800bhp; 4 x electric motors, 1,440shp, two shafts.
Performance: surface – 24kt, 3,000nm/13.5kt; submerged – 9kt, 13.5nm/9kt; maximum operational depth 200ft (61m).
Weapons: 10 x 18in (457mm) TT (bow – 4; beam – 4; revolving mount – 2) (16 torpedoes); 2 x 4in (102mm) guns; 1 x 3in (76mm) AA.
Complement: 59.
Specifications are for K-class, as built.

History: The Royal Navy remained committed to a high surface speed, now increased to 24kt. This could be achieved only with eight of the latest diesel engines, which was clearly impracticable; so a further attempt was made at steam-propulsion, the outcome being the notorious K-class. By the standard of the day, they were large and very complicated boats and were officially described as double-hulled although, in fact, the outer hull was abreast the upper half of the pressure hull only, and did not totally envelope it. As originally built, the K-class had a long low bow (similar to the Nautilus-class), with a narrow superstructure from the enclosed bridge (the first in the Royal Navy) aft to include the funnels. It was originally intended to mount 21in (533mm) torpedo tubes but only 18in (457mm) tubes were available and were used instead, with four in the bow, four in the beam and two in a rotating mount in the superstructure, intended for use in night surface operations. There was a single 4in (102mm) mount fore and aft and a 3in (76mm) mount on the superstructure.

The steam units worked well but became excessively hot and humid, while the funnels, watertight hatches and vents could be closed in 30 seconds although small obstructions could prevent the latter closing, thus endangering the boat and its crew. Normal diving time was about 5 minutes, although one boat achieved 3 minutes 25 seconds. A major feature was the auxiliary diesel, which was used for a quick get-away while steam was being raised, either from port or after surfacing, which took about 20 minutes. Most boats could exceed

Below: K-3 in original condition with low bow.

Above: K-26 *had many modifications, including a raised bow.*

23kt on the surface but endurance submerged was very poor – 30nm at 4kt and 45nm at 1.5kt.

Problems were quickly found once the first boats entered service. The bow shape resulted in a very "wet" boat, so a new bulbous "swan" bow was added, which required another deck-level on the bridge to see over the top. The forward 4in (102mm) gun and the revolving torpedo mount in the superstructure proved unusable and were removed. There was some talk of mounting a single 5.5in (140mm) gun but as far as is known this never happened, although some boats were fitted with depth-charge throwers in 1918. In addition, extra fans were fitted in the boiler room to reduce temperature and humidity.

A total of 17 K-class boats was completed, of which 13 survived World War I to be sold between 1921-26. *K-1* was lost in a collision with *K-4* off the Danish coast (November 1917) and *K-5* foundered in the Bay of Biscay (January 1921), while *K-13* sank during builder's trials but was raised and returned to service as *K-22,* being sold in 1926. The most infamous event in the K-class history, however, was the ironically named "Battle of May Island" (31 January 1918) when nine K-class boats put to sea from Rosyth, Scotland, in company with a number of battlecruisers, at night and at a speed of 20kt. During this operation *K-14*'s helm jammed, initiating a complicated series of collisions that resulted in the sinking of two K-class boats, severe damage to three more and the loss of over 100 lives – and all without any enemy involvement whatsoever.

In an effort to overcome all the shortcomings a modified class was designed, of which only *K-26* was actually completed. The hull was longer (351ft/107m) and displacement increased to 2,530 tons. All three 4in (102mm) guns were mounted on the superstructure, which was lengthened and raised 3ft (0.9m) compared with the earlier boats. Torpedo armament was strengthened by installing six 21in (533mm) tubes in the bow (12 torpedoes), although the four 18in (457mm) beam tubes (eight torpedoes) were retained, but were removed in 1929. The machinery was the same, resulting in a slightly slower maximum speed, while a rearrangement of the tanks made diving very much quicker. The improved design was considered superior in every way and six were ordered in 1918, although only *K-26* was ever completed. She entered service in 1923 and was scrapped in 1931.

Nuclear-powered Attack Submarines (SSNs)

From the very first, submariners dreamt of a vessel that would be completely free of the surface for long periods, but they were frustrated by three factors. Electric storage batteries consumed no oxygen, but could hold only a strictly limited charge before they had to be replenished. Such recharging could only be done by diesel engines, which needed oxygen to work, and this meant that the boat had to surface, thus becoming vulnerable to enemy action. Third, these batteries could not produce enough power both to propel the vessel and to sustain life for a protracted period. Nuclear power, however, changed all that and its potential for use in submarines was seen from about 1942 onwards.

The first American nuclear-powered submarine (SSN) was completed in 1954 after an almost unparalleled development effort, giving the USA an estimated five years' lead over the Soviet Union. Later in the Cold War the Soviet Union overtook the United States in numbers of SSNs and by the 1980s was approaching the United States in terms of quality as well – perhaps being even ahead in some areas. But the end of the Cold War and the collapse of the Soviet Union, both politically and financially, has left the United States Navy pre-eminent.

The main stream of development has been large, multi-purpose boats, powered by pressurised-water nuclear reactors, but there have been numerous attempts to find different or more effective solutions. Both the Americans and the former Soviet Union tried liquid metal-cooled reactors, which hold out the promise of considerably greater efficiency and power for a given weight. An early U.S. attempt was *Seawolf* (SSN-575) but this was abandoned after only

two years and the reactor replaced by a conventional pressurised-water system. The Soviets tested their system in the remarkable Alfa-class SSNs, but this proved highly complicated to operate, the type achieving the unusual distinction of requiring an all-officer crew.

In the early years of the 21st century the U.S. Navy is equipped almost exclusively with Los Angeles-class SSNs, with just two of the older Sturgeons left and two out of three Seawolf (SSN-21)-class in service and a third approaching completion, while work on the first four Virginia-class has already started. Together these form the largest and most capable attack submarine force in the world. In contrast, the Russian Navy is now but a shadow of its former self. In its heyday, the Soviet Navy operated a large, well-equipped and effective force of attack submarines, and in the 1970s and '80s their SSNs were the world leaders. But that is no more and today they probably have fewer than 20 SSNs even nominally in service. Many of those are in a sad state of disrepair, and there is no certainty that a successor class will ever reach production.

Among the second rank navies the British operate a small and efficient SSN flotilla, as do the French. Both have a successor class under development. The only other navy with SSNs in service is China's PLA-N, and its force will undoubtedly increase in both quantity and quality. India is known to have an SSN under development and Brazil is known to aspire to such status.

Below: British Swiftsure-class SSN, HMS Splendid.

Han-class

Total built: 5.
Completed: 1970-90.
Displacement: surfaced 4,500 tons; submerged 5,000 tons.
Dimensions: length 295ft 4in (90.0m); beam 29ft 6in (9.0m); draught 24ft 4in (7.4m).
Propulsion: 1 x pressurised-water nuclear reactor, 48mW; 2 x steam turbines, 12,000shp; one shaft.
Performance: surface – 25kt; submerged – 30kt; maximum operating depth 984ft (300m).
Weapons: 6 x 21in (533mm) TT (bow).
Complement: 75.
Specifications for #401, as built.

History: This was a most important project, being not only China's first indigenous submarine design, but also her first nuclear-powered submarine. The Chinese Navy (PLA-N) had acquired Soviet diesel-electric submarines in the late 1940s and started to produce Soviet designs under license in the 1950s, but despite being such beginners the high command quickly understood the importance of nuclear propulsion. As a result, a national programme was started in the mid-1950s, which led to the first SSN being laid down in 1968 and launched in 1971, although it did not become fully operational until the early 1980s, due to problems with the propulsion system. Construction then continued slowly with the second hull being launched in 1977, but both then underwent a lengthy refit/reconstruction in the 1980s. Meanwhile, three more were launched (in 1983, 1987 and 1990, respectively) which were 26ft 3in (8.0m) longer than the first two and incorporated additional weapons and equipment.

This was not only the PLA-N's first nuclear-propelled submarine design, but was also the first with a shorter, fatter "Albacore" hull and single propeller in

Below: The Han-class was a sophisticated design for its era.

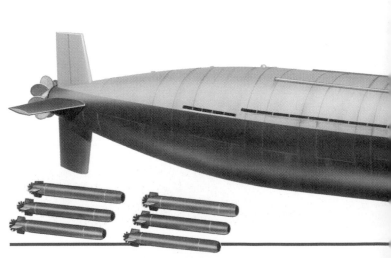

Above: Han-class SSN of the Chinese PLA-Navy.

place of the traditional long, thin, twin-propeller design. The Han is certainly not a copy of any other design, but it is of classic SSN layout, with an Albacore-type hull and diving planes mounted high on the forward-mounted sail. All five were built at Huladao, entering service in 1974 (#401), 1980 (#402), 1984 (#403), 1988 (#404) and 1991 (#405); all serve in the North Sea Fleet.

In one well-publicised incident a Han-class boat tracked the USS *Kitty Hawk* carrier battle-group in the Yellow Sea for several days in October 1994. A U.S. Navy S-3 Viking patrol aircraft detected the submarine when it was some 450nm from the carrier and heading in the direction of the carrier at periscope depth. The submarine came within 20nm of *Kiitty Hawk* before turning away and it seems clear that its commander meant to be seen so as to make it clear that there was a new challenge to U.S. naval supremacy in the area. A successor class (Project 093) is being designed with assistance from the Rubin Design Bureau of St. Petersburg, Russia.

Rubis/Amethyste-classes (SNA-72)

FRANCE

Total built: Rubis 4; Amethyste 2.
Completed: Rubis 1983-88; Amethyste 1992-93.
Displacement: surfaced (Rubis) 2,388 tons, (Amethyste) 2,410 tons; submerged (both) 2,670 tons.
Dimensions: length (Rubis) 236ft 6in (72.1m), (Amethyste) 241ft 6in (73.6m); beam (both) 24ft 10in (7.6m); draught (both) 21ft 0in (6.4m).
Propulsion: 1 x CAS 48 pressurised-water nuclear reactor, 48mW; 2 x turbo-alternator sets, each 3,950kW; 1 x electric motor, 9500shp; 1 x SEMT-Pielstick/Jeumont Schneider 8PA4V185SM diesel-electric auxiliary engine, 450kW; 1 x battery-driven emergency motor; one shaft.
Performance: submerged – 25kt; operational diving depth 984ft (300m).
Weapons: 4 x 21in (533mm) TT (bow); 14 x missiles/torpedoes.
Complement: 66 (two crews).

History: In France, President De Gaulle exerted such strong pressure on the French Navy to produce a nuclear deterrent capability that all efforts were concentrated on development of ballistic missiles and the submarines to carry them, and the development of nuclear-propelled attack submarines was deliberately postponed. Thus, it was not until 1974 that an SSN development programme was started, with the first of the Rubis-class being laid down in December 1976 and launched in 1979; it then underwent extensive trials and did not join the fleet until 1983.

As built, the Rubis-class were the smallest SSNs in any navy, their hull design, armament, sonar and fire control systems being closely based on those of the Augusta-class diesel-electric submarines (qv). However, the design proved to be

Below: The original Rubis-class proved to be somewhat noisy, leading to the more refined and quieter Amethyste-class.

Above: French Amethyste-class SSN.

surprisingly noisy, which led to the *Amethyste* programme (<u>AME</u>lioration <u>T</u>actique <u>HY</u>drodynamique <u>S</u>ilence <u>T</u>ransmission <u>E</u>coute), which was introduced into the fifth of class (coincidentally also called *Amethyste*) and the sixth, *Perle,* while building. The *Amethyste* programme also involved changes to sonar and other ASW equipment to match the change in role from anti-ship to anti-submarine.

Amethyste and *Perle* are longer than the earlier boats – 241.5ft (73.6m) as opposed to 236.5ft (72.1m) – and have a revised bow form, a new sonar, a towed sonar array, a more streamlined superstructure, and improved electronics. Once the new build standard had proved itself, the first four boats were rebuilt between 1989 and 1995, with a new bow section which increased their length to that of *Amethyste*. *Saphir* recommissioned in July 1991, *Rubis* in February 1993, *Casabianca* in June 1994 and *Emeraude* in late 1995. All six boats are based at Toulon but frequently deploy to the Atlantic and, unusually among SSNs, they are operated with two crews. Normal endurance is limited to 45 days by the stock of food that can be carried, although this can be extended to 60 days if operationally necessary.

Rubis collided with a tanker on 17 July 1993 and had to undergo extensive repairs. *Emeraude* suffered a serious steam leak on 30 March 1994 while submerged, which caused 10 deaths among the crew, including that of the commanding officer. The casualties were in the compartment containing the two turbo-alternators and were not associated with the nuclear plant.

The next class of French SSN is to be known as the Barracuda-class and, according to current information, will have a displacement of 4,500 tons. Six boats are scheduled to be built, with the Rubis-class being stricken one-for-one as the new boats enter service between 2010 and 2020.

Dreadnought-class

GREAT BRITAIN

Total built: 1.
Completed: 1963.
Displacement: surfaced 3,000 tons; submerged 4,000 tons.
Dimensions: length 265ft 9in (81.0m); beam 32ft 3in (9.8m); draught 26ft 0in (7.9m).
Propulsion: 1 x Rolls-Royce/Westinghouse S5W pressurised-water nuclear reactor, 2 x geared steam turbines, 15,000shp; diesel-electric auxiliary propulsion; one shaft.
Performance: surface – 15kt; submerged – 28kt.
Weapons: 6 x 21in (533mm) TT (bow); 24 x torpedoes.
Complement: 88.

History: Britain initiated the study of the possibility of nuclear propulsion for submarines in 1946, although for several years it was considered that the Walter system might provide a viable and less expensive alternative (see Explorer-class). It was soon realised that systems based on hydrogen peroxide were too dangerous and in 1953 a naval section was established at the Atomic Warfare Research Establishment (AWRE), Harwell, which initiated studies in cooperation with the Admiralty, Vickers-Armstrong, Rolls-Royce and Foster-Wheeler. The outcome was a land-based prototype submarine reactor, built at the nuclear research establishment at Dounreay in Scotland; work started in spring 1958 and it went critical in 1965.

Design of this British propulsion system was based on that of the U.S. Navy's Westinghouse S5W pressurised water-cooled reactor, but it was not

Valiant-class

GREAT BRITAIN

Total built: 5.
Completed: 1966-71.
Displacement: surfaced 4,000 tons; submerged 4,900 tons.
Dimensions: length 285ft 0in (86.9m); beam 33ft 3in (10.1m); draught 27ft 0in (8.2m).
Propulsion: 1 x Rolls-Royce PWR.1 pressurised-water nuclear reactor, geared steam-turbine, 15,000shp; 1 x diesel-electric propulsion system; 1 x 112-cell battery; one shaft.
Performance: surfaced – 20kt; submerged – 28kt.
Weapons: 6 x 21in (533mm) TT (bow); 26 x torpedoes.
Complement: 103.

History: The Valiants were the first class of entirely British SSNs, the first boat being ordered in August 1960 and completed in June 1966, followed by the second, *Warspite*, completed in 1967. There was then a three-year gap before the last three, *Churchill, Conqueror* and *Courageous*, were completed in 1970-71, and these are sometimes listed as a separate class, although the differences were no more than progressive modifications to be expected in any lengthy production run and they are shown here as one class. The design was generally similar to that of *Dreadnought*, but the hull was 19ft (5.8m) longer, mainly in order to accommodate the slightly larger Rolls-Royce PWR.1 nuclear reactor. The crew was also larger – 103 compared to 88.

In 1967 *Valiant* travelled 10,000 miles (16,100km) submerged from Singapore to the UK in 28 days. *Conqueror* is the only SSN in any navy to have sunk an enemy warship in combat, having launched two Mk VIII torpedoes

Above: **Dreadnought**, *the Royal Navy's first SSN.*

ready in time for HMS *Dreadnought*. So, in order to get a British SSN to sea as quickly as possible, a complete S5W was bought from the USA and installed in *Dreadnought*, which was launched in October 1960 and commissioned in April 1963. The bow section of this boat, containing the Type 2001 sonar, was of entirely British design and was much blunter than contemporary U.S. designs.

Dreadnought was a fully operational attack submarine. She was laid up in 1983, the nuclear reactor was dismantled and the core removed; she was then placed in storage, where she remains.

against the Argentinian cruiser *General Belgrano* on 2 May 1982 during the Falklands War.

Starting in 1988 the reactors began to show signs of age and it was decided not to modernise these boats, as had been previously planned. They were accordingly decommissioned between 1990 and 1992 and their reactors decored.

Right: Valiant-class SSN loads a torpedo. One of this class, **Conqueror,** *is the only SSN to sink an enemy ship in combat.*

Swiftsure-class

Total built: 6.
Completed: 1973-81.
Displacement: surfaced 4,400 tons; submerged 4,900 tons.
Dimensions: length 272ft 0in (82.9m); beam 32ft 4in (9.8m); draught 27ft 0in (8.2m).
Propulsion: 1 x Rolls-Royce PWR.1 pressurised-water nuclear reactor, 2 x GEC-Alsthom geared steam-turbines, 15,000shp; Paxman auxiliary diesel, 4,000bhp; 1 x 112-cell battery; one shaft.
Performance: surface – 20kt; submerged – 30kt.
Weapons: 5 x 21in (533mm) TT (bow); 21 x torpedoes, 4 x Sub-Harpoon or Tomahawk SLCM.
Complement: 116.

History: The third class of British SSNs was the six-strong Swiftsure-class, the first of which joined the fleet in April 1973. The hull was 13ft (4m) shorter than the Valiants with a flat outer casing giving a completely different appearance to that of the humped-back of the earlier SSN classes. This new, shorter, fatter shape is evidence of the greater internal volume of the pressure hull, giving more equipment space and better living conditions. The diving planes are set very much lower and are not visible when the boats are on the surface. There are five torpedo tubes and 25 weapons are carried, usually, 21 torpedoes and four missiles.

These boats introduced a number of significant improvements over previous British submarines. One of these was a conformal covering of anechoic tiles on the hull and sail, which was intended to pro-vide a dramatic re-

Trafalgar-class

Total built: 7.
Completed: 1983-91.
Displacement: surfaced 4,740 tons; submerged 5,208 tons.
Dimensions: length 280ft 2in (85.4m); beam 32ft 2in (9.8m); draught 27ft 3in (8.3m).
Propulsion: 1 x Rolls-Royce PWR.1 pressurised-water nuclear reactor, two GEC steam turbines, 11.2mW (15,000bhp); two Paxman diesel alternators, 2.1mW (2,800hp); one shaft, pump-jet propulsor.
Performance: submerged – 32kt.; maximum diving depth in excess of 985ft (300m).
Endurance: 85 days.
Weapons: 5 x 21in (533mm) TT (bow); 25 x torpedoes, Sub-Harpoon or Tomahawk SLCM.
Complement: 130.

History: Seven Trafalgar-class boats were completed between 1983 and 1991, making this the largest class of SSNs built for the Royal Navy. All were constructed by VSEL at Barrow-in-Furness and they replaced the original *Dreadnought* and the Valiant-class. The design was essentially an "improved Swiftsure" but with refinements to ensure that it was both faster and much quieter, as well as having greater endurance. One of the quietening measures is that both the pressure hull and all outer surfaces are covered with conformal anechoic noise reduction tiles using new adhesives which reduces the number of tiles lost on a voyage.

The Trafalgar-class have the same beam as the Swiftsure-class, but are 8ft

Right: **Superb**, *of the Swiftsure-class. UK SSNs do not have sail-mounted hydroplanes.*

duction in the acoustic signature. These were also the first boats to be fitted with a pump-jet propulsor – in essence a truncated conical shroud surrounding the propeller blades – a major design feature which has now been adopted by many other navies.

Swiftsure was undergoing a long refit in the early 1990s when a major problem with the reactor was discovered; as a result, she was retired in 1992. The remainder were all refitted in the 1990s, which included being modified to launch Tomahawk cruise missiles. A number have suffered from problems with their nuclear reactors, mainly cracking, which have required fairly extensive repairs, thus reducing operational availability. Retirement dates are: *Splendid* – 2003; *Sovereign* – 2005; *Spartan* – 2006; *Superb* – 2007; and *Sceptre* – 2008.

Above: Trafalgar-class SSN, **Tireless.**

1in (2.5m) longer, and are built of NQ-1 steel, which is equivalent to the U.S. Navy's HY80. There are three decks divided into four pressure-tight compartments, with escape hatches fore and aft. The forward hydroplanes are retractable and the sail is strengthened for under-ce operations.

The Royal Navy had been engaged in debate for some time about the next

November-class
(Project 627A)

RUSSIA

Total built: 14.
Completed: 1959-63.
Displacement: surfaced 4,500 tons; submerged 5,300 tons.
Dimensions: length 363ft 11in (110.0m); beam 29ft 6in (9.0m); draught 25ft 3in (7.7m).
Propulsion: 2 x VI-A pressurised-water nuclear reactors, each 70mW;
2 x turbines, each 17,500shp; 2 x creep electric motors , each 450shp; two shafts.
Performance: surface – 15kt; submerged – 30kt; maximum operational diving depth 984ft (300m).
Weapons: 8 x 21in (533mm) TT (bow); 24 torpedoes.
Complement: 80.

History: These large and generally conservatively designed boats were the first Soviet submarines to have nuclear propulsion. All were built at Severodvinsk between 1959 and 1963. To a certain degree the technology was based on information gained through espionage from the United States in 1955, although it would seem that, at that time, the Soviet designers failed to appreciate the

generation submarine to replace the Swiftsure-class. Initially, there was going to be an entirely new design, the "SSN-20" (also known as the "W-class"), which, among other features, would have been powered by a modified version of the PWR-2 used in the Vanguard-class SSBNs. By 1990, however, it had become clear that unit cost (not including R&D) would be of the order of £400 million and this, coupled with the rapidly reducing defence budget led to the project being cancelled in 1991. It was then decided to go for a less ambitious design, which was originally known as the "Batch 2 Trafalgar-class" (frequently abbreviated to "B2TC"), which implies that the submarines will be straight developments of the original Trafalgars (which, by inference, have now become "Batch 1 Trafalgars"). The name has, however, been changed to the Astute-class, of which three are currently under construction with scheduled in-service dates of 2005, 2007 and 2008, with a further three to be ordered shortly.

The new SSN will be powered by a derivative of the PWR.2 which powers the Vanguard-class SSBNs, and it will incorporate all the weapon systems, sensor and command-and-control improvements going into the Trafalgar-class. The Astute-class will also have fully reelable towed arrays rather than the clip-on type currently used.

Left: Trafalgars can launch a wide array of weapons, and in addition to the torpedoes, mines and Sub-Harpoon seen here, can now launch Tomahawk land-attack cruise-missiles.

Above: The November-class were the first Soviet SSNs.

advantages of the "teardrop" hull, which had been under test in the United States since 1953 (see Albacore-class). Accordingly, the November-class had the classic long, conventional hull with two propellers. There were two separate power-trains, both of which were required for maximum speed, but through cross connections one turbine could power both shafts in the cruise regime. The nuclear reactors were the VI-A and were identical to those used in

Above: A November-class SSN in distress in October 1970.

the contemporary SSBNs and SSGNs, hence the NATO designation HEN (Hotel-Echo-November). By 1963 a total of 14 had been built, the production run continuing despite the fact that the design had been overtaken by later

Victor I/II/III-classes RUSSIA

History: The first Victor was laid down in 1965 and entered service in 1967, following which the class was built at the Admiralty Yard, Leningrad, at a rate of two per year until 1974, when it was succeeded on the ways by the Victor II class. The Victor was the first Soviet submarine with a "body-of-revolution" hull, similar to, but by no means based on, the U.S. Navy's Albacore hull-form. It was also the first Soviet SSN to have its two nuclear reactors positioned side-

Class	Victor I	Victor II	Victor III
Project	671	671RT	671RTM
Total built	15	7	26
Completed	1967- 76	1972-1978	1977-1991
Displacement surfaced submerged	4,300 tons 5,100 tons	4,500 tons 5,700 tons	4,900 tons 6,000 tons
Dimensions length beam draught	311ft 8in (95.0m) 32ft 10in (10,0m) 23ft 0in (7.0m)	334ft 6in (102m) 32ft 10in (10.0m) 23ft 0in (7.0m)	341ft 2in (104m) 32ft 10in (10.0m) 23ft 0in (7.0m)

technology, illustrating the inflexibility of Soviet construction programmes, allied to their preference for long production runs.

Four of the class suffered from reactor accidents and one, *K-8*, sank in the Atlantic off Cape Finisterre in April 1970 after a reactor-related fire; all the crew were saved. The surviving boats were stricken between 1989 and 1991.

Propulsion		
reactor	2 x VM-4P nuclear	
steam-turbines	two sets	
power	30,000shp	
shafts	one	
creep motor	two (2 x 505shp)	
battery	2 x 112 cells (8,000 amp/hour)	
Performance		
submerged	30kt	28kt
maximum		
operating depth	1,312ft (400m)	
Endurance	80 days	
Weapons		
tubes	6 x 21in (533mm)	2 x 21in (533mm), 2 x torpedoes
torpedoes	18 x torpedoes	4 x 25in (650mm), 12 x SS-N-16
Complement:	94	

by-side, which not only reduced the length, but also provided an excess of power, which came in very useful later in the development of the longer-hulled Victor II and III. Armament consisted of six 21in (533mm) torpedo tubes, positioned in two horizontal rows, with two in the top row, four in the lower, but

Above: Successor to the November, a Victor-class SSN at sea.

Right: Victor I was highly effective at the time it appeared.

the two outer tubes in the bottom row were outside the pressure hull and thus non-reloadable. The main shaft ended in a five-bladed propeller, and there were also two more auxiliary propulsion units for "creep" movement. One Victor I was damaged beyond repair during refit in 1985 and the remainder were stricken between 1993 and 1996.

The Victor II was redesigned and lengthened in order to accommodate the SS-N-16 system. These missiles were launched from 25.6in (650mm) tubes, which replaced the four internally mounted and reloadable tubes. The two externally mounted, non-reloadable 21in tubes remained, being used for either conventional torpedoes or the ultra high-speed *Shkval* missile. Seven Victor IIs were built and all were stricken between the early 1990s and 1997.

Below: The Victors were the first Soviet SSNs with "body-of-revolution" hull. Note also the large pod on the rudder which housed a trailing-wire sonar and its winch.

Finally came the Victor III, which was essentially a longer and tidied-up version of Victor II with a more comprehensive sensor fit and improved silencing; a total of 26 units were built. The Victor III was 43ft (13.2m) longer than Victor II, but the most visible difference was a large streamlined pod mounted atop the stern fin, which housed a towed sonar array dispenser. Water environment sensors were also mounted at the front of the fin and on the forward casing as in the Akula II and Sierra classes (qqv). Incremental improvements were made to the design and the last nine of the class were even quieter than the others. One of the class had a trials installation for SS-N-21 SLCM mounted on the forward casing and was sometimes referred to as

Alfa-class (Project 705)   RUSSIA

Total built: 7.
Completed: 1972-83.
Displacement: surfaced 2,800 tons; submerged 3,680 tons.
Dimensions: length 267ft 1in (81.4m); beam 31ft 2in (9.5m); draught 23ft 0in (7.0m).
Propulsion: 2 x liquid-metal cooled nuclear reactors, 45,000shp; one shaft.
Performance: submerge – 43-45kt; maximum operating depth 2,300ft (700m).
Weapons: 6 x 21in (533mm) TT (bow); 18 x torpedoes/SS-N-15 missiles.
Complement: 31 (all officers).

History: The Alfa-class was remarkable for its time in three respects. First was its very high speed which was due to its very powerful, liquid-metal cooled nuclear reactors. Second, was its deep diving depth, which was made possible by the exceptional strength of its titanium hull. Finally, there was its very small crew of 31 men, the result of an exceptional degree of automation, although, uniquely, they were all officers. The first boat was completed in 1971 and underwent three years' trials before being broken up in 1974, possibly because the liquid metal coolant was inadvertently allowed to solidify. The remaining six boats, all of which took much longer than usual to build, entered service between 1979 and 1983.

The relatively short overall length (267ft/81m compared to 312ft/95m for a Victor I), combined with the high submerged speed of some 45kt, indicated very sophisticated hydrodynamic design and the use of laminar flow techniques. The hull was constructed of titanium, a material which combines lightness with great strength and resulted in the great diving depth

the Victor IV (Type 671 RTMK). Early Victor IIIs had a seven-bladed propeller, but some Victor IIs and most Victor IIIs had an unusual propeller, which consisted of two, tandem, four-blade, co-rotating units mounted at 22.5 degrees to each other on the same shaft. It is assumed that this offered some acoustic advantage, although it was not repeated on any other Russian submarines, and was replaced by a seven-bladed type in the surviving Victor IIIs in the late 1990s. A total of 26 Victor IIIs were built, but by 2002 only eight remained in service.

Below: Victor III; the pod caused great interest in the West.

Above: Alfa-class, powered by liquid-metal nuclear reactors.

(2,460ft/750m crush depth), but this metal is very difficult to work and even the great Russian metallurgical expertise did not allow production of more than a few of these submarines.

The lead-bismuth liquid-metal reactors provided exceptional power density, giving these boats an underwater speed well in excess of 40kt. This was demonstrated when one ran under a NATO convoy during an exercise in the North Atlantic; it was a deliberate demonstration of its performance, and one which caused consternation in Western naval circles. The Alfa generated considerable noise at such a speed, which enabled surface warships to track its progress with great precision, but it also showed them that in war they would have no means of counteracting it. This led to urgent NATO programmes to develop much deeper diving and faster torpedoes, resulting in the British Spearfish and the U.S. Navy's Mk48 ADCAP and Mk50.

One boat was scrapped in 1988 and another four were defuelled and scrapped in 1992/93. The remaining boat had an accident in 1982 which led to a very lengthy rebuild in which she was fitted with an experimental type of pressurised-water reactor. After a period of trials, she, too, was scrapped in the mid-1990s.

Below: The Alfa's exceptional performance – it once went under a NATO convoy at over 40 knots – led to vast expenditure in Western navies to developing submarines and torpedoes that could catch it.

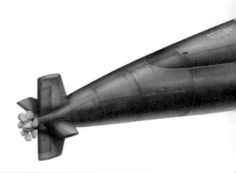

Sierra I/II-class (Project 945)

RUSSIA

History: The Sierra-class was built in parallel to the Akula-class (qv), with two Sierra Is completed in 1984 and 1987, followed by two Sierra IIs in 1990 and 1993. A fifth boat (Project 945B, which would probably have received the NATO

Class	Sierra I	Sierra II
Project	945	945A
Total built	2	2
Completed	1987	1990-93
Displacement surfaced submerged	6,300 tons 8,300 tons	6,470 tons 8,500 tons
Dimensions length beam draught	351 ft 0in (107.0m) 54ft 2in (16.5m) 28ft 11in (8.8m)	362ft 6in (110.5m) 54ft 2in (16.5m) 30ft 9in (9.4m)

Propulsion		
reactor	1 x OK-650A pressurised-water	1 x OK-650B pressurised-water
turbo-alternators	two	two
power	190mW	190mW
shafts	one	one
creep motor	two (2 x 750shp)	two (2 x 750shp)
Performance		
surface	12kt	12kt
submerged	33.6kt	33.6kt
maximum		
operating depth	1,804ft (550m)	1,970ft (600m)
Endurance	90 days	100 days
Weapons		
tubes	4 x 25.6in (650mm) 4 x 21in (533mm)	8 x 25.6in (650mm)
torpedoes	40 x torpedoes/SS-N-16 missiles	40 x torpedoes/SS-N-16 missiles
Complement	59	61

designation Sierra III) was cancelled during construction in 1992 and scrapped.
The original Sierra I was slightly smaller than the Akula and its primary

mission was to attack U.S. and other NATO naval task groups, with a secondary mission against coastal targets. Its performance and capabilities were generally comparable with the U.S. Navy's earlier Los Angeles-class SSNs, although its internal quietening systems and a coating of anechoic tiles, designated "Cluster Guard" by NATO, were reported to give it a superior acoustic performance. A huge torpedo room gave it a capacity of no fewer than 40 torpedoes and missiles for its eight torpedo tubes, four 21in (533mm) and four 25.6in (650mm) tubes. Like the Alfa-class it had a titanium hull. Two were built, followed by the two Sierra IIs some years later.

Below: The Sierra shows its weapons and sensors.

Akula-class

RUSSIA

Class	Akula I	Improved Akula I	Akula II
Project No	971	971U	971A
Total built (see text)	6	3	1
Completed	1984-90	1992-95	1996-2000
Displacement surfaced submerged	8,140 tons 10,700 tons		9,830 tons 12,390 tons
Dimensions length beam draught	361ft 11in (110.3m) 44ft 7in (13.6m) 31ft 9in (9.7m)		375ft 0in (114.3m) 44ft 7in (13.6m) 31ft 9in (9.7m)
Propulsion reactor/ power shafts	1 x IK-650B pressurised-water nuclear reactor, 190mW 1 x GT3A turbine, 35mW 2 x auxiliary diesels, each 750bhp one		

Above: Four Sierras were built; the Akula design was better.

Performance			
surface		10kt	
submerged		35kt	
maximum			
operating depth		1,970ft (600m)	
Endurance		80 days	
Weapons			
tubes internal	4 x 26.4in (650mm)	4 x 26.4in (650mm)	4 x 26.4in (650mm)
	4 x 21in (533mm)	4 x 21in (533mm)	4 x 21in (533mm)
tubes external	–	6 x 21in (533mm)	6 x 21in (533mm)
Complement		73	

History: The Akula-class was divided into three groups: Akula (Project 971) – 7 boats; Improved Akula I (Project 917U) – 4 boats; Akula II (Project 971A) – 2 boats. The Akula-class (Project 971), designed by the St. Petersburg-based Malakhit Design Bureau, was the follow-on to the Victor III-class, and the largest SSN ever built for the Soviet Navy. It was built in parallel to the Sierra-class (qv) but was constructed from low-magnetic steel rather than the much more expensive and difficult to work titanium. One of the most notable visual features of the Akula class is the long fin, which is carefully faired into the hull, whereas in most other SSN designs the fin/hull junction is a stark 90 degrees. This was almost certainly a product of the long-standing Russian study into aquatic life-forms such as whales, sharks and porpoises, and is almost certainly intended to cut down hydrodynamic swirl – and thus noise. All Akulas also have a large pod on the vertical stern fin for the Skat 3 thin-line, towed sonar array and a rescue pod for the crew in the sail.

Earlier Russian submarines were notorious for their noise signatures, but the Akula-class changed that and the design was continually improved with reduced noise levels, boundary-layer suppression and active noise cancellation in the later groups. One of the major reasons for the 3.7 m (12.14 ft) longer hull in the Akula II is to enable it to accommodate yet further noise reduction measures.

Below: An Akula I with its assembly of weapons.

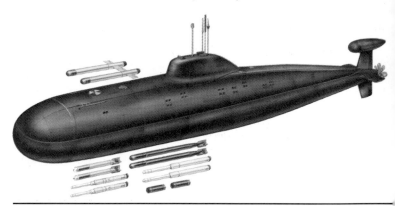

Nautilus-class

UNITED STATES

Total built: 1.
Completed: 1954.
Displacement: surfaced 3,674 tons; submerged 4,092 tons.
Dimensions: length 323ft 0in (98.5m); beam 27ft 0in (8.2m); draught 22ft 0in (6.7m).
Propulsion: 1 x S2W pressurised-water nuclear reactor, ca. 15,000shp; two shafts.
Performance: surfaced – 18kt; submerged – 23kt; maximum operational diving depth 400ft (122m).
Weapons: 6 x 21in (533mm) TT (bow).
Complement: 111.

History: From the earliest days in the U.S. nuclear programme it had been realised that, apart from its use for the most powerful explosions ever known, nuclear reactions could be controlled and thus used as a source of power. One particularly advantageous application would be in submarines and as soon as World War II ended a naval research and development team assembled at the Oak Ridge nuclear research centre, led by Captain Hyman G. Rickover, U.S. Navy, an outspoken but hitherto little known electrical engineer.

Rickover forced the pace and eventually contracts were placed with the Electric Boat Company for the first SSN and with Westinghouse for the first powerplant. This led to an operational reactor, the Submarine Thermal Reactor Mark II, which under the designation S2W was installed in the hull of *Nautilus* during her 27-month construction period. USS *Nautilus* (SSN-571) was

Above: Akula is now the Russian Navy's only SSN class.

The original Akula has four 26.4in (650mm) and four 21in (533mm) torpedo tubes, but Improved Akula Is and the Akula IIs both a further six 21in tubes mounted in the forward casing and outside the pressure hull, which adds to the firepower, but makes them impossible to reload at sea. In addition, in all three types the 26.4in tubes can be fitted with liners to enable them to launch 21in torpedoes.

One of the distinguishing features of the Akula II is the number of prominent non-acoustic sensors on the leading edge of the sail and on the forward casing, which are similar to devices tested on a Hotel II in the early 1980s.

The first Akula I ran trials for several years and was then stricken, so that only six of this first group actually entered service. Five Improved Akula Is were laid down but it appears that, at most, only three were completed and the other two, partially complete, are being leased to India in 2002-07.

Above: **Nautilus***, the world's first nuclear-propelled submarine.*

launched on 21 January 1954 and on 17 January 1955 was able to send her historic signal: "Underway on nuclear power."

Nautilus was designed with what was at that time a conventional long, streamlined hull, not dissimilar to that of the German Type XXI. Her great power drove her through the water at a speed of about 23kt, but she then began to experience the control problems inherent in such a design.

Despite her revolutionary power-plant, *Nautilus* was always considered to be an operational attack boat and was a great success. Within three months of her first run on nuclear power she made a 1,381nm (2,558km) underwater voyage from New London to San Juan, Puerto Rico, in 90 hours at an average speed of some 16kt. By August 1958 there was sufficient confidence in her nuclear plant for her to make the first-ever Polar transit, starting from Pearl Harbor, Hawaii, and finishing at Portland, England. She steamed 62,562nm (115,865km) on her first nuclear core, 91,324nm (169,132km) on her second, and some 150,000nm (277,800km) on the third. After a very successful career she was withdrawn from active service in 1980 and is now at a museum at Groton, Connecticut.

Right: USS Nautilus *married the great power of nuclear propulsion to the out-dated traditional and inherently slow long/thin hull. It was the Albacore "teardrop" design that resolved the problem.*

Seawolf (SSN-575)-class UNITED STATES

Total built: 1.
Completed: 1955.
Displacement: surfaced 3,741 tons; submerged 4,287 tons.
Dimensions: length 337ft 6in (102.9m); beam 27ft 8in (8.4m); draught 22ft 0in (6.7m).
Propulsion: 1 x S2G liquid sodium-cooled nuclear reactor, ca.15,000shp; two shafts.
Performance: submerged – 20kt.
Weapons: 6 x 21in (533mm) TT (bow).
Complement: 105.
Specifications are for Seawolf (SSN-575), as built.

History: *Seawolf* (SSN-575) was authorised, designed and built in parallel with *Nautilus* (qv) in order to provide valid comparisons between the latter's pressurised-water and nuclear reactor and a different type of reactor using liquid sodium. Using a molten metal (with a graphite moderator) was considered a promising alternative because it offered a ten-fold increase in temperature in the reactor, which would lead to a much more efficient transfer of heat to the steam in the secondary circuit. However, it suffered from a general problem in that the sodium had to be maintained in a molten state at all times; it also was considered less reliable than the pressurised-water alternative and suffered at least one leak. Apart from her power-plant, *Seawolf* was a very conventional design, similar but not identical to *Nautilus*, with a long, thin hull, twin propellers and a stepped fin similar to many Guppy submarines. Unilke *Nautilus*, she had a distinct rise in the bow with an externally mounted sonar dome.

Above: **Seawolf *(SSN-575)* had a liquid sodium reactor.**

Seawolf was used on trials for two years but was then rebuilt with an S2Wa pressurised-water nuclear reactor. In 1969 four externally mounted thrusters were added (two forward, two aft), indicating a new role requiring very precise positioning, which may have been related to intelligence-gathering activities. Thus, despite the lack of success of her original powerplant, she had a long and useful career and was eventually decommissioned in 1987. (It should be noted that the Soviet Navy later tried liquid-metal reactors in its Alfa-class (qv)).

Skate-class

Total built: 4.
Completed: 1957-59.
Displacement: surfaced 2,550 tons; submerged 2,848 tons.
Dimensions: length 267ft 8in (81.6m); beam 25ft 0in (7.6m); draught 20ft 7in (6.3m).
Propulsion: 1 x pressurised-water nuclear reactor, S3W (*Skate, Sargo),* S4W (*Swordfish, Seadragon*), ca. 6,600shp; two shafts.
Performance: submerged – 20kt.
Weapons: 8 x 21in (533mm) TT (bow – 6; stern – 2).
Complement: 84.

History: Following the design of *Nautilus* and *Seawolf*, the U.S. Navy turned to its first series production SSN, the Skate-class. This was a considerably smaller design, very similar in size to the contemporary U.S. Navy Tang-class diesel-electric submarines. The only smaller operational SSNs have been the French Navy's Rubis-class (qv). One surprising feature of the design was the reversion to stern torpedo tubes, which was practicable only because of the twin propeller design.

Despite their size, the four Skate-class boats served for many years and established a number of "firsts" including the first ever surfacing at the North Pole by USS *Skate* (SSN-578) on 17 March 1959. All underwent a number of refits and refuellings, and were eventually decommissioned between 1984 and 1989.

Right: **Skate** *and* **Seadragon** *at the North Pole, August 1962.*

Skipjack-class

UNITED STATES

Total built: 6.
Completed: 1959-61.
Displacement: surfaced 3,070 tons; submerged 3,500 tons.
Dimensions: length 251ft 9in (76.8m); beam 31ft 8in (9.7m); draught 25ft 3in (7.7m).
Propulsion: 1 x S5W pressurised-water nuclear reactor, ca. 15,000shp; one shaft.
Performance: submerged – ca. 30kt.
Weapons: 6 x 21in (533mm) TT (bow); 24 x torpedoes.
Complement: 85.

History: The six Skipjack-class boats benefited from a number of major advances in submarine technology. First, they adopted the "tear-drop" hull and single propeller which had been proven by USS *Albacore* (AGSS-569) (qv); second, they introduced the new S5W nuclear reactor; and, third, they adopted, for the first time in a major U.S. operational submarine, a single-hull design. The result was a great success and for the first time the U.S. Navy possessed a submarine capable of travelling for long periods at the same speed (perhaps, even faster) as a surface task group, thus finally realising the dream of the "fleet submarine". Their maximum submerged speed of 30+kt was not exceeded until the advent of the Los Angeles-class some 20 years later, while the manoeuvrability remains unparalleled. The single propeller meant that stern torpedo tubes were no longer practicable.

A further demonstration of the success of the design was that it proved a fairly simple process to adapt a number of Skipjacks already under construction

Above: Snook *(SSN-621) enters Rio de Janeiro harbour.*

and add a totally new missile section to produce the equally successful George Washington-class SSBNs (qv).

One of this Skipjack-class of boats, *Scorpion* (SSN589), was lost. She underwent an extended overhaul from October 1967 to February 1968 and then operated in the Mediterranean until early May, when she set out to return to the USA. Her last position report was from a point some 50nm south of the Azores and after

Below: The Skipjack-class was the first to adopt the "teardrop" hull – compare with Nautilus *on page 365.*

Thresher (Permit)-class   UNITED STATES

Total built: 14.
Completed: 1961-67.
Displacement: surfaced 3,750 tons; submerged 4,311 tons.
Dimensions: length 278ft 6in (84.9m); beam 31ft 8in (9.7m); draught 25ft 2in (7.7m).
Propulsion: 1 x S5W pressurised-water nuclear reactor, ca. 15,000shp; one shaft.
Performance: surfaced – 20kt; submerged – 27kt; maximum operating depth 1,300ft (396m).
Weapons: 4 x 21in (533mm) TT (amidships); torpedoes, SubRoc, plus Sub-Harpoon missiles in some.
Complement: 94.

History: The first four of the Thresher-class were originally ordered as SSGNs to carry the Regulus II cruise missile, but when that weapon was cancelled in 1958 they were re-ordered and re-designed as SSNs. They were initially known as the Thresher-class, but when the nameship of the class was lost (see below), they were renamed the Permit-class. This accident also caused the design to be re-examined and the last three were delayed in construction to incorporate the lessons learned. The principal ASW weapon system was SubRoc, conrtrolled by the BQQ-2 sonar system. Four torpedo tubes were mounted amidships, two on each beam, and angled outwards.

Jack (SSN-605) of this class had a modified hull, 296ft 9in (90.5m) long, and was fitted with contra-rotating propellers, with one shaft inside the other and turning in the opposite direction. This was one of the U.S. Navy's numerous

six days of no further transmissions she was declared overdue. After a huge search the hulk of the submarine was found at the end of October; it was lying at a depth of some 10,000ft (3,050m) about 400nm SW of the Azores, in three major pieces: the forward part including the control room; the after part including the engineroom; and the sail. No explanation for the tragedy, which cost the lives of all 99 men aboard, has ever been found. The surviving Skipjacks were decommissioned between 1986 and 1990.

Above: Thresher-class Haddock (SSN-621) in Subic Bay

attempts to find a really quiet propulsion system and although apparently reasonably successful it was not repeated.

Thresher (SSN-593) was lost on 10 April 1963, while undergoing post-overhaul trials off the United States' East Coast. It was the first SSN loss in any navy and took the lives of 129 people; 112 Navy and 17 civilians. The remaining boats in the class had successsful service careers and were withdrawn from service between 1989 and 1996.

Right: **Permit** *(SSN-594). Note the subtle change in hull shape compared to the Skipjack-class (pp 368-9) and much higher position of the forward hydroplanes on the sail.*

Sturgeon-class   UNITED STATES

Total built: 36.
Completed: 1967-75.
Displacement: surfaced 4,250 tons; submerged 4,780 tons.
Dimensions: length 292ft 0in (89.0m); beam 31ft 8in (9.7m); draught 28ft 10in (8.8m).
Propulsion: 1 x S5W pressurised-water nuclear reactor, 2 x steam turbines; 15,000shp; one shaft.
Performance: surface – 15kt; submerged – 28kt.
Weapons: 4 x 21in (533mm) TT (amidships); torpedoes, Harpoon, Tomahawk SLCM.
Complement: 136.
Specifications for SSN-637 to SSN-687, as built.

History: The 36 Sturgeon-class SSNs were slightly enlarged and improved versions of the Permit-class, with an elongated teardrop hull, torpedo tubes set amidships and the bow taken up with the various components of the conformal sonar system. Sturgeons could be distinguished visually from Permits by their taller fin (the top was 20ft 6in/6.3m above the hull), which accommodated more masts of various types and was suitable for under-ice operations. The diving planes were set further down than in the Permit-class, and rotated to the vertical for ice penetration.

Several problems were experienced between the builders and the U.S. Navy over this class: *Pogy* (SSN-647) was reallocated to another yard for completion, while *Guitarro* (SSN-655) was delayed for more than two years after sinking in 35ft (10.7m) of water while fitting-out, an incident described by

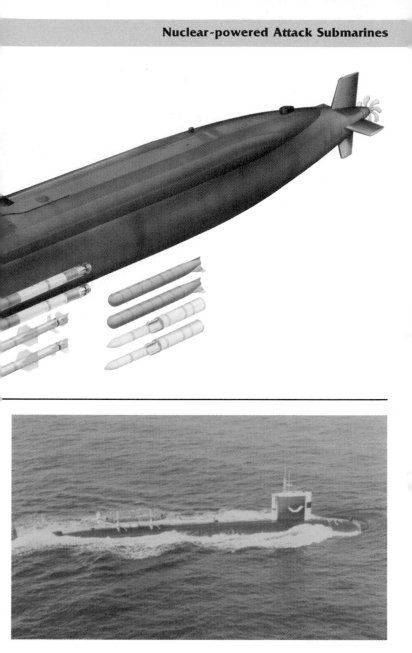

Above: **Pintado *(SSN-672)* with Deep-Sea Rescue Vehicle.**

a Congressional committee as "totally avoidable".

The last 10 units in the class, SSN-678 to SSN-687, were built some 10ft 0in (3.1m) longer, giving an overall length of 302ft 0in (92.1m), and displacement increased to 4,460 tons surfaced and 4,960 tons submerged. However, this was not to accommodate extra equipment but to improve habitability, and to provide extra volume for future developments.

Right: Sturgeon-class Richard B Russell (SSN-687).

Numerous conversions were made, including four to take one DDS each for use by SEALs, and at least four were modified to accept a Deep-Sea Rescue Vehicle (DSRV), if required. *Silversides* (SSN-679) was fitted with an extension abaft the sail, the purpose of which has never been revealed. The most radical modification was given to *Parche* (SSN-683) between 1987 and 1991, when she was given a 100ft (30.5m) extension forward of the sail, together with a large hump on the foredeck. Her official mission is "research and development" and this is understood to include intelligence gathering activities, such as recovering debris from the ocean floor (including from foreign missile tests) using a grapple. The only two Sturgeons still in service in 2002 are one of the DDS conversions, *L. Mendel Rivers* (SSN-686), and *Parche*. The latter is due to be decommissioned in 2003.

Tullibee/Lipscomb/ Narwhal-classes

UNITED STATES

Class	Tullibee	Narwhal	Glenard P Lipscomb
Hull No	SSN-597	SSN-671	SSN-685
Total built	1	1	1
Completed	1960	1969	1974
Displacement surfaced submerged	2,316 tons 2,670 tons	5,284 tons 5,830 tons	5,800 tons 6,480 tons
Dimensions length beam draught	272ft 10in (83.2m) 23ft 4in (7.1m) 21ft 0in (6.4m)	314ft 11in (96m) 37ft 9in (11.5m) 25ft 11in (7.9m)	365ft 0in (111.3m) 31ft 9in (9.7m) 31ft 0in (9.5m)
Propulsion reactor power shafts	1 x S2C PWR ca. 2,500 shp one	1 x S5G PWR ca 17,000shp one	1 x S5Wa PWR one

Performance			
surface	15kt	25kt	18kt
submerged	15-18kt	30kt	25kt
Weapons tubes - 21in (533mm)	4 amidships torpedoes	4 amidships torpedoes/SUBROC	4 amidships torpedoes/SUBROC
Complement	56	120	120

History: These three "one-offs" were not related to each other, but are treated here together. *Tullibee* (SSN-597), one of the smallest SSNs ever built, was the final stage in the U.S. Navy's search for a hunter-killer (SSK) (see Barracuda-class). These were intended to wait outside Soviet ports or in narrow straits and ambush enemy submarines as they left on patrol; this required detection by long-range sonar and then sinking by high-speed, homing torpedoes. *Tullibee* displaced only 2,640 tons submerged, its small size meaning that, although she was very manoeuvrable, she was also very slow, with a submerged speed of just 15kt, while the lack of space meant that newer, more sophisticated and thus almost inevitably larger, equipment and electronics could not be accommodated. She was the first to be fitted with BQQ-2 sonar, whose conformal array took up most of the space in the bow, thus displacing the torpedo tubes to an amidships position, a practice followed in all subsequent U.S. Navy SSNs. She was also fitted with the PUFFS system, with its characteristic "shark's fin" sonar domes. Propulsion used the specially developed S2C reactor, whose size constraints meant that it had only a comparatively low power output, and turbo-electric drive in order to eliminate the self-generated noise made by reduction gearing in earlier SSNs. Despite its disadvantages and unique design, *Tullibee* served for some 28 years, splitting her time between home waters, where she carried out training and ASW development work, and four operational deployments to the Mediterranean. She was decommissioned in 1988 and scrapped in 1989, and was the U.S. Navy's last attempt to produce a small ASW submarine.

Narwhal (SSN-671) was an experimental SSN, built in 1967-69 to test the ultra-quiet S5G natural-circulation reactor, which had no pumps, making the boat the quietest in any navy at that time. This system proved a success and was adtoped for the S8G reactor in the Ohio-class SSBNs (qv). The hull design was based on that of the Sturgeon-class, but somewhat larger, while the sensors, weapons and equipment were the same, thus making for valid comparisons. *Narwhal* was always regarded as a fully operational attack boat. She was modifed to conduct "special operations" which included operating a remotely operated vehicle (ROV). A large "hump" was installed aft, which according to some reports housed the ROV, although it was also claimed that it housed the reel for a new type of towed sonar array. After many years' service, *Narwhal* was decommissioned 1999.

The third boat, USS *Glenard P. Lipscomb* (SSN-685), was the U.S. Navy's second attempt to find a staifactory Turbo-Electric Drive (TED) the first having been the *Tullibee* (see above). *Lipscomb* was generally similar to the Sturgeon-class, but somewhat larger, the major difference being the TED. The machinery was larger and heavier and power output was considerably lower than in the Sturgeons, with the result that speed was lower. *Lipscomb* was a fully combat-capable submarine and served for many years, but the more traditional pumping systems were adopted for the Los Angeles-class. *Lipscomb* was decommissioned in 1990 and stricken in 1997.

Above and below: Tullibee (SSN-597) was one of the smallest and (being underpowered) slowest SSNs ever, having been designed specifically for the ASW mission; note the three "sharks fin" PUFFS sonar domes.

Los Angeles-class

Class	Los Angeles-class				Improved Los Angeles-class	
Hull No	SSN 688-699	SSN 700-714	SSN 715-718	SSN 719-725, +750	SSN 751-770	SSN 771-773
Total built	12	15	4	8	20	3
Completed	1976-81	1981-83	1983-85	1985-89	1988-95	1995-96
Displacement surfaced submerged	6,080 tons 6,927 tons	6,130 tons 6,977 tons	6,165 tons 7,012 tons	6,255 tons 7,102 tons	6,300 tons 7,147 tons	6,330 tons 7,177 tons
Dimensions length beam draught	360ft 0in (109.7m) 33ft 0in (10.1m) 32ft 0in (9.8m)					
Propulsion reactor power shafts	1 x S6G pressurised-water nuclear reactor ca 30,000shp one					
Performance submerged maximum op depth	ca 33kt 1,480ft (450m)					
Endurance	90 days					
Weapons 21in (533mm) TT Vert launch tubes Load Torpedoes/ missiles Tomahawk Mine capable	4 – 22 – no	4 – 22 – no	4 – 22 – no	4 12 22- 12 no	4 12 22* 12 yes**	4 12 22* 12 yes
Complement	141					

* May also include further Tomahawks, but at expense of torpedoes.

** From SS-756 onwards.

History: This was one of the most expensive of all the defence programmes undertaken during the Cold War, and, with 62 units, is the largest class of SSNs ever built; indeed, since 1945 only the Soviet diesel-electric Whiskeys and Foxtrots were built in larger quantities. Hull numbers ran continuously from SSN-688, completed in November 1976, to SSN-733, completed in September 1996 – a 20-year production run unprecedented in submarine history. There

Above: Santa Fe *(SSN-763) of the SSN-688 Improved-class.*

was, however, a gap in the numerical sequence since numbers #726 to #749 were allocated to Ohio-class SSBNs. The overall cost of the programme would be almost impossible to calculate, but the building costs of a single boat (in "then-year" U.S. dollars) were: 1976 – $221million; 1979 – $326million; 1981 – $496million; and 1990 – $900million. (However, it should be noted that the new Virginia-class will cost an estimated $2billion each and SSN-23 over $3billion.)

The Los Angeles-class boats were much larger than any previous U.S. Navy SSN, primarily in order to accommodate the larger and much more powerful S6G nuclear reactor, which was needed to raise the maximum speed. Officially the maximum underwater speed was stated to be "20+ knots" but it is widely accepted that the boats were actually capable of some 32kt, making them the first class to exceed the speed of the Skipjacks, built in the late 1950s. It was originally intended to construct them of HY-100 steel but this proved too difficult with the technology that then existed and in the event HY-80 was used, except that the pressure hulls of SSN-753 and -754 were partially fabricated from HY100 to test the construction processes for the Seawolf-class. The entire bow area of these new boats was taken up by the dome for the BQQ-5 sonar system, while a towed array was carried in a sheath on the outside of hull, a neater and more hydrodynamically efficient arrangement than the large pods on Soviet SSNs. The torpedo tubes were located amidships and used to launch the SubRoc ASW weapon, as well as the Mk48 and Mk48ADCAP conventional torpedoes. Weapons load was later increased to include Sub-Harpoon and Tomahawk missiles. Despite the increase in size, however, they are considered quite cramped, with a number of crewmen having to use sleeping bags. All the boats have a Fairbanks-Morse 38D8Q diesel-generator and batteries for emergency propulsion.

Naturally, in a programme involving so many boats produced over such a long period, there have been changes, but the class can be divided into three broad groups, plus one boat converted for special purposes. The first group consisted of 32 boats (SSN-688 to SSN-718) which, apart from changes of detail, were identical. When the Tomahawk SLCM was introduced, the weapons were stored in the torpedo room and launched from the torpedo tubes. The next eight boats (SSN-719 to SSN-725 and SSBN-750) incorporated a major change in the weapons arrangements. When Tomahawks were carried internally it could only be at the expense of torpedoes, so it was decided that from SSN-719 onwards 12 Tomahawks would be carried in vertical launch tubes positioned between the sonar dome and the pressure hull in space that had previously been occupied by ballast tanks. These boats also had a longer-life core for their nuclear reactors.

More changes were made in the third group (23 hulls, SSN-751 - SSN-773), which is referred to as the "Improved Los Angeles" or "688I"class (I = Improved). The most important of these changes was that they were made "Arctic capable" by installing a strengthened sail and by relocating the diving planes from the sail to the bows. In addition, quietening was greatly improved, the sonar suite was enhanced and two anhedral stern fins were added, as in the Seawolf-class. Some of the later units in this group also have shrouded

pump-jet propulsors. All these have the 12 vertical tubes for Tomahawk, but from SSN-756 onwards they also have a mine-laying capability. The fourth group comprises just one boat – USS *Memphis* (SSN-691) – which was completed as a standard SSN in 1977, but in 1981 was reroled as a dedicated trials boat and has since carried out a large number of trials. It retains its combat capability and is therefore still designated SSN, although its actual employment would be bettter indicated by an auxiliary (AGSSN) designation.

During their Cold War service Los Angeles-class boats carried out missions in all oceans of the world, the great majority of them of a clandestine nature. Their activities usually came to light only through mishaps, such as collisions with Soviet submarines, two known occurrences affecting *Augusta* (SSN-710) in the Atlantic (October 1986) and *Baton Rouge* (SSN-689) in the Barents Sea

Below: The launch of Miami *(SSN-755), 12 November 1988.*

(February 1992). Two came to prominence when they launched Tomahawk Land-Attack Missiles (TLAM) against Iraq in the Gulf War, *Louisville* (SSN-724) launching eight and *Pittsburgh* (SSN-720) four. Closer to home, *San Juan* (SSN-751) collided with *Kentucky* (SSBN-737) off Long Island in March 1998.

During the production run of the Los Angeles-class many plans for alternatives were considered, one example being in the early 1980s when Congress forced the Navy to examine designs for a small, cheaper SSN, but none of these ever came to anything. Later, when it became clear just how expensive the successor Seawolf- and Virginia-classes would be, it was proposed that production of the 688I should continue instead, but this, too, came to nought because there was no potential for system growth left in what had become a 25-year-old design.

All Los Angeles-class boats were built for a 30-year life, although experience suggests that, with proper refits, recores of the reactor and modernisation, they could actually be expected to last for up to 50 years. However, a mixture of factors, including the end of the Cold War, the resulting requirement to reduce operating costs and manning requirements, and a desire to avoid the costs of recoring during refits, have resulted in a reduction in the fleet. The U.S. Navy started to retire ships of the original Los-Angeles class in the mid-1990s, the past retirements and future forecast up to 2008 being: 1995 – 2; 1996 – 1; 1997 – 3; 1998 – 3; 1999 – 2; 2000 – 1; 2001 – 3; 2005 – 1; 2006 – 1; 2007 – 1; 2008 – 1. Thus, by 2008, some 19 boats will have been retired, all of them of the original SSN-688 to SSN-750 group, leaving 34 in commission (11 SSN-688; 23 SSN-688I). A number of those which the Navy intends to keep have been modified to carry one Dry Deck Shelter (DDS) plus a detachment of SEALs: SSN-688, SSN-690, SSN-700, SSN-701 and SSN-715.

Below: **Los Angeles** *(SSN-688). The* **artwork does not give a true** **impression of the great size of this** **boat which is 360ft (110m) long and** **some 33ft (10m) in diameter.**

Above: USS Phoenix *(SSN-702) in the Atlantic, May 1982.*

Above: Birmingham *(SSN-695) surfaces dramatically.*

Seawolf (SSN-21)-class UNITED STATES

Total built: 3.
Completed: 1997-2004.
Displacement: surfaced 7,467 tons; submerged 9,137 tons.
Dimensions: length 353ft 0in (107.6m); beam 42ft 0in (12.8m); draught 36ft 0in (11.0m).
Propulsion: 1 x S6W pressurised-water nuclear reactor, 200mW; one pump-jet propulsor, 45,500shp.
Performance: submerged – 35+kt; maximum operating depth 1,970ft (600m).
Weapons: 8 x 26.5in (673mm) TT (amidships); ca. 50 Mk 48ADCAP torpedoes or Tomahawk SLCM, or up to 100 mines.
Complement: 133.
Specifications for SSN-21, as built.

History: The Seawolf-class, the most advanced submarines currently at sea, had a troubled inception. The project for a Los Angeles-class successor started in the 1980s but there was constant discussion about the requirement and the costs, and then, when these had been resolved, there was a serious dispute over which yard – Newport News or Electric Boat – should build it. Then, during construction of the first-of-class, there were delays due to welding difficulties and these were followed by problems with the covers for the flank sonar arrays. At a less important level, traditionalists were upset by the numbers allocated – SSN-21,~SSN -22, SSN-23 – which are totally out of sequence in the U.S. Navy's excellent and well-established hull-numbering system, apparently having arisen out of the project title "SSN for the 21st Century" which was abbreviated to "SSN-21." The name of the third boat, *Jimmy Carter* (SSN-23), was also considered inappropriate by many, even though the ex-president was a former nuclear-qualified officer in the submarine service.

The Seawolf-class hull is of generally the same shape as that of the Los Angeles-class and is entirely covered in anechoic tiles. The sail is specially strengthened for under-ice operations and incorpoates a large fillet at the forward end, designed to improve the waterflow over the structure. A shrouded propulsor

Above: **Seawolf** *(SSN-21) prior to launch.*

replaces the customary propeller, and there are six fins: the customary cruciform, plus one at 135 degrees and one at 225 degrees.

The first two boats of the Seawolf-class are 7ft 0in (2.13m) shorter than the Los Angeles-class, but with a greater diameter to give a considerable increase in internal volume. Nevertheless, even this proved insufficient and the third boat, *Jimmy Carter* (SSN-23), will incorporate a 27ft (8.23m) plug abaft the sail to enable her to carry a 50-

strong Special Operations Forces detachment and their equipment. There will also be facilities for operating and controlling a variety of remotely operated vehicles (ROVs). This boat will not now be delivered until June 2004, some 2 years 3 months behind the original schedule and will cost, for this one boat, $US3.2billion.

The Seawolf-class is armed with eight 26in (660mm) torpedo tubes and carries a total of approximately 50 weapons, the actual mix of Tomahawk cruise missiles, Harpoon anti-ship missiles and Mk48ADCAP torpedoes depending upon the operational situation, although the normal load-out of Tomahawks is 12. Mines can also be carried on a basis of two mines replacing each torpedo.

It was originally planned to build 12 SSN-23 class boats and a figure of 29 was under consideration at one time. In the event, only three are actually being built and these will be followed by the Virginia-class, of which 30 are currently planned, with the first due for delivery in 2004. Even well before the first-of-class was completed work had started on its successor, currently dubbed "SSXN", which is scheduled to start joining the fleet in the 2020s.

Left: SSN-21 submerged. Note the triple flank-array sonars, forward hydroplanes and midships position of torpedo tubes.

Cruise Missile Carriers

The Germans were the first to examine the possibility of launching rocket-powered missiles from submarines, when some short-range army rockets were launched from *U-551* in 1942. Although both surface and submerged launches were successful the idea was not pursued, but in 1943 the *Kriegsmarine* produced a plan to launch the pulsejet-powered, winged V-1 from U-boats, with New York as the principal target, but the missile was a *Luftwaffe* project and they flatly refused to cooperate. The concept was picked up immediately after the war by both the Soviet and United States navies.

The U.S. Navy used a Japanese-designed aircraft shelter, which was the right size to accommodate a V-1 missile, mounted on the after deck of a modified fleet submarine. Known as the "Loon" system, this was installed aboard two submarines and was tested from 1947-53. Most launches were successful but it was overtaken by the American-developed Regulus programme, which became operational aboard converted fleet submarines, the two purpose-built Grayback-class diesel-electric SSGs and the sole nuclear-powered Halibut-class SSGN. But only a few years later the Regulus system was halted due to the success of the Polaris programme and the U.S. Navy then concentrated on the SSBN/SLBM combination.

The Americans saw Loon and Regulus as land-attack missiles, but the Soviet Navy was much more interested in anti-ship missiles to counter the threat from U.S. carrier groups operating close to the Soviet littoral. Following tests with the German V-1, Soviet designers developed the SS-N-3 (Shaddock) cruise missile and produced some very inelegant Whiskey-class conversions to get them to sea. This was followed by a succession of increasingly effective

nuclear-powered cruise missile carriers, the Echo-class (and its diesel-electric back-up, the Juliett-class), Charlie-class, the one-off Papa-class and, finally, the very powerful Oscar-class. There was also the Yankee Notch, in which the Soviet Navy made use of four surplus SSBNs to produce four vessels carrying land-attack missiles. In the 1990s the Russian Navy had plans for a successor cruise missile submarine, the Severodvinsk-class, but construction of the first has been suspended and in view of the financial situation it seems highly improbable that it will ever be completed.

The only other navy to develop a dedicated cruise missile carrier is the Chinese Navy, which produced the one-off Wuhan-class diesel-electric powered boat in the 1980s. This has, however, remained a prototype and no further boats of this type have been built.

Having rejected the SLCM in the 1960s, the U.S. Navy later returned to it in the 1980s, but this time it was to be launched out of a standard torpedo tube, where the missile became part of the standard load-out of Los Angeles-class SSNs. This reduced the number of torpedoes that could be carried, so external vertical launch tubes for the SLCMs were developed, which were fitted in the later Los Angeles-class. A recently announced future project, however, is a return to the specialised cruise missile carrier, with a projected conversion of four surplus Ohio-class SSBNs to carry a battery of 154 Tomahawk land-attack missiles, together with facilities for a 66-strong SEAL force. This would be an extremely powerful warship posing a very strong threat to any country within the Tomahawk's 1,400nm range.

Below: Grayback (SSG-574), an early cruise missile carrier.

Wuhan-class (Project 033G)   CHINA

Total built: 1.
Converted: 1987.
Displacement: surfaced 1,650 tons; submerged 2,100 tons.
Dimensions: length 251ft 3in (76.6m); beam 24ft 11in (7.6m); draught 17ft 5in (5.3m).
Propulsion: 2 x Type 1Z38 diesels, 2 x 2,400bhp; 2 x electric motors, 2 x 1,350shp; 2 x "creep" motors, 2 x 100shp; two shafts.
Performance: surface – 15kt, 14,000nm at 9kt; submerged – 10kt; range 330nm at 4kt.
Weapons: 8 x 21in (533mm) TT (bow – 6, stern – 2) (14 torpedoes); 6 x C-801 cruise-missiles.
Complement: 58.

History: The Wuhan SSG was a converted Romeo (qv), rebuilt as a "proof-of-concept" boat for a surface-launched cruise missile platform, with the launch tubes for the six C-801 missiles built into the raised casing abreast the sail. An additional mast for a Snoop Tray radar antenna was mounted between the two periscopes to provide target data. This was essentially a Chinese version of the concept employed by the Soviet Navy in the Juliett-class SSGs and, like the Juliett, this Chinese submarine had to surface in order to acquire the target and then fire the missiles. This would undoubtedly have rendered the submarine vulnerable to detection and attack by a sophisticated enemy, but against most Asian navies, particularly those lacking any form of seaborne air surveillance, it could have proved effective. This submarine was stationed with the North Sea Fleet and may still be there although

Whiskey-class Conversions   RUSSIA

Class	Whiskey Single-cylinder	Whiskey Twin-cylinder	Whiskey Long-bin
Project No	613Kh	644	665
Converted	1956	1958-60	1960-63
Number Converted:	1	6	6
Displacement: surfaced submerged	1,050 tons 1,340 tons	1,070 tons 1,360 tons	1,200 tons 1,500 tons
Dimensions: length beam draught	249ft 4in (76.0m) 20ft 8in (6.3m) 16ft 5in (5.0m)	249ft 4in (76.0m) 20ft 8in (6.3m) 16ft 5in (5.0m)	274ft 11in (83.8m) 20ft 8in (6.3m) 16ft 5in (5.06m)
Propulsion	2 x Type 37-D diesels, 4,000bhp 2 x electric motors, 2,700shp 2 x creep motors, 100shp two shafts		

Above: Chinese Wuhan-class cruise-missile carrier.

it is questionable whether it would be used in a conflict.

The missile was the Mach 0.9 C-801Ying Ji (Eagle Strike) for which there were six launchers, three each side of the sail. This was a rocket- propelled missile with a rocket booster, and on launch it climbed to about 164ft (50m) then descended to 65-100ft (20-30m) until its radar seeker acquired the target. It then descended further to a height of some 16-23ft (5-7m), from which point it used the nose-mounted, monopulse radar seeker for the terminal approach phase.

It was proposed at one time to produce a similarly converted version of the Ming-class (qv) but this has not been proceeded with.

Performance:			
surface			
speed	18.3kt,	18.3kt,	13.5kt
range	8,580nm/10kt	8,580nm/10kt	n/k
submerged			
speed	13.1kt	13.1kt	8kt
range	335nm/2kt	335nm/2kt	n/k
maximum			
operational depth	656ft (200m)	656ft (200m)	656ft (200m)
Weapons			
torpedo tubes	8 x 21in (533mm) (bow – 4; stern – 2)		
torpedoes	12 torpedoes/22 mines		
cruise missiles	1 x SS-N-3	2 x SS-N-3	4 x SS-N-3
Complement	53	56	60

History: The Whiskey-class (qv) design proved to be very suitable for modifications and a number were used as launchers for the Chelomey P-5 cruise missile, known to NATO as the SS-N-3 "Shaddock". The first boat to be converted was a trials unit which carried one missile in a simple elevating tube on top of the casing abaft the sail. The aft-facing tube normally rested on the deck, but prior to launch it was raised to about 40 degrees and the two heavy end-caps were raised by electric motors. The turbojet-powered SS-N-3 flew at about 470kt (later increased to over 600kt) and was armed with a 200kT warhead. Successful trials with the single missile version led to a service version with two launchers (Whiskey Twin-cylinder), which were also abaft the sail, but mounted each side of the casing. Again, the tubes faced aft, with large blast deflectors at the forward end. The whole installation was crude and created a great deal of underwater noise, which made them easy for Western submarines to detect. One of these boats sank with all hands in January 1961, but was found in 1969 and raised the following year.

Next came a much more substantial rebuild in which the hull was lengthened by 25ft 7in (7.8m) and the four launch cylinders were fixed and facing forward, with two on each side of a greatly enlarged sail. This was the Soviet Navy's Project 665, which was known to NATO as "Whiskey Long-bin". Six were completed but they did not remain long in service.

Right: An early SSG, Whiskey Long Bin carried four SS-N-3.

Juliett-class (Project 651)   RUSSIA

Total built: 16.
Completed: 1960-68..
Displacement: surfaced 3,000 tons; submerged 3,750 tons.
Dimensions: length 295ft 3in (90.0m); beam 32ft 10in (10.0m); draught 23ft 0in (7.0m).
Propulsion: 3 x Type 37-D diesels, 7,000bhp; 3 x electric motors, 5,000shp; two shafts.
Performance: surface – 16.0kt, 9,000nm/7kt; submerged – 17.0kt, 300nm/2.8kt; maximum operational depth 1,300ft (396m).
Weapons: 6 x 21in (533mm) TT (bow) (16 torpedoes); 4 x 16in (406mm) TT (aft) (12 torpedoes); 4 x SS-N-3B cruise missiles.
Complement: 78.

History: The conventionally powered Juliett was the non-nuclear equivalent to the Echo-class (qv), but carried only half the number (ie, four) of SS-N-3 missiles. These were mounted in forward-facing bins which were raised for launch. Defects in the design included the large cavities of the thrust-deflectors at the after end of each tube, which were open to the sea at all times and created considerable noise.

The Julietts had three main engines; the two

outer engines powered the propellers, while the centreline engine powered a generator, which could either drive the two propellers in a low speed mode, or charge the battery. There were unconfirmed reports that towards

Below: Juliett: missiles raised, radar open, ready for launch.

the end of their lives some
Julietts were given an air-
independent propulsion (AIP)
plant. Most boats had Punch Bowl
satellite targeting system and all
had the Front Door/Front Piece
missile guidance radar in the
forward edge of the sail. They also
carried a full sonar and torpedo
outfit, the latter consisting of six
21in (533mm) tubes forward and
four 16in (406mm) tubes aft.
These 16in torpedoes were
specifically intended for use
against attacking ASW escorts.

A total of 16 were built, and
these were originally deployed
with half in the Black Sea fleet and
half in the Northern Fleet.
However, the surviving Northern
Fleet boats were transferred to
the Baltic in the 1980s, indicating
a change from a strategic to a
theatre-level role against targets
in Western Europe. All were
scrapped between 1989 and
1994.

Echo-class
(Projects 659/675)

RUSSIA

Total built: Echo I – 5; Echo II – 29.
Completed: Echo I – 1961-62; Echo II – 1962-67.
Displacement: surfaced 5,000 tons; submerged 6,000 tons.
Dimensions: length 377ft 4in (115.0m); beam 29ft 6in (9.0m); draught 24ft 7in (7.5m).
Propulsion: 1 x HEN nuclear reactor, 24,000shp; two shafts.
Performance: surface – 20kt; submerged – 23kt.
Weapons: 6 x 21in (533mm) TT (bow) (12 torpedoes); 2 x 16in (406mm) TT (aft) (8 torpedoes); 8 x SS-N-3a cruise missiles.
Complement: 90.
Specifications for Echo II, as built.

History: The Echo I (Project 659) armed with six SS-N-3 missiles was intended
for the strategic attack role and lacked the necessary sensors for an anti-ship
role. Five were built and all were later converted to the attack (SSN) role, the
survivors being scrapped in the early 1990s.

The Echo II (Project 675) had the same weapons systems as the Echo I but
was some 13ft (4.0m) longer and with a 500-ton greater submerged
displacement. This enabled it to incorporate an additional pair of launchers as
well as the sensors necessary for anti-ship missions. This class were the Soviet
Navy's primary anti-carrier submarines in the 1960s and 1970s. The missiles,
which could be launched only while the submarine was on the surface, were

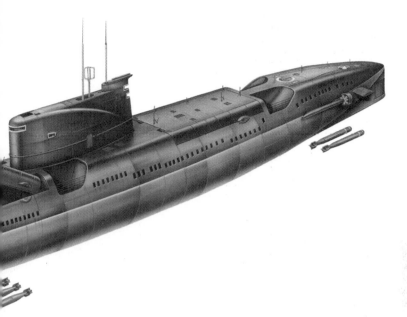

Above: Juliett with front tubes raised, SS-N-3B just launched.

Above: Echo II, back in port after a reactor problem in 1989.

mounted in pairs on top of the pressure hull and elevated prior to launch. Guidance was by means of the Front Door radar, whose antenna was mounted in the forward end of the sail on a base which rotated through 180 degrees. A total of 14 were converted to take SS-N-12 missiles and some were also adapted to take the Punch Bowl satellite targeting system. All surviving boats were disposed of in the early 1990s.

Both Echo I and II had the HEN nuclear propulsion system (which was also fitted in the Hotel- and November-classes) and suffered a number of accidents,

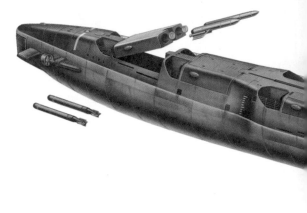

Charlie-class
(Projects 670/670M)

RUSSIA

Total built: Charlie I – 11; Charlie II – 6.
Completed: Charlie I – 1968-73; Charlie II – 1973-80.
Displacement: surfaced 4,300 tons; submerged 5,100 tons.
Dimensions: length 340ft 0in (103.6m); beam 32ft 10in (10.0m); draught 26ft 3in (8.0m).
Propulsion: 1 x VM-4-1 pressurised-water nuclear reactor; 18,800shp; one shaft.
Performance: surface – 15kt; submerged – 20kt; maximum operational depth 1,300ft (400m).
Weapons: 4 x 21in (533mm) TT (bow) (12 torpedoes); 2 x 16in (406mm) TT (bow) (4 torpedoes); 8 x SS-N-9 cruise missiles.
Complement: 98.
Specifications for Charlie II, as built.

History: The shortcomings of the Echo II class were readily apparent to the Soviet Navy and the next class of SSGN – the Charlie-class – largely rectified them. They had the same hull form and machinery as the Victor I-class SSNs and a similar high speed. The major advance over earlier Soviet SSGNs was that the missiles were mounted in launch tubes which were fully faired into the bow casing and there were no deep thrust deflector wells, making them much quieter, although still not as quiet as contemporary Western submarines.

Charlie I was armed with eight SS-N-7 anti-ship cruise missile, an

although none was actually lost. Two Echo Is suffered underwater fires, while six Echo IIs had nuclear-related accidents. In addition, four were involved in collisions: two with U.S. submarines, one with a Soviet research ship, and one with an unknown object while submerged. The final problem was a leak in the nuclear primary reactor circuit in 1989 which was so serious that it resulted in all submarines equipped with the HEN reactor being withdrawn from service.

Below: Echo II was powered by the dangerous HEN reactor.

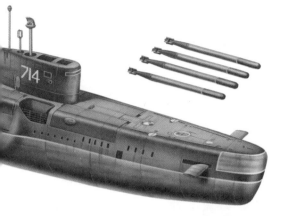

Right: One Charlie-class SSGN was lent to India in the 1980s.

underwater-launched version of the SS-N-2 Styx missile used by numerous classes of Soviet surface warships, which was developed in a rush due to the failure of the *Amethyst* missile which was being developed for the Papa-class SSGN (qv). The Charlie II was armed with the SS-N-9 (Siren), which had a much superior performance.

A unique event in the Charlie history is that one was lent to the Indian Navy, who named it INS *Chakra*. The Indians wished to learn how to operate a nuclear-powered submarine, but this was frustrated by the reported Soviet refusal to allow the Indian crew into either the missile control room or the nuclear reactor compartment. As a result, the Indians refused to renew the lease when it ended in 1991.

One Charlie I sank in the Pacific in 1983, was raised, sank again in port and was then raised for a second time, but was thereafter used as a training vessel. Most Charlie Is and IIs were stricken in the early 1990s, but one Charlie II remains in service in 2002.

Papa-class (Project 661)   RUSSIA

Total built: 1.
Completed: 1969.
Displacement: submerged 5,197 tons.
Dimensions: length 350ft 9in (106.9m); beam 372ft 9in (11.5m); draught 26ft 3in (8.0m).
Propulsion: 2 x pressurised-water nuclear reactor; 80,000shp; 2 x 153-cell batteries; two shafts.
Performance: surface – 16kt; submerged – 42kt; maximum operational depth 1,300ft (400m).
Weapons: 4 x 21in (533mm) TT (bow) (12 torpedoes); 10 x SS-N-9 cruise missiles.
Complement: 82.

History: The single Papa-class SSGN, *K-162,* established the world underwater speed record of 44.7kt (51.5mph/83km/h) in 1970-71, an incredible achievement. As far as is known, the record still stands. Design work started in 1959 for an SSGN with a titanium hull, deep operating depth and high speed, armed with the *Amethyst* missile. Design and construction proved to be lengthy, partly because of delays in the supply of titanium, but also because the submarine incorporated so many new systems. The forward end consisted of two cylinders in a vertical figure-8 installation, with the missile tubes alongside the upper cylinder and fully encased within the outer casing, as in the Charlie-class.

   The Papa was one of the few nuclear-powered submarines to have two

Yankee Notch-class (Project 667AT)   RUSSIA

Total built: 3.
Converted: 1984-88.
Displacement: surfaced 9,250 tons; submerged 11,500 tons.
Dimensions: length 464ft 2in (141.5m); beam 38ft 1in (11.6m); draught 26ft 7in (8.1m).
Propulsion: 2 x VM-4 pressurised-water nuclear reactors, 155mW; two GT- 3A-635; 38.2mW (50,000hp); two shafts.
Performance: surface – 12kt; submerged – 26kt; maximum operational depth 1,050ft (320m).
Weapons: 6 x 21in (533mm) TT (bow) (18 torpedoes); 8 x 21in (533mm) (amidships) TT for cruise missiles; 32 x SS-N-21 (Sampson) cruise- missiles.
Complement: 120.

History: The "Yankee Notch" was a conversion applied to three surplus Yankee-class SSBNs in the mid-1980s to produce a dedicated cruise missile carrier for the SS-N-21 (Sampson) land-attack cruise missile. This was the Russian equivalent of the U.S. Tomahawk. It was launched from a 21in (533mm) torpedo tube and flew at a speed of Mach 0.7 and a height of some 650ft (200m) to a range of 1,620nm (3,000km).

   The conversion resulted in an increase in length of 39.4ft (12m) as a result of the "notch waisted" central section, despite the removal of the ballistic missile section. The new section housed four 21in tubes amidships on each

Above: One Papa-class was built; it carried SS-N-9 missiles.

independent nuclear propulsion systems, each generating some 40,000shp, and each driving its own propeller. The design speed was 38kt but 42kt was achieved on trials, and, as mentioned above, 44.7kt was eventually achieved. However, there was considerable buffeting above about 35kt, which in protracted runs led to damage in the upper casing and would have generated noise which would have been detected many miles away. Only one was built and this was retired in 1991, but is apparently still in reserve in 2002.

Right: Three Yankee-class SSBNs were converted to Yankee Notch SSGNs; they carried 32 x SS-N-21 (Sampson) cruise missiles.

beam, with an internal magazine holding an additional 24 SS-N-21s, but it is believed that this magazine could accommodate additional torpedoes or mines instead of missiles. Further elements of the modification included the replacement of the two 16in (406mm) torpedo tubes by a further pair of 21in tubes and the lengthening of the sail, probably to accommodate a new type of communications buoy.

The Yankee Notch conversions reached the end of their lives because, unlike the U.S. Navy's Tomahawk, the SS-N-21 had only nuclear warheads and thus had to be withdrawn as a result of the various nuclear weapons reduction treaties. Two submarines were retired in 1996 and the other in 1997.

Oscar-class (Project 949)

RUSSIA

Total built: Oscar I – 1980-82; Oscar II – 1986-97.
Completed: Oscar I – 2; Oscar II – 11.
Displacement: surfaced 14,700 tons; submerged 19,400 tons.
Dimensions: length 505ft 3in (154.0m); beam 59ft 8in (18.2m); draught 30ft 2in (9.2m).
Propulsion: 2 x OK-650B pressurised-water nuclear reactors, 2 x 190mW; two OK-9 steam turbines, 98,000shp; two shafts.
Performance: surface – 15kt; submerged – 31kt; maximum operational depth 2,000ft (600m).
Weapons: 4 x 21in (533mm) TT (bow); 4 x 25.6in (650mm) TT (bow); total of 28 SS-N-16 missiles or torpedoes; 24 x SS-N-19 (Stallion) cruise missiles.
Complement: 107.
Specifications are for Oscar II, as built.

History: The Oscar I was introduced in 1980 and represented a major advance on the Echo II, having 24 "over-the-horizon" submerged-launch SS-N-19 missiles in a hull which, at the time, made it the third largest submarine in the world. Only two were built and these were followed by the even larger Oscar II with a 36ft (11m) increase in hull length and 4,000-ton increase in submerged displacement. These huge submarines are designated *Atomniy Podvodny Kresery I Ranga* (nuclear-powered submarine cruisers of the first rank) and were intended to play a major role in the battle against U.S. carrier battle groups. The choice of the word "cruiser" is interesting and indicates a role which includes a major commitment to surface action.

The missile tubes are in two banks of 12 running down each side of and outside the 27.9ft (8.5m) diameter pressure hull, which results in a gap of some 9.8ft (3m) between the outer and inner hulls, and in a very large beam. The gap between the hulls is filled with rubber, which results in excellent anti-torpedo protection and good sound reduction. The SS-N-19 missile tubes are inclined at 40 degrees, with one hatch covering each pair and the targeting data was to be provided by radar satellite downlink to the Punch Bowl antenna.

The reason for the longer Oscar II is not clear, but may have been either the result of some shortcoming in the first-of-class (which could not be corrected in time to change hull number two) or may have been the result of a plan (never realised) to install SS-N-24 missiles in due course. All but the first Oscar I had a

Below: Oscar-class, armed with 24 SS-N-19 cruise missiles.

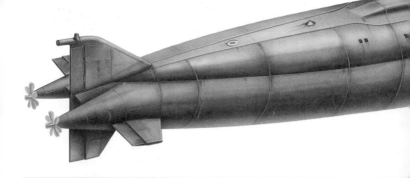

Above: Oscar-class SSGN; note the missile bins.

tube atop the rudder fin used to dispense a thin-line towed sonar array.

The two Oscar Is were based in the Northern Fleet but became non-operational in 1995 and were stricken in 1996/97, while the 11 Oscar IIs were divided between the Pacific Fleet (7) and the Northern Fleet (4). On 12 August 2000, however, *Kursk* sank while on exercise with surface units in the Barents Sea. All 118 aboard died in the tragedy, whose cause has yet to be determined.

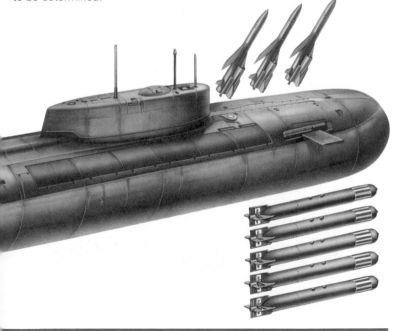

Fleet Submarine Cruise Missile Conversions

UNITED STATES

Total built: Loon – 2; Regulus – 2.
Converted: Loon – 1948; Regulus – 1952-55.
Displacement: surfaced 1,525 tons; submerged 2,130 tons.
Dimensions: length 312ft 0in (95.1m); beam 27ft 4in (8.3m).
Propulsion: 4 x Fairbanks-Morse 10-cylinder 2-stroke diesel engines, 2 x 1,600bhp; 2 x General Electric electric motors, 2,740shp; battery 2x 126-cell Exide cells; two shafts.
Performance: surface – 14kt; submerged – 9kt.
Weapons: 6 x 21in (533mm) TT (bow); 2 x Regulus I cruise missiles.
Complement: 85.
Specifications are for SSG-317 (Regulus I), as converted.

History: During World War II the Germans conceived the idea of submarine-launched cruise missiles (SLCM), but failed to pursue it, and it was left to the U.S. Navy to bring the idea to reality. The first missile to be used was a U.S.-made copy of the German pulsejet-powered, winged V-1 missile and this was successfully launched from a ramp on the afterdeck of *Cusk* (SS-348) on 15 February 1947. *Cusk* and *Carbonaro* (SS-337) were then fitted with a cylindrical hangar and launching ramp for a development of Loon, which could be given in-flight course corrections from modified submarines. The Loon programme ended in 1953, to be replaced by Regulus I, which was similar in concept to Loon but larger and considerably more sophisticated.

Above: **Tunny** *(SSG-282), Gato-class converted to SSG.*

Tunny (SSG-282) followed by *Barbero* (SSG-17) were converted to carry the new missile, the work including a snorkel, missile launch ramp, hangar for two missiles, and control, guidance and servicing facilities. *Tusk* received a new streamlined sail during conversion, but *Barbero* did not receive hers until later. To make way for the new equipment, the stern torpedo tubes and various other equipment were removed, including one main engine in *Tunny* and two in *Barbero.*

The Regulus programme was a success and the missile was also deployed aboard *Grayback* (SSG-574) (qv) and *Halibut* (SSGN-587) (qqv), but the programme was halted in 1964, with the success of the Polaris system.

Below: **Carbonero** *(SS-337) converted to trial Loon missile.*

Grayback-class

Total built: 2.
Completed: 1958.
Displacement: surfaced 2,540 tons; submerged 3,515 tons.
Dimensions: length 322ft 4in (98.3m); beam 30ft 0in (9.1m); draught 17ft 4in (5.3m).
Propulsion: 3 x Fairbanks-Morse 10-cylinder 2-stroke diesel engines, 3 x 1,500bhp; 2 x Elliott electric motors, 2 x 2,800shp; two shafts.
Performance: surface – 20kt; submerged – 12kt.
Weapons: 8 x 21in (533mm) TT (bow —6; stern – 2); 4 x Regulus I or II cruise missiles.
Complement: 84.
Specifications are for SSG-574 (Regulus II), as built.

History: These two submarines were originally intended to be sister-ships to the attack submarine *Darter* (qv), but were converted to SSGs during construction by inserting a plug and adding a large, ungainly bow structure housing two cylindrical hangars. This increased their length, *Grayback* by 50ft (15.3m) and *Growler* by 54ft (16.5m). Each missile cylinder was 70ft (21.3m) long and 11ft (3.4m) high and contained two Regulus I or II missiles. These could be launched only from the surface. As soon as the upper casing was clear of the water the watertight doors were opened, following which a missile was extracted rearwards onto a launching ramp sited in the well between the raised bow and the sail. Once the missile was secure the ramp was turned to the beam for launch. Not surprisingly, this was a time-consuming process.

Halibut-class

Total built: 1.
Completed: 1960.
Displacement: surfaced 3,846 tons; submerged 4,895 tons.
Dimensions: length 360ft 0in (106.7m); beam 29ft 6in (9.0m); draught 20ft 9in (65.3m).
Propulsion: 1 x Westinghouse S3W nuclear reactor, 6,600shp (approx); two shafts.
Performance: surface – 15kt; submerged – 15.5kt.
Weapons: 6 x 21in (533mm) TT (bow – 4; stern – 2); 5 x Regulus I or 2 x Regulus II cruise missiles.
Complement: 111.

History: The single nuclear-powered Halibut-class SSGN was the last boat to be built for the Regulus missile. She was laid down as the third in the conventionally-powered Grayback-class (qv), albeit with a larger missile compartment faired into the foredeck, but was redesigned to take nuclear power. She was fitted with a Westinghouse S3W nuclear plant, similar to that in the Skate-class SSNs and also driving two shafts. She carried either five Regulus I or two Regulus II missiles, which were brought up a ramp to be launched from a rotating launcher, and she launched numerous training missiles in the years 1961-65.

On the termination of the Regulus programme in 1965 the missile equipment was removed, a ducted bow-thruster (for precise manoeuvring) was installed and *Halibut* was reroled as a research submarine, although she was given an SSN designation. There is, however, good reason to believe that she

Above: **Grayback** *(SSG-574) with Regulus I on launcher.*

Each submarine conducted nine deterrent patrols armed with Regulus I missiles before the Regulus programme was halted in 1964. *Grayback* was then re-roled as an amphibious transport (LPSS), for which she was lengthened by 11ft 8in (3.5m) and the missile containers converted into Swimmer Delivery Vehicle (SDV) hangars. The conversion included raising the sail and the installation of the PUFFS sonar system with its characteristic three fins on the upper casing. Due to the expense involved, *Growler* was not converted. Both submarines were stricken in 1984.

Above: The SSGN, Halibut*, carried five Regulus I missiles.*

was actually engaged in intelligence-gathering and it is reported that it was a submersible launched from *Halibut* that found the sunken Soviet Golf-class submarine in the Pacific; she may also have been employed in recovering expended Soviet missile warheads. She was decommissioned in 1976 and later scrapped. A further three improved SSGNs were cancelled in 1965 and reordered as Permit-class SSNs.

Ballistic Missile Carriers

In the early 1950s it appeared that strategic warfare – by which was meant the ability of the USA and the Soviet Union to conduct direct attacks on each other's homelands – belonged to long-range bombers and land-based intercontinental ballistic missiles (ICBMs). However, both systems suffered form a fundamental disadvantage, since both the airfields and the missile sites were clearly known and could be targeted in a pre-emptive strike. The introduction of submarine-launched ballistic missiles (SLBMs), particularly when the submarine was nuclear-powered (SSBN), totally changed all that since the launch platform was inherently stealthy and, while a potential enemy might be able to locate one or two at a time, the chances of being able to locate 10 or more were extremely remote. These odds became even greater as the range of the missiles increased, thus enabling submarines to launch their missiles from areas dominated by their own ASW forces.

The idea of launching ballistic missiles from the sea originated in 1942 with a German named Lafferenz, who suggested that a V-2 rocket should be placed inside a submersible barge which would then be towed across the Atlantic by a U-boat. Once in position, both would surface, and the barge would be flooded to bring it upright; the missile would be then be fuelled and launched against New York. Somewhat surprisingly, this suggestion was given a low priority by the Germans. After the war both the United States and the Soviet Union examined the barge concept and the latter actually produced some prototypes, but the tests resulted in premature explosions and that particular idea was abandoned. These studies did, however, lead both navies to realise the strategic potential of a submarine armed with ballistic missiles and the Soviet Navy forged ahead to become the first to produce a workable solution, the Zulu V, a converted diesel-electric submarine. This carried two liquid-fuelled missiles in vertical tubes extending from the keel to the top of the sail. This early system required the submarine to be on the surface, where the missile was raised on an elevator until clear of the tube, a slow procedure which had obvious operational limitations, but it was a start. The Soviet Navy then progressed rapidly through in-tube launches to submerged launches, with accompanying improvements in range, payload and accuracy.

In the early 1950s the U.S. Navy, in collaboration with the U.S. Army, started development of a navalised Jupiter ICBM, the plan being to mount three of these 60ft (18.3m) liquid-fuelled missiles in a 10,000-ton, nuclear-powered submarine. Fortunately, the development of solid fuel and miniaturised components offered greater potential, and when a project team led by Admiral W. F. Raborn was formed in the early 1950s it decided from the start to opt for missiles with solid propellants which would be ejected from a vertical tube while the submarine was submerged. The resulting Polaris project, however, involved much more than this, including lightweight ablative RVs, inertial guidance and miniaturised nuclear warheads. For the submarine, new systems of navigation, noise reduction, deployments and launch procedures were required. Despite its complexity, the whole project came together without any serious hitches and Polaris became operational in November 1960. Improvement programmes led to Polaris A-2 and A-3, then Poseidon, followed by Trident I and the current Trident II. What is so impressive, however, is that Admiral Raborn and his team of naval officers and scientists got the concept so exactly right in the 1950s that today's Ohio/Trident combination is instantly recognisable as a lineal descendant of the original Polaris/Washington of 50 years ago.

Soviet progress was slower and required more interim steps before reaching the fully-fledged SSBN/SLCM combination with the Yankee/SS-N-6. Thereafter, progress was rapid and led to a large fleet of SSBNs, the bulk of

Above: **Typhoon,** *by far the largest submarine ever built.*

which were of the Yankee- and Delta-classes, although the latter were lineal descendants of the Yankee design. The balance of the fleet was made up of six Typhoons, the largest submarines ever built.

The British Polaris force of four Resolution-class SSBNs was commissioned between 1967 and 1969, with the Polaris missiles being bought direct from the Unites States, although the re-entry vehicles and warheads were designed, developed and produced entirely in the United Kingdom. This force was kept in service rather longer than had been planned, but was eventually replaced in the 1990s by the Vanguard-class.

France's nuclear deterrent was developed entirely within her own resources, a remarkable achievement. The first SSBN, *Le Redoutable*, became operational in 1971 and was followed by further boats in 1973, 1974 and 1976, respectively. However, unlike the British, the French then decided to build a fifth ship, which became operational in 1980. A sixth, *L'Inflexible*, was built to a more advanced design, joining the fleet in 1985, but the next was a totally new class, the Le Triomphant-class.

The end of the Cold War saw a sharp reduction in the number of operational SSBNs and a slowing down in the pace of development of new systems.

Despite this the importance of the SSBN has grown as the emphasis on bombers and ICBMs has decreased. Thus, the position in 2002 was that the U.S. had a force of 14 Ohio-class boats, but with the possibility of either reducing to 12 or maintaining the figure at 14, but with single crews. Her former opponent, Russia, nominally operates seven Delta IVs and eight Delta-IIIs but most of these are of doubtful operational value; possibly no more than four Delta-IVs and two Delta-IIIs are actually in a usable state.

The two European nuclear powers continue to operate their smaller SSBN fleets, although it should be noted that the advent of MIRVs has given them a proportionally greater capability than with their first generation systems. Thus, the British have a force of four Vanguard-class SSBNs armed with 16 Trident II SLBMs, while the French have six ships, armed with French SLBMs, which will reduce to four in 2004. In Asia, China has operated a single SSBN for some years, but a new class is under development, while persistent rumours of the development of missiles and nuclear-propulsion in India may lead to an SSBN/SLBM in due course.

Below: Ohio-class SSBN, USS **Michigan** *(SSBN-727).*

Daqingyu (Xia)-class (Project 092)

CHINA

Total built: 1.
Completed: 1988.
Displacement: submerged 7,000 tons.
Dimensions: length 393ft 8in (120.0m); beam 32ft 9in (10.0m); draught 26ft 2in (8.0m).
Propulsion: 1 x pressurised-water nuclear reactor, 58MW; 2 x steam turbines; one shaft.
Performance: submerged – 22kt; maximum operating depth 985ft (300m).
Weapons: 6 x 21in (533mm) TT (bow); missiles – 12 x missile tubes.
Complement: ca 100.
Specifications for Xia (#406), as built.

History: The Chinese Daqingyu-class, pennant *#406,* is the first SSBN to be designed and built in Asia, being constructed at Huladao, a major shipbuilding centre some 120 miles (200km) north-east of Beijing. Laid down in 1978, the submarine was launched in 1981, but then spent a lengthy period fitting out and conducting tests with its 12 JL-1 (CSS-N-3) missiles. The system suffered several problems, not surprising in a first-generation system, and did not become operational until 1987. It would appear that, just as the USA lengthened the hull of a Skipjack-class SSN to produce the first Washington-class SSBNs, so the Chinese lengthened the hull of the Han-class SSN to

Le Redoutable-class

FRANCE

Total built: 6.
Completed: 1971-85.
Displacement: surfaced 8,045 tons; submerged 8,940 tons.
Dimensions: length 422ft 0in (128.0m); beam 35ft 0in (10.6m); draught 33ft 0in (10.0m).
Propulsion: 1 x pressurised-water nuclear reactor; 2 x steam turbines, 2 x turbo-alternators, 1 x electric motor, 15,000shp; 1 x auxiliary diesel, 2,670bhp; one shaft.
Performance: surfaced – 20kt; submerged – 22kt; maximum operating depth 656ft (200m).
Weapons: 4 x 21.7in (550mm) TT (bow) (18 torpedoes); missiles – 16 x missile tubes.
Complement: 135.
Specifications for Le Redoutable, as built.

History: In the early 1960s France embarked on the development of a *Force de Dissuasion* (deterrent force) which was initially based on five SSBNs. The overall design was similar to that of the U.S. Navy's Lafayette-class (qv) – a single hull design with a 16-missile SLBM compartment located directly abaft the sail, the machinery spaces aft and a single shaft. The propulsion system was, however, different from contemporary U.S. and British designs in that the single pressurised-water nuclear reactor did not drive geared steam turbines, but drove two turbo-alternators instead, these, in turn, providing the power for a single large electric motor. The fourth and fifth boats, *L'Indomptable* and *Le Tonnant,* had a metallic reactor core in place of the oxide cores in the earlier

Right: **Daqingyu,** *China's first* *operational SSBN.*

produce the Daqingyu. Only one boat is known for certain to have been constructed. This entered service in 1987. It then went into a long refit at Huladao in 1985, where the work, which was still in progress in early 2002, involved installing the new JL-2 (CSS-NX-4) missile system, as well as general updating.

Western intelligence reports have suggested that a second Xia-class SSBN may have been launched in 1981 and that one of the two was lost at sea in 1985. This has never been confirmed and the only extant submarine became operational in the late 1980s and served with the North Sea Fleet until going into refit. A new class of SSBN (Type 093) is now under construction.

In order to maintain one submarine on continuous patrol a navy requires a minimum of four, preferably five, hulls. While the Daqingyu programme falls far short of this criterion, it does represent a major national achievement and is a valuable first step for a country which traditionally takes a very long-term view.

Above: **L'Inflexible,** *sixth of the French Le Redoutable-class.*

boats, while the sixth, *L'Inflexible*, was of an improved design and is sometimes regarded as a separate class.

The first two units, *Le Redoutable* and *Le Terrible*, initially carried the two-stage, single-warhead M1 missile with a range of 1,350nm, but this was superceded in the third unit, *Le Foudroyant*, by the more capable M2 missile. The fourth and fifth units carried a mix of M2 and M20 missiles, the latter differing only in having a single 1mT thermonuclear warhead, with the first three later carrying the same mix. The sixth, *L'Inflexible*, carried the M4, a totally new missile, with greater range and a payload of six 150kT MRVs.

The first four ships were stricken between 1991 and 1999, leaving just two in service in 2002: *L'Indomptable* and *L'Inflexible*. These will strike in 2004 and 2007, respectively.

Right: **Le Tonnant***, one of the first five French SSBNs which carried 16 M2/M20 ballistic missiles. They also carried L5 and F17 torpedoes for self-defence.*

Le Triomphant-class FRANCE

Total built: 4.
Completed: 1996-2008.
Displacement: surfaced 12,640 tons; submerged 14,335 tons.
Dimensions: length 452ft 8in (138.0m); beam 41ft 0in (12.5m); draught 34ft 8in (10.6m).
Propulsion: 1 x K15 pressurised-water nuclear reactor; 1 x electric motor, 41,500shp; 2 x SEMT-Pielstick 8 PA-4 V200 stand-by diesels, 2 x 1,225bhp; one shaft (pump-jet).
Performance: submerged – 25+kt; maximum operational diving depth 1,640ft (500m).
Weapons: 4 x 21in (533mm) (bow) (18 cruise missiles/torpedoes); missiles – 16 x missile tubes.
Complement: 121.

History: *L'Indomptable* was the last of the first series of French SSBNs and production then switched to a totally new second-generation design, with the first ship, *Le Triomphant*, being laid down in 1989, entering service in 1996 and carrying out its first operational patrol in 1997. The French Navy originally planned to build five, but it was announced in 1992 that only four would be built. Following a series of delays for budgetary reasons, the last will now enter service in 2008.

The Le Triomphant-class hull is constructed of NLES-100 steel and is of a better hydrodynamic shape than earlier designs, with a prop-jet propulsor

Right: **Le Triomphant***, first of the latest French SSBN class.*

and end plates on the horizontal stabilisers. Internally, power is provided by the new K15 pressurised-water nuclear reactor, with all mechanical elements mounted on "rafts" to isolate them from the hull in order to reduce radiated noise. The final stage is a pump-jet propulsor, which provides both improved hydrodynamic efficiency and a greatly reduced acoustic signature.

The first three boats carry 16 of the new M45 SLBMs, but the fourth will have the M51 missile, which will then be retrofitted into the first three. The M51 will have a range of 3,240nm and carry 10-12 TN-75 MIRVs.

Right: Le Triomphant. The pump-jet propulsor is carefully screened from view.

Resolution-class

GREAT BRITAIN

Total built: 4.
Completed: 1966-80.
Displacement: surfaced 7,500 tons; submerged 8,400 tons.
Dimensions: length 425ft 0in (129.5m); beam 33ft 0in (10.1m); draught 30ft 1in (9.1m).
Propulsion: 1 x Vickers/Rolls-Royce PWR.2 pressurised-water nuclear reactor, ca. 27,500shp; one pump-jet.
Performance: surface – 20kt; submerged – 25kt.
Weapons: 6 x 21in (533mm) TT (bow); missiles – 16 x missile tubes.
Complement: 143 (two crews).

History: In the late 1950s it was planned that the British Royal Air Force would provide the British strategic nuclear deterrent into the 1960s and 1970s, using V-bombers armed with Skybolt air-to-surface nuclear missiles. But at the Nassau conference in 1962, President John F. Kennedy told British Prime Minister Harold MacMillan that the USA was abandoning Skybolt, due to apparently insuperable development problems. It was then agreed that the United States would supply Britain with Polaris SLBMs, for which the British would build their own SSBNs, but that the missiles would have entirely British front-ends (ie, nuclear warhead and guidance package), thus giving the British government total control over the use and targeting of the weapons.

Four submarines were built of a planned total of five, the last boat being cancelled in the Labour Government's 1965 defence review. Much technical

Right: British Resolution-class SSBN approaches its base.

assistance was provided by the United States and the Resolution-class is generally similar to the American Lafayette-class, although the actual design is based on that of the Valiant-class SSN, but with a missile compartment between the control centre and the reactor room.

First-of-class *Resolution* was laid down in February 1964 and completed in October 1967, exactly on schedule. She then fired her first Polaris A-3 missile off Cape Kennedy on 15 February 1968 and sailed on her first operational patrol on 15 June that year. Later, she was the third to receive the Chevaline update (1984) and created a record in 1991 when she conducted the longest-ever Polaris patrol, lasting 108 days. She paid off in October 1994 after 69 patrols.

Repulse underwent her Chevaline update in 1982 and completed the British 200th Polaris patrol in August 1990. One of her achievements was to take part in trials of the U.S. Navy's Deep Submergence Rescue Vehicle (DSRV), named *Avalon*, which was flown in from the United States and installed on *Repulse's* after casing. Once in deep water, *Avalon* disengaged, moved to HMS *Odin*, simulating a sunken submarine and took a number of *Odin's* crew to *Repulse* in an entirely successful operation. *Repulse* completed the last Polaris patrol, and her own 69th, on 5 May 1996 and paid off in August 1996.

Renown was the first of the four ships to be fitted with the Chevaline conversion and successfully tested the system in early 1982. She paid off in 1995. *Revenge* launched her first Polaris missile in June 1970 and started her first operational patrol three months later. She was the last to receive her Chevaline update (1988) but became the first to be paid off in May 1992, having completed 56 deterrent patrols.

Right: The British operated four Resolution-class SSBNs.

Below: Resolution *was armed with 16 Polaris A3TK SLBMs.*

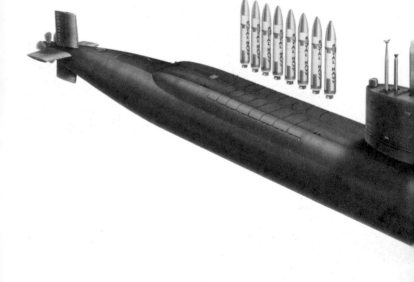

Vanguard-class

Total built: 4.
Completed: 1993-99.
Displacement: submerged 15,850 tons.
Dimensions: length 490ft 0in (149.3m); beam 42ft 0in (12.8m); draught 33ft 1in (10.1m).
Propulsion: 1 x Vickers/Rolls-Royce PWR.2 pressurised-water nuclear reactor, ca. 27,500shp; one pump-jet.
Performance: submerged – 25kt.
Weapons: 4 x 21in (533mm) TT (bow) (Harpoon/Spearfish/Tigerfish torpedoes); missiles – 16 x missile tubes.
Complement: 135 (two crews).

History: After many years of discussion it was announced in 1980 that the British government had selected the Trident missile as the replacement for its Polaris A3TK missiles (Polaris A-3 with British Chevaline warhead). Initial plans were to buy the Trident I C-4, but this was later changed to Trident II D-5 to ensure long-term compatibility with the U.S. Navy. This required a new submarine, considerably larger than the Resolution-class it replaced – in fact, by far the largest submarine ever built in the UK – but still armed with 16 missiles, unlike the U.S. Navy's Ohio-class which has 24 missiles.

The arrangement for the missiles is unique and demonstrates the extremely close relationship between the Royal and U.S. navies. Under this, the UK did not purchase a specific number of Trident missiles which would then have been the sole property of the British government. Instead, the UK purchased a share of a common USN/RN pool which is held at King's Bay, Georgia. Thus, when a British SSBN requires missiles it sails to King's Bay

Above: **Vanguard,** *first of the UK's second class of SSBNs.*

Above: British SSBNs are armed with 16 Trident II SLBMs.

where it is loaded with the next 16 available missiles, less their warheads, there being no differentiation between British and American missiles. The ship then returns to Coulport on the west coast of Scotland, where the missiles are fitted with British warheads. At the end of the commission the reverse process is followed, with the British warheads remaining in the UK and the missiles being returned to the USA.

First-of-class HMS *Vanguard* was launched on 4 March 1992 and sailed on its first operational patrol in December 1994. The second, *Victorious*, entered service in December 1995, followed by *Vigilant* in November 1996 and *Vengeance* in November 1999. All four are based at Faslane in the Gareloch off the River Clyde in Scotland.

The class was just coming into service as the Cold War ended, and this led to a number of major changes in deployment. According to the Ministry of Defence, "...each submarine will deploy with no more than 96 warheads and may carry significantly fewer." This was followed by an announcement that the

Vanguard-class will have a "sub-strategic" mission..." which would involve "...the limited and highly selective use of nuclear weapons in a manner that fell demonstrably short of a strategic strike, but with a sufficient level of violence to convince an aggressor who had already miscalculated (British) resolve and attacked us that he should halt his aggression and withdraw or face the prospect of a devastating strategic strike." This involves fitting some Trident missiles with a single warhead, which could be used to detonate the primary system with a yield of less than 10kT and thus used as a demonstration of resolve to "go all the way" unless the aggressor ceased his attack. This means that a proportion of the 16 missiles will carry an average of five warheads each, while the remainder carry one warhead each; thus, one load-out might comprise 14 missiles with five warheads plus two single warheads, for a total of 72 warheads.

Below: The escorting boats give the scale of this huge SSBN.

Zulu V-class (Project 611)   RUSSIA

Total converted: 5.
Converted: 1954-58.
Displacement: surfaced 1,900 tons; submerged 2,350 tons.
Dimensions: length 324ft 1in (98.8m); beam 24ft 7in (7.5m); draught 17ft 1in (5.2m).
Propulsion: 3 x diesel engines, each 2,000bhp; 3 x electric motors, 5,200shp; three shafts.
Performance: surface – 18.0kt; submerged – 12,5kt, 20,000nm/8kt; maximum operating depth 656ft (200m).
Weapons: 10 x 21in (533mm) TT (bow – 6, stern – 4) (10 torpedoes); missiles – 2 x missile tubes.
Complement: 83.

History: The first launch of a ballistic missile from a submarine took place on 16 September 1955, one of many significant achievements by the Soviet Navy during the Cold War period. It was launched from a modified Zulu IV patrol submarine (qv), which was fitted with a single tube in the sail for a standard Soviet Army R-11 (Scud) tactical missile, which was mounted on an elevator

developed fom a battlecruiser gun mounting. Once in position, with the submarine on the surface and only in relatively calm seas, the end-cap was removed by an electric motor and the missile raised, held firmly in the grip of a two-part cradle until the motor had fired.

Having achieved success in these trials with the Zulu IV, five Zulu-class boats were converted with two tubes in a lengthened sail, each carrying a navalised Scud, designated R11FM. Generally known under their NATO reporting name of "Zulu V", these boats were slightly longer than the earlier Zulus, and no spare torpedoes were carried. The R11FM (also known as D-1) had a range of approximately 80nm (150km), carried a non-nuclear warhead and had an accuracy (circular error probable – CEP) of 4nm (8km). Only one missile could be raised and launched at a time, which meant that the submarine would have had to expose itself for some 10-15 minutes very close to the enemy shore while launching two relatively small and very inaccurate missiles. This missile was replaced by the R-13 (D-2) in 1967/68, known to NATO as SS-N-4 (Sark). This had a range of some 350nm (650km) and carried a 1mT nuclear warhead.

Below: Zulu V carried 2 x SS-N-4 in its enlarged sail.

Golf-class (Project 628)

RUSSIA

Total built: 23 (plus 1 in PRC).
Completed: 1958-62.
Displacement: surfaced 2,350 tons; submerged 2,850 tons.
Dimensions: length 328ft 1in (99.0m); beam 27ft 11in (8.0m); draught 21ft 8in (6.6m).
Propulsion: 3 x diesel engines, each 2,000bhp; 3 x electric motors, 5,200shp; three shafts.
Performance: surface – 17kt, 9.500nm/5kt; submerged – 12kt; maximum operating depth 656ft (200m).
Weapons: 10 x 21in (533mm) TT (bow – 6, stern – 4) (16 torpedoes); missiles – 3 x missile tubes.
Complement: 59.
Specifications for Golf I, as built.

History: The Golf I diesel-electric submarines were built using many Foxtrot-class components, in parallel to the Hotel-class (qv) and as an insurance against the failure of the latter's nuclear propulsion system. The early Golf Is carried three RF-11M (Scud) missiles in vertical tubes in the sail until the SS-N-4 became available. Even this new missile also had a short range and 13 boats (known to NATO as Golf II) were converted to take three SS-N-5 (Serb) missiles. The SS-N-5 Soviet D-4 (R-21) not only had much greater range but could also be launched when the submarine was submerged, limits being a depth of 200ft (60m) and a forward speed of 4kt. Missile range was some 760nm (1,400km).

Some of the remaining hulls were used to test new msssile systems. Golf III was lengthened by 33ft (10m) and carried three SS-N-8 (Sawfly), while Golf IV was lengthened by 60ft (18.3m) to carry six SS-NX-13 and Golf V carried just one of the much larger SS-N-20. One curiosity about these three was that the missiles in the Golf II and III were counted under U.S./USSR SALT-I agreement,

Above: Golf II carried 3 x SS-N-5 (Serb) SLBMs in its sail.

Above: Golf II on patrol; note huge sail and radio masts.

but the hulls were not, while neither the Golf V nor its single missile were countable. Two of these boats were converted in the late 1970s by having their missile and torpedo tubes removed and much communications equipment added to be employed as communications relays – they were designated Golf I (Modified) or Golf SSQ by NATO. One Golf-class submarine is known to have been assembled in China as part of that country's SLBM programme and there have been persistent rumours that a second was also built, and that one of the two exploded in the South China Sea in mid-1981.

One Soviet Golf II sank in the central Pacific in 1968. Part of it was later recovered by the specially built *Glomar Explorer*, owned by Howard Hughes, but funded and controlled by the CIA. According to reports, this ship recovered the bow section, two nuclear-tipped torpedoes and a number of bodies, which were given formal funerals.

In the 1970s, late in the Golf II's career, six were deployed to the Baltic as theatre assets to be used in direct support of any land battle in central Europe. The Golfs left service in the late 1980s, except for the three SSQs, which survived into the 1990s.

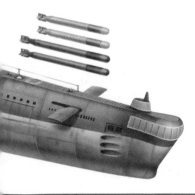

Hotel-class (Project 658)   RUSSIA

Total built: 6.
Completed: 1960-64.
Displacement: surfaced 5,000 tons; submerged 6,000 tons.
Dimensions: length 377ft 4in (115.0m); beam 29ft 6in (9.0m); draught 23ft 0in (7.0m).
Propulsion: 1 x HEN pressurised-water nuclear reactor; 2 x electric motors, 30,000shp; two shafts.
Performance: surface – 20kt; submerged – 25kt.
Weapons: 6 x 21in (533mm) TT (bow) (16 torpedoes); 2 x 16in (406mm) TT (stern); missiles – 3 x missile tubes.
Complement: 80.
Specifications for Hotel I, as built.

History: The first Soviet nuclear-powered ballistic missile submarines, the Hotel I-class carried three SS-N-4 (Sark) SLBMs, with the tubes stretching from the keel to the top of the sail. The missiles were launched from the surface, being raised clear of the sail by an elevator, as in the Zulu-V- and Golf-class SSBs. Six were built, all at Severodvinsk, and all were powered by the same nuclear plant as used in the other two first-generation nuclear classes, leading to the NATO designation of HEN (Hotel-Echo-November). The six boats were rebuilt in the mid-1960s: five were converted to take three SS-N-5 (Serb) missiles each and were redesignated by NATO as Hotel II. The sixth was converted to serve as trials boat for SS-N-8 (Sawfly), which subsequently was deployed aboard Yankee- and Delta-class SSBNs. This boat, which was lengthened to 426ft (130m), was designated Hotel III by NATO.

The Hotel IIs were deployed off the western and eastern seaboards of the

Below: The nuclear-powered Hotel II carried 3 x SS-N-5.

Above: Hotel II in distress, one of many to suffer accidents.

United States, posing a major threat to U.S. strategic bomber bases, since the flight times would have been some 6-10 minutes. First-of-class *K-19* had such an appalling safety record that she was known as "*Hiroshima*" throughout the Soviet Navy. She suffered two very serious nuclear-related accidents with 10 personnel dying in one (July 1961) and 29 in another (February 1972), and also collided with USS *Gato* (SSN-615) in the White Sea (November 1969). In 1973 one unit was disabled off the coast of Newfoundland and towed back to Northern Russia. These boats were affected by the SALT agreements: two were scrapped in 1982-83 and all surviving boats had their missile facilities removed by 1989. Two were re-roled as communications relays (SSQN) for a short period.

Yankee-class (Project 667) RUSSIA

Total built: 34.
Completed: 19670-72.
Displacement: surfaced 8,000 tons; submerged 9,600 tons.
Dimensions: length 426ft 6in (30.0m); beam 39ft 4in (12.0m); draught 29ft 10in (8.8m).
Propulsion: 1 x VM-4 pressurised-water nuclear reactor, 90MW; 2 x electric motors, 29,000shp; two shafts.
Performance: submerged – 27kt.
Weapons: 4 x 21in (533mm) TT (bow) (16 torpedoes); 2 x 16in (406mm) TT (bow); missiles – 16 x missile tubes.
Complement: 120.
Specifications for Yankee I, as built.

History: The Soviet Navy lost its early lead over the U.S. Navy in SSBN/SLBM development when the first of the Polaris submarines went to sea in 1960, and it was not until the Yankee-class became operational in 1967 that the Soviets had their first submarines to mount SLBMs totally within the hull. The missile tubes were arranged in two vertical rows abaft the fin, the first 20 ships being armed with 16 SS-N-6 Mod I (Sawfly) SLBM, each of which had one 2mT warhead with a range of some 1,500nm and which, for the first time in a Soviet SLBM, were launched while submerged. The next 14 boats carried 16 of the longer-ranged SS-N-6 Mod 3, with two MRV warheads.

Like all Soviet submarines, the Yankees were noisier than their Western counterparts and were correspondingly easier to detect. The relatively short range of the SS-N-6, even in its later versions, meant that the Yankees would have had to approach the American coasts in order to launch their missiles, although they were less vulnerable than the earlier types which had to surface to launch their missiles. As the new Deltas entered service, the Yankees were progressively withdrawn from the strategic role, starting in 1980, SSBNs in service being: 1980 – 34; 1991 – 12; 1992 – 6; 1993 – 0.

As they retired from strategic service, many of the Yankees were modified for different roles. One was armed with 12 SS-N-17 in a trial installation (Yankee II), while four were converted into carriers for SS-N-21 cruise missiles; the NATO designation was Yankee Notch (qv). Another was converted to take 12 SS-NX-24 in vertical tubes in a new and much larger mid-body. Two others became Yankee Pod, designed to test new sonars, and Yankee Stretch, lengthened by 97ft 6in (29.7m), which was used as a support vessel for mini-submarines. The five remaining boats were converted to SSNs by removing the central missile section, shortening them by 95ft (28.9m), becoming Yankee III.

Yankees suffered a number of accidents in service, two of them in the missile tubes (31 August 1973; 6 October 1986). One had a serious reactor problem which led to the boat being rebuilt, becoming the sole Yankee II.

Right: A Yankee on fire off Bermuda in 1986. Note that the sail- mounted hydroplanes are swung to the vertical, a capability necessary to penetrate the ice when surfacing in the Arctic.

Delta-class (Project 667B) RUSSIA

Class	Delta I	Delta II	Delta III	Delta IV
Project	667B	667BD	667BDR	667BDRM
Total built	18	4	14	7
Completed	1972-77	1975	1976-81	1985-92
Displacement surfaced submerged	9.000 tons 11,750 tons	10,000 tons 12,750 tons	10,500 tons 13,250 tons	11,740 tons 15.500 tons
Dimensions: length beam draught	459ft 4in (140.0m) 39ft 4in (12.0m) 28ft 7in (8.7m)	508ft 6in (155.0m) 39ft 4in (12.0m) 28ft 10in (8.8m)	508ft 6in (155.0m) 38ft 5in (11.7m) 28ft 7in (8.7m)	548ft 0in (167.0m) 39ft 4in (12.0m) 28ft 6in (8.7m)
Propulsion: reactor power shafts	2 x VM-4S 50,000shp 2	2 x VM-4S 50,000shp 2	2 x VM-4S 50,000shp 2	2 x VM-4SG 60,000shp 2
Performance submerged maximum operating depth	25kt	24kt	24kt 1,250ft (380m)	24kt
Endurance	80 days			
Weapons: 21in (533mm) TT torpedoes 406mm TT torpedoes missiles	4 12 2 6 12 x SS-N-8	4 12 2 6 16 x SS-N-8	4 12/SS-N-16 2 6 16 x SS-N-18	4 12/SS-N-16 – – 16 x SS-N-23
Complement:	120	126	130	135

History: The Soviet Navy's Delta-class has been one of the most successful of all SSBNs, with 43 built over a 20-year period. It was the mainstay of the Soviet/Russian deterrent force throughout the 1980s and 1990s, exerting a major influence on the strategic nuclear balance. By Soviet Navy standards the Yankee-class SSBN was a very satisfactory design, so when a new class of SSBN was required to take the new SS-N-8 missile to sea it was decided to avoid disruption in the shipyards by producing an evolutionary development of the Yankee, thus avoiding the complications of a new missile *and* a new submarine. As a result, the Delta had the same forward end (torpedo tubes, sonar, command centre and accommodation) and after end (nuclear reactors, propulsion) as the Yankee, but with a totally new mid-section housing 12 missiles. Because the SS-N-8 was longer than the SS-N-6, however, the missile section had to be higher and was covered by a raised casing, known in the West as a "turtleback".

Above: Delta III heads North on patrol under the Arctic ocean.

When the Delta I/SS-N-8 combination became operational in 1973, it ended the superiority in both quality and performance which the U.S. Navy had enjoyed since the appearance of the Washington/Polaris in 1960. The early Soviet SLBMs had short ranges which meant that the SSBNs had to patrol close off the U.S. coastline, where they were naturally more vulnerable. However, the SS-N-8 missile with its range of more than 4,800nm (7,720km) and a CEP of only 0.84nm (1.5km) enabled the Soviets to threaten the USA from "bastions" in the Sea of Okhotsk and the Barents Sea, close to their own shores and thus much more easily protected by their own defensive measures.

Eighteen Delta Is were built, which were split equally between the Northern and Pacific Fleets, the nine latter boats being the last SSBNs to be constructed at Komsomols'k in the Soviet Far East; once these had been completed construction of all later SSBNs was concentrated at Severodvinsk. The Delta Is served from the mid-1970s to 1991 when nine were retired, following by the remaining nine in 1992.

Next came four Delta IIs, an interim design which was lengthened to enable them to carry four more SS-N-8 missiles, thus matching Western SSBNs. They were all built at Severodvinsk and all served in the Northern Fleet, entering service in 1974-75 and retiring in 1993-94.

The Delta III introduced the SS-N-18 missile, which mounted either a large single or a number of MIRVed warheads (see table on page 430). The new missile was longer than the SS-N-8, requiring an even larger "turtleback". All 14 Delta IIIs were built at Severodvinsk, being completed between 1976 and 1982, but the force was split equally between the Northern and Far East Fleets. The first to be stricken went in 1996, followed by another five until in 2002 only eight remained nominally in service, although very few of these were actually fit to go to sea.

Delta IVs were the last and largest of the Deltas. At least 10 were ordered, of which seven were completed between 1985 and 1992, while the construction of another two was stopped on the stocks. All seven served in the Northern Fleet and their planned use was to deploy under the Arctic ice and then to surface to launch their missiles. In 2002 all seven were still nominally operational.

In 1993 one Delta-class boat collided with the U.S. Navy's Sturgeon-class attack submarine, USS *Grayling* (SSN-646). In 1998 one unit, *K-407*, was used to launch a Russian RSM-54 missile carrying a German telecommunications satellite.

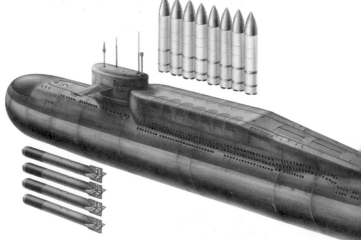

Above: First of a long line, Delta I armed with 12 x SS-N-8.

Below: Delta III armed with 16 x SS-N-8 Stingray SLBMs.

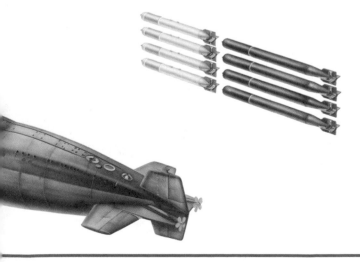

Missile	SS-N-8		SS-N-18			SS-N-23
	Sawfly		Stingray			Skiff
	Mod 1	Mod 2	Mod 1	Mod 2	Mod 3	Mod 1
SSBN	Delta I/II		Delta III			Delta IV
Stages	2					
Propellant	Stored liquid					
Length	42ft 6in (13.0m)		46ft 3in (14.1m)			48ft 6in (14.8m)
Diameter	5ft 11in (1.8m)		5ft 11in (1.8m)			6ft 2in (1.9m)
Weight	73,413lb (33,300kg)		77,822lb (35,300kg)			88,845lb (40,300kg)
IOC	1973	1977	1977	1979	1979	1986
Range	4,200nm (7,800km)	4,900nm (9,100km)	3,500nm (6,480km)	4,300nm (7,960km)	3,500nm (6,480km)	4,500nm (8,300km)
RVs	1 x RV	1 x RV	1 x RV	3 x MIRV	7 x MIRV	4 x MIRV
Yield per RV	800kT	800kT	450kt	200kt	100kT	100kT
CEP (estimate)	5,250ft (1,600m)	5,250ft (1,600m)	2,950ft (900m)	2,950ft (900m)	2,950ft (900m)	500ft (152m)

Above: Delta IV carries 16 x SS-N-23 (Skiff) missiles.

Below: Delta II carried 16 SS-N-8 (Sawfly) missiles.

Typhoon-class (Project 491)

Total built: 6.
Completed: 1981-89.
Displacement: surfaced 23,200 tons; submerged 33,800 tons.
Dimensions: length 566ft 11in (172.8m); beam 76ft 1in (23.2m); draught 37ft 8in (11.5m).
Propulsion: 2 x OK-650 pressurised-water nuclear reactor; 2 x steam turbines, 100,000shp; two shafts (shrouded propellers).
Performance: surface – 12kt; submerged – 25kt; maximum operating depth 1,300ft (400m).
Weapons: 2 x 21in (533mm), 4 x 24.8in (630mm) TT (bow) (22 weapons); missiles – 20 x missile tubes.
Complement: 179.

History: In the late 1970s there were persistent rumours in the West that the Soviet Navy was constructing a new class of submarines of huge proportions, but when the design was revealed in November 1980 it still came as a major surprise. Overall, the most astonishing factor was its enormous size – it was far bigger than any other submarine before or since, and for many years there were arguments as to whether it had one or two

Below. Typhoon's size caused great alarm in the West.

Above: Typhoon is 76ft (23m) wide, 567ft (173m) long.

hulls inside the outer casing. Next, it was the first SSBN to have the missiles located forward of the sail, and the number of missiles – 20 – was greater than any of its contemporaries, until the advent of the U.S. Navy's Ohio-class.

The mysteries were gradually revealed, the main one being that there were two identical and interconnected hulls, each 27ft 11in (8.5m) in diameter containing a full propulsion system, accommodation and other services. In addition, there were three pressure containers, housing the torpedo tubes forward, sail and command centre amidships, and a smaller one aft for the steering and hydroplane control machinery. The missile tubes were located in two parallel rows of 10 between the two main pressure hulls and forward of the massive sail.

The Typhoons were designed to operate under the Arctic ice-cap, using their enormous size to force their way to the surface in order to launch their missiles. The missile was the SS-N-20 (Sturgeon), a three-stage, solid fuel missile with a range of 4,470nm (8,300km) and a payload of 10 100kT MIRVs.

The main machinery comprised two quite separate power-trains, one in each hull, each unit comprising an OK-650 pressurised-water nuclear reactor (190mW) driving a steam turbine (50,000hp) and two 3,200kW turbo-generators. Each unit also includes stand-by power from a single 800kW diesel generator coupled to the shaft line. Each power-train culminates in a seven-bladed, fixed-pitch shrouded propeller. In order to assist navigation at slow speeds, there were built-in bow and stern thrusters, each powered by a 750kW motor.

Six Typhoons were built at Severodvinsk on the White Sea near Archangelsk, completion dates being: *TK-208* – 1981, *TK-202* – 1983, *TK-12* – 1984, *TK-13* – 1985, *TK-17* – 1987 and *TK-20* – 1989. Work on a seventh – *TK-210* – stopped in 1990 and it was then broken up. All were based with the Russian Northern Fleet at Litsa Guba. First-of-class *TK-208* started a refit in 1992, which included conversion to take SS-N-28 missiles, but work was later suspended and the combination of a shortage of funds and cancellation of the SS-NX-28 mean that it will never be completed. *TK-12* and *TK-13* were stricken in 1996, since funds were not available for a refit. Work on scrapping most of these ships started in the late 1990s, the Russian Navy being assisted by the United States under the Co-operative Threat Reduction Programme, with U.S. funding being particularly earmarked for the processing facilities to remove nuclear material and convert it into forms suitable for either re-use or long-term storage.

Below: In essence, Typhoon consists of two parallel hulls, each containing its own missiles and nuclear power-train, with a third command compartment on top and all encased, as always in Russian submarines, in a second, outer hull.

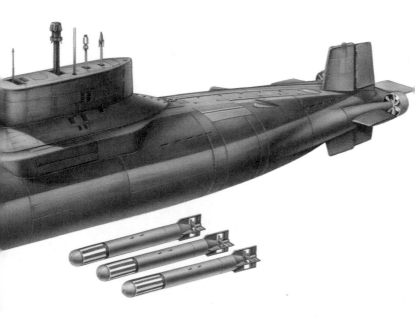

George Washington-class   UNITED STATES

Total built: 5.
Completed: 1959-61.
Displacement: surfaced 5,959 tons; submerged 6,709 tons.
Dimensions: length 381ft 8in (116.4m); beam 33ft 0in (10.1m); draught 26ft 8in (8.1m).
Propulsion: 1 x Westinghouse S5W pressurised-water nuclear reactor; ca. 15,000shp; 1 x electric motor; one shaft.
Performance: submerged – 20kt.
Weapons: 6 x 21in (533mm) TT (bow); missiles – 16 x missile tubes.
Complement: 112 (two crews).

History: This historic design established a pattern which has been followed by the great majority of subsequent SSBNs, with 16 missiles mounted vertically in two rows of eight abaft the sail. Having decided in favour of the principle, the U.S. Navy was desperate to get SSBNs to sea as quickly as possible and the first-of-class was constructed by taking the hull of Skipjack-class USS *Scorpion* (SSN-589), which was already under construction, and adding a new 130ft (40m) missile section, while retaining the original powerplant and much of the SSN-type equipment. The result was an outstanding success and four more to the same design were completed between 1959 and 1961, each armed with 16 Polaris A-1 missiles. Such was the pace of progress, however, that by the mid-1960s the relatively short range of their first-generation SLBMs was making them vulnerable to Soviet countermeasures, so during their first re-coring they were fitted to launch the 2,855nm (4,595km) Polaris A-3. Their electronics and other systems were also upgraded.

These five boats were physically unsuitable for

conversion to take Poseidon missiles, so they were deactivated in 1980-81, and several plans for their future were considered, including conversion to cruise-missile carriers. In the event, *Theodore Roosevelt* (SSBN-600) and *Abraham Lincoln* (SSBN-602) were cut in two and have since been scrapped, while the other three had their missile tubes filled with concrete and were reclassified as SSNs. They were then used as training boats for several years, but the last was decommissioned in 1985.

Below: **George Washington** *SSBN receives a Polaris SLBM* .

Ethan Allen-class

UNITED STATES

Total built: 5.
Completed: 1961-63.
Displacement: surfaced 6,946 tons; submerged 7,884 tons.
Dimensions: length 410ft 5in (125.1m); beam 33ft 0in (10.1m); draught 24ft 7in (8.4m).
Propulsion: 1 x Westinghouse S5W pressurised-water nuclear reactor; ca. 15,000shp; 1 x electric motor; one shaft.
Performance: submerged – 20kt.
Weapons: 4 x 21in (533mm) TT (bow); missiles – 16 x missile tubes.
Complement: 110 (two crews).

History: Whereas the George Washington-class was built to a modified SSN design in order to get the Polaris missile into service as quickly as possible, the five Ethan Allen SSBNs were designed specifically as SSBNs. They were generally similar to the earlier class, but were some 28ft 9in (8.7m) longer, and when first commissioned were armed with the Polaris A-2 missile, which had a range of 1,725nm (2,776km). They had greatly improved crew quarters, an important consideration in a boat intended to spend 60 days at a time submerged. *Ethan Allen* (SSBN-08) was the first SSBN to launch a live SLBM (6 May 1962) which detonated successfully on the Christmas Island test range. These boats were later converted to take the Polaris A-3 missile, but could not be further converted to take Poseidon.

In 1980-81 they were redesignated SSNs, but it was not until 1982 that their missile tubes were filled with concrete and their missile launch and fire control equipment removed. Two never returned to service, but the other three served until 1990-91 as SSNs, of which two – *Sam Houston* (SSBN-609) and *John Marshall* (SSBN-611) – were each capable of carrying 66 SEALs and could mount two Dry Deck Shelters on the upper casing. The last was decommissioned in 1992.

Below: Ethan Allen-class SSBNs carried 16 missiles.

Right: Ethan Allen-class carried Polaris A-1 or A-3 missiles.

Lafayette-class

Total built: 31.
Completed: 1963-67.
Displacement: surfaced 7,325 tons; submerged 8,251 tons.
Dimensions: length 425ft 0in (129.6m); beam 33ft 0in (10.1m); draught 27ft 10in (8.5m).
Propulsion: 1 x Westinghouse S5W pressurised-water nuclear reactor; ca. 15,000shp; 1 x electric motor; one shaft.
Performance: submerged – 20kt.
Weapons: 4 x 21in (533mm) TT (bow); missiles – 16 x missile tubes.
Complement: 140 (two crews).

History: The 31 Lafayette-class SSBNs were the definitive U.S. SSBNs of the 1960s and 1970s. The first 19 to be built were slightly improved and enlarged versions of the Ethan Allen design and were, at least outwardly, virtually indistinguishable from the earlier class. The last 12 (ie, from SSBN-640 onwards) differed considerably, with improved, quieter machinery, many minor improvements and 28 more crewmen, and are sometimes referred to as the

*Below: Earlier Lafayette-class SSBNs retained their original Poseidon C-3 missiles, but later boats, like **Daniel Boone** (SSBN-629) seen here, were retrofitted to take Trident I C-4 .*

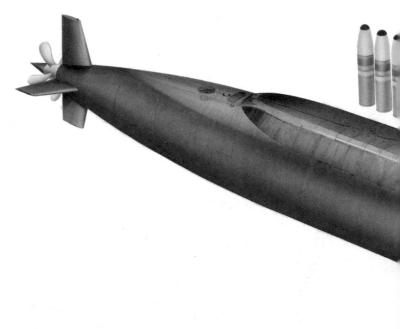

Above: Lafayette-class, George Washington Carver.

Benjamin Franklin-class, but are here treated as one.

The missiles were progressively improved. As built, the first eight Lafayettes (SSBN-616 – SSBN-625) carried Polaris A-2 SLBMs, while the remaining 23 had the improved Polaris A-3, which had a range of 2,855nm (4,594km) and three 200kT MRV warheads. Then, between 1970 and 1978, all Lafayettes were converted to take the Poseidon C-3 missiles, which had a better range of about 3,230nm (5,200km) but, much more significantly, carried 10 50kT MIRVs, giving a very marked improvement in strategic capability. Finally, 12 were refitted yet again (1978-1982), this time to take the larger, three-stage Trident C-4 with a range of 4,400nm (7,100km) and carried eight 100kT MIRVs. The first of these to be completed, *Francis Scott Key* (SSBN-657), began the first Trident patrol on 20 October 1979. Another significant improvement was that, while the first five boats used compressed-air to eject the missiles from the tubes (as had been the case in the Washington- and Ethan

Above: **Benjamin Franklin,** *first of the modified Lafayettes.*

Allen-classes), the remainder had the now-standard rocket-motor, which produced a gas-steam mixture. Although these SSBNs did not have the same underwater performance as an SSN they had a respectable self-defence capability against surface ships or other submarines, and were armed with conventional or wire-guided torpedoes and SubRoc. Normally, however, they would attempt to evade detection or contact.

Daniel Webster (SSBN-626) of this class was fitted with diving planes on a raised and reinforced bow sonar dome, instead of on the fin. Although successful, this was not copied on other SSBNs.

SSBN-623, -635 and -636 were deactivated in the mid-1980s and the remainder in 1990-1994, the only exceptions being SSBN-642 and -645, which were reclassified as SSNs, and converted to SEAL transports.

Ohio-class

Total built: 18.
Completed: 1981-97.
Displacement: surfaced 16,764 tons; submerged 18,750 tons.
Dimensions: length 560ft 0in (170.7m); beam 42.0in (12.8m); draught 3ft 0in (11.3m).
Propulsion: 1 x General Electric S8G natural-circulation, pressurised-water nuclear reactor; turbo-reduction drive, ca. 35,000shp; one shaft.
Performance: submerged – 25kt; maximum operational diving depth 984ft (300m).
Weapons: 4 x 21in (533mm) TT (amidships); missiles – 24 x missile tubes.
Complement: 163 (two crews).

History: While the programme to upgrade the later Polaris SSBNs to carry Poseidon missiles was under way in the early 1970s, development of an entirely new missile was started. This was to have a much greater range, which required a larger missile, and this in turn required a larger submarine to take full advantage of its capabilities. At first, Congress baulked at the immense cost of the new missile, but its view was transformed into support when the Soviet Navy introduced first the SS-N-8 (4,200nm/6,760km) followed shortly afterwards by the SS-N-18 (4,846nm/7,800km). The U.S. Navy then speeded up its programme and the first Ohio-colas ship was laid down on 10 April 1976. However, a variety of factors caused delays and first-of-class USS *Ohio* (SSBN-726) did not start trials until 17 June 1981; it fired its first

Above: Fourth in the Ohio-class, USS Georgia (SSBN-729).

Below: Caps lift to expose the Ohios' awesome power.

Above: The dedication of USS West Virginia *(SSBN-736).*

successful missile on 17 January 1982 and sailed on its first operational deterrent patrol on 1 October 1982. This was considerably behind schedule and both submarine and missile were subjected to considerable criticism at the time, but since then this has proved to be one of the most successful naval weapons systems ever to enter service.

The Ohio-class boats are huge, being only marginally shorter than a Ticonderoga-class cruiser – 560ft (170.7m) compared to 567ft (172.9m) – but with a very much greater displacement – 16,747 compared to 9,466 tons. Their immense destructive power, however, lies in their 24 Trident II D-5 missiles, each capable of carrying eight 475kT W-88 MIRVed warheads.

Eighteen were built, joining the fleet between 1981 and 1997, of which eight were armed with the Trident I C-4 missile and 10 with the Trident II D-5 missile. In 2002, the plan was to retire the first four ships (SSBN-726 – SSBN-729) and to rearm the second four (SSBN-730 – SSBN-733) with Trident II D-5 missiles. This will leave the U.S. Navy's deterrent force comprising 14 ships, with each of the 24 missiles carrying five warheads, for a grand total of 1,680 warheads. Of these warheads, some 400 are W-88s with a 300-475kT yield, while the remainder are W-76s with a yield of some 100kT.

The Trident force is split equally between the east and west coasts of the United States, with nine based at Bangor, Washington, and nine at King's Bay, Georgia. Of these, five are on station, five proceeding to or returning from patrol (but still capable of launching their missiles) and the others are in port or undergoing overhaul. Each boat has two crews, known as Blue and Gold.

In early 2002 the future of some elements of the Ohio-class was uncertain. There have been periodic proposals to either reduce the active force to 12 boats, or to reduce the crewing of all 14 to one crew each. This would produce a totally new deployment cycle and reduce the numbers available on station at any one time; it would also drastically reduce both the manpower requirement and the annual operating costs.

Right: **Tennessee** *outward bound on deterrent patrol.*

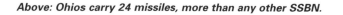

Above: Ohios carry 24 missiles, more than any other SSBN.

Special Role Submarines

Gun-armed Cruisers
In 1917 the German Navy started developing "U-cruisers" armed with large calibre guns to attack enemy merchant shipping in remote areas. The British also developed the M-class (one 12in/305mm) followed by X-1 (two twin 5.2in/132mm), but neither proved satisfactory. The U.S. Navy considered very large submarines mounting 8in (203mm) guns, but the only outcome was the Narwhal-class with two 6in (152mm) guns. Largest of them all was the French *Surcouf* with two 8in (203mm) guns but, like the others, she was a failure.

Minelayers
The first specialised submarine minelayer was the Russian *Krab* laid down in 1908, followed by the German UC I-class in 1915, and small numbers of minelayers were subsequently built for most navies. The Russians used a horizontal conveyor belt atop the hull which moved the mines to the stern where they simply fell off, while the U.S. Navy, used a system in which mines were ejected along a tube. One German system used tubes on the boat's centreline, but this required holes in the pressure hull, open at both ends. The fourth was the simplest, using vertical tubes in the submarine's side tanks. The specialised minelayer disappeared because small minefields could be laid more effectively by aircraft, and mines were developed which could be laid from torpedo tubes.

Aircraft-carrying Submarines
Aircraft-carrying submarines were conceived to extend the observation range of submarines, and both the British and Germans experimented with taking aircraft to sea aboard submarines during World War I. Nothing came of the idea until after the war, when several navies produced submarines carrying a small floatplane in a cylindrical hangar, with the submarine surfacing to launch and recover the aircraft. The U.S. Navy conducted experiments in the early 1920s with the submarine *S-1* (SS-105) and Martin MS-1 floatplane but did not pursue the idea. The British converted the monitor *M-2*, but after she was lost with all hands, they, too, abandoned the idea. In the mid-1930s the French built the *Surcouf*, which carried a small floatplane, but when war broke out the aircraft was removed. The Japanese built by far the most aircraft-carrying submarines which saw a great deal of action in World War II. A completely different approach was taken by the Germans in World War II who used a one-man, rotary-winged kite (Focke-Achgelis Bachstelze) which was assembled on deck and then towed aloft. The problem with all these schemes was that it took a relatively long time to assemble and launch the aircraft and to recover, dismantle and stow it after landing, during which the submarine was very vulnerable to attack..

Radar Pickets
Another special role for submarines was as radar

pickets, a mission originated by the U.S. Navy which needed both to detect incoming *kamikaze* attacks, and provide forward control for carrier aircraft operations. After heavy losses among surface warships, the role was passed to submarine radar pickets (SSR), operating radars while awash; they could submerge if threatened with air attack. Two boats (out of an intended 24) were converted during the war and a few more conversions followed in the late 1940s. In the 1950s three purpose-built radar pickets were commissioned, two conventionally powered (SSR) and one nuclear-powered (SSRN). The only other navy to develop submarine radar pickets was the Soviet Navy, but this was to meet a totally different operational requirement.

Transport, Cargo and Oiler Submarines

Finally, throughout the 20th century submarines have had to transport people or materiel, most often by misemploying operational boats. Some specialist transports have been produced, eg, German World War I Deutschland-class and Italian World War II Romolo-class, while the Germans also produced the Type VIIF, a torpedo transport. The German Type XIV resupply submarines posed a particular threat, but the Allied breaking of Enigma codes enabled these boats to be sunk comparatively quickly. Another concept tried at various times by the German, Japanese and U.S. navies was the use of submarines as floating refuelling stations for seaplanes, but without great success.

Below: USS **Redfin** *converted to radar picket (SSR).*

Surcouf-class

FRANCE

Total built: 1.
Commissioned: 1935.
Displacement: surfaced 3,252 tons; submerged 4,304 tons.
Dimensions: length 360ft 1in (110.0m); beam 29ft 6in (9.0m); draught 23ft 9in (7.25m).
Propulsion: 2 x Sulzer diesel engines, 7,600bhp; 2 x electric motors, 3,400shp; two shafts.
Performance: surface – 18.5kt, 10,000nm/10kt; submerged – 10kt, 75nm/4.5kt; maximum depth 262ft (80m).
Weapons: 8 x 21.7in (550mm) TT (14 torpedoes); 4 x 15.7in (400mm) TT (8 torpedoes); 2 x 8in/50 (203mm) guns (600 rounds); 2 x 37mm guns (1,000 rounds); 4 (2 x 2) 13.2mm AAMG.
Aircraft: 1 x Besson MB 411 floatplane.
Complement: 118.

History: *Surcouf* was designed for world-wide commerce-raiding, mounting two 8in (203mm) guns in a twin turret forward and carrying a purpose-built Besson floatplane, whose role was to obtain targets and to provide corrections for gun engagements. She was the largest submarine of her time and was superficially impressive, but suffered from a number of disadvantages. First, it took some 2-3 minutes to get the guns into action following surfacing and, second, the low height of the stereoscopic rangefinder limited effective fire to 12,300yd (11,265m). Next, the aircraft was small and under-powered, and took all of 10 minutes to disassemble prior to submerging. The basic problem, however, was that it was never clear which nations' merchant shipping *Surcouf*

Above: **Surcouf's main armament was two 8in (203mm) guns.**

might be required to attack. If war was declared against the most likely enemy, Germany, that country's merchant fleet would be swept from the sea in a matter of weeks by surface warships, while no other potential enemy had a merchant fleet worth attacking.

Torpedo armament consisted of eight 21.7in (550mm) tubes, four in the bow and four external aft, and four 15.7in (400mm) in a rotating mount on the after deck, the latter being intended for use against merchant ships. In World War II *Surcouf* served as a convoy escort but on the French collapse went to Plymouth, England, where, after several weeks delay, she was forcibly taken over by the British. She served for some months in the Caribbean but was then ordered to the Pacific and was en route to her new operating area when she disappeared with all hands, the result of a collision with a U.S. freighter.

Below: **A spotter plane was built for Surcouf, but never used.**

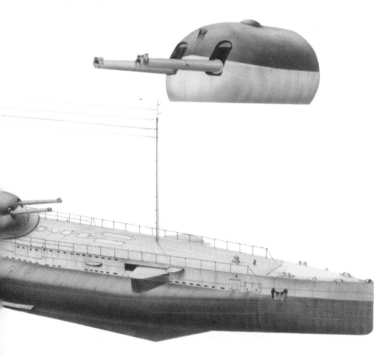

U-151-class

Total built: 7.
Commissioned: 1917.
Displacement: surfaced 1,512 tons; submerged 1,875 tons.
Dimensions: length 213ft 3in (65.0m); beam 29ft 2in (8.9m); draught 17ft 4in (5.3m).
Propulsion: 2 x Germania 6-cylinder, 4-stroke diesel engines, 800bhp; 2 x electric motors, 800shp; two shafts.
Performance: surface – 12.4kt, 25,000nm/5.5kt; submerged – 5.2kt, 65nm/3kt; maximum depth 164ft (50m).
Weapons: *U-155* – 6 x 19.7in (500mm) TT, remainder – 2 x 19.7in (500mm) TT (18 torpedoes); 2 x 5.9in/45 (150mm) guns (2 x 1); 2 x 3.45in/45 (88mm) guns.
Complement: 56 (plus 20 prize crew).

History: The Deutschland-class boats were originally designed as submarine freighters, for which they were built to mercantile standards, managed by a commercial company and manned by civilian crews. They mounted no armament and could carry some 740 tons of cargo. First-of-class *Deutschland* made two successful return voyages to the United States in 1916, but the second to be completed, *Bremen*, disappeared without trace on her first voyage. When the USA entered the war on the Allied side it was decided to convert the remaining boats into long-range, gun-armed U-cruisers. *Deutschland* was converted (becoming *U-151*) and the remainder were completed to the new design as *U-152 – U-157*, all seven becoming operational in late 1917.

M-class

Total built: 3.
Commissioned: 1917.
Displacement: surfaced 1,600 tons; submerged 1,950 tons.
Dimensions: length (M-1/2) 295ft 9in (90.1m), (M-3/4) 303ft 0in (92.4m); beam 24ft 8in (7.5m); draught 15ft 1in (4.8m).
Propulsion: 2 x Vickers 12-cylinder diesel engines, 2,400bhp; 2 x electric motors, 1,600shp; 336 lead-acid cells; two shafts.
Performance: surface – 14kt, 3,800nm/10kt; submerged – 8kt, 80nm/2kt; maximum depth 200ft (61m).
Weapons: M-1/2 – 4 x 18in (457mm) TT (bow) (10 torpedoes), M-3/4 – 4 x 21in (533mm) TT (8 torpedoes); 1 x 12in/40 (305mm) gun (40 rounds); 1 x 3in (76mm) gun (72 rounds); 1 x 0.303in Lewis MG.
Complement: 68.

History: The original idea for the M-class was for a submarine armed with a single 12in (305mm) gun with 50 rounds, which could be used against either sea or land targets. The hull was a new design, but the diesel and electric motors were taken from the L-class. Four boats were laid down in 1916 and on trials with the first-of-class the gun proved to be successful, being capable of elevation between +12 and -5 degrees, and training over 15 degrees. The diving time was a surprisingly short 90 seconds.

Four were laid down in 1916, of which *M-1* was completed in 1917 and saw brief war service in late 1918 in the Mediterranean; it served on until 1925. *M-2* was to the same design as *M-1*, but *M-3* and *M-4* were lengthened by some 10ft (3m) to accommodate the new 21in (533mm)

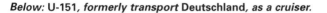

All mounted two 5.9in (150mm) and two 88mm guns, but while *U-151* had six torpedo tubes (three per side) mounted under the upper deck and angled out at 15 degrees, the remainder had two conventional bow-mounted, ahead-firing tubes. There were two war losses, *U-154* being torpedoed by British submarine *E-35*, while *U-156* was mined; the remaining five were ceded to the Allies (UK – 3, France – 2) and were sunk or broken up in the early 1920s.

**Below: U-151*, formerly transport* **Deutschland*, as a cruiser.*

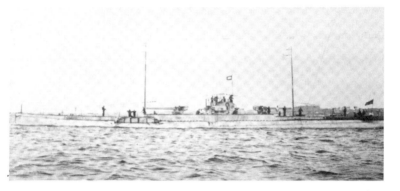

Above: British M-1 armed with a single 12in (305mm) gun.

torpedo tubes. *M-2* and *M-3* were both too late to see war service and were converted in 1927-28, *M-2* to a seaplane carrier (qv), and *M-3* to a minelayer. *M-1* was rammed and sunk by a freighter in 1925 with the loss of all hands. *M-4* was cancelled while building and scrapped. Somewhat surprisingly, despite this clear rejection of the concept by the British, the French built the *Surcouf* (qv) which was virtually identical in concept, and was, similarly, a failure.

X~1~class

Total built: 1.
Commissioned: 1925.
Displacement: surfaced 3,050 tons; submerged 3,600 tons.
Dimensions: length 360ft 6in (110.8m); beam 29ft 10in (9.1m); draught 15ft 9in (4.8m).
Propulsion: 2 x Admiralty diesel engines, 6,000bhp; 2 x M.A.N. auxiliary diesels, 2,600bhp; 2 x G.E.C. electric motors, 2,400shp; two shafts.
Performance: surface – 20kt, 18,700nm/8kt; submerged – 9kt, 50nm/4kt; maximum operating depth 350ft (107m).
Weapons: 6 x 21in (533mm) TT (bow) (12 torpedoes); 4 x 5.2in/42 (132mm) guns (2 x 2).
Complement: 109.

History: The German World War I concept of the lone submarine roaming the world's sealanes had its attractions for the British who ordered *X-1* in 1921, armed with four 5.2in (132mm) guns in two twin turrets, which were supposed

to enable her to survive against destroyers and to attack enemy merchant shipping. She proved to have excellent handling characteristics both on the surface and when submerged, and provided a stable gun platform, while her range-finder could be raised by 9ft (2.7m) to provide good gun control over adequate ranges. However, she suffered from severe mechanical problems: the main diesels and the electric motors proved to be unreliable, while the M.A.N. battery charging diesels never produced their design output power. In addition, the eternal fuel tanks leaked badly, leaving a tell-tale oil slick on the surface.

Once in service it became clear that her intended role against destroyers would prove hazardous in the extreme, while it was unclear which nation's merchant ships she could be used against. As a result, she completed one four-year commission in the Mediterranean, but was then placed in reserve, stricken in 1935 and scrapped in 1936.

Below: British X-1, with 4 x 5.2in (132mm) guns.

Pierre Chailley/
Saphir-classes

Total built: Pierre Chailley – 1; Saphir – 6.
Completed: Pierre Chailley – 1922 ; Saphir – 1928-35.
Displacement: surfaced 761 tons; submerged 925 tons.
Dimensions: length 216ft 2in (65.9m), beam 23ft 7in (7.2m); draught 14ft 1in (4.3m).
Propulsion: 2 x Normand-Vickers diesels, 1,300bhp; 2 x electric motors, 1,000shp; two shafts.
Performance: surface – 12kt, 4,000nm/12kt; submerged – 9kt, 80nm/4kt; maximum depth 250ft (76m).
Weapons: 2 x 21.7in (550mm) TT (bow); 1 x 21.7in (550mm) TT ; 2 x 15.7in (400mm) TT (rotating mount aft); 1 x 3in (76mm) gun; mines– 32.
Complement: 42.
Specifications for Saphir-class, as built.

History: *Pierre Chailley*, ordered in 1917 and completed in 1921, was the first French purpose-built minelayer. It used the Normand-Fenaux system of externally mounted, vertical mine-tubes, which proved both safe and efficient in practice. There were 20 tubes, each containing two 441lb (200kg) mines. The Saphir-class was a modified version, with 16 mine-tubes, each containing two mines. *Pierre Chailley* was stricken in 1936, but the six Saphir-class boats served on routine peacetime tasks until the outbreak of World War II, when

UC-1-class (Project 35a)   GERMANY

Total built: 15.
Completed: 1915.
Displacement: surfaced 168 tons; submerged 183 tons.
Dimensions: length 111ft 6in (34.0m); beam 10ft 4in (3.2m); draught 10ft 0in (3.0m).
Propulsion: 1 x Daimler 6-cylinder 4-stroke diesel, 90bhp; 1 x electric motor, 175shp; one shaft.
Performance: surface – 6.25kt, 780nm/5kt; submerged – 5.2kt, 50nm/4kt; maximum operating depth 164ft (50m).
Weapons: Mine tubes – 6 x 39.4in (100cm) sloped tubes (forward); 12 x UC/120 mines.
Complement: 14.

History: The German land attack on France in the early months of World War I was most successful on its right wing. In early September it was proposed that small minelaying U-boats should be built to take advantage of the newly captured naval bases on the Belgian coast. The first proposal was for an 80 ton boat driven by battery power alone, but was this was shelved and by October the requirement was for a 150 ton boat based on the newly completed Type UB design. This would have a totally new forward section housing six tubes, each containing two mines. It was decided that the mines would be laid while the boat was moving slowly forwards, so the tubes were angled aft at 26 degrees from the vertical, even though this caused some construction problems.

   Despite the novelty of the concept, the project proceeded with remarkable speed: the requirement was stated on 14 October 1914; orders for 15 were

Above: **Rubis** *was the most successful minelayer in any navy.*

two took up minelaying duties in the North Sea and four in the Mediterranean.

Following the French armistice in June 1940, two served with the Free French Navy, of which *Perle* was sunk in error by the RAF in July 1944, while *Rubis* became the most successful minelaying submarine in any navy, her mines accounting for 10 minor warships and 14 merchant ships. The other four served in the Vichy Navy; one was scuttled in November 1942 and the other three were captured in Bizerta in 1942. Two of these were then used as battery-charging hulks by the Italian Navy, but all three were scuttled in 1943. *Rubis* survived the war, to be stricken in 1949. These were the only purpose-built minelayers built for the French Navy.

Above: **German UC-1-class minelayer had sloping tubes.**

placed on 23 November; the first to be completed left the yard on 26 April 1915; and the last was completed in July. They were built by Vulkan (10) and Weser (5) and were broken down into sections and despatched by train, *UC-1 – UC- 11* to Flanders and *UC-12 – UC-15* to Pola on the Adriatic. Apart from the mines, the Type UC-1 boats were unarmed except for one of the Flanders boats, *UC-11*, which was fitted with a single external 17.7in (45cm) tube aft in 1916. *UC-2* sank off Yarmouth, England, on 2 July 1915 and was detected and raised by the British, their first indication that submarines were being used to lay mines.

UC-III-class (Project 41a) GERMANY

Total built: 29 (see notes).
Completed: 1918.
Displacement: surfaced 491 tons; submerged 571 tons.
Dimensions: length 214ft 10in (56.5m); beam 18ft 0in (5.5m); draught 12ft 6in (3.8m).
Propulsion: 2 x M.A.N. 6-cylinder 4-stroke diesels, 2 x 300hp; 2 x electric motors, 2 x 385hp; 2 x 62-cell batteries; two shafts.
Performance: surface – 11.5kt, 9,850nm/7kt; submerged – 6.6kt, 40nm/4.5kt; maximum depth 246ft (75m).
Weapons: 3 x 19.7in (500mm) TT (see notes) (7 torpedoes); 1 x 4.1in/45 (105mm) gun; mine tubes – 6 x 39.4in (100cm) (forward); 18 UC/200 mines.
Complement: 32.
Specifications for UC-90 group, as built.

History: Even the UC-II boats did not prove totally satisfactory and, in any case, the German Navy needed more boats to replace the high loss rate among minelayers already in service. A requirement was therefore stated for new boats with a more powerful armament, greater surface speed and increased submerged endurance. There was also feedback from the UC-II crews, who criticised the diving time, adverse conditions for watchkeepers on the bridge during winter, and discomfort for the men below when the boats were travelling on the surface. The result was a revised UC-II design, with a new hull shape, a 4.1in (105mm) gun on a raised mounting, and with the two forward torpedo tubes brought back to abreast the conning tower, where they were angled

U-117-class (Project 45) GERMANY

Total built: 10.
Completed: 1917-18.
Displacement: surfaced 1,164 tons; submerged 1,512 tons.
Dimensions: length 267ft 4in (81.5m); beam 24ft 3in (7.4m); draught 24ft 3in (4.2m).
Propulsion: 2 x M.A.N. 6-cylinder diesels, 23 x 1,200bp; 2 x electric motors, 2 x 600hp; two shafts.
Performance: surface – 14.7kt, 9,400nm/8kt; submerged – 7kt, 35nm/4.5kt; maximum operating depth 246ft (75m).
Weapons: 4 x 19.7in (500mm) TT (bow) (12 torpedoes); 1 x 5.9in/45 (150mm) gun; mine tubes – 2 x 39.4in (100cm) horizontal tubes (stern); 42 mines (plus 30 mines in deck stowage).
Complement: 40.
Specifications for U-117 group, as completed.

History: A requirement for an improved and more reliable minelayer arose in 1916, leading to Project 45, which began as essentially a marriage of the main features of Project 43 (U-155-class) to the large mine storage space and twin, aft-mounted mine tubes of Project 38 (U-71-class). As with Project 38 there were two tubes, each of which carried three mines, plus 36 mines in the store room. One of the curious features of this design, however, was that there were also storage bins in special troughs on the upper deck abaft the conning tower, which could accommodate either 10 spare torpedoes or 30 additional mines. The latter were launched manually over the stern of the surfaced submarine.

Above: UC-103*, a UC-III-class minelayer, after the war.*

outwards at some 10 degrees. The boats' flooding and ballast arrangements were improved, but the mine tubes and other internal arrangements remained unchanged.

A total of 39 boats were ordered (*UC-80 – UC-118*), but, in the event only *UC-90 – UC-118*, all built by Blohm + Voss, were completed before the war's end, those at Weser (3) and Danzig (9) being broken-up on the slips in 1919. None of the completed boats was lost in combat, although one was lost in an accident, and the remainder were allocated to the Allies, including two to the Japanese Navy, which used them as the basis for their KRS-class minelayers.

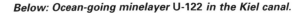

The first five of these boats (*U-117 – U-121*) were built by Vulkan, Hamburg and the second five (*U-122 – U-126*) by Blohm + Voss, the latter being 20in (0.5m) longer and having a slightly shorter range. All served in World War I and were then allocated to the Allies: France – 3; Japan – 1; UK – 4; U.S. – 1.

At one point in the war the demand for U-cruisers became greater than that for minelayers and certain of these Project 45 boats were converted for such a role, with the mine storage space being used to accommodate the prize crews and additional fuel.

Below: Ocean-going minelayer U-122 *in the Kiel canal.*

Type XB-classes

Total built: 8.
Completed: 1941-43.
Displacement: surfaced 1,755 tons; submerged 2,143 tons.
Dimensions: length 294ft 7in (89.8m); beam 30ft 3in (9.2m); draught 15ft 5in (4.7m).
Propulsion: 2 x Germania 9-cylinder, 4-stroke diesels, 2 x 2,100bhp; 2 x electric motors, 2 x 550shp; two shafts.
Performance: surface – 16.4kt, 14,450nm/12kt; submerged – 7.0kt, 188nm/2kt; maximum operating depth 394f t (120m).
Weapons: 2 x 21in (533mm) TT (stern) (15 torpedoes); 1 x 4.1in/45 (105mm) gun; 1 x 20mm C30 cannon; mine tubes – 30 x 4ft 4in (1.33m) diameter tubes (6 x 3-mine tubes forward; 12 x 2-mine tubes in each side tank); 66 x SMA mines.
Complement: 52.

History: The largest submarine built in Germany, the Type X was designed specifically to carry the SMA anchored mine. The original design (Type XA) was an update of the World War I Project 45 (qv) and was based on the need to set the SMA mechanism by hand immediately prior to launch, which necessitated the mines being held in a large storage chamber aft. When this need for manual setting was overcome the entire design was recast, resulting in the Type XB. There were six vertical tubes forward, each containing three mines, which protruded about 12in (305mm) from the foredeck and were open above and below. There were a further 24 tubes, 12 in each side tank, holding two mines

---

Porpoise/
Grampus-classes

Total built: Porpoise – 1; Grampus – 5.
Completed: Porpoise – 1933; Grampus-class – 1936-39.
Displacement: surfaced 1,520 tons; submerged 2,157 tons.
Dimensions: length 293ft 0in (89.3m); beam 25ft 6in (7.8m); draught 17ft 3in (5.3m).
Propulsion: 2 x Admiralty diesel engines; 2 x 3,300bhp; 2 x electric motors, 2 x 1,630shp; battery 3 x 112 4,560AH cells; two shafts.
Performance: surface – 15.8kt, 5,880nm/9.3kt; submerged – 8.8kt, 64nm/4kt; maximum operating depth 300ft (91m).
Weapons: 6 x 21in (533mm) TT (bow) (12 torpedoes); 1 x 4in/40 (102mm) gun; mine system – one horizontal conveyor-belt; 50 x Mk XVI mines.
Complement: 59.
Specifications for Grampus-class, as built.

History: *Porpoise* had a hull based on that of the Parthian-class (qv) combined with an improved version of the conveyor system tested aboard *M-3* (qv).There was only one conveyor carrying 50 mines and this ran down the centreline of the boat, requiring the tower and periscopes to be offset to starboard with balancing weights carried on the port side. The design was improved yet further and the next five boats were longer, had a revised internal design and a straight-through casing, whereas *Porpoise* had a small step near the bow. *Porpoise* and the five Grampus-class boats had a very busy war, laying a total of 2,599 mines,

Right: A Type XB minelayer sailing into Portsmouth, NH, in May 1945.

each. The two torpedo tubes were situated aft and the boats originally mounted a 105mm gun, although this was later removed.

The large size of the Type XBs made them suitable for other uses and they were often employed as supply boats; indeed, all six war losses were due to enemy action while serving in this role. The other two boats were converted for use as transport boats on the Far East run, one of them, *U-219*, actually reaching Malaya in 1944 and still there at the time of the German surrender, when it was taken over by the Japanese as *I-505*. The last boat, *U-234*, left for the Far East in April 1945 and was in mid-Atlantic when Germany capitulated. The captain surrendered to the United States and on arrival at Portsmouth, NH, his boat was found to be carrying a large quantity of uranium, whose origin, intended use in Japan, and actual use in the USA all remain mysteries to this day.

Above: British minelayer, Rorqual, *is launched, 21 July 1936.*

but losses were heavy. Two were sunk by Italian surface units: *Cachalot* (30 July 1941) and *Grampus* (16 June 1940). Two more fell victim to aircraft: the Luftwaffe sank *Narwhal* (23 July 1940) and Japanese naval aircraft sank *Porpoise* (19 January 1945). The fifth loss was *Seal*, which was sunk by a mi~~ (4 May 1940) but brought back to the surface, where it was unable to proce~~ and was captured by the Germans, who later employed it for a time as training boat. That left *Rorqual*, which was scrapped in December 1945.

Above: **Rorqual's** *conveyor-belt dropped mines over the stern.*

X-2-class

ITALY

Total built: 2.
Completed: 1917-18.
Displacement: surfaced 403 tons; submerged 468 tons.
Dimensions: length 139ft 9in (42.6m); beam 18ft 1in (5.5m); draught 10ft 2in (3.1m).
Propulsion: 2 x Sulzer diesel engines, 2 x 650bhp; 2 x electric motors, 2 x 325shp; two shafts.
Performance: surface – 8.2kt; submerged – 6.3kt.
Weapons: 1 x 3in/30 (76mm) AA gun; mine system – 9 x sloping tubes; 18 x Italian AE1916/125t mines.
Complement: 25.

History: The German UC I-class minelayer, *UC-12*, was transported to the Adriatic where it operated under the Austro-Hungarian flag as *U-24*, but with its original German crew. While operating off Taranto on 16 March 1916, it hit one of its own mines and sank, but was subsequently raised by the Italians and completely rebuilt, joining the Italian Navy on 9 December 1916 as *X-1*. This led the Italian Navy to develop its own submarine-launched mines and to design a new class of boat to deliver them. The new boats, the

X-2-class, were somewhat larger than the German UC-1-class, enabling them to accommodate nine tubes (18 mines) as opposed to six tubes (12 mines) in the German boat. Main armament was a 3in (76mm) AA gun mounted abaft the tower. As built, no torpedo tubes were fitted, but in 1918 two 17.7in (450mm) torpedoes were carried on the upper casing.

Below: Italian X-3 carried 18 mines in nine vertical tubes.

Bragadin-class

Total built: 2.
Completed: 1930-31.
Displacement: surfaced 965 tons; submerged 1,008 tons.
Dimensions: length 235ft 7in (71.5m); beam 20ft 2in (6.2m); draught 16ft 4in (5.0m).
Propulsion: 2 x Tosi diesel engines, 2 x 750bhp; 2 x Marelli electric motors, 2 x 500shp; two shafts.
Performance: surface – 11.5kt, 4,800nm/6.5kt; submerged – 7.0kt, 86nm/2.2kt; maximum operating depth 288ft (90m).
Weapons: 4 x 21in (533mm) TT (6 torpedoes); 1 x 4in/35 (102mm) AA gun; 2 x 13.2mm MG; mine system – 2 x horizontal tubes; 16-24 mines.
Complement: 55.

History: These were Italy's first post-World War I minelayers and were designed by Bernardis, who had been responsible for the rebuilding of the ex- German X-1 and the design and construction of the X-2-class. Those earlier boats had used vertical tubes, but the new boats used a horizontal system, with two tubes, ejecting the mines at the stern. They were designed for short-range operations in the Mediterranean, and were developed from the Pisani-class, with a single hull and saddle-tanks. The design was not satisfactory and after several years' service they underwent major modification, with the stern being shortened by some 12ft

---

KiRai-Sen (KRS)-class

Total built: 4.
Completed: 1927-28.
Displacement: surfaced 1,142 tons; submerged 1,768 tons.
Dimensions: length 279ft 6in (85.2m), beam 24ft 8in (7.5m); draught 14ft 6in (4.4m).
Propulsion: 2 x M.A.N. 6-cylinder, 4-stroke diesel engines, 2 x 1,200bhp; 2 x electric motors, 2 x 550shp; two shafts.
Performance: surface – 14.5kt, 10,500nm/8kt; submerged – 7kt, 40nm/4.5kt; maximum operating depth 250ft (76m).
Weapons: 4 x 21in (533mm) TT (bow) (12 torpedoes); 1 x 5.5in/40 (140mm) gun; mine system – 2 x horizontal tubes; 42 x Type 88 mines.
Complement: 51-70.

History: One of the ex-German U-boats allocated to Japan in 1919 was U-125, a U-117-class minelayer (qv), which was renumbered O-6 and served until 1922. Experience with this boat prompted the IJN to build a class of its own, designated KRS, which were slightly larger, but otherwise identical to the original German design. They had two relatively short mine tubes aft, each of which carried three mines, with the balance of 36 mines in a large store room. The Japanese boats were not particularly successful and in 1940 they were given the additional task of refuelling reconnaissance seaplanes, for which they were fitted with deck-mounted aviation fuel tanks. This task required them to rendezvous with seaplanes in remote islands and replenish them so that they could carry out very long-range reconnaissance flights, but the submarines retained their full minelaying capability.

(4m) and a watertight compartment installed in a raised bow to improve surface sea-keeping. They were not used as minelayers during the war, being employed instead to transport supplies to North Africa and the Aegean.

Below: Modified Bragadin-class, with raised bow, short stern.

All four boats took part in the offensive operations in December 1941, *I-21* and *I-22* being part of the Malayan invasion, while *I-23* and *I-24* were with the Philippines attack. All laid mines at strategic points and then became part of the surveillance force. In January 1942 all four boats laid mines off the northern shores of Australia, in the course of which *I-24* was attacked and sunk. Up to this point the boats were numbered *I-21* to *I-24*, but in May 1942, in common with other Japanese submarines, they were renumbered, becoming *I-121* to *I-124*, respectively. *I-123* was sunk off Guadalcanal on 29 August 1942. From 1943 the two survivors were relegated to training, in which role *I-122* was torpedoed by a U.S. submarine on 10 June 1945. The only surviving boat, *I-121*, was broken up in 1946.

Below: Japanese KRS-class, the only minelayers built by the IJN, although they were employed during World War II as transports.

O-19-class

Total built: 2.
Completed: 1939.
Displacement: surfaced 998 tons; submerged 1,536 tons.
Dimensions: length 265ft 9in (81.0m); beam 24ft 7in (7.5m); draught 163t 1in (4.0m).
Propulsion: 2 x Sulzer diesel engines, 2 x 2,600bhp; 2 x electric motors, 2 x 500shp; two shafts.
Performance: surface – 19.3kt; submerged – 9kt; maximum operating depth 320ft (100m).
Weapons: 8 x 21in (533mm) TT (bow – 4, stern – 2, amidships in rotating mount – 2) (14 torpedoes); 1 x 3.4in/45 (88mm) gun; 2 x 40mm Bofors AA; mine system – 20 x vertical tubes; 40 x mines.
Complement: 55.

History: These were the RNethN's first and only minelaying submarines, the overall design being based on that of the Orzel-class, then building for the Polish Navy, but with the addition of mine tubes. The 20 tubes were mounted within the saddle tanks, 10 on each side, with two mines in each tube. These boats were principally intended for use in the Far East and particularly powerful diesel engines were installed to give a very high surface speed and a long range. The boats were also among the first to be fitted with air-breathing tubes – the prototypes of today's snorkels – which were intended to enable them to travel just submerged to avoid the heat of the tropical sun, but while continuing to use the diesel engines. Both boats spent the greater part of their service lives in the

Krab-class

Total built: 1.
Completed: 1915.
Displacement: surfaced 512 tons; submerged 740 tons.
Dimensions: length 173ft 3in (52.8m); beam 14ft 0in (4.3m); draught 12ft 9in (3.9m).
Propulsion: 4 x gasoline engines, 4 x 300bhp; 2 x electric motors, 2 x 200shp; two shafts.
Performance: surface – 11.8kt, 1,700nm/7kt; submerged – 7.1kt, 82nm/4kt.
Weapons: 2 x 18in (457mm) TT (bow); 2 x Drzewiecki drop-collars (4 torpedoes); 1 x 3in (75mm) gun; 2 x MG; mine system – 2 x horizontal tubes; 60 x mines.
Complement: 50.

History: *Krab*, the world's first submarine minelayer, was designed by a railway engineer named Nalyetev, who not only conceived a very effective laying system, but also designed the submarine that carried it, which had notably clean lines for its time. Work, however, proceeded at a very slow pace; the proposal was accepted in 1906, but construction did not begin at the Admiralty Yard, Nikolayev, until 1908. She was launched in 1912 but was not completed until January 1915, by which time the German UC-I-class (qv) was already in service. The Nalyetev system consisted of two electrically driven conveyor belts mounted under the upper casing, which propelled the mines aft until they fell over the stern, a system which eventually proved more versatile than the vertical tubes, and was adopted by more navies.

alen/Delfinen/
eptun-classes

SWED

ss	Valen	Delfinen	Neptun
l built	1	3	3
leted	1925	1934-35	1942-43
cement: d ged	548 tons 730 tons	540 tons 720 tons	550 tons 730 tons
ons	187ft 4in (57.1m) 23ft 4in (7.1m) 10ft 2in (3.1m)	207ft 0in (63.1m) 21ft 0in (6.4m) 11ft 2in (3.4m)	205ft 5in (62.6r 21ft 0in (6.4m) 11ft 2in (3.4m)
rs	2 x 670bhp (Atlas) 2 x 350shp 2	2 x 600bhp (M.A.N.) 2 x 400shp 2	2 x 900bhp (M.A 2 x 500shp 2
	14.8kt 7.4kt	15kt 9kt	15kt 10kt
	4 x 17.7in (450mm) 1 x 75mm/42 1 x 25mm AA 20	4 x 21in (533mm) 1 x 57mm 1 x 25mm AA 20	5 x 21in (533mm 1 x 40mm Bofors 1 x 20mm AA 20
	31	34	35

n's first minelayer, designed by I.v.S.

Above: Dutch O-19 carried 40 mines in 20 vertical tubes.

Far East. *O -20* had to be scuttled after a depth-charge attack by a Japanese destroyer on 20 December 1941, but *O-19* served until 8 July 1945 when it was wrecked in a storm in the South China Sea.

Krab proved somewhat unreliable in service but carried out several mining operations in the Black Sea in 1915-16, which sank several hostile vessels. In the Revolution, she was captured first by the Ukrainians and then by the Germans, who surrendered her to the British. The latter scuttled her in April 1918 but she was raised and scrapped by the Soviets in 1935.

Below: Russian minelayer Krab carried 60 mines.

Series II, XI, XIII, XIIIbis

RUSSIA

Type	Series II	XI	XIII	XIIIbis
Completed	1931	1935-36	1937-38	194041
Total built	6	6	7	6
Displacement surfaced submerged	1,040 tons 1,335 tons	1,100 tons 1,400 tons	1,123 tons 1,414 tons	1,123 tons 1,414 tons
Dimensions length beam draught	265ft 8in ((81.0m) 22ft 7in (6.9m) 13ft 8in (4.2m)		273ft 3in (83.3m) 23ft 0in (7.0m) 13ft 5in (4.1m)	
Propulsion diesels electric motors shafts	2 x 1,100bhp 2 x 525shp 2	2 x 1,100bhp 2 x 725shp 2	2 x 2,100bhp 2 x 1200hp 2	
Performance surface submerged depth	14kt 9kt 246ft (75m)	14kt 9kt 246ft (75m)	18kt 10kt 246ft (75m)	18kt 10kt 246ft (75m)
Range: surface submerged	6,000nm/9kt 135nm/2kt		14,000nm/9kt 130nm/2kt	
Weapons: torpedo tubes torpedoes guns Mines	6 12 1 x 100mm 1 x 45mm 20	6 12 1 x 100mm 1 x 45mm 20	8 12 1 x 100mm 1 x 45mm 2 x 0.3 MG 20	8 12 1 x 100mm 1 x 45mm 2 x 0.3 MG 20
Complement	54	55	55	55

Above: Leninetz-class, one of many Soviet-buil

and another six were built in Nikolayev and alloc
remaining boats were prefabricated in Leningrad
(1), and the parts were then sent by rail to the [
they were assembled and delivered to the Pa
major logistics undertaking. Nine were lost
scrapped in the 1950s.

Below: Series II; a conveyor belt laid

Below: Valen, Swede

472

History: The Leninetz-class consisted of three groups – Series II, Series XI and Series XIII – together with a modified version of the last, Series XIIIbis. There had been no submarine construction in the USSR following the Revolution until the Series I Dekabrist-class of 1926 (qv), which proved unsatisfactory. The Soviet Navy then raised the British submarine *L-55* which had been sunk off Kronstadt in 1919 and, having returned the bodies of the crew to Britain with complete correctness, they returned the boat to service and closely examined its construction and operation. The lessons learnt were then used in the construction of the next class, the Series II minelayers. These boats used a virtually unaltered version of the Nalyetev conveyor system, as used in *Krab* (qv), with two horizontal conveyors under the upper casing, dropping mines though holes in the stern.

The boats had hull numbers *L-1 – L- 25* and all were fabricated in yards in the western USSR. Six boats were built in Leningrad and allocated to the Baltic Fleet

Above: Delfinen-class carried 20 mines in 10 tubes.

Above: The Neptun-class were Sweden's last minelayers.

History: The first purpose-built minelayer for the RSwedN was the *Valen*, which was laid down in 1923 and completed in 1925. The Swedes are known to have had some dealings with the Netherlands-based German design office, I.V.S., in the early 1920s and it is probable that German know-how was involved in the design. It was a straightforward design, using the French Normand-Fenaux system of vertical tubes mounted in the side tanks, five each side, with two mines per tube, and four 17.7in (450mm) torpedo tubes, all in the bow.

This was followed by the three-strong Delfinen-class, a conventional design prepared by I.V.S., but built in Sweden by Kockums to Swedish standards. Like *Valen*, they had 10 mine tubes, but this time they were armed with four 21in (533mm) torpedo tubes (3 bow, 1 stern). Ordered in 1930, they were launched in 1934-35 and completed in 1936-37. The last of the minelayers was the Neptun-class, three of which were laid down in 1942 and completed in 1943. The mission of these boats was to lay mines in the Baltic if Sweden's neutrality was threatened, an event which never arose. *Valen* was stricken in 1944, followed by the three Delfinen-class boats in 1956-58, and the last of the line, the three Neptun-class boats, in 1966.

Argonaut-class (V-4)

UNITED STATES

Total built: 1.
Completed: 1928.
Displacement: surfaced 2,710 tons; submerged 4,164 tons.
Dimensions: length 381ft 0in (116.1m); beam 33ft 10in (10.3m); draught 15ft 4in (4.7m).
Propulsion: 2 x M.A.N. 6-cylinder, 4-stroke diesel engines; 2 x 1,400bhp; 2 x Ridgeway electric motors, 2 x 1,100shp; 2 x 120-cell Elide ULS37; two shafts.
Performance: surface – 15kt, 18,000nm/8kt; submerged – 8kt, 10nm/8kt; maximum operational depth 300ft (91m).
Weapons: 4 x 21in (533mm) TT (bow) (12 torpedoes); 2 x 6in/53 (152mm) Mk XII Mod 2 guns; 2 x 0.3in MG (see notes); mine system – 2 x horizontal 40in (102mm) tubes; 60 x Mk XI mines.
Complement: 88.

History: The U.S. Navy followed an international fashion in the 1920s when it constructed a large minelayer, USS *Argonaut* (SS-166). She was designed for operations in the Pacific, which required long range and 90-day endurance, and the overall design was based on that of the Barracuda-class, but incorporating lessons learned from examination of surrendered German U-boats. The minelaying apparatus was of American design, in which mines were moved in a hydraulic system involving rotating cages and loaded, four at a time, into two 40in (106mm) diameter tubes, from which they were ejected just under the stern. There was also a complicated water compensation system to maintain the boat's trim during the laying process. The submarine was theoretically

M-2-class

GREAT BRITAIN

Type: aircraft-carrying submarine.
Total converted: 1.
Converted: 1928.
Displacement: surfaced 1,788 tons; submerged 1,950 tons.
Dimensions: length 295ft 9in (90.1m); beam 24ft 6in (7.5m); draught 15ft 9in (4.8m).
Propulsion: 2 x Vickers 12-cylinder diesel engines, 2 x 1,200bhp; 2 x electric motors, 2 x 1,300shp; 336 lead-acid cells; two shafts.
Performance: surface – 14kt, 3,700nm/10kt; submerged – 6.5kt, range 24nm/4kt; maximum depth 200ft (61m).
Weapons: 4 x 18in (457mm) TT (bow) (10 torpedoes); 1 x 3in (76mm) gun (72 rounds), 2 x 0.303in Lewis MG.
Aircraft: 1 x Parnall Peto 2-seat floatplane.
Complement: 55.

Right: British M-2, converted to aircraft-carrier, lost in 1932.

Above: Built as a minelayer, Argonaut *was used as a transport.*

capable of laying eight mines in every 10 minutes, but the system was complicated and difficult to operate, although if well-maintained it was very effective.

Argonaut's engines were never sufficiently reliable or powerful for her to attain her design speed and this, coupled with the complexity of the minelaying gear, meant that she was never particularly successful as a minelayer. She was given a major refit in early 1942, which included installing four General Motors diesels in place of the unreliable M.A.N. machines, plus two new external torpedo tubes aft. It was then decided to employ her as a transport and she carried 120 Marines on the successful Makin Island raid. Next, she went to the South-West Pacific to continue serving as a transport and it was there that she was sunk on 10 January 1943 with the loss of 120 lives, the U.S. Navy's worst ever submarine disaster.

History: The British carried out trials in 1916 in which two small aircraft were carried to sea aboard a submarine and then floated off, but there seemed little future for the idea and it was shelved. The concept was, however, resurrected in the 1920s and the M-class monitor HMS *M-2* was converted, since it was of a suitable size and it was no longer required in its original role (see M-1 entry). It was reconstructed between April and November 1928, when the 12in (305mm) gun and the associated equipment were removed and replaced by a watertight, cylindrical hangar, which was so large that the bridge had to be raised to enable watchkeepers to see forward. A short launching rail was also fitted on the foredeck.

To launch the aircraft, the submarine was brought to the surface, where the bottom-hinged hangar door was lowered, following which the aircraft on its wheeled trolley was pushed forward onto the catapult. The submarine then turned into wind and the aircraft was launched. This process took about five minutes. For recovery, the aircraft landed on its floats and taxied

J1M/J2-classes

JAPAN

Total built: J1M – 1; J2 – 1.
Completed: J1M – 1932; J2 – 1935.
Displacement: surfaced 2,080 tons; submerged 2,921 tons.
Dimensions: length 308ft 5in (94.0m); beam 29ft 9in (9.1m); draught 16ft 2in (4.9m).
Propulsion: 2 x M.A.N. 10-cylinder, 4-stroke diesel engines, 2 x 3,00bhp; 2 x electric motors, 2 x 1,300shp; two shafts.
Performance: surface – 18kt, 24,00nm/10kt; submerged – 8kt, 60nm/3kt; maximum operational depth 260ft (80m).
Weapons: 6 x 21in (533mm) TT (bow) (10 torpedoes); 1 x 5.5in/40 (140mm) gun.
Aircraft: 1 x 2-seat floatplane.
Complement: 93.
Specifications are for J1M, as built.

History: From the early 1920s onwards the IJN laid great emphasis on long-range scouting and one outcome was the development of aircraft-carrying submarines. The first was the J1Mboat, *I-5*, whose design was based on the J1 scouting submarine (qv), but with the after 5.5in (140mm) gun deleted and replaced by facilities to carry a two-seat floatplane. There were two containers

Above: Dutch O-19 carried 40 mines in 20 vertical tubes.

to the submarine wh
hangar. This recover
could be protracted.
seat, twin-float biplar
and six production m
performance, experie
low ceiling.

M-2 was on exerc
Subsequent investigat
hatch into the pressur
preparing to launch the
made to recover the w
aircraft-carrying subma
the Japanese made a
a very strong operatio

immediately abaft the
wings and minor item
the aircraft had to be
crane, since there w
power and on comple
procedure was rever:
consuming, and no su
the surface in enem
following which I-5 s
USS Wyman (DE-38)

The single J2-cla
design, marginally la
surface speed by 2k
there was a single flc
on the after deck, a
that take-off was ove
the pilot of the assi
campaign until it was

Below: I-5, before c

Far East. O -20 had to be scuttled after a depth-charge attack by a Japanese destroyer on 20 December 1941, but O-19 served until 8 July 1945 when it was wrecked in a storm in the South China Sea.

Krab proved somewhat unreliable in service but carried out several mining operations in the Black Sea in 1915-16, which sank several hostile vessels. In the Revolution, she was captured first by the Ukrainians and then by the Germans, who surrendered her to the British. The latter scuttled her in April 1918 but she was raised and scrapped by the Soviets in 1935.

Below: Russian minelayer Krab carried 60 mines.

Class
Total built
Completed
Displacement: surfaced submerged
Dimensions length beam draught
Propulsion diesels electric motors shafts
Performance surface submerged
Weapons torpedo tubes guns mines
Complement

Below: **Valen, Swe**

AM-class
JAPAN

Total built: 2.
Completed: 1944-45.
Displacement: surfaced 2,620 tons; submerged 4,762 tons.
Dimensions: length 373ft 5in (113.7m); beam 38ft 5in (11.7m); draught 19ft 4in (5.9m).
Propulsion: 2 x Kampon 10-cylinder, 4-stroke diesel engines, 2 x 2,200bhp; 2 x electric motors, 2 x 300shp; two shafts.
Performance: surface – 16.7kt, 21,000nm/16kt; submerged – 5.5kt, 60nm/3kt; maximum operational depth 330ft (100m).
Weapons: 6 x 21in (533mm) TT (bow) (12 torpedoes); 1 x 5.5in/40 (140mm) gun; 7 x 25mm AAMG.
Aircraft: 2 x 2-seat floatplanes.
Complement: 114.

History: Originally planned to be a class of four, only two AM-class boats were Completed: *I-13* and *I-14*. They were even larger than the A2-class, and like them were intended to combine the roles of advanced scouts, headquarters and aircraft- carrier. Once again, less powerful machinery was fitted in order to enhance the surface range, although this was now slightly less than in the A2-class. The hull was generally similar to that of the A2-class, but was fitted with bulges to increase the reserve buoyancy and to give greater freeboard on the surface. A major innovation was the installation of a schnorkel, consisting of two tubes, one for air intake, one for exhaust, but this early Japanese model was considerably less

B1/B2/B3-classes
JAPAN

Total built: B1 – 20; B2 – 6; B3 – 3.
Completed: B1 1940-43; B2 1943-44; B3 1944.
Displacement: surfaced 2,198 tons; submerged 3,654 tons.
Dimensions: length 356ft 7in (108.7m); beam 30ft 6in (9.3m); draught 16ft 10in (5.1m)
Propulsion: 2 x Kampon 10-cylinder, 4-stroke diesel engines, 2 x 6,200bhp; 2 x electric motors, 2 x 1,000shp; two shafts.
Performance: surface – 24kt, 14,000nm/16kt; submerged – 8kt, 96nm/3kt; maximum operational depth 330ft (100m).
Weapons: 6 x 21in (533mm) TT (bow) (12 torpedoes); 1 x 5.5in/40 (140mm) gun; 2 x 25mm AAMG.
Aircraft: 1 x 2-seat floatplane.
Complement: 101.
Specifications for B1-class, as built.

History: These were by far the most numerous classes of aircraft-carrying submarines built by any navy. All three groups had identical hulls and armament, but, compared to the B1-class, the B2s had marginally less powerful engines (11,000bhp), while the B3s had engines of much less power (4,700bhp) in order to increase bunkerage and thus extend the surface range to 21,000nm at 16kt.

The hangar was on the centreline with the bridge above it and to port, and all boats were fitted with a schnorkel. In common with many other aircraft-carrying submarines of the IJN, a number of these boats were converted in 1941-42 to patrol submarines by deleting the hangar and adding a second 5.5in

sophisticated than that developed by the Germans. The aircraft facilities were, however, altered with a larger hangar accommodating two aircraft. The hangar was offest slightly to starboard and faired into the forward part of the sail which was offset to port to compensate. *I-13* was sunk by U.S. surface forces on 16 July 1945, while *I-14* surrendered at sea on 27 August 1945.

Below: I-15; *note hangar below bridge, ramp on the foredeck.*

Below: I-37 dockside in 1939; refitted as a kaiten carrier in 1944.

(140mm) gun; later in the war some were converted into *kaiten* transports. A number were also converted into transports for resupplying isolated garrisons in the Pacific. One, *I-30,* undertook the voyage to France and returned successfully to Singapore, only to hit a mine within hours of leaving that port on the final leg back to Japan. The loss rate was very high and of the 29 boats completed just one (*I-36*) survived the war, all the remainder being sunk by U.S. forces, except for *I-27* and *I-34* which were sunk by the British.

STo-class

Total built: 3.
Completed: 1944-45.
Displacement: surfaced 5,233 tons; submerged 6,560 tons.
Dimensions: length 400ft 3in (122.0m); beam 39ft 4in (12.0m); draught 23ft 0in (7.0m).
Propulsion: 4 x Kampon 10-cylinder, 4-stroke diesel engines, 4 x 1,920bhp; 2 x electric motors, 2 x 1,200shp; two shafts.
Performance: surface – 18.8kt, 37,500nm/14kt; submerged – 6.5kt, 60nm/3kt; maximum operational depth 330ft (100m).
Weapons: 8 x 21in (533mm) TT (bow) (20 torpedoes); 1 x 5.5in/40 (140mm) gun; 10 x 25mm AAMG.
Aircraft: 3 x 2-seat floatplanes.
Complement: 144.

History: These remain, by a wide margin, the largest diesel-electric submarines ever built and were the outcome of a plan made by Admiral Yamamoto, the IJN's commander-in-chief, to attack the locks on the Panama Canal, thus cutting the shortest sea link between the USA's East and West coasts. The original design, started in 1942, would have carried two aircraft, but this was later enlarged to take three, plus the parts for a fourth. These were housed in a 110ft (33.5m) long, 11ft 6in (3.5m) diameter cylindrical hangar, offset slightly to starboard, with the bridge above and to port. The aircraft were warmed up in the hangar and then pulled forward in turn onto the 85ft (25.9m) catapult track, where their wings were rotated through 90 degrees and then extended, following which the pylons and floats were attached. Following training all three aircraft could be launched within 15 minutes of surfacing.

The aircraft specifically designed for this class was the Aichi M6A1 Seiran, a single-engined, two-place monoplane, which was unquestionably the best aircraft ever deployed aboard any submarine. The twin floats were detached for storage, but were not, as some reports state, capable of being jettisoned in flight when on a suicide mission. The Seiran had a top speed of nearly 300mph (483km/h) and could carry one 800kg (1,288lb) or several smaller bombs.

I-400 and *I-401* took part in an attempted raid against the U.S. naval base at Ulithi, but the Japanese surrendered while they were en route and they had no choice but to surrender. A third boat – *I-402* – was completed as a fuel tanker.

Below: STo-class shows huge hangar and long launch ramp.

Above: Dutch **O-19** *carried 40 mines in 20 vertical tubes.*

Far East. *O -20* had to be scuttled after a depth-charge attack by a Japanese destroyer on 20 December 1941, but *O-19* served until 8 July 1945 when it was wrecked in a storm in the South China Sea.

Krab proved somewhat unreliable in service but carried out several mining operations in the Black Sea in 1915-16, which sank several hostile vessels. In the Revolution, she was captured first by the Ukrainians and then by the Germans, who surrendered her to the British. The latter scuttled her in April 1918 but she was raised and scrapped by the Soviets in 1935.

Below: Russian minelayer **Krab** *carried 60 mines.*

Series II, XI, XIII, XIIIbis   RUSSIA

Type	Series II	XI	XIII	XIIIbis
Completed	1931	1935-36	1937-38	194041
Total built	6	6	7	6
Displacement surfaced submerged	1,040 tons 1,335 tons	1,100 tons 1,400 tons	1,123 tons 1,414 tons	1,123 tons 1,414 tons
Dimensions length beam draught	265ft 8in ((81.0m) 22ft 7in (6.9m) 13ft 8in (4.2m)		273ft 3in (83.3m) 23ft 0in (7.0m) 13ft 5in (4.1m)	
Propulsion diesels electric motors shafts	2 x 1,100bhp 2 x 525shp 2	2 x 1,100bhp 2 x 725shp 2	2 x 2,100bhp 2 x 1200hp 2	
Performance surface submerged depth	14kt 9kt 246ft (75m)	14kt 9kt 246ft (75m)	18kt 10kt 246ft (75m)	18kt 10kt 246ft (75m)
Range: surface submerged	6,000nm/9kt 135nm/2kt		14,000nm/9kt 130nm/2kt	
Weapons: torpedo tubes torpedoes guns Mines	6 12 1 x 100mm 1 x 45mm 20	6 12 1 x 100mm 1 x 45mm 20	8 12 1 x 100mm 1 x 45mm 2 x 0.3 MG 20	8 12 1 x 100mm 1 x 45mm 2 x 0.3 MG 20
Complement	54	55	55	55

History: The Leninetz-class consisted of three groups – Series II, Series XI and Series XIII – together with a modified version of the last, Series XIIIbis. There had been no submarine construction in the USSR following the Revolution until the Series I Dekabrist-class of 1926 (qv), which proved unsatisfactory. The Soviet Navy then raised the British submarine L-55 which had been sunk off Kronstadt in 1919 and, having returned the bodies of the crew to Britain with complete correctness, they returned the boat to service and closely examined its construction and operation. The lessons learnt were then used in the construction of the next class, the Series II minelayers. These boats used a virtually unaltered version of the Nalyetev conveyor system, as used in *Krab* (qv), with two horizontal conveyors under the upper casing, dropping mines though holes in the stern.

The boats had hull numbers *L-1 – L- 25* and all were fabricated in yards in the western USSR. Six boats were built in Leningrad and allocated to the Baltic Fleet

Above: Leninetz-class, one of many Soviet-built minelayers.

and another six were built in Nikolayev and allocated to the Black Sea Fleet. The remaining boats were prefabricated in Leningrad (10), Nikolayev (2) and Sevastopol (1), and the parts were then sent by rail to the Dalzavod Yard in Vladivostok, where they were assembled and delivered to the Pacific Fleet, in what must have been a major logistics undertaking. Nine were lost in the war and the survivors were scrapped in the 1950s.

Below: Series II; a conveyor belt laid mines over the stern.

Valen/Delfinen/ Neptun-classes

Class	Valen	Delfinen	Neptun
Total built	1	3	3
Completed	1925	1934-35	1942-43
Displacement: surfaced submerged	548 tons 730 tons	540 tons 720 tons	550 tons 730 tons
Dimensions length beam draught	187ft 4in (57.1m) 23ft 4in (7.1m) 10ft 2in (3.1m)	207ft 0in (63.1m) 21ft 0in (6.4m) 11ft 2in (3.4m)	205ft 5in (62.6m) 21ft 0in (6.4m) 11ft 2in (3.4m)
Propulsion diesels electric motors shafts	2 x 670bhp (Atlas) 2 x 350shp 2	2 x 600bhp (M.A.N.) 2 x 400shp 2	2 x 900bhp (M.A.N.) 2 x 500shp 2
Performance surface submerged	14.8kt 7.4kt	15kt 9kt	15kt 10kt
Weapons torpedo tubes guns mines	4 x 17.7in (450mm) 1 x 75mm/42 1 x 25mm AA 20	4 x 21in (533mm) 1 x 57mm 1 x 25mm AA 20	5 x 21in (533mm) 1 x 40mm Bofors AA 1 x 20mm AA 20
Complement	31	34	35

Below: Valen, Sweden's first minelayer, designed by I.v.S.

to the submarine where it was lifted onto its trolley and returned to the hangar. This recovery process was very dependent on the sea-state and could be protracted. The specially developed Parnall Peto aircraft was a two-seat, twin-float biplane, powered by a single 135hp engine; two prototypes and six production models were built. It was underpowered and had a poor performance, experiencing difficulty in taking-off and having a particularly low ceiling.

M-2 was on exercise on 26 January 1932 when it was lost with all hands. Subsequent investigation showed that the door of the hangar and the internal hatch into the pressure hull were both open, suggesting that the boat had been preparing to launch the aircraft and had been accidentally flooded. Attempts were made to recover the wreck but failed. The British never again experimented with aircraft-carrying submarines. Most of the major navies followed this path but only the Japanese made a success of it. The basic reason for this was that they had a very strong operational requirement; the others did not.

immediately abaft the sail, with the fuselage and twin floats in one and the wings and minor items in the other. The submarine surfaced, following which the aircraft had to be assembled on the open deck and then hoisted out by a crane, since there was no catapult. The aircraft then took off under its own power and on completion of its mission landed beside the submarine where the procedure was reversed. These arrangements were very awkward and time consuming, and no submarine commander likes to have to expose his boat on the surface in enemy waters. The aircraft facilities were removed in 1940, following which *I-5* served as a normal patrol submarine until it was sunk by USS *Wyman* (DE-38) on 19 July 1944.

The single J2-class submarine – *I-6* – was a development of the J1M design, marginally larger and with more powerful engines, which increased surface speed by 2kt but resulted in a decreased range of 4,000nm. Again, there was a single floatplane, but this time there was a long ramp and catapult on the after deck, a slightly more satisfactory arrangement than in *I-5*, except that take-off was over the stern, a most peculiar arrangement, since it deprived the pilot of the assistance of a head wind. *I-6* served through the Pacific campaign until it was sunk on 14 July 1944.

Below: I-5, *before conversion to the IJN's first aircraft carrier.*

AM-class

Total built: 2.
Completed: 1944-45.
Displacement: surfaced 2,620 tons; submerged 4,762 tons.
Dimensions: length 373ft 5in (113.7m); beam 38ft 5in (11.7m); draught 19ft 4in (5.9m).
Propulsion: 2 x Kampon 10-cylinder, 4-stroke diesel engines, 2 x 2,200bhp; 2 x electric motors, 2 x 300shp; two shafts.
Performance: surface – 16.7kt, 21,000nm/16kt; submerged – 5.5kt, 60nm/3kt; maximum operational depth 330ft (100m).
Weapons: 6 x 21in (533mm) TT (bow) (12 torpedoes); 1 x 5.5in/40 (140mm) gun; 7 x 25mm AAMG.
Aircraft: 2 x 2-seat floatplanes.
Complement: 114.

History: Originally planned to be a class of four, only two AM-class boats were Completed: *I-13* and *I-14*. They were even larger than the A2-class, and like them were intended to combine the roles of advanced scouts, headquarters and aircraft-carrier. Once again, less powerful machinery was fitted in order to enhance the surface range, although this was now slightly less than in the A2-class. The hull was generally similar to that of the A2-class, but was fitted with bulges to increase the reserve buoyancy and to give greater freeboard on the surface. A major innovation was the installation of a schnorkel, consisting of two tubes, one for air intake, one for exhaust, but this early Japanese model was considerably less

B1/B2/B3-classes

Total built: B1 – 20; B2 – 6; B3 – 3.
Completed: B1 1940-43; B2 1943-44; B3 1944.
Displacement: surfaced 2,198 tons; submerged 3,654 tons.
Dimensions: length 356ft 7in (108.7m); beam 30ft 6in (9.3m); draught 16ft 10in (5.1m)
Propulsion: 2 x Kampon 10-cylinder, 4-stroke diesel engines, 2 x 6,200bhp; 2 x electric motors, 2 x 1,000shp; two shafts.
Performance: surface – 24kt, 14,000nm/16kt; submerged – 8kt, 96nm/3kt; maximum operational depth 330ft (100m).
Weapons: 6 x 21in (533mm) TT (bow) (12 torpedoes); 1 x 5.5in/40 (140mm) gun; 2 x 25mm AAMG.
Aircraft: 1 x 2-seat floatplane.
Complement: 101.
Specifications for B1-class, as built.

History: These were by far the most numerous classes of aircraft-carrying submarines built by any navy. All three groups had identical hulls and armament, but, compared to the B1-class, the B2s had marginally less powerful engines (11,000bhp), while the B3s had engines of much less power (4,700bhp) in order to increase bunkerage and thus extend the surface range to 21,000nm at 16kt.

The hangar was on the centreline with the bridge above it and to port, and all boats were fitted with a schnorkel. In common with many other aircraft-carrying submarines of the IJN, a number of these boats were converted in 1941-42 to patrol submarines by deleting the hangar and adding a second 5.5in

sophisticated than that developed by the Germans. The aircraft facilities were, however, altered with a larger hangar accommodating two aircraft. The hangar was offest slightly to starboard and faired into the forward part of the sail which was offset to port to compensate. *I-13* was sunk by U.S. surface forces on 16 July 1945, while *I-14* surrendered at sea on 27 August 1945.

Below: **I-15; *note hangar below bridge, ramp on the foredeck.***

Below: **I-37 *dockside in 1939; refitted as a kaiten carrier in 1944.***

(140mm) gun; later in the war some were converted into *kaiten* transports. A number were also converted into transports for resupplying isolated garrisons in the Pacific. One, *I-30,* undertook the voyage to France and returned successfully to Singapore, only to hit a mine within hours of leaving that port on the final leg back to Japan. The loss rate was very high and of the 29 boats completed just one (*I-36*) survived the war, all the remainder being sunk by U.S. forces, except for *I-27* and *I-34* which were sunk by the British.

STo-class

Total built: 3.
Completed: 1944-45.
Displacement: surfaced 5,233 tons; submerged 6,560 tons.
Dimensions: length 400ft 3in (122.0m); beam 39ft 4in (12.0m); draught 23ft 0in (7.0m).
Propulsion: 4 x Kampon 10-cylinder, 4-stroke diesel engines, 4 x 1,920bhp; 2 x electric motors, 2 x 1,200shp; two shafts.
Performance: surface – 18.8kt, 37,500nm/14kt; submerged – 6.5kt, 60nm/3kt; maximum operational depth 330ft (100m).
Weapons: 8 x 21in (533mm) TT (bow) (20 torpedoes); 1 x 5.5in/40 (140mm) gun; 10 x 25mm AAMG.
Aircraft: 3 x 2-seat floatplanes.
Complement: 144.

History: These remain, by a wide margin, the largest diesel-electric submarines ever built and were the outcome of a plan made by Admiral Yamamoto, the IJN's commander-in-chief, to attack the locks on the Panama Canal, thus cutting the shortest sea link between the USA's East and West coasts. The original design, started in 1942, would have carried two aircraft, but this was later enlarged to take three, plus the parts for a fourth. These were housed in a 110ft (33.5m) long, 11ft 6in (3.5m) diameter cylindrical hangar, offset slightly to starboard, with the bridge above and to port. The aircraft were warmed up in the hangar and then pulled forward in turn onto the 85ft (25.9m) catapult track, where their wings were rotated through 90 degrees and then extended, following which the pylons and floats were attached. Following training all three aircraft could be launched within 15 minutes of surfacing.

The aircraft specifically designed for this class was the Aichi M6A1 Seiran, a single-engined, two-place monoplane, which was unquestionably the best aircraft ever deployed aboard any submarine. The twin floats were detached for storage, but were not, as some reports state, capable of being jettisoned in flight when on a suicide mission. The Seiran had a top speed of nearly 300mph (483km/h) and could carry one 800kg (1,288lb) or severral smaller bombs.

I-400 and *I-401* took part in an attempted raid against the U.S. naval base at Ulithi, but the Japanese sur-rendered while they were en route and they had no choice but to surrender. A third boat – *I-402* – was completed as a fuel tanker.

Below: STo-class shows huge hangar and long launch ramp.